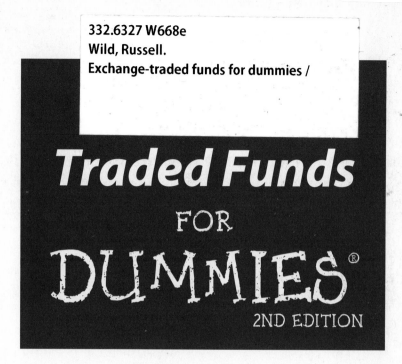

Traded Funds

FOR

DUMMIES®

2ND EDITION

by Russell Wild, MBA

WILEY

John Wiley & Sons, Inc.

Exchange-Traded Funds For Dummies®, 2nd Edition

Published by
John Wiley & Sons, Inc.
111 River St.
Hoboken, NJ 07030-5774
www.wiley.com

Copyright © 2012 by John Wiley & Sons, Inc., Hoboken, New Jersey

Published by John Wiley & Sons, Inc., Hoboken, New Jersey

Published simultaneously in Canada

For general information on our other products and services, please contact our Customer Care Department within the U.S. at 877-762-2974, outside the U.S. at 317-572-3993, or fax 317-572-4002.

For technical support, please visit www.wiley.com/techsupport.

Wiley publishes in a variety of print and electronic formats and by print-on-demand. Some material included with standard print versions of this book may not be included in e-books or in print-on-demand. If this book refers to media such as a CD or DVD that is not included in the version you purchased, you may download this material at http://booksupport.wiley.com. For more information about Wiley products, visit www.wiley.com.

Library of Congress Control Number: 2011943588

ISBN 978-1-118-10424-8 (pbk); ISBN 978-1-118-21446-6 (ebk); ISBN 978-1-118-21450-3 (ebk); ISBN 978-1-118-21451-0 (ebk)

Manufactured in the United States of America

10 9 8 7 6 5 4 3 2 1

WILEY

About the Author

Russell Wild is a NAPFA-certified financial advisor and principal of Global Portfolios, an investment advisory firm based in Allentown, Pennsylvania. He is one of only a handful of wealth managers in the nation who is both fee-only (takes no commissions) and welcomes clients of both substantial *and* modest means. He calls his firm Global Portfolios to reflect his ardent belief in international diversification — using exchange-traded funds to build well-diversified, low-expense, tax-efficient portfolios.

Wild, in addition to the fun he has with his financial calculator, is also an accomplished writer who helps readers understand and make wise choices about their money. His articles have appeared in many national publications, including *AARP The Magazine, Consumer Reports, Details, Maxim, Men's Health, Men's Journal, Cosmopolitan, Reader's Digest,* and *Real Simple.* He writes a regular finance column for *The Saturday Evening Post.* And he has also contributed to numerous professional journals, such as *Financial Planning, Financial Advisor,* and the *NAPFA Advisor.*

The author or coauthor of two dozen nonfiction books, Wild's last work (prior to the one you're holding in your hand) was *One Year to an Organized Financial Life,* coauthored with professional organizer Regina Leeds, published by Da Capo Press. He also wrote two other Dummies titles in addition to this one: *Bond Investing For Dummies* and *Index Investing For Dummies.* No stranger to the mass media, Wild has shared his wit and wisdom on such shows as *Oprah, The View, CBS Morning News,* and *Good Day New York,* and in hundreds of radio interviews.

Wild holds a Master of Business Administration (MBA) degree with a concentration in finance from The Thunderbird School of Global Management, in Glendale, Arizona (consistently ranked the #1 school for international business by both *U.S. News and World Report* and *The Wall Street Journal*); a Bachelor of Science (BS) degree in business/economics magna cum laude from American University in Washington, D.C.; and a graduate certificate in personal financial planning from Moravian College in Bethlehem, Pennsylvania (America's sixth-oldest college). A member of the National Association of Personal Financial Advisors (NAPFA) since 2002, Wild is also a long-time member and past president of the American Society of Journalists and Authors (ASJA).

The author grew up on Long Island and now lives in Allentown, Pennsylvania. His son Clayton attends George Washington University in Washington, D.C. His daughter Adrienne is in high school. His dog Norman, a standard poodle, protects their home from killer squirrels. His website is www.global portfolios.net.

Dedication

To the small investor, who has been bamboozled, bullied, and beaten up long enough.

Author's Acknowledgments

Although I've written many books, the first edition of this book was my first *Dummies* book, and writing a first *Dummies* book is a bit like learning to ride a bicycle — on a very windy day. If it weren't for Joan Friedman, project editor, who kept a steady hand on the back of my seat, I would surely have fallen off a curb and been run over by a pickup truck flying a Confederate flag. Joan, hands down, is one of the best editors I've ever worked with. She's a very nice person, too. For those reasons, I was absolutely thrilled when I learned that Joan would be project editor on this second edition, as well. If there's ever a third edition . . . Joan?

Other nice people that I'd also like to tip my bicycle helmet to include Marilyn Allen of Allen O'Shea Literary Agency (she calls me "babe," just like agents do in movies; I love that) and Stacy Kennedy, acquisitions editor at Wiley. If these two gals hadn't gotten together, I wouldn't have had a bicycle to ride.

Thanks, too, to Paul Justice, CFA, editor of Morningstar's ETFInvestor newsletter. Paul, who knows a heck of a lot about ETFs, was the official technical editor on this book, and he checked every chapter to make certain that this remained strictly a work of nonfiction. Fellow fee-only financial advisor and good friend Neil Stoloff then double checked. You da man, Neil.

I'd like to thank Morningstar — all the folks there aside from Paul — for extreme generosity in providing fund industry data and analysis. Additional good data came from the various ETF providers, such as Vanguard, State Street, BlackRock, and T. Rowe Price, as well as a few non-ETF providers, such as Dimensional and the U.S. Treasury. Thanks, all.

I'd also like to thank Donald Bowles, my old professor of economics at American University, for showing me that supply and demand curves can be fun. Sorry we lost touch, but I haven't forgotten you.

And finally, I'd like to thank my old man, attorney Lawrence R. Wild, both my most beloved and most difficult client, who, if he told me once, told me a thousand times: 'Rich or poor, it's good to have money. It took me years, Dad, to discover the profound wisdom in that statement.

Publisher's Acknowledgments

We're proud of this book; please send us your comments at http://dummies.custhelp.com. For other comments, please contact our Customer Care Department within the U.S. at 877-762-2974, outside the U.S. at 317-572-3993, or fax 317-572-4002.

Some of the people who helped bring this book to market include the following:

Acquisitions, Editorial, and Vertical Websites

Project Editor: Joan Friedman

Acquisitions Editor: Stacy Kennedy

Assistant Editor: David Lutton

Editorial Program Coordinator: Joe Niesen

Technical Editor: Paul Justice

Senior Editorial Manager: Jennifer Ehrlich

Editorial Manager: Carmen Krikorian

Editorial Assistants: Rachelle S. Amick, Alexa Koschier

Cover Photos: © iStockphoto.com/ Yong Hian Lim

Cartoons: Rich Tennant (www.the5thwave.com)

Composition Services

Project Coordinator: Kristie Rees

Layout and Graphics: Lavonne Roberts

Proofreaders: Laura Albert, Nancy L. Reinhardt

Indexer: Potomac Indexing, LLC

Publishing and Editorial for Consumer Dummies

    Kathleen Nebenhaus, Vice President and Executive Publisher

    Kristin Ferguson-Wagstaffe, Product Development Director

    Ensley Eikenburg, Associate Publisher, Travel

    Kelly Regan, Editorial Director, Travel

Publishing for Technology Dummies

    Andy Cummings, Vice President and Publisher

Composition Services

    Debbie Stailey, Director of Composition Services

Contents at a Glance

Table of Contents

Part II: Building the Stock (Equity) Side of Your Portfolio.. 69

Introduction

*E*very month, it seems, Wall Street comes up with some newfangled investment idea. The array of financial products (replete with 164-page prospectuses) is now so dizzying that the old lumpy mattress is starting to look like a more comfortable place to stash the cash. But there is one relatively new product out there definitely worth looking at. It's something of a cross between an index mutual fund and a stock, and it's called an *exchange-traded fund,* or ETF.

Just as computers and fax machines were used by big institutions before they caught on with individual consumers, so it was with ETFs. They were first embraced by institutional traders — investment banks, hedge funds, and insurance firms — because, among other things, they allow for the quick juggling of massive holdings. Big traders like that sort of thing. Personally, playing hot potato with my money is not my idea of fun. But all the same, over the past several years, I've invested most of my own savings in ETFs, and I've suggested to many of my clients that they do the same.

I'm not alone in my appreciation of ETFs. They have grown exponentially in the past few years, and they will surely continue to grow and gain influence. While I can't claim that my purchases and my recommendations of ETFs account for much of the growing $1 trillion+ ETF market, I'm happy to be a (very) small part of it. After you've read this second edition of *Exchange-Traded Funds For Dummies,* you may decide to become part of it as well, if you haven't already.

Since the First Edition . . .

Many changes have taken place in the investment world, both on Wall Street and Main Street, since the first edition of this book was published in 2007. For one thing, a much larger pot of money is now invested in ETFs: $1.1 trillion as of this writing (up from a mere $300 billion in 2007). Also, when I introduce myself as the author of *Exchange-Traded Funds For Dummies,* I no longer get a look as if I'm speaking some strange language with a lisp. Many people today, perhaps most, are at least somewhat familiar with the term *exchange-traded funds.* ETFs have, after all, made a few headlines.

Out of the shadows

The rising popularity of ETFs has been a news story in and of itself. Many educated folks are now aware that ETFs are low-cost investment vehicles that can serve as building blocks for a diversified portfolio.

But ETFs have gotten a bad rap, too, especially for the role they played in the infamous "flash crash" of May 6, 2010 (see Chapter 2) and for the ongoing role they are playing in the increasingly nauseating volatility of the markets. According to one 2010 report from the Ewing Marion Kauffman Foundation, "ETFs are choking the recovery and may pose unrecognized risks to the financial markets."

Well, I'm not so sure about that (especially given that the stock market shot up 10 percent in the six months immediately following the Kauffman report). I discuss the overall effect that ETFs have had on financial markets, but what I concentrate on most in this second edition is how changes in the ETF market affect *you* — the individual investor. And in that arena, without question, there have been many changes both positive and negative.

Filling the investment voids

One very positive change in the past several years is that the "black holes" that I identified in the first edition of this book have largely been filled. That is, half a decade ago, you could not buy an ETF that would give you exposure to tax-free municipal or high-yield bonds. Or international bonds. Or international REITs. All that has changed. There are now ETFs that represent all those asset classes, and many more. Building an entire well-diversified portfolio out of ETFs was not humanly possible several years ago; it is very possible today. I've done it numerous times!

Another very positive development: ETFs have recently been making a grand entrance into employer-sponsored 401(k) plans, where many of America's hard-working people store the bulk of their savings. And they've been appearing lately in college-saving 529 plans, too. Insurance companies have also jumped into the fray, offering ETFs in some of their annuity plans (which, unfortunately, are still often overpriced).

Creations of dubious value

Many of the newer ETFs are bad investments, pure and simple. They were introduced to take advantage of the popularity of ETFs. They are overly expensive, and they represent foolish indexes (extremely small segments of the market, or indexes constructed using highly questionable methodologies). Much of this book is designed to help you tell the good from the bad.

Many of the newer ETFs are also specifically designed for short-term trading — which you would know if you read the really small print at the bottom of the advertisements — and short-term trading usually gets small investors into big trouble.

A scary number of the newer ETFs are based on "back-tested" models: They track whatever indexes, or invest in whatever kinds of assets, have done the best in recent months or years. These ETFs (or the indexes they track) have shining short-term performance records, which induce people to buy. But past short-term performance is a very, very poor indicator of future performance.

Morphing into new creatures

Actively managed ETFs have been slower to take off than Wall Street had hoped but have made inroads since the first edition of this book. These ETFs differ radically from the original index ETFs. Actively managed ETFs don't track any indexes at all but instead have portfolios built and regularly traded by managers attempting to beat the indexes. Active management, study after study has shown, usually doesn't work all that well for investors, even though the managers themselves often get very rich (more in Chapter 2).

And finally, many of the newer exchange-traded products aren't ETFs at all but very different financial instruments called _exchange-traded notes_ (ETNs). ETNs aren't bad, per se, but they represent risks that ETFs do not . . . and that too few people understand (see my discussion in Chapters 14 and 15).

About This Book

As with any other investment, you're looking for a certain payoff in reading this book. In an abstract sense, the payoff will come in your achieving a thorough understanding and appreciation of a powerful financial tool called an exchange-traded fund. The more concrete payoff will come when you apply this understanding to improve your investment results.

What makes me think ETFs can help you make money?

  ✔ **ETFs are intelligent.** Most financial experts agree that playing with individual stocks can be hazardous to one's wealth. Anything from an accounting scandal to the CEO's sudden angina attack can send a single stock spiraling downward. That's why it makes sense for the average investor to own lots of stocks — or bonds — through ETFs or mutual funds.

- ✔ **ETFs are cheap.** At least 150 ETFs charge annual management expenses of 0.20 percent or lower, and a few charge as little as 0.06 percent a year. The average actively managed mutual fund, in contrast, charges 1.33 percent a year. Index mutual funds generally cost a tad more than their ETF cousins. Such cost differences, while appearing small on paper, can make a huge impact on your returns over time. I crunch some appropriate numbers in Chapter 2.

- ✔ **ETFs are tax-smart.** Because of the very clever way ETFs are structured, the taxes you pay on any growth are minimal. I crunch some of those numbers as well in Chapter 2.

- ✔ **ETFs are open books.** Quite unlike mutual funds, an ETF's holdings are readily visible. If this afternoon, for example, I were to buy 100 shares of the ETF called the SPDR (pronounced "spider") S&P 500, I would know that exactly 3.44 percent of my money was invested in Exxon Mobil Corp, 2.59 percent was invested in Apple, Inc., and 1.77 percent was invested in General Electric Co. You don't get that kind of detail when you buy most mutual funds. Mutual fund managers, like stage magicians, are often reluctant to reveal their secrets. In the investment game, the more you know, the lower the odds you will get sawed in half.

  (News flash: Regulators are still debating just how open the portfolios of the newer actively managed ETFs will have to be. For the time being, however, most ETFs track indexes, and the components of any index are readily visible.)

And speaking of open books, if the one you're now reading were like some (but certainly not all) mutual funds, it would be largely unintelligible and expensive. (It might be doubly expensive if you tried to resell the book within 90 days!) Luckily, this book is more like an ETF. Here's how:

- ✔ *Exchange-Traded Funds For Dummies* **is intelligent.** I don't try to convince you that ETFs are your best investment choice, and I certainly don't tell you that ETFs will make you rich. Instead, I lay out facts and figures and summarize some hard academic findings, and I let you draw your own conclusions.

- ✔ *Exchange-Traded Funds For Dummies* **is cheap.** Hey, top-notch investment advice for only $26.99 (plus or minus any discounts, shipping, and tax) . . . Where else are you going to get that kind of deal? *And* should you come to the conclusion after reading this book that ETFs belong in your portfolio, you'll likely get your $26.99 (plus any shipping costs and tax) back — in the form of lower fees and tax efficiency — in no time at all.

- ✔ *Exchange-Traded Funds For Dummies* **is tax-smart.** Yes, the money you spent for this book, as all other outlays you make for investment advice, may be deducted from your federal income taxes (provided you itemize your deductions). Go for it!

- ✔ *Exchange-Traded Funds For Dummies* **is an open book.** We've already established that!

If you've ever read a *For Dummies* book before, you have an idea of what you're about to embark on. This is not a book you need to read from front to back. Feel free to jump about and glean whatever information you think will be of most use. There is no quiz at the end. You don't have to commit it all to memory.

Conventions Used in This Book

To help you navigate this text as easily as possible, I use the following conventions:

- Whenever I introduce a new term, it appears in *italic*. You can rest assured that I provide a definition or explanation nearby.

- If I want to share some interesting information that isn't crucial to your understanding of the topic at hand, I place it in a *sidebar,* a gray box with its own heading that is set apart from the rest of the text. (See how this whole italic/definition thing works?)

- All website addresses appear in `monofont` so they're easy to pick out if you need to go back and find them.

Keep in mind that when this book was printed, some web addresses may have needed to break across two lines of text. If that happened, rest assured that we haven't put in any extra characters (such as hyphens) to indicate the break. So, when using one of these web addresses, just type in exactly what you see in this book, pretending as though the line break doesn't exist.

What You're Not to Read

When my computer is ill, and I call "Tom" (Dell's man somewhere in India or the Philippines), all I want is for Tom to fix my problem, whatever that is. I'm not in the market for explanations. On the ETF front, however, I really like knowing all the technical ins and outs. That may not be your thing. You may be like me with my computer problems: "Just tell me how to make money with these things, and keep the technical stuff to yourself, Russ." Okay, I do that. Sort of.

Throughout this book, you usually find the heavy technical matter tucked neatly into sidebars. But if any technicalities make it into the main text, I give you a heads up with a Technical Stuff icon so you can skip over that section, or just speed-read it if you wish.

Foolish Assumptions

I assume that most of the people reading this book know a fair amount about the financial world. I think that's a fairly safe assumption. Why else would you have bought an entire book about exchange-traded funds?

If you think that convertible bonds are bonds with removable tops and that the futures market is a place where fortunetellers purchase crystal balls, I help you along the best I can by letting you know how to find out more about certain topics. However, you may be better off picking up and reading a copy of the basic nuts-n-bolts *Investing For Dummies* by Eric Tyson (published by Wiley). After you spend some time with that title, c'mon back to this book. You'll be more than welcome!

How This Book Is Organized

Here's a down-and-dirty look at what's in store in the next 350 or so pages.

Part 1: The ABCs of ETFs

Just what *is* an ETF, after all? The beginning of the book would seem like a logical place to cover that topic, and I do. You also find out what makes an ETF different — more sleek and economical — than a mutual fund. (Think Prius versus SUV.) This section of the book also begins the discussion of how to actually buy ETFs — the very best of them — hold them, and, when necessary, cash them out.

Part II: Building the Stock (Equity) Side of Your Portfolio

You wouldn't want a closet filled with nothing but black slacks or red sweaters, and similarly, you don't want a portfolio filled with, say, nothing but tech stocks (remember 2000–2003 when your tech portfolio suddenly went poof?). ETFs are wonderful diversification tools, if used right. In Part II, I show you how to mix and match your stock ETFs to build a portfolio that will serve you well in both good times and bad.

Part III: Adding Bonds, REITs, and Other ETFs to Your Portfolio

In this part, I walk you through the construction of a portfolio beyond its stock components. I introduce you to a bevy of bond, real estate (otherwise known as *REIT*), and commodity ETFs, and I show you how to massage those into your portfolio for maximum diversification. (Oh, have I not mentioned that diversification is all-important?) Afterward, I discuss non-ETF investments (such as mutual funds, individual stocks, and exchange-traded notes) and how to determine if those are appropriate and desirable additions to your portfolio.

Part IV: Putting It All Together

Here, you find sample portfolios. You may find one that fits you like a glove. Or you may find one that you can tinker with to make it your own. After that business is done with, you enter a section of this book that I almost titled "Zen and the Art of ETF Portfolio Maintenance." After all, after you have your ETF portfolio, you need to know how to maintain it, tweak it from time to time, and use it to serve both your material and spiritual needs — preferably with a cool head and calm spirit. Part IV helps you to address those needs.

Part V: The Part of Tens

A classic feature in the *For Dummies* series, The Part of Tens offers concise advice and food for extra thought, all in handy dandy list form.

Part VI: Appendixes

Here's where you find websites you can visit to get even more information about this investment tool and a glossary to help you navigate any ETF resource.

Icons Used in This Book

Throughout the book, you find little globular pieces of art in the margins called *icons*. These admittedly cutesy but handy tools give you a heads up that certain types of information are in the neighborhood.

Although this is a how-to book, you also find plenty of whys and wherefores. Any paragraph accompanied by this icon, however, is guaranteed pure, 100 percent, unadulterated how-to.

The world of investments offers pitfalls galore. Wherever you see the bomb, know that there is a risk of your losing money — maybe even Big Money — if you skip the passage.

Read twice! This icon indicates that something important is being said and is really worth putting to memory.

If you don't really care about the difference between standard deviation and beta, or the historical correlation between U.S. value stocks and REITs, feel free to skip or skim the paragraphs with this icon.

The world of Wall Street is full of people who make money at other people's expense. Where you see the pig face, know that I'm about to point out an instance where someone will likely be sticking a hand deep in your pocket.

Where to Go from Here

Where would you like to go from here? If you wish, start at the beginning. If you're interested only in stock ETFs, hey, no one says that you can't jump right to Part II. Bond ETFs? Go ahead and jump to Part III. It's entirely your call.

Part I
The ABCs of ETFs

The 5th Wave   By Rich Tennant

"Thank goodness it's not his investment portfolio."

In this part . . .

*I*n these first few ground-laying chapters, you find out what makes exchange-traded funds different from other investment vehicles. You discover the rationale for their being, why they are popular with institutional investors, why they are rapidly becoming so popular with non-institutional folk, and why the author of this book likes them almost as much as he does milk chocolate.

Although the art and science of building an ETF portfolio come later in the book, this first part introduces you to how ETFs are bought and sold and helps you ponder whether you should even be thinking about buying them.

Chapter 1

The (Sort of Still) New Kid on the Block

There are, no doubt, a good number of pinstriped ladies and gentlemen in and around Wall Street who froth heavily at the mouth when they hear the words *exchange-traded fund*. In a world of very pricey investment products and very well paid investment-product salespeople, ETFs are the ultimate killjoys.

Since their arrival on the investment scene in the early 1990s, more than 1,300 ETFs have been created, and ETF assets have grown faster than those of any other investment product. That's a good thing. ETFs enable the average investor to avoid shelling out fat commissions or paying layers of ongoing, unnecessary fees. And they've saved investors oodles and oodles in taxes.

Hallelujah.

In the Beginning

When I was a lad growing up in the 'burbs of New York City, my public school educators taught me how to read, write, and learn the capitals of the 50 states. I also learned that anything and everything of any importance in this world was, ahem, invented in the United States of America. I've since learned that, well, that isn't entirely true. Take ETFs. The first ETF was introduced in Canada. It was a creation of the Toronto Stock Exchange — no Wall Streeters were anywhere in sight!

I'm afraid that the story of the development of ETFs isn't quite as exciting as, say, the story behind penicillin or the atomic bomb. As one Toronto Stock Exchange insider once explained to me, "We saw it as a way of making money by generating more trading." Thus was born the original ETF known as TIP, which stood for Toronto Index Participation Unit. It tracked an index of large Canadian companies (Bell Canada, Royal Bank of Canada, Nortel, and 32 others) known as the Toronto 35. That index was then the closest thing that Canada had to the Dow Jones Industrial Average index that exists in the United States.

Enter the traders

TIP was an instant success with large institutional stock traders, who saw that they could now trade an entire index in a flash. The Toronto Stock Exchange got what it wanted — more trading. And the world of ETFs got its start.

TIP has since morphed to track a larger index, the so-called S&P/TSX 60 Index, which — you probably guessed — tracks 60 of Canada's largest and most liquid companies. The fund also has a different name, the iUnits S&P/TSX 60 Index Fund, and it trades under the ticker XIU. It is now managed by BlackRock, Inc., which, upon taking over the iShares lineup of ETFs from Barclays in 2009 (part of a juicy $13.5 billion deal), has come to be the biggest player in ETFs in the world. I introduce you to BlackRock and other ETF suppliers in Chapter 3. (A completely different BlackRock-managed U.S. ETF now uses the ticker TIP, but that fund has nothing to do with the original TIP; the present-day TIP invests in U.S. Treasury Inflation-Protected Securities.)

Moving south of the border

The first ETF didn't come to the United States for three or so years after its Canadian birth. (Oh, how my public school teachers would cringe!) On January 22, 1993, the Mother of All U.S. ETFs was born on the American Stock Exchange (which, in January 2009 — a big year for mergers and acquisitions — became part of NYSE Euronext). The first U.S.-based ETF was called the S&P Depositary Receipts Trust Series 1, commonly known as the SPDR (or Spider) S&P 500, and it traded (and still does) under the ticker symbol SPY.

The SPDR S&P 500, which tracks the S&P 500 index, an index of the 500 largest U.S. companies, was an instant darling of institutional traders. It has since branched out to become a major holding in the portfolios of many individual and institutional investors — and a favorite of favorites among day-traders.

SPDRs, DIAMONDS, Qubes . . . Why the plurals?

Many ETFs have names that end in an *s*. I don't refer to ETFs this way in this book because doing so can be confusing, but you will often hear people talk about the DIAMONDS and the Qubes. Why is that? After all, you would never refer to the Fidelity Magellan Fund as *Magellans*. So why the plural when talking about a single ETF? The convention refers not just to the fund but to the components of the fund. Thus, *DIAMONDS* refers to the 30 companies that make up the Dow Jones Industrial Average index. *Qubes* refers to the 100 companies that make up the NASDAQ-100 Index. But rest assured that when brokers talk about DIAMONDS and Qubes, they are talking about a single ETF.

Fulfilling a Dream

ETFs were first embraced by institutions, and they continue to be used big-time by banks and insurance companies and such. Institutions sometimes buy and hold ETFs, but they are also constantly buying and selling ETFs and options on ETFs for various purposes, some of which I touch on in Chapter 18. For us noninstitutional types, the creation and expansion of ETFs has allowed for similar juggling (usually a mistake for individuals); but more importantly, ETFs allow for the construction of portfolios possessing institutional-like sleekness and economy.

Goodbye, ridiculously high mutual fund fees

The average mutual fund investor with a $150,000 portfolio filled with actively managed funds will likely spend $2,000 (1.33 percent) or so in annual expenses. By switching to an ETF portfolio, that investor may incur trading costs (because trading ETFs generally costs the same as trading stocks) of perhaps $100 or so to set up the portfolio, and maybe $50 or so a year thereafter. But now his ongoing annual expenses will be about $375 (0.25 percent). That's a difference, ladies and gentlemen of the jury, of big bucks. We're looking at an overall yearly savings of $1,575, which is compounded every year the money is invested.

Loads, those odious fees that some mutual funds charge when you buy or sell their shares, simply don't exist in the world of ETFs.

Capital gains taxes, the blow that comes on April 15th to many mutual fund holders with taxable accounts, hardly exist. In fact, here's what my clients and I have paid in capital gains taxes in the past three years: $0.00.

In Chapter 2, I delve much deeper into both the cost savings and the tax efficiency of ETFs.

Hello, building blocks for a better portfolio

In terms of diversification, my own and my clients' portfolios include large stocks; small stocks; micro cap stocks; English, French, Swiss, Japanese, and Korean stocks; intermediate-term bonds; short-term bonds; and real estate investment trusts (REITs) — all held in low-cost ETFs. I discuss diversification and how to use ETFs as building blocks for a class A portfolio, in Part II.

Yes, you could use other investment vehicles, such as mutual funds, to create a well-diversified portfolio. But ETFs make it much easier because they tend to track very specific indexes. They are, by and large, much more "pure" investments than mutual funds. An ETF that bills itself as an investment in, say, small growth stocks is going to give you an investment in small growth stocks, plain and simple. A mutual fund that bills itself as an investment vehicle for small growth stocks may include everything from cash to bonds to shares of General Electric (no kidding, and I give other examples in the next chapter).

Will you miss the court papers?

While scandals of various sorts — hidden fees, "soft-money" arrangements, after-hours sweetheart deals, and executive kickbacks — have plagued the world of mutual funds and hedge funds, this is the number of ETF scandals that have touched my life or the lives and fortunes of my clients: 0. That's because the vast majority of ETFs' managers, forced to follow existing indexes, have very little leeway in their investment choices. Unlike many investment vehicles, ETFs are closely regulated by the U.S. Securities and Exchange Commission. And ETFs trade during the day, in plain view of millions of traders — not after hours, as mutual funds do, which can allow for sweetheart deals when no one is looking.

In Chapter 2, I discuss in greater detail the transparency and cleanliness of ETFs.

Not Quite as Popular as the Beatles, But Getting There

With all that ETFs have going for them, I'm not surprised that they have spread like wildfire on a hot day in July. From the beginning of 2000, when there were only 80 ETFs on the U.S. market, to the end of August 2011, when there were slightly more than 1,300 ETFs, the total assets invested in ETFs rose from $52 billion to just about $1.1 trillion.

Certainly, $1.1 trillion pales in comparison to the $12 trillion or so invested in mutual funds. But if current trends continue, ETFs may indeed become as popular as were John, Paul, George, and Ringo.

The little kid is growing fast: ETFs' phenomenal growth

Following are a few facts and figures from the Investment Company Institute that indicate how the ETF market compares with the mutual fund market and how rapidly ETFs are gaining in popularity.

The amount of money invested in U.S.-based ETFs and mutual funds as of August 2011:

- ✔ ETFs: $1.1 trillion

- ✔ Mutual funds: $12 trillion (Index mutual funds: $1 trillion)

The total number of U.S.-based ETFs and mutual funds as of August 2011:

- ✔ ETFs: 1,300

- ✔ Mutual funds: 7,600 (Index mutual funds: 366)

The number of U.S.-based ETFs in recent years:

- ✔ 2006: 359

- ✔ 2007: 629

- ✔ 2008: 728

- ✔ 2009: 797

- ✔ 2010: 923

- ✔ August 2011: 1,301

The total net assets invested in ETFs in recent years:

- ✔ 2006: $442.6 billion

- ✔ 2007: $608.4 billion

- ✔ 2008: $531.3 billion

- ✔ 2009: $777.1 billion

- ✔ 2010: $992.0 billion

- ✔ August 2011: $1.1 trillion

Part of ETFs' popularity stems from the growly bearish market of the first decade of this millennium. Investors who had been riding the double-digit annual returns of the 1990s suddenly realized that their portfolios weren't going to keep growing in leaps and bounds, and perhaps it was time to start watching investment costs. There has also been a greater awareness of the triumph of *indexing* — investing in entire markets or market segments — over trying to cherry-pick stocks. Much more on that topic in Chapter 2.

Moving from Wall Street to Main Street

In the world of fashion, trendsetters — movie stars or British royals — wander out into public wearing something that most people consider ridiculous, and the next thing you know, everyone is wearing that same item. Investment trends work sort of like fashion trends, but a bit slower. It took from 1993 until, oh, 2001 or so (around the time I bought my first ETF) for this newfangled investment vehicle to really start moving. By about 2003, insiders say, the majority of ETFs were being purchased by individual investors, not institutions or investment professionals.

BlackRock, Inc., which controls about 45 percent of the U.S. market for ETFs, estimates that approximately 60 percent of all the trading in ETFs is done by individual investors. The other 40 percent is institutions and fee-only financial advisors, like me.

(*Fee-only,* by the way, signifies that a financial advisor takes no commissions of any sort. It's a very confusing term because *fee-based* is often used to mean the opposite. Check out Chapter 20, where I talk about whether and what kind of financial professional you need to build and manage an ETF portfolio.)

Actually, individual investors — especially the buy-and-hold kind of investors — benefit much more from ETFs than do institutional traders. That's because institutional traders have always enjoyed the benefits of the very best deals on investment vehicles. That hasn't changed. For example, institutions often pay much less in management fees than do individual investors for shares in the same mutual fund. (Fund companies often refer to *institutional class* versus *investor class* shares. All that really means is "wholesale/low price" versus "retail/higher price.")

Keeping up with the Vanguards

It may sound like I'm pushing ETFs as not only the best thing since sliced bread but as a replacement for sliced bread. Well, not quite. As much as I like ETFs, good old mutual funds still enjoy their place in the sun. That's especially true of inexpensive index mutual funds, such as the ones offered by Vanguard and Fidelity. Mutual funds, for example, are clearly the better option when you're investing in dribs and drabs and don't want to have to pay for each trade you make . . . although a number of brokerage houses, including Charles Schwab, TD Ameritrade, and Fidelity, allow customers to trade certain ETFs for free.

One of the largest purveyors of ETFs is The Vanguard Group, the very same people who pioneered index mutual funds. In the case of Vanguard (and only Vanguard at this point), shares in the company's ETFs are the equivalent of shares in one of the company's index mutual funds. In other words, they are different share classes of the same fund — the same representation of companies but a different structure and generally slightly lower management fees for the ETFs.

In addition, Vanguard allows its customers to trade all Vanguard ETFs for free.

Because Vanguard funds allow for an apples-to-apples comparison of ETFs and index mutual funds, and because the company presumably has no great stake in which you choose, Vanguard may be a good place to turn for objective advice on which investment is better for you. But rest assured — a point that I'll make again in this book — this ain't rocket science. For most buy-and-hold investors, ETFs will almost always be the better choice, at least in the long run. I look more closely at the ETFs-versus-mutual-funds question when I design specific portfolios and give actual portfolio examples in Chapters 15 and 16.

The ripple effect: Forcing down prices on other investment vehicles

You don't need to invest in ETFs to profit from them. They are doing to the world of investing what Chinese labor has done to global manufacturing wages. That is, they are driving prices down. Thanks to the competition that ETFs are giving to index mutual funds (ETFs now claim about one-half of the $2 trillion or so invested in all index funds), mutual fund providers have been lowering their charges.

Fidelity Investments, for example, has over the past several years lowered the expense ratio on some of its index funds from as much as 0.47 percent down to as low as 0.07 percent. With many mutual funds, however, you must keep a minimum balance. Fidelity's minimum for its lowest-cost index funds ranges from $10,000 to a whopping $100,000. ETFs impose no such restrictions.

Ready for Prime Time

Although most investors are now familiar with ETFs, mutual funds remain the investment vehicle of choice by a margin of 12:1. The reasons for the dominance of mutual funds are several. First, mutual funds have been around a lot longer and so got a good head start. Second, largely as a corollary to the first reason, most company retirement plans and pension funds still use mutual funds rather than ETFs; as a participant, you have no choice but to go with mutual funds. And finally, the vast majority of ETFs are index funds, and index funds are not going to become the nation's favorite investment vehicle anytime soon. They should, but they won't. People just aren't that logical.

Index mutual funds, which most closely resemble ETFs, have been in existence since 1976 when Vanguard first rolled out the Index Investment Trust fund. Since that time, Vanguard and other mutual fund companies have created hundreds of index funds tracking every conceivable index. Yet index funds remain relatively obscure. According to figures from the Investment Company Institute, index mutual funds hold less than 8 percent of all money invested in mutual funds.

Why would anyone want to invest in index funds or index ETFs? After all, the financial professionals who run actively managed mutual funds spend many years and tens of thousands of dollars educating themselves at places with real ivy on the walls, like Harvard and Wharton. They know all about the economy, the stock market, business trends, and so on. Shouldn't we cash in on their knowledge by letting them pick the best basket of investments for us?

Good question! Here's the problem with hiring these financial whizzes, and the reason that index funds or ETFs generally kick their ivy-league butts: When these whizzes from Harvard and Wharton go to market to buy and sell stocks, they are usually buying and selling stock (not directly, but through the markets) from *other* whizzes who graduated from Harvard and Wharton. One whiz bets that ABC stock is going down, so he sells. His former classmate bets that ABC stock is going up, so he buys. Which whiz is right? Half the time, it's the buyer; half the time, it's the seller. Meanwhile, you pay for all the trading, not to mention the whiz's handsome salary while all this buying and selling is going on.

Economists have a name for such a market; they call it "efficient." It means, in general, that there are soooo many smart people analyzing and dissecting and studying the market that the chances are slim that any one whiz — no matter how whizzical, no matter how thick his Cambridge accent — is going to be able to beat the pack.

Can you pick next year's winners?

Okay, study after study shows that most actively managed mutual funds don't do as well in the long run as the indexes. But certainly some do much better, at least for a few years. And any number of magazine articles will tell you exactly how to pick next year's winners.

Alas, if only it were that easy. Sorry, but studies show rather conclusively that it is anything but easy. Morningstar, on a great number of occasions, has earmarked the top-performing mutual funds and mutual fund managers over a given period of time and tracked their performance moving forward. In one representative study, the top 30 mutual funds for sequential five-year periods were evaluated for their performance moving forward. In each and every five-year period, the "30 top funds," as a group, did worse than the S&P 500 in subsequent years.

That, in a nutshell, is why actively managed mutual funds tend to lag the indexes, usually by a considerable margin. If you want to read more about why stock-pickers and market-timers almost never beat the indexes, I suggest picking up a copy of the seminal *A Random Walk Down Wall Street* by Princeton economist Burton G. Malkiel. The book, now in something like its 200th edition, is available in paperback from W. W. Norton & Company. There's also a website — www.indexfunds.com — run by something of an indexing fanatic (hey, there are worse things to be) that is packed with articles and studies on the subject. You could spend days reading!

The proof of the pudding

One study, done in 2010 by Wharton finance professor Robert F. Stambaugh and University of Chicago finance professor Lubos Pastor, looked back over 23 years of data. The conclusion: Actively managed funds have trailed, and will likely continue to trail, their indexed counterparts (whether mutual funds or ETFs) by nearly 1 percent a year. That may not seem like a big deal, but compounded over time, 1 percent a year can be *HUGE*.

Let's plug in a few numbers. An initial investment of $100,000 earning, say, 7 percent a year, would be worth $386,968 after 20 years. An initial investment of $100,000 earning 8 percent for 20 years would be worth $466,096. That's $79,128 extra in your pocket, all things being equal, if you invest in index funds. And if that investment were held in a taxable account, the figure would likely be much higher after you account for taxes. (Taxes on actively managed funds can be considerably higher than those on index funds.)

Moving from the world of academia and theory to the real world, let's look at that very first ETF introduced in the United States, the SPDR S&P 500 (SPY). Since inception in January 1993, that fund has enjoyed an average annual return of 8.26 percent — not bad, considering that it survived two very serious bear markets (2000–2002 and 2008–2009). Very few actively managed funds can match that record. (You'll find some performance specifics in the next chapter.)

By the way, SPY, as well as it has performed, has several flaws that make it far from my first choice of ETF for most portfolios; I will divulge these in Chapter 5. But despite its flaws — and I'm certainly not the only investment professional privy to them — SPY remains by far the largest ETF on the market, with total assets of $90 billion. (The largest fund of any kind is the PIMCO Total Return mutual fund [PTTRX], with total net assets of $136 billion.) In terms of number of shares traded daily, nothing even comes close to SPY.

The major players

In Parts II and III of this book, I provide details about many of the ETFs on the market. Here, I want to introduce you to just a handful of the biggies. You will likely recognize a few of the names.

In Table 1-1, I list the six largest ETFs on the market as of mid-August 2011, as calculated by the number of shares traded.

Table 1-1	The Six Largest ETFs by Number of Shares Traded	
Name	**Ticker**	**Average daily trading volume**
SPDR S&P 500	SPY	244 million shares
Financial Select Sector SPDR	XLF	100 million shares
iShares Russell 2000 Index	IWM	76 million shares
PowerShares QQQ	QQQ	70 million shares
iShares MSCI Emerging Markets Index	EEM	60 million shares
iShares Silver Trust	SLV	40 million shares

In Table 1-2, I list the six largest ETFs based on their assets. You'll notice some overlap with the funds listed in Table 1-1.

Table 1-2	The Six Largest ETFs by Assets	
Name	**Ticker**	**Assets (in billions of dollars)**
SPDR S&P 500	SPY	$78.6
SPDR Gold Shares	GLD	$70.4
Vanguard MSCI Emerging Markets ETF	VWO	$44.8
iShares MSCI EAFE Index	EFA	$35.4
iShares MSCI Emerging Markets Index	EEM	$33.4
iShares S&P 500 Index	IVV	$25.6

Twist and shout: Commercialization is tainting a good thing

Innovation is a great thing. Usually. In the world of ETFs, a few big players (BlackRock, State Street Global Advisors, Vanguard) jumped in early when the going was hot. Now, in order to get their share of the pie, a number of new players have entered the fray with some pretty wild ETFs. "Let's invest in all companies whose CEO is named Fred!" Okay, there's no Fred portfolio, but the way things are going, it could happen.

I tend to like my ETFs vanilla plain, maybe with a few sprinkles. I like them to follow indexes that make sense. And, above all, I like their expense ratios looooow. At present, plenty of ETFs carry expense ratios of 0.20 percent or less. Some of the newer, more complicated ETFs, however, have expense ratios edging up into the ballpark of what you usually see for mutual funds. There are now several dozen ETFs charging 0.75 percent a year or higher, and at least six carry net expense ratios of 1 percent or more.

I'm not saying that all ETFs must follow traditional indexes. The ETF format allows for more variety than that. (Actually, when I think about it, some of the traditional indexes, like the Dow, are darn dumb. I explain why in Chapter 3.) But the ETF industry has lost some of its integrity over the past few years with higher expenses and some awfully silly investment schemes.

The rest of this book will help you to sidestep the greed and the silliness — to take only the best parts of ETF investing and put them to their best use.

RIP these ETFs

New ETFs are being born every week, but at the same time, others are dying. About 150 ETFs in the past several years have been zipped up, closed down, folded, and sent to that Great Brokerage in the Sky. No need to shed tears for the investors; they are okay.

If you are holding shares in a particular ETF that closes down, you will generally be given at least several weeks notice. You can sell, or you can wait till the final day and receive whatever is the value of the securities held by the ETF at that point. It isn't like holding a bond (or an exchange-traded note) that goes belly up. You may have a bit of a hassle redoing your portfolio, and you may face sudden tax consequences. If the ETF tracks a very small segment of the market, there may be a bit of investor panic that could depress prices. But you aren't going broke.

As for the purveyors of the ETFs that have closed, I may shed only a crocodile tear or two. Most of the ETFs that have gone under are exactly the kinds of ETFs that I try to steer you away from in this book: They tracked narrow segments of the market (companies based in Oklahoma, for example); or they tracked somewhat silly and complex indexes (dividend rotation); or they were highly leveraged, exposing investors to excessive risk; or they were overpriced; or all of the above! The public simply would not buy. Bravo, public.

Here is just a small sampling from the ETF graveyard:

- Bear Stearns Current Yield Fund (YYY)
- Claymore/Beacon Global Exchanges, Brokers & Asset Managers ETF (EXB)
- Claymore/Robb Report Global Luxury Index ETF (ROB)
- Claymore/Zacks Country Rotation ETF (CRO)
- Claymore/Zacks Dividend Rotation ETF (IRO)
- Direxion Daily 2-Year Treasury Bull 3x ETF (TWOL)
- Geary Oklahoma ETF (OOK)
- Geary Texas Large Companies ETF (TXF)
- JETS DJ Islamic Market International ETF (JVS)
- Guggenheim Inverse 2x Select Sector Energy ETF (REC)
- WisdomTree Earnings Top 100 Fund (EEZ)

On the Internet, where there's a blog for anything and everything, I found a blog called ETF Deathwatch. According to ETF Deathwatch, any ETF that is at least six months old that has an "Average Daily Value Traded" of less than $100,000 for three consecutive months — or that has assets under management of less than $5 million for three consecutive months — is probably not an ETF you should get overly attached to. To find the Deathwatch blog, go to www.investwithanedge.com, and type "deathwatch" in the search box.

Chapter 2

What the Heck Is an ETF, Anyway?

*B*anking your retirement on stocks is risky enough; banking your retirement on any individual stock, or even a handful of stocks, is Evil Knievel-jumping-the-Snake-River investing. Banking on individual bonds is typically less risky (maybe Evil Knievel jumping a creek), but the same general principle holds. There is safety in numbers. That's why teenage boys and girls huddle together in corners at school dances. That's why gnus graze in groups. That's why smart stock and bond investors grab onto ETFs.

In this chapter, I explain not only the safety features of ETFs but also the ways in which they differ from their cousins, mutual funds. By the time you're done with this chapter, you should have a pretty good idea of what ETFs can do for your portfolio.

The Nature of the Beast

Just as a deed shows that you have ownership of a house, and a share of common stock certifies ownership in a company, a share of an ETF represents ownership (most typically) in a basket of company stocks. To buy or sell an ETF, you place an order with a broker, generally (and preferably, for cost reasons) online, although you can also place an order by phone. The price of an ETF changes throughout the trading day, which is to say from 9:30 a.m. to 4:00 p.m. New York City time, going up or going down with the market value of the securities it holds. (Sometimes there can be a little sway — times when the price of an ETF doesn't exactly track the value of the securities it holds — but that situation is rarely serious, at least not with ETFs from the better purveyors.)

Originally, ETFs were developed to mirror various indexes:

✔ The SPDR S&P 500 (ticker SPY) represents stocks from the S&P (Standard & Poor's) 500, an index of the 500 largest companies in the United States.

✔ The DIAMONDS Trust Series 1 (ticker DIA) represents the 30 underlying stocks of the Dow Jones Industrial Average index.

✔ The NASDAQ-100 Trust Series 1, which was renamed the PowerShares QQQ Trust Series 1 (ticker QQQ), represents the 100 stocks of the NASDAQ-100 index.

Since ETFs were first introduced, many others, tracking all kinds of things, including some rather strange things that I dare not even call investments, have emerged.

The component companies in an ETF's portfolio usually represent a certain index or segment of the market, such as large U.S. value stocks, small growth stocks, or micro cap stocks. (If you're not 100 percent clear on the difference between *value* and *growth,* or what a micro cap is, rest assured that I define these and other key terms in Part II.)

Sometimes, the stock market is broken up into industry sectors, such as technology, industrials, and consumer discretionary. ETFs exist that mirror each sector.

Regardless of what securities an ETF represents, and regardless of what index those securities are a part of, your fortunes as an ETF holder are tied, either directly or in some leveraged fashion, to the value of the underlying securities. If the price of Exxon Mobil Corporation stock, U.S. Treasury bonds, gold bullion, or British Pound futures goes up, so does the value of your ETF. If the price of gold tumbles, your portfolio (if you hold a gold ETF) may lose some glitter. If GE stock pays a dividend, you are due a certain amount of that dividend — *unless* you happen to have bought into a leveraged or inverse ETF.

As I discuss in Chapter 11, some ETFs allow for leveraging, so that if the underlying security rises in value, your ETF shares rise doubly or triply. If the security falls in value, well, you lose according to the same multiple. Other ETFs allow you not only to leverage but also to *reverse* leverage, so that you stand to make money if the underlying security falls in value (and of course lose if the underlying security increases in value). I'm not a big fan of leveraged and inverse ETFs, for reasons I make clear in Chapter 11.

Choosing between the Classic and the New Indexes

Some of the ETF providers (Vanguard, iShares, Schwab) tend to use traditional indexes, such as those I mention in the previous section. Others (Invesco PowerShares, WisdomTree, Guggenheim) tend to develop their own indexes.

For example, if you were to buy 100 shares of an ETF called the iShares S&P 500 Growth Index Fund (IVW), you'd be buying into a traditional index (large U.S. growth companies). At about $68 a share (at this writing), you'd plunk down $6,800 for a portfolio of stocks that would include shares of Apple, International Business Machines, Microsoft Corp, The Coca-Cola Company, Google, Oracle, and Johnson & Johnson. If you wanted to know the exact breakdown, the iShares prospectus found on the iShares website (or any number of financial websites, such as http://finance.yahoo.com) would tell you specific percentages: Apple, 5.25 percent; International Business Machines, 3.25 percent; Microsoft Corp, 3.07 percent, The Coca-Cola Company, 2.49 percent; and so on.

Many ETFs represent shares in companies that form foreign indexes. If, for example, you were to own 100 shares of the iShares MSCI Japan Index Fund (EWJ), with a market value of about $10 per share as of this writing, your $1,000 would buy you a stake in large Japanese companies such as Toyota Motor, Honda Motor, Mitsubishi UFJ Financial Group, Canon, and Sony. Chapter 9 is devoted entirely to international ETFs.

Both IVW and EWJ mirror standard indexes: IVW mirrors the S&P 500 Growth Index, and EWJ mirrors the MSCI Japan Index. If, however, you purchase 100 shares of the PowerShares Dynamic Large Cap Growth Portfolio (PWB), you'll buy roughly $1,700 worth of a portfolio of stocks that mirror a very unconventional index — one created by the PowerShares family of exchange-traded funds. The large U.S. growth companies in the PowerShares index don't include Apple, International Business Machines, or Microsoft, but rather companies like Union Pacific, Caterpillar, and Visa. Invesco PowerShares refers to its custom indexes as "enhanced."

A big controversy in the world of ETFs is whether the newfangled, customized indexes offered by companies like Invesco PowerShares make any sense. Most financial professionals are skeptical of anything that's new. We are a conservative lot. Those of us who have been around for a while have seen too many "exciting" new investment ideas crash and burn. But I, for one, try to keep an open mind. For now, let me continue with my introduction to ETFs, but rest assured that I address this controversy later in the book (in Chapter 3 and throughout Part II).

Another big controversy is whether you may be better off with an even newer style of ETFs — those that follow no indexes at all but rather are "actively" managed. As I make clear in Chapter 1, I prefer index investing to active investing, but that's not to say that active investing, carefully pursued, has no role to play. More on that topic later in this chapter and throughout the book.

Other ETFs — a distinct but growing minority — represent holdings in assets other than stocks, most notably bonds and commodities (gold, silver, oil, and such). And then there are exchange-traded notes (ETNs), which allow you to venture even further into the world of alternative investments — or speculations — such as currency futures. I discuss these products in Part III of the book.

Preferring ETFs over Individual Stocks

Okay, why buy a basket of stocks rather than an individual stock? Quick answer: You'll sleep better.

You may recall that in August 2010, HP CEO Mark Hurd suddenly resigned over a sex scandal. The stock plummeted, and HP shareholders lost billions. A few years before that, the always fashionable Martha Stewart was convicted of obstruction of justice and lying to investigators in an insider-trading case involving a small company called ImClone. Within hours, shares in Stewart's namesake firm, Martha Stewart Living Omnimedia, tumbled 23 percent.

Those sorts of things — sometimes much worse — happen every day in the world of stocks.

A company I'll call ABC Pharmaceutical sees its stock shoot up by 68 percent because the firm just earned an important patent for a new diet pill; a month later, the stock falls by 84 percent because a study in the *New England Journal of Medicine* found that the new diet pill causes people to hallucinate and think they are Genghis Khan — or Martha Stewart.

Compared to the world of individual stocks, the stock market as a whole is as smooth as a morning lake. Heck, a daily rise or fall in the Dow of more than a percent or two (well, maybe 2 or 3 percent these days) is generally considered a pretty big deal.

If you, like me, are not especially keen on roller coasters, then you are advised to put your nest egg into not one stock, not two, but many. If you have a few million sitting around, hey, you'll have no problem diversifying — maybe individual stocks are for you. But for most of us commoners, the only way to effectively diversify is with ETFs or mutual funds.

Distinguishing ETFs from Mutual Funds

So what is the difference between an ETF and a mutual fund? After all, mutual funds also represent baskets of stocks or bonds. The two, however, are not twins. They're not even siblings. Cousins are more like it. Here are some of the big differences between ETFs and mutual funds:

✔ ETFs are bought and sold just like stocks (through a brokerage house, either by phone or online), and their prices change throughout the trading day. Mutual fund orders can be made during the day, but the actual trading doesn't occur until after the markets close.

✔ ETFs tend to represent indexes — market segments — and the managers of the ETFs tend to do very little trading of securities in the ETF. (The ETFs are *passively* managed.) Most mutual funds are actively managed.

✔ Although they may require you to pay small trading fees, ETFs usually wind up costing you much less than mutual funds because the ongoing management fees are typically much less, and there is never a *load* (an entrance and/or exit fee, sometime an exorbitant one) as you find with many mutual funds.

✔ Because of low portfolio turnover and also the way ETFs are structured, ETFs generally declare much less in taxable capital gains than mutual funds.

Table 2-1 provides a quick look at some ways that investing in ETFs differs from investing in mutual funds and individual stocks.

Table 2-1   ETFs Versus Mutual Funds Versus Individual Stocks

	ETFs	*Mutual Funds*	*Individual Stocks*
Priced, bought, and sold throughout the day?	Yes	No	Yes
Offer some investment diversification?	Yes	Yes	No
Is there a minimum investment?	No	Yes	No
Purchased through a broker or online brokerage?	Yes	Yes	Yes
Do you pay a fee or commission to make a trade?	Typically	Sometimes	Yes
Can that fee or commission be more than a few dollars?	No	Yes	No
Can you buy/sell options?	Sometimes	No	Sometimes
Indexed (passively managed)?	Typically	Atypically	No
Can you make money or lose money?	Yes	Yes	You bet

Why the Big Boys Prefer ETFs

When ETFs were first introduced, they were primarily of interest to institutional traders — insurance companies, hedge fund people, banks — who often have investment needs considerably more complicated than yours and mine. In this section, I explain why ETFs appeal to the largest investors.

Trading in large lots

Prior to the introduction of ETFs, a trader had no way to buy or sell instantaneously, in one fell swoop, hundreds of stocks or bonds. Because they trade both during market hours and, in some cases, after market hours, ETFs made that possible.

Institutional investors also found other things to like about ETFs. For example, ETFs are often used to put cash to productive use quickly or to fill gaps in a portfolio by allowing immediate exposure to an industry sector or geographic region.

Savoring the versatility

Unlike mutual funds, ETFs can also be purchased with limit, market, or stop-loss orders, taking away the uncertainty involved with placing a buy order for a mutual fund and not knowing what price you're going to get until several hours after the market closes. See the sidebar "Your basic trading choices (for ETFs or stocks)" if you're not certain what limit, market, and stop-loss orders are.

And because many ETFs can be sold short, they provide an important means of risk management. If, for example, the stock market takes a dive, *shorting* ETFs — selling them now at a locked-in price with an agreement to purchase them back (cheaper, you hope) later on — may help keep a portfolio afloat. For that reason, ETFs have become a darling of hedge fund managers who offer the promise of investments that won't tank should the stock market tank. See Chapter 18 for more on this topic.

Your basic trading choices (for ETFs or stocks)

Buying and selling an ETF is just like buying and selling a stock; there really is no difference. Although you can trade in all sorts of ways, the vast majority of trades fall into these categories:

✔ **Market order:** This is as simple as it gets. You place an order with your broker or online to buy, say, 100 shares of a certain ETF. Your order goes to the stock exchange, and you get the best available price.

✔ **Limit order:** More exact than a market order, you place an order to buy, say, 100 shares of an ETF at $23 a share. That is the maximum price you will pay. If no sellers are willing to sell at $23 a share, your order will not go through. If you place a limit order to sell at $23, you'll get your sale if someone is willing to pay that price. If not, there will be no sale. You can specify whether an order is good for the day or until canceled (if you don't mind waiting to see if the market moves in your favor).

✔ **Stop-loss (or stop) order:** Designed to protect you should the price of your ETF

or stock take a tumble, a stop-loss order automatically becomes a market order if and when the price falls below a certain point (say, 10 percent below the current price). Stop-loss orders are used to limit investors' exposure to a falling market, but they can (and often do) backfire, especially in very turbulent markets. Proceed with caution.

✔ **Short sale:** You sell shares of an ETF that you have borrowed from the broker. If the price of the ETF then falls, you can buy replacement shares at a lower price and pocket the difference. If, however, the price rises, you are stuck holding a security that is worth less than its market price, so you pay the difference, which can sometimes be huge.

For more information on different kinds of trading options, see the U.S. Securities and Exchange Commission discussion at `www.sec.gov/investor/alerts/trading101basics.pdf`.

Why Individual Investors Are Learning to Love ETFs

Clients I've worked with are often amazed that I can put them into a financial product that will cost them a fraction in expenses compared to what they are currently paying. Low costs are probably what I love the most about ETFs. But I also love their tax efficiency, their transparency (you know what you're buying), and the long track record of success for indexed investments.

The cost advantage: How low can you go?

In the world of actively managed mutual funds (which is to say most mutual funds), the average annual management fee, according to Morningstar, is 1.33 percent of the account balance. That may not sound like a lot, but don't be misled. A well-balanced portfolio with both stocks and bonds may return, say, 7 percent over time. In that case, paying 1.33 percent to a third party means that you've just lowered your total investment returns by about one-fifth. In a bad year, when your investments earn, say, 1.33 percent, you've just lowered your investment returns to *zero*. And in a *very* bad year . . . you don't need me to do the math.

I'm astounded at what some mutual funds charge. Whereas the average is 1.33 percent, I've seen charges 10 times that amount. Crazy. Investing in such a fund is tossing money to the wind. Yet people do it. The chances of your winding up ahead after paying such high fees are next to nil. Paying a *load* (an entrance and/or exit fee) that can total as much as 8.50 percent is just as nutty. Yet people do it.

In the world of index funds, the expenses are much lower, with index mutual funds averaging 0.64 percent and ETFs averaging 0.50 percent, although many of the more traditional domestic indexed ETFs cost no more than 0.20 percent a year in management fees. A handful are under 0.10 percent.

Some fees, as you can see in Table 2-2, are so low as to be negligible. Each ETF in this table has a yearly management expense of 0.12 percent or less.

Table 2-2	The Rock Bottom ETFs	
ETF	**Ticker**	**Total Annual Management Expense**
Focus Morningstar U.S. Market Index	FMU	0.05%
Focus Morningstar Large Cap Index	FLG	0.05%
Schwab U.S. Broad Market	SCHB	0.06%
Vanguard S&P 500	VOO	0.06%
Vanguard Total Stock Market	VTI	0.07%
Schwab U.S. Large-Cap	SCHX	0.08%
SPDR S&P 500 Index	SPY	0.09%
iShares S&P 500 Index	IVV	0.09%
PIMCO 1–3 Year U.S. Treasury Index	TUZ	0.09%
Vanguard Large Cap	VV	0.12%
Vanguard Short-Term Bond	BSV	0.12%

Numerous studies have shown that low-cost funds have a huge advantage over higher-cost funds. One study by Morningstar looked at stock returns over a five-year period. In almost every category of stock mutual fund, low-cost funds beat the pants off high-cost funds. Do you think that by paying high fees you're getting better fund management? Hardly. The Morningstar study found, for example, that among mutual funds that hold large blend stocks (*blend* meaning a combination of value and growth . . . an S&P 500 fund would be a blend fund, for example), the annualized gain was 8.75 percent for those funds in the costliest quartile of funds; the gain for the least costly quartile was 9.89 percent.

Why ETFs are cheaper

The management companies that bring us ETFs, such as BlackRock, Inc. and Invesco PowerShares, are presumably not doing so for their health. No, they're making a good profit. One reason they can offer ETFs so cheaply compared to mutual funds is that their expenses are much less. When you buy an ETF, you go through a brokerage house, not BlackRock or Invesco PowerShares. That brokerage house (Merrill Lynch, Fidelity, TD Ameritrade) does all the necessary paperwork and bookkeeping on the purchase. If you have any questions about your money, you'll likely call Schwab, not BlackRock. So unlike a mutual fund company, which must maintain telephone operators, bookkeepers, and a mailroom, the providers of ETFs can operate almost entirely in cyberspace.

ETFs that are linked to indexes do have to pay some kind of fee to Dow Jones or MSCI or whoever created the index. But that fee is *nothing* compared to the exorbitant salaries that mutual funds pay their stock pickers, er, market analysts.

An unfair race

Active mutual funds really don't have much chance of beating passive index funds — whether mutual funds or ETFs — over the long run, at least not as a group. (There are individual exceptions, but it's virtually impossible to identify them before the fact.) Someone once described the contest as a race in which the active mutual funds are "running with lead boots." Why? In addition to the management fees that eat up much of any gains, there are also the trading costs. Yes, when mutual funds trade stocks or bonds, they pay a spread and a small cut to the stock exchange, just like you and I do. That cost is passed on to you, and it's on top of the annual management fees previously discussed.

It's been estimated that annual turnover costs for active mutual funds typically run about 0.8 percent. And active mutual fund managers must constantly keep some cash on hand for all those trades. Having cash on hand costs money, too: The opportunity cost is estimated to be in the neighborhood of 0.4 percent.

So you take the 1.33 percent average management fee, and the 0.8 percent hidden trading costs, and the 0.4 percent opportunity cost, and you can see where the lead boots come in. Add taxes to the equation, and while some actively managed mutual funds may do better than ETFs for a few years, over the long haul I wouldn't bank on many of them coming out ahead.

Uncle Sam's loss, your gain

Alas, unless your money is in a tax-advantaged retirement account, making money in the markets means that you have to fork something over to Uncle Sam at year's end. That's true, of course, whether you invest in individual securities or funds. But before there were ETFs, individual securities had a big advantage over funds in that you were required to pay capital gains taxes only when you actually enjoyed a capital gain. With mutual funds, that isn't so. The fund itself may realize a capital gain by selling off an appreciated stock. You pay the capital gains tax regardless of whether you sell anything and regardless of whether the share price of the mutual fund increased or decreased since the time you bought it.

There have been times (pick a bad year for the market — 2000, 2008 . . .) when many mutual fund investors lost a considerable amount in the market yet had to pay capital gains taxes at the end of the year. Talk about adding insult to injury! One study found that over the course of time, taxes have wiped out approximately 2 full percentage points in returns for investors in the highest tax brackets.

In the world of ETFs, such losses are very unlikely to happen. Because most ETFs are index-based, they generally have little turnover to create capital gains. To boot, ETFs are structured in a way that largely insulates shareholders from capital gains that result when mutual funds are forced to sell in order to free up cash to pay off shareholders who cash in their chips.

No tax calories

The structure of ETFs makes them different than mutual funds. Actually, ETFs are legally structured in three different ways: as exchange-traded open-end mutual funds, exchange-traded unit investment trusts, and exchange-traded grantor trusts. The differences are subtle, and I elaborate on them somewhat in Chapter 3 and throughout Part II. For now, I want to focus on one seminal difference between ETFs and mutual funds, which boils down to an extremely clever setup whereby ETF shares, which represent stock holdings, can be traded without any actual trading of stocks. In a way it's like fat-free potato chips (remember Olestra?), which have no fat calories because the fat just passes through your body.

Perhaps a better analogy is to the poker player who can play all night and, thanks to the miracle of chips, not have to touch any cash.

Capital gains, investor pains

If you hold a mutual fund, and that fund sells shares for more than their purchase price, you, as an existing shareholder, will likely get slapped with a capital gains tax. How much that tax will be depends on several factors:

✔ **The 0 percent rate.** *Eligibility:* You are in the 10 percent and 15 percent federal income tax brackets, and the capital gains you've incurred come from selling investment securities held for more than one year. After 2012, however, your capital gains rate is most likely going to jump to 10 percent.

✔ **The 15 percent rate.** *Eligibility:* You are in the 25 percent federal income tax bracket or higher, and the capital gains you've incurred come from selling investment securities held for more than one year. After 2012, however, your rate on short-term capital gains, along with your income-tax bracket, is likely going to jump to 28 percent, and on long-term capital gains it's going to jump to 20 percent.

✔ **Rates as high as 35 percent.** *Suckerability:* The capital gains come from selling investment securities held for less than one year, in which case you will be taxed at the same rate you are taxed for other income. After 2012, the top tax bracket is scheduled to rise to 39.6 percent.

Market makers and croupiers

In the world of ETFs, we don't have croupiers, but we have market makers. *Market makers* are people who work at the stock exchanges and create (like magic!) ETF shares. Each ETF share represents a portion of a portfolio of stocks, sort of like poker chips represent a pile of cash. As an ETF grows, so does the number of shares. Concurrently (once a day), new stocks are added to a portfolio that mirrors the ETF. See Figure 2-1, which may help you envision the structure of ETFs and what makes them such tax wonders.

When an ETF investor sells shares, those shares are bought by a market maker who turns around and sells them to another ETF investor. By contrast, with mutual funds, if one person sells, the mutual fund must sell off shares of the underlying stock to pay off the shareholder. If stocks sold in the mutual fund are being sold for more than the original purchase price, the shareholders left behind are stuck paying a capital gains tax. In some years, that amount can be substantial.

In the world of ETFs, no such thing has happened or is likely to happen, at least not with the vast majority of ETFs, which are index funds. Because index funds trade infrequently, and because of ETFs' poker-chip structure, ETF investors rarely see a bill from Uncle Sam for any capital gains tax. That's not a guarantee that there will never be capital gains on any index ETF, but if there ever are, they are sure to be minor.

Traditional Mutual Fund

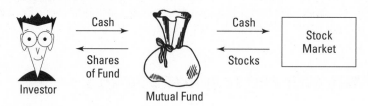

Exchange-Traded Fund

Figure 2-1:
The secret
to ETFs' tax
friendliness
lies in their
very
structure.

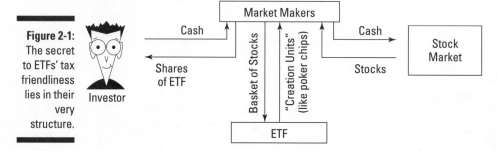

The actively managed ETFs — currently a very small fraction of the ETF market, but almost certain to grow — may present a somewhat different story. They are going to be, no doubt, less tax friendly than index ETFs but more tax friendly than actively managed mutual funds. Exactly where will they fall on the spectrum? It may take another year or two (or three) before we really know.

Tax efficient does not mean tax-free. Although you won't pay capital gains taxes, you will pay taxes on any dividends issued by your stock ETFs, and stock ETFs are just as likely to issue dividends as are mutual funds. In addition, if you sell your ETFs and they are in a taxable account, you have to pay capital gains tax (15 percent for most folks; 20 percent after 2012) if the ETFs have appreciated in value since the time you bought them. But hey — at least you get to decide when to take a gain, and when you do, it's an actual gain.

ETFs that invest in taxable bonds and throw off taxable bond interest are not likely to be very much more tax friendly than taxable-bond mutual funds.

ETFs that invest in actual commodities, holding real silver or gold, tax you at the "collectible" rate of 28 percent. And ETFs that tap into derivatives (such as commodity futures) and currencies sometimes bring with them very complex (and costly) tax issues.

Taxes on earnings — be they dividends or interest or money made on currency swaps — aren't an issue if your money is held in a tax-advantaged account, such as a Roth IRA. I love Roth IRAs! More on that topic when I get into retirement accounts in Chapter 19.

What you see is what you get

A key to building a successful portfolio, right up there with low costs and tax efficiency, is diversification, a subject I discuss more in Chapter 4. You cannot diversify optimally unless you know exactly what's in your portfolio. In a rather infamous example, when tech stocks (some more than others) started to go belly up in 2000, holders of Janus mutual funds got clobbered. That's because they learned after the fact that their three or four Janus mutual funds, which gave the illusion of diversification, were actually holding many of the same stocks.

Style drift: An epidemic

With a mutual fund, you often have little idea of what stocks the fund manager is holding. In fact, you may not even know what *kinds* of stocks he is holding. Or even if he is holding stocks! I'm talking here about *style drift,* which occurs when a mutual fund manager advertises his fund as aggressive, but over time it becomes conservative, and vice versa. I'm talking about the mutual fund manager who says he loves large value but invests in large growth or small value.

One classic case of style drift cost investors in the all-popular Fidelity Magellan Fund a bundle. The year was 1996, and then fund manager Jeffrey Vinik reduced the stock holdings in his "stock" mutual fund to 70 percent. He had 30 percent of the fund's assets in either bonds or short-term securities. He was betting that the market was going to sour, and he was planning to fully invest in stocks after that happened. He was dead wrong. Instead, the market continued to soar, bonds took a dive, Fidelity Magellan seriously underperformed, and Vinik was out.

One study by the Association of Investment Management concluded that a full 40 percent of actively managed mutual funds are not what they say they are. Some funds bounce around in style so much that an investor would have almost no idea where her money was. The Parnassus Fund, for example, was once placed by Morningstar in the small cap blend category. Then it moved to small cap value. Later it moved to mid cap blend. Later still, the fund was reclassified as mid cap growth.

ETFs are the cure

When you buy an indexed ETF, you get complete transparency. You know exactly what you are buying. No matter what the ETF, you can see in the prospectus or on the ETF provider's website (or on any number of independent financial websites) a complete picture of the ETF's holdings. See, for example, either www.etfconnect.com or http://finance.yahoo.com. If I go to either website and type the letters *IYE* (the ticker symbol for the iShares Dow Jones U.S Energy Sector ETF) in the box in the upper right of the screen, I can see in an instant what my holdings are. You can see too, in Table 2-3.

Table 2-3	Holdings of the iShares Dow Jones U.S. Energy Sector ETF as of 04/14/2011	
Name	*% Net Assets*	*Market Value in U.S. $*
Exxon Mobil Corp.	23.3	269,550,164.40
Chevron Corp.	11.95	138,256,608.80
Schlumberger Ltd.	6.86	79,338,333.72
ConocoPhillips	5.97	69,068,598.06
Occidental Petroleum Corp.	4.75	54,922,347.27
Apache Corp.	2.9	33,510,937.80
Halliburton Co.	2.64	30,527,847.28
Anadarko Petroleum Corp.	2.34	27,048,345.60
Devon Energy Corporation	2.29	26,483,537.22
Marathon Oil Corp.	2.26	26,110,651.59

You simply can't get that information on most actively managed mutual funds. Or if you can, the information is both stale and subject to change without notice.

Transparency also discourages dishonesty

The scandals that have rocked the mutual fund world over the years have left the world of ETFs untouched. There's not a whole lot of manipulation that a fund manager can do when his picks are tied to an index. And because ETFs trade throughout the day, with the price flashing across thousands of computer screens worldwide, there is no room to take advantage of the "stale" pricing that occurs after the markets close and mutual fund orders are settled. All in all, ETF investors are much less likely ever to get bamboozled than are investors in active mutual funds.

Getting the Professional Edge

I don't know about you, but when I take the kids bowling and — as happens on very rare occasion — I bowl a strike, I feel as if a miracle of biblical proportions has occurred. And then I turn on the television, stumble upon a professional bowling tournament, and see guys for whom *not* bowling a strike is a rare occurrence. The difference between amateur and professional bowlers is huge. The difference between investment amateurs and investment professionals can be just as huge. But you can close much of that gap with ETFs.

Consider a few impressive numbers

By investment professionals, Lord knows I'm not talking about stockbrokers or variable-annuity salesmen, or my barber, who always has a stock recommendation for me. I'm talking about the managers of foundations, endowments, and pension funds with $1 billion or more in invested assets. By amateurs, I'm talking about the average U.S. investor with a few assorted and sundry mutual funds in his 401(k).

Let's compare the two: During the 20-year period 1990 through 2009, the U.S. stock market, as measured by the S&P 500 Index, provided an annual rate of return of 8.2 percent. Yet the average stock mutual fund investor, according to a study by Dalbar, earned an annual rate of 3.2 percent over that same period, just barely keeping up with the inflation rate of 2.8 percent a year. Bond-fund investors did much worse. Why the pitiful returns? There are several reasons, but two main ones:

- ✔ Mutual fund investors pay too much for their investments.
- ✔ They jump into hot funds in hot sectors when they're hot and jump out when those funds or sectors turn cold. (In other words, they are constantly buying high and selling low.)

Professionals tend not to do either of those things. To give you an idea of the difference between amateurs and professionals, consider this: For that very same 20-year period in which the average stock mutual fund investor earned 3.2 percent, and the average bond mutual fund investor earned 1 percent, the multibillion-dollar stock-and-bond-and-real-estate California Public Employees' Retirement System (CALPERS) pension fund, the largest in the nation, earned nearly 8 percent a year.

You can do what they do!

Professional managers, you see, don't pay high expenses. They don't jump in and out of funds. They know that they need to diversify. They tend to buy indexes. They know exactly what they own. And they know that asset allocation, not stock picking, is what drives long-term investment results. In short, they do all the things that an ETF portfolio can do for you. So do it. Well, maybe . . . but first read the rest of this chapter!

Passive versus Active Investing: Your Choice

Surely, you've sensed by now my preference for index funds over actively managed funds. Until recently, all ETFs were index funds. And in the past few years, most index funds have been ETFs.

On March 25, 2008, Bear Stearns introduced an actively managed ETF: the Current Yield ETF (YYY). As fate would have it, Bear Stearns was just about to go under, and when it did, the first actively managed ETF went with it. Prophetic? Perhaps. In the three years since, about two dozen actively managed ETFs have hit the street, with very little commercial success. At the time of this writing, however, a number of companies, many of them new to the ETF market, have sought permission from the U.S. Securities and Exchange Commission to launch ETFs that follow no indexes. These players include PIMCO, BlackRock, Eaton Vance, T. Rowe Price, and Dreyfus.

I don't think this development is necessarily a bad thing, but I'm not frothing at the mouth to invest in actively managed ETFs, either.

Let's looks at a few of the pros and cons.

The index advantage

The superior returns of indexed mutual funds and ETFs over actively managed funds have had much to do with the popularity of ETFs to date. Index funds (which buy and hold a fixed collection of stocks or bonds) consistently outperform actively managed funds. One study done by Fulcrum Financial tracked mutual fund performance over ten years and found that 81 percent of value funds underperformed the indexes, as did 63 percent of growth funds. And that is just one of many, many studies that present similar results.

Here are some reasons that index funds (both mutual funds and ETFs) are hard to beat:

- ✔ They typically carry much lower management fees, sales loads, or redemption charges.

- ✔ Hidden costs — trading costs and spread costs — are much lower when turnover is low.

- ✔ They don't have cash sitting around idle (as the manager waits for what he thinks is the right time to enter the market).

- ✔ They are more — sometimes much more — tax efficient.

- ✔ They are more "transparent" — you know exactly what securities you are investing in.

Perhaps the greatest testament to the success of index funds is how many allegedly actively managed funds are actually index funds in (a very expensive) disguise. I'm talking about closet index funds. According to a report in *Investment News,* a newspaper for financial advisers, the number of actively managed stock funds that are closet index funds has tripled over the past several years. As a result, many investors are paying high (active) management fees for investment results that could be achieved with low-cost ETFs.

R squared is a measurement of how much of a fund's performance can be attributed to the performance of an index. It can range from 0.00 to 1.00. An R squared of 1.00 indicates *perfect correlation*: When a fund goes up, it's because the index was up — every time; when the fund falls, it's because the index fell — every time. An R squared of 0.00 indicates no such correlation. This measurement is used to assess tracking errors and to identify closet index funds.

According to Morningstar data as interpreted by *Investment News,* nearly 28 percent of all large cap funds carry a three-year R squared of 0.95 or higher relative to the S&P 500 stock index. That kind of number makes them closet index funds. And if you look at the entire mutual fund industry, it is apparent that the triumph of indexing is becoming well known. Recently, the average large cap fund had an R squared of almost 0.90. That number is up from 0.74 only a decade or so ago.

The allure of active management

Speaking in broad generalities, actively managed mutual funds have been no friend to the small investor. Their dominance remains a testament to people's ignorance of the facts and the enormous amount of money spent on (often deceptive) advertising and PR that give investors the false impression that buying this fund or that fund will lead to instant wealth. The media often plays into this nonsense with splashy headlines, designed to sell magazine copies or attract viewers, that promise to reveal which funds or managers are currently the best.

Still, active management can make sense — and that may be especially true when some of the best aspects of active management are brought to the ETF market. Some managers actually do have the ability to "beat the markets" — they are just few and far between, and the increased costs of active management often nullify any and all advantages these market-beaters have. If those costs can be minimized, and if you can find such a manager, you may wind up ahead of the game. Active management in ETF form may also be both more efficient and more transparent than it is in mutual fund form.

And finally, with some kinds of investments, such as commodities and possibly bonds, active management may simply make better sense in certain cases. I talk about these scenarios in Part III.

Why the race is getting harder to measure . . . and what to do about it

Unfortunately, the old-style "active versus passive" studies that consistently gave passive (index) investing two thumbs up are getting harder and harder to do. What exactly qualifies as an "index" fund anymore, now that many ETFs are set up to track indexes that, in and of themselves, were created to outperform "the market" (traditional indexes)? And whereas index investing once promised a very solid cost savings, some of the newer ETFs, with their newfangled indexes, are charging more than some actively managed funds. Future studies are likely to become muddier and muddier.

Here's my advice: Give a big benefit of the doubt to index funds as the ones that will serve you the best in the long run. If you want to go with an actively managed fund, follow these guidelines:

- ✔ Keep your costs low.
- ✔ Don't believe that a manager can beat the market unless that manager has done so consistently for years, and for reasons that you can understand. (That is, avoid "Madoff" risk!)
- ✔ Pick a fund company that you trust.
- ✔ Don't go overboard! Mix an index fund or two in with your active fund(s).
- ✔ All things being equal, you may want to choose an ETF over a mutual fund. But the last section of this chapter can help you to determine that. Ready?

Do ETFs Belong in Your Life?

Okay, so on the plus side of ETFs we have ultra-low management expenses, super tax efficiency, transparency, and a lot of fancy trading opportunities, such as shorting, if you are so inclined. What about the negatives? In the sections that follow, I walk you through some other facts about ETFs that you should consider before parting with your precious dollars.

Calculating commissions

I talk a lot more about commissions when I compare and contrast various brokerage houses in Chapter 3, but I want to give you a heads up here: You may have to pay a commission every time you buy and sell an ETF.

Here's the good news: Trading commissions for stocks and ETFs (it's the same commission for either) have been dropping faster than the price of desktop computers. What once would have cost you a bundle, now — if you trade online, which you definitely should — is really pin money, perhaps as low as $4 a trade, and sometimes nothing at all. However, you can't simply ignore trading commissions. They aren't always that low, and even $4 a pop can add up. In most cases, you shouldn't agonize over the cost of trading ETFs; merely keep an eye on them.

Moving money in a flash

The fact that ETFs can be traded throughout the day like stocks makes them, unlike mutual funds, fair game for day-traders and institutional wheeler-dealers. For the rest of us common folk, there isn't much about the way that ETFs are bought and sold that makes them especially valuable. Indeed, the ability to trade throughout the day may make you more apt to do so, perhaps selling or buying on impulse. As I discuss in detail in Chapter 17, impulsive investing, although it can get your endorphins pumping, is generally not a profitable way to proceed.

Understanding tracking error

At times, the value of the securities held by the ETF may trade above or below the index it follows. This situation is called *tracking error*. At times, an ETF may also sell at a price that is a tad higher or lower than what that price should be given the prices of all the securities held by the ETF. This situation is called selling at a *premium* (when the price of the ETF rides above the value of the securities) or selling at a *discount* (when the price of the ETF drops below the value of the securities). Both foreign-stock funds and bond funds are more likely to run off track, either experiencing tracking error or selling at a premium or discount. But the better funds do not run off track to any alarming degree.

In Chapter 3, I offer a few trading tricks for minimizing "off track" ETF investing, but for now, let me say that it is not something to worry about if you are a buy-and-hold ETF investor — the kind of investor I want you to become.

Making a sometimes tricky choice

In Parts II, III, and IV of this book, I give you lots of detailed information about how to construct a portfolio that meets your needs. Here, I just want to whet your appetite with a couple of very basic examples of decisions you may be facing.

The infamous "flash crash" of 2010

On the afternoon of May 6, 2010, the stock market, if you'll indulge me for a moment and allow for the use of a highly technical term, went kablooey. No terrorist attacks occurred that day — no earthquakes or tsunamis or heart attacks in the White House either. With no real reason to explain it, the stock market suddenly plunged by nearly 10 percent. Some ETFs had fallen in value to mere pennies on the dollar. It seemed like the start of another Great Depression.

Ooops.

The "flash crash" of 2010 was just a big mistake — a few computer glitches, essentially — and within 10 minutes, the market nearly recovered. Trades made in those 10 minutes were corrected, and life went on as normal. Sort of. For months that followed, market authorities scratched their collective chins, trying to figure out what exactly went wrong and how to make sure that it didn't happen again. They've since, they assure us, instituted circuit breakers so that the same kind of swift movement again will result in the temporary shutting down of the market, allowing troublesome computer glitches to be addressed.

So now you're safe. Maybe.

Still, if you feel nervous about another "flash crash," perhaps one in which trades won't be corrected, exercise caution when trading your ETF holdings. A "stop order" tells your broker to sell your ETF if it drops below a certain price — say, for example, below $10 a share. In theory, that protects you from a market crash. But in reality, it may actually subject you to a crash. If, say, the price of your ETF shares drops precipitously enough, as prices did on May 6, 2010, your order to sell if the price dips below $10 may kick in at 10 *cents* a share. Solution: Instead of a "stop order" use a "stop-limit" order, which tells the broker to sell your ETF if the price drops below, say, $10 a share, but not to sell if you can't get, say, at least $9 a share.

Or — perhaps a better solution — don't use stop orders at all. Rather, be prepared for some bumps in the road, and only invest in the stock market money that you or your family won't need for a good time to come. More on risk control in Chapter 4.

The index mutual fund trap

Some brokerage houses, such as Vanguard and Fidelity, offer wonderful low-cost index mutual funds. But a problem with them is that you either can't buy them at other financial "supermarkets" (such as Charles Schwab or T. Rowe Price), or you have to pay a substantial fee to get into them. So building an entire portfolio of index mutual funds can be tough. If you want both Fidelity and Vanguard funds, you may be forced to pay high fees or to open up separate accounts at different supermarkets, which means extra paperwork and hassle. With ETFs, you can buy them anywhere, sell them anywhere, and keep them — even if they are ETFs from several different providers — all parked in the same brokerage house. I know of no major brokerage house that now charges more than $10 to make an online ETF trade.

Say you have a choice between investing in an index mutual fund that charges 0.15 percent a year and an ETF that tracks the same index and charges the same amount. Or say you are trying to choose between an actively managed mutual fund and an ETF with the very same manager managing the very same kind of investment, with the same costs. What should you invest in?

If your money is in a taxable account, go with the ETF, provided you are investing at least a few thousand dollars and you plan to keep your money invested for at least several years. If you're investing less, and/or if you think you may need to tap the money anytime soon, you may be better off with the index mutual fund that won't charge you commissions to buy and sell shares.

But say you have, oh, $5,000 to invest in your IRA. (All IRA money is taxed as income when you withdraw it in retirement, and therefore the tax efficiency of securities held within an IRA isn't an issue.) An ETF charges you a management fee of 0.15 percent a year, and a comparable index mutual fund charges 0.35, but buying and selling the ETF will cost you $7.95 at either end. Now what should you do?

The math isn't difficult. The difference between 0.15 and 0.35 (0.20 percent) of $5,000 is $10. It will take you less than one year to recoup your trading fee of $7.95. If you factor in the cost of selling (another $7.95), it will take you 1.6 years to recoup your trading costs. At that point, the ETF will be your lower-cost tortoise, and the mutual fund your higher-cost hare.

In general, building an entire portfolio out of ETFs usually makes sense starting in the ballpark of $50,000. Anything less than that, and you are most likely better off with mutual funds or a mix of mutual funds and ETFs. The exception would be, say, a portfolio of all Vanguard ETFs held at Vanguard, where there would be no trading fees. Or a portfolio of all Schwab ETFs held at Schwab, with the same deal. In these cases, the ETF portfolio may make sense for even the smallest of accounts.

Warning: If you have a trigger finger, and you are the kind of person who is likely to jump to trade every time there's a blip in the market, you would be well advised to go with mutual funds (that don't impose short-term redemption fees). You're less likely to shoot yourself in the foot!

Chapter 3

Getting to Know the Players

I love to shop on Christmas Eve. It's the only time the entire year when men — husbands and boyfriends who finally realize that they need to buy a gift, quickly — outnumber women at the mall. I see these hulking figures, some in bright orange hunting jackets, walking the halls of the Lehigh Valley Mall, looking themselves like scared prey. "Where's the lingerie?" they ask, eyes to the ground.

Sometimes, when I suggest to a client that he buy a few ETFs for his portfolio, I see the same look of dire trepidation. I need to reassure him that buying ETFs isn't that difficult. In this chapter, I want to do the same for you.

This chapter is something of a shopper's guide to ETFs — a mall directory, if you will. I don't suggest which specific ETFs to buy (I will, I will — but that's for later chapters). Instead, I show you where to find the brokerage houses that allow you to buy and sell ETFs; the financial institutions that create ETFs; the indexes on which the financial institutions base their ETFs; and the exchanges where millions of ETF shares are bought, sold, and borrowed each day.

Creating an Account for Your ETFs

You — you personally — can't just buy a share of an ETF as you would buy, say, a negligee. You need someone to actually buy it for you and hold it for you. That someone is a broker, sometimes referred to as a *brokerage house* or a *broker-dealer.* Some broker-dealers, the really big ones, are sort of like financial department stores or supermarkets where you can buy ETFs, mutual funds, individual stocks and bonds, or fancier investment products like puts and calls. You'll recognize, I'm sure, the names of such financial department stores: Fidelity, Vanguard, TD Ameritrade, and T. Rowe Price.

ETFs are usually traded just as stocks are traded. Same commissions. Mostly the same rules. Same hours (generally 9:30 a.m. to 4:00 p.m., Manhattan Island time). Through your brokerage house, you can buy 1 share, 2 shares, or 10,000 shares. Here's one difference between ETFs and stocks: Although people today rarely do it, you can sometimes purchase stocks directly from a company, and you may even get a pretty certificate saying you own the stock. (I *think* some companies still do that!) Not so with ETFs. Call BlackRock or State Street and ask to buy a share of an ETF, and they will tell you to go find yourself a broker. Ask for a certificate, and . . . well, don't even bother.

The first step, then, prior to beginning your ETF shopping expedition, is to find a brokerage house, preferably a financial department store where you can keep all your various investments. It makes life a lot easier to have everything in one place, to get one statement every month, and to see all your investments on one computer screen.

Answering a zillion questions

The first question you have to answer when opening an account is whether it will be a retirement account or a non-retirement account. If you want a retirement account, you need to specify what kind (IRA? Roth IRA? SEP?). I cover the ins and outs of retirement accounts — and how ETFs can fit snuggly into the picture — in Chapter 19. A non-retirement account is a simpler animal. You don't need to know any special tax rules, and your money isn't committed for any time period unless you happen to stick something like a CD into the account.

The next question you have to answer is whether you want to open a *margin* account or a *cash* account. A margin account is somewhat similar to a checking account with overdraft protection. It means that you can borrow from the account or make purchases of securities (such as ETFs, but generally not mutual funds) without actually having any cash to pay for them on the spot. Cool, huh?

Unless you have a gambling addiction, go with margin. You never know when you may need a quick (and, compared to credit cards, inexpensive) and potentially tax-deductible loan. If you think you may have a gambling addiction, however, read the sidebar "Don't margin your house away!"

Don't margin your house away!

I once knew a woman whose husband handled all of the finances. Then they divorced. Divorcing couples usually split the family assets, but they also split the liabilities. This woman had no idea, until she divorced, that her hubbie had been playing with stocks and ETFs, buying them on margin. Suddenly, she inherited a rather enormous debt. "Buying on margin" means that the brokerage house is lending you money, and charging you interest, so you can purchase securities. Ouch. One of the often touted "advantages" of ETFs is that you can buy them on margin — something you often can't do with mutual funds. Margin buying is very dangerous business. The fact that you can buy an ETF on margin is *not* an advantage as I see it. The stock market is risky enough. Don't ever compound that risk by borrowing money to invest. You may wind up losing not only your nest egg but also your home. This woman was able to save hers; not everyone is so lucky.

Two things about margin you should know:

✔ The brokerage house can usually change the rate of interest you're paying without notice.

✔ If your investments dip below a certain percentage of your margin loan, the brokerage house can sell your stocks and bonds right from under you.

It can be dangerous business. Margin only with great caution.

You're also asked questions about beneficiaries and titling (or registration), such as whether you want your joint account set up with rights of survivorship. I'll just say one quick word about naming your beneficiaries: Be certain that who you name is who you want to receive your money if you die.

Beneficiary designations supercede your will. In other words, if your will says that all your ETFs go to your spouse, and your beneficiary designation on your account names someone else, your spouse loses; all the ETFs in your account will go to someone else.

For more information on what happens to your assets when you die, I recommend *Estate Planning For Dummies* by N. Brian Caverly, Esq. and Jordan S. Simon (Wiley).

Finally, you're asked all kinds of personal questions about your employment, your wealth, and your risk tolerance. Don't sweat them! Federal securities regulations require brokerage houses to know something about their clients. Honestly, I don't think anyone ever looks at the personal section of the forms. I've never heard any representative of any brokerage house so much as whisper any of the information included in those personal questions.

Placing an order to buy

After your account is in place, which should take only a few days, you're ready to buy your first ETF. Most brokerage houses give you a choice: Call in your order, or do it yourself online. Calling is typically much more expensive, as it requires the direct assistance of an actual person. Being the savvy investor that you are, you're not going to throw money away, so place all your orders online! If you need help, a representative of the brokerage house will walk you through the process step-by-step — for free!

Keep in mind when trading ETFs that the trading fees charged by the brokerage, although usually not all that much, can nibble seriously into your holdings. Even if you work with a brokerage house that waives charges for trading particular ETFs, there will still be a small cost called the *spread* that you don't readily see. The spread is where you may lose a penny or two or three to middlemen working behind the scenes of each trade. Spreads can nibble at your portfolio just as the more visible fees do. Here's how to avoid getting nibbled:

- ✔ **Don't trade often.** Buy and hold, more or less (see Chapter 17). Yes, I know that a number of headlines since 2008 have declared that "buy and hold is dead." That's nonsense. Don't believe it. "Buy and hold," by the way, doesn't mean you *never* trade. But if you're making more than a few trades every few months, that's too much.

- ✔ **Know your percentages.** In general, don't bother with ETFs if the trade is going to cost you anything more than one-half of one percent. In other words, if making the trade is going to cost you $8 (an average amount for an online trade), you want to invest at least $1,600 at a pop. If you have only $1,000 to invest, or less, you are often better off purchasing a no-load mutual fund, preferably an index fund, or waiting until you've accumulated enough cash to make a larger investment. Alternatively, you might choose a no-commission ETF, even if it's slightly less attractive than the ETF you'd have to pay a commission for. You may swap for the better alternative down the road, especially if you are funding a retirement account where swapping will have no tax consequences.

- ✔ **Be a savvy shopper.** Keep the cost of your individual trades to a minimum by shopping brokerage houses for the lowest fees, placing all your orders online, and arguing for the best deals. Yes, you can often negotiate with these people for better deals, especially if you have substantial bucks. Also know that many brokerage houses offer special incentives for new clients: Move more than $100,000 in assets and get your first 50 trades for free, or that sort of thing. Always ask.

But wait just a moment!

Please don't be so enthralled by anything you read in this book that you rush out, open a brokerage account, and sell your existing mutual funds or stocks and bonds to buy ETFs. Rash investment decisions almost always wind up being mistakes. Remember that whenever you sell a security, you may face serious tax consequences. (Vanguard offers a unique advantage here; see the sidebar "The Vanguard edge" in this chapter.) If you decide to sell certain mutual funds, annuities, or life insurance policies, there may also be nasty surrender charges. If you're unsure whether selling your present holdings would make for a financial hit on the chin, talk to your accountant or financial planner.

Trading ETFs like a pro

If you're familiar with trading stocks, you already know how to trade ETFs. If you aren't, don't sweat it. Although there are all kinds of fancy trades you could make, and we'll touch on a few later, I'm going to ask you now to familiarize yourself with only the two most basic kinds of trades: market orders and limit orders.

A *market order* to buy tells the broker that you want to buy. Period. After the order is placed, you will have bought your ETF shares . . . at whatever price someone out there was willing to sell you those shares.

A *limit order* to buy asks you to name a price above which you walk away and go home. No purchase will be made. (A limit order to sell asks you to name a price below which you will not sell. No sale will be made.)

Market orders are fairly easy. As long as you are buying a domestic ETF that isn't too exotic (the kind of ETFs I'll be recommending throughout this book); as long as you aren't trading when the market is going crazy; as long as you aren't trading right when the market opens or closes (9:30 a.m. and 4:00 p.m., Manhattan time weekdays); you should be just fine.

A limit order may be a better option if you are placing a purchase for an ETF where the "bid" and the "ask" price may differ by more than a few pennies (indicating the middlemen are out to get you), or where there may be more than a negligible difference between the market price of the ETF and the net asset value of the securities it is holding. This would include foreign-stock ETFs, junk-bond ETFs, and any other ETFs that trade not that many shares — especially on a day when the market seems jumpy. The risk with limit orders is that you may not get your price, and so the order may not go through.

To execute a limit order without risk that you'll miss out on your purchase, place the order slightly above the last sale. If your ETF's last sale was for $10 a share, you may offer $10.01. If you're buying 100 shares, you may have just blown a whole dollar, but you'll have your purchase in hand.

Introducing the Shops

I've read that the motorcycle industry boasts the highest level of consumer loyalty in the United States. A Harley man would *never* be caught dead on a Yamaha. Not being a motorcyclist, I have no idea why that is. In the world of brokerage houses, after someone has a portfolio in place at a house such as Fidelity, Vanguard, or Schwab, that client is often very hesitant to switch. I know *exactly* why that is: Moving your account can sometimes be a big, costly, and time-consuming hassle. So, whether you're a Harley man or a Yamaha mama, if you have money to invest, it behooves you to spend some serious time researching brokerage houses and to choose the one that will work best for you. Perhaps I can help.

What to look for

Here's what you want from any broker who is going to be holding your ETFs:

- Reasonable prices
- Freebies, including free trades on certain ETFs
- Good service, meaning they answer the phone without putting you through answering-system hell
- A user-friendly website
- Good advice, if you think you're going to need advice
- A service center near you, if you like doing business with real people
- Incentives for opening an account, which can run the gamut from a certain number of fee-free trades to laptop computers
- Financial strength

Financial strength really isn't as important as the others because all brokerage houses carry insurance. Still, a brokerage house that collapses under you can be a problem, and it may take time to recoup your money. See the sidebar "Can you lose your ETFs if your brokerage house collapses?"

I give you my take on some of the major brokerage houses in just a moment, but I first want to talk a bit about prices, which can be downright devilish to compare and contrast.

Can you lose your ETFs if your brokerage house collapses?

Brokerage houses, as part of their registration process with the federal government, are automatically insured through the Securities Investor Protection Corporation (SIPC). Each individual investor's securities are protected up to $500,000 should the brokerage house go belly up. Almost all larger brokerage houses carry supplemental insurance that protects customers' account balances beyond the half-million that SIPC covers. TD Ameritrade,

for example, has insurance through Lloyd's of London that protects each customer's account up to $150 million.

Note: Neither SIPC coverage nor any kind of supplemental insurance will protect the value of your account from a market downfall! For additional information on SIPC, you can order a free brochure by calling 1-800-934-4448 or check out its website at www.sipc.org.

A price structure like none other

Shopping for shoes? Beer? Pickled herring? Go to one store. Go to another. Or open up an issue of *Consumer Reports.* Compare the prices. Easy business.

Comparing the prices at brokerage houses is anything but easy. At Vanguard, for example, you'll pay from $2 to $7 per ETF trade, depending on how much money you have with Vanguard. But if you are trading a Vanguard ETF at Vanguard, you'll pay nothing for the trade. At TD Ameritrade, there are 100 ETFs that you can buy and pay nothing for the trade. But beware! If you don't hold on to them for a full 30 days, you'll be assessed a $20 charge. At ShareBuilder, you can pay only $4 a trade, but you need to commit to a schedule of regular trades that occur only on Tuesdays. (That's right, only on Tuesdays.) This is *not* easy business.

It would take me many pages to relay to you the complicated price structures of the various brokerage houses. I'll pass. Instead, in the following sections, I give you a short summary of the pricing and then leave you to do some leg work. Always look at the entire brokerage package. That includes not only the price of trades but total account fees. You need to do some comparing and contrasting on your own, but with the tools I give you in the following sections, it shouldn't take an eternity. Please turn to Appendix A for websites and phone numbers of the financial supermarkets listed next.

The Vanguard Group

I mention Vanguard frequently in this book for a number of reasons. For one, I like Vanguard because of its leadership role in the world of index investing.

Vanguard is also both an investment house that serves as a custodian of ETFs and is itself a provider of ETFs. (That's also true of Schwab and soon will be true of T. Rowe Price, too.) There's also "The Vanguard edge" (which I discuss in a sidebar later in this chapter). And — perhaps most important to the theme of this book — Vanguard's ETFs are top-notch products. But more on that in a few pages. Right now, I'm here to discuss Vanguard as a shop where you can buy and hold your ETFs.

Incidentally, buying and holding Vanguard ETFs at Vanguard offers an advantage over buying and holding those ETFs elsewhere, in that you won't pay any fees to trade. But Vanguard ETFs can be held at any brokerage, and typically the trading charges will be minimal, so Vanguard the shop and Vanguard the ETF supplier really should be assessed separately.

As for Vanguard the shop, the trading commissions (that apply to ETFs other than Vanguard's own) are reasonable — $2 to $7 a trade, depending on the size of your Vanguard account — and the service is middle of the road (and better than that if you have big bucks with the company). What really shines about Vanguard is, well, two things . . . first, its broad array of top-rated index mutual funds. I know, I know, this is a book about ETFs. But index mutual funds and ETFs are close cousins, and sometimes it makes sense to have both in a portfolio. (More on that subject in Chapter 15.)

If you do wish to hold Vanguard index mutual funds alongside your ETFs, Vanguard is an awfully logical place to hold them because you can buy and sell Vanguard funds, provided you don't do it often, at no charge. At Fidelity, in contrast, buying any Vanguard mutual fund will typically cost you $75.

I also like the very structure of the company. Vanguard is owned "mutually" by its shareholders, unlike, say, Fidelity, which is privately owned, or just about all the other brokerage houses, which are publicly owned. The mutual ownership means that investors are shareholders in the company, and that means the Vanguard elite, although well paid, for sure, have an obligation to serve your best interests. That gives me trust in the company.

One thing about Vanguard drives me a bit crazy. For some strange reason, the company feels compelled to place your funds into two separate accounts: All Vanguard mutual funds go into one account; all mutual funds of other companies and all ETFs (whether from Vanguard or another firm) go into a separate "brokerage" account. This schizo system can make Vanguard statements somewhat harder to read than those of other brokerage houses.

Fidelity Investments

I like this brokerage house a lot. In fact, I house my own ETFs at Fidelity. The service, at least for me, is fabulous. (Okay, I admit it, my clients and I have a fair amount of money there.) The cost of trading at Fidelity is very competitive. Like Vanguard, Fidelity also has some excellent low-cost index funds of its own, which you may wish to keep alongside your ETF portfolio. And the Fidelity website has some really good tools — some of the best available — for analyzing your portfolio and researching new investments.

At present, 30 of BlackRock's iShares ETFs can be traded at Fidelity with no fees. All other ETFs will cost you $7.95 to trade. Fidelity, however, is quite liberal in granting free trades to new customers. Although the policy changes from time to time, recent clients of mine who have opened up fresh accounts at Fidelity were given 200 free trades . . . enough to last a very good while.

Charles Schwab

"Invest with Chuck" Schwab offers a lineup of 13 low-cost, sensible ETFs of its own creation, and they trade free if you open an account with this brokerage. All other ETFs cost $10 per online trade.

Whenever I've had occasion to do business with "Chuck's" staff, I find them friendly and knowledgeable. I just wish I could forgive Chuck for investing — and losing — so much of its clients' money in the mortgage crisis of 2008, and then admitting no wrong and making no restitution until being strong-armed by the court. (For those familiar with the case, I'm referring to Schwab's YieldPlus Fund debacle.)

T. Rowe Price

This Baltimore-based shop has several claims to fame, including its bend-over-backwards friendliness to small investors and its plethora of really fine financial tools, especially for retirement planning, available to all customers at no cost. The price of trading is a wee bit higher than average for a discount broker. ETFs cost $9.95 to $19.95 per online trade, depending on how much money you have invested and how often you trade. At the time of this writing, T. Rowe Price was gearing up to launch its own lineup of ETFs, which rumor has it will all be actively managed.

The service at this firm is excellent (reps tend to be very chummy). If you decide that part of your portfolio should be in mutual funds, you can do a lot worse than going with T. Rowe Price's lineup of entirely load-free funds.

TD Ameritrade

For a number of years, TD Waterhouse and Ameritrade were known as the discount kings of the brokerage biz. They merged several years ago to form TD Ameritrade. The trading prices at TD are just about middle of the pack.

Although I've never had occasion to work with TD, the service is reputedly quite high. The website has a very clean and crisp feel to it. On the down side (in my opinion, of course), the TD culture and many of the articles on the website promote frequent trading, as opposed to, say, Vanguard, where the culture is decidedly more buy-and-hold. (The same two philosophies exist among different providers of ETFs, as I discuss shortly.)

At the moment, this firm is offering commission-free online trades on 100 ETFS (certain iShares, Vanguard products, SPDRs, and PowerShares funds), BUT you must hold them for at least 30 days or you'll need to cough up $20 per trade. All other ETFs cost $10 per online trade. In 2010, the firm acquired online futures brokerage *thinkorswim*, where ETFs trade for $5 and no-load mutual funds trade fee-free regardless of their sponsor.

Scottrade

In March 2011, Scottrade rolled out its own lineup of 15 ETFs, called FocusShares, which you can trade online with no commissions. All other ETFs cost $7 to trade online. You will need other ETFs: The FocusShares offerings, although they boast some of the lowest ongoing management fees in the business, cannot in and of themselves form a complete portfolio. There is not a single non-U.S. fund in the lot (although I imagine that Scottrade will introduce foreign funds over time).

Like TD Ameritrade (I suppose the "trade" in both names is something of a giveaway), the culture at Scottrade doesn't seem to promote wise investor behavior. The home page of the website, for example, is filled with offers for the latest apps to allow you to make trades from your cell phone.

Other brokerage houses

The houses I discuss in the previous sections aren't the only players in town. Here are a few more to consider:

- ✔ **eTrade:** 800-387-2331; www.etrade.com. Not only can you house your ETFs here, but you can refinance the mortgage on your house, as well.

- ✔ **TIAA-CREF:** 800-927-3059; www.tiaa-cref.org. A good company, but I can't work with them directly because I'm not a teacher. This brokerage house works only with people who have chalk under their fingernails. (If you're married to such a person, you qualify, too.)

✔ **Folio Investing:** 888-973-7890; www.folioinvesting.com. This is a very different kind of brokerage house, where you pay a flat rate ($29 a month) and then perhaps a nominal trading charge. It also offers pre-fab, ready-to-go ETF portfolios for the laziest investors. (I comment on these portfolio options in Chapter 16.)

✔ **TradeKing:** 877-495-5464; www.tradeking.com. Despite the somewhat hokey name, this newcomer to the industry is offering the lowest trading prices — $5 per ETF trade, regardless of whether that's online or by phone — and customer service is reportedly excellent.

✔ **ShareBuilder:** At $4 a trade, or even less if you're willing to pay a monthly fee, it's hard to beat ShareBuilder, a subsidiary of ING Bank, on price. The catch is that you have to commit to regular trades. You need to make trades (investing as little as $25) once a week or once a month. And therein lies the problem.

If you're putting in money each week or month, chances are you're not putting in a whole lot. You're a drib-and-drab investor, and drib-and-drab investors, although likely better off with ShareBuilder than most other brokers, should be investing in mutual funds, not ETFs. Do the math. Even if you are saving a very impressive $200 every week out of your paycheck, at $4 a trade, you're losing 2 percent right off the top.

ShareBuilder, alas, also took last place in a customer-service ranking published by *SmartMoney* magazine in 2010.

Presenting the Suppliers

There are dozens and dozens of mutual fund providers. Some of the firms may offer just one fund, and they sometimes give the impression that the entire business is run out of someone's garage. Not so with ETFs. Fewer providers exist (currently 48), they tend to be larger companies, and the top four providers (BlackRock, State Street, Vanguard, and Invesco PowerShares) control 92 percent of the market. Why is that? In large measure it's because ETFs' management fees are so low that a company can't profit unless it enjoys the economies of scale and multiple income streams that come from offering a bevy of ETFs.

It's okay to mix and match — with caution

I want to emphasize that while picking a single brokerage house to manage your accounts makes enormous sense, there is no reason that you can't own ETFs from different sources. Like your favorite professional sports team or clothing store, each supplier of ETFs has its own personality. A portfolio with a combination of BlackRock, Vanguard, and State Street ETFs can work just fine. In fact, I would recommend *not* wedding yourself to a single ETF supplier but being flexible and picking the best ETFs to meet your needs in each area of your portfolio.

(Note that brokerage houses typically do not sell every available mutual fund. But I've never heard of a brokerage house limiting which ETFs it will sell. The reason is simple: When you buy or sell an ETF, you pay a trading fee directly to the brokerage house. The more ETFs they can offer, the merrier.)

When mixing and matching ETFs, I would just caution that you don't want holes in your portfolio, and you don't want overlap. Mixing and matching, say, a total U.S. stock fund from one ETF provider with a European stock fund of another provider would be just fine because there's virtually no chance for either overlap or gaps. However, I would recommend that in putting together, say, a U.S. value and a U.S. growth fund, or a U.S. large cap and a U.S. small cap fund, in the hopes of building a well-rounded portfolio, you may want to choose ETFs from the same ETF provider, using the same index providers (Russell, Morningstar, S&P, and so on). That's because each indexer uses slightly (and sometimes not so slightly) different definitions of "value," "growth, "large," and "small." So mixing and matching funds from different providers may be less than ideal. More on this topic in Chapter 16.

Table 3-1 offers a handy reference to the largest ETF providers, which I introduce you to in a moment. Note that I list the companies in order of the total assets each has in all its ETFs.

Table 3-1	Providers of ETFs		
Company	*Number of ETFs*	*Average Expense Ratio*	*Claim to Fame*
BlackRock iShares	222	0.42	Biggest variety of funds
State Street Global Advisors	100	0.35	Oldest and single-largest ETF
Vanguard	65	0.18	Sensibility and economy
Invesco PowerShares	120	0.60	Quirky indexes
ProShares	119	0.95	Woooeee . . . High volatility with leveraged and inverse ETFs
Van Eck	35	0.60	Alternative investments galore
WisdomTree	50	0.52	Dividend mania

Check your passport

A quick word for you readers who live outside of the United States: All ETFs (and mutual funds) sold in the United States must be approved by the U.S. Securities and Exchange Commission. Other countries have their equivalent governmental regulatory authorities. None of the ETFs listed in this section or in Part II of this book are sold beyond the borders of the United States. Some of the ETF providers mentioned — particularly BlackRock — do sell ETFs in other countries, but they go by different names (*iShares* in Canada are known as *iUnits*), and they likely have different structures.

BlackRock iShares

With 222 ETFs for sale and $475 billion in ETF assets (about 45 percent of the U.S. ETF market), iShares is the undisputed market leader. The firm behind iShares, BlackRock, Inc., merged in 2009 with Barclays Global Investors, the mega-corporation that is now one of the largest investment banks in the world ($3.5+ trillion in assets under management). Through its iShares, BlackRock offers by far the broadest selection of any ETF provider. You can buy iShares that track the major S&P indexes for growth and value, large cap and small cap stocks. Other iShares equity ETFs track the major Russell and Morningstar indexes. You can also find industry-sector iShares ETFs from technology and healthcare to financial services and software.

In the international arena, you can buy an iShares ETF to track either an intercontinental index, such as the MSCI EAFE (Europe, Australia, and the Far East), or much narrower markets, such as the Malaysian or Brazilian stock markets. iShares also offer a broad array of fixed-income (bond) ETFs, with six offerings ranging from long-term conventional Treasury bonds and inflation-protected securities (TIPS) to corporate bonds and foreign bonds.

Management fees vary from a low of 0.09 percent for the plain-vanilla large cap U.S. stock funds, such as the iShares S&P 500 (IVV), to a high of 0.89 percent for the much more exotically flavored iShares S&P India Nifty 50 Index (INDY).

Russell's review: You can't go too wrong with iShares. My only beef is with the price of some of the international funds where BlackRock has enjoyed a monopoly thus far. On the other hand, the firm has done an outstanding job of tracking indexes and offering variety. It also has done a good job of maintaining tax efficiency. I caution you, however, not to get sucked into the iShares candy store. Some of the ETFs track very small markets and market segments and clearly don't belong in most people's portfolios. I suggest that you think twice, for example, before making the iShares MSCI All Peru Capped Index Fund (EPU) a major part of your portfolio.

For more information, call 800-474-2737 or visit www.ishares.com.

State Street Global Advisers (SSgA) SPDRs

State Street's flagship ETF, the first ETF on the U.S. market, is the SPDR S&P 500 (SPY). It boasts almost $80 billion in net assets, nearly twice the assets of any other stock ETF on the market. I suspect that status will change over time, but for now, SSgA's pet spider gives it a firm perch as the second-largest provider of ETFs. State Street's ETFs follow traditional indexes, carry reasonable fees, and are varied enough to allow for a very well-diversified portfolio, at least on the domestic equity side. All told, SSgA's 100 U.S.-based ETFs hold about $245 billion in assets.

Russell's review: The management expenses — 0.35 percent on average — are reasonable, and I like the variety of funds, from which, if you were so inclined, you could build an entire portfolio. The Select Sector SPDRs offer a very efficient way of investing in various industry sectors (if that's your thing). The websites are topnotch, and the SPDRs website in particular — www.spdrs.com — offers some fabulous portfolio-construction tools, such as the *Correlation Tracker,* which allows you to find ETFs that best complement your existing portfolio.

One drawback to SSgA's offerings is the legal structure of some of its ETFs. The oldest ETFs, such as SPY, are set up as unit investment trusts rather than open-end funds as most of the newer ETFs are. That means the older funds can't reinvest dividends on a regular basis, creating a cash drag that can bring down long-term total returns by a smidgen and a half. (It's hard to actually measure the impact.)

For more information, call 866-787-2257 or visit www.streettracks.net or www.spdrs.com.

Vanguard ETFs

It goes without saying that these people know something about index investing. In 1976, Vanguard launched the first index-based mutual fund for the retail investor, the Vanguard Index Trust 500 Portfolio. (Wells Fargo already had an index fund, but it was available only to endowments and other institutions.) In 2001, Vanguard launched its first ETF. Why Vanguard wasn't exactly in the ETF vanguard is anyone's guess, but by the time Vanguard ETFs were introduced to the market, iShares (then under Barclays) had already taken a solid lead. But Vanguard ETFs, due largely to their incredibly low costs, are quickly moving up. As of this writing, 65 Vanguard ETFs held $165 billion in assets, making Vanguard the third-largest ETF provider. And in 2010, Vanguard claimed 50 cents of every dollar that flowed into ETFs. Indeed, Vanguard is winning the growth battle.

How low is low cost? The lowest-cost Vanguard ETFs — the Vanguard S&P 500 ETF (VOO) and the Vanguard Total Stock Market ETF (VTI) — will set you back 0.06 and 0.07 percent in total management expenses per year, respectively. (That's 60 to 70 cents per $1,000 invested.) As far as I know, that may be the lowest cost noninstitutional investment vehicle anywhere in the world, except for two FocusShares ETFs that charge 10 cents less per $1,000 per year. The average expense ratio for Vanguard ETFs is 0.18 percent, making them the cheapest to own in the major leagues.

Russell's review: I *love* Vanguard's low costs. Who wouldn't? (Although two newcomers to the industry, Schwab and FocusShares, are coming to market with fees just a bit lower.) Vanguard's lineup of ETFs, in line with Vanguard's corporate personality, is sensible and direct. The company uses reasonable indexes, tracks them well, and takes the utmost care to avoid capital gains taxes and make certain that all dividends paid are "qualified" dividends subject to a lower tax rate.

For more information, call 877-662-7447 or visit www.vanguard.com.

The Vanguard edge

If you own a Vanguard mutual fund and you want to convert to the Vanguard ETF that tracks the same index, you can do so without any tax ramifications. The conversion is tax-free because you will actually be exchanging one class of shares for another class of shares, all within the same fund. You can do this *only* with Vanguard ETFs. Vanguard actually has a U.S. patent that gives it a monopoly on this share structure.

For example, if you own shares in the Vanguard Total Stock Market Index Fund (VTSMX), and you decide that you want to exchange them for the Vanguard Total Stock Market ETF (VTI), you can do so and not worry about having to take any tax hit. So should you do it? The expense ratio on the mutual fund is 0.18. The expense ratio on the ETF is 0.07. If you have, say, $20,000 in the account, moving from the mutual fund to the ETF will save you $22 a year in management fees. And the conversion may also possibly save you a dollar or two a year in taxes. It would be worth your trouble to make the exchange only if you were looking to keep your investment for more than a couple of years.

Note that the tax-free transfer works in only one direction. If you have ETF shares that have appreciated in value, you can't convert them to mutual fund shares without incurring a taxable gain (unless you hold them in a retirement account).

Invesco PowerShares

Invesco PowerShares, number four in size and number two in number of ETF offerings, hesitates to call all but five of its 120 ETFs "actively managed" and instead refers to them as "dynamic." The ETFs track "enhanced" indexes, or, to use the company's own jargon, "Intellidexes." An Intellidex is a custom-made index, which, according to Invesco PowerShares, "quantitatively chooses stocks for their capital appreciation potential, evaluating and selecting stocks based on multiple valuation criteria, rather than simply by market cap alone."

Multiple valuation criteria. Hmmm. That means potential high turnover and some added trading expenses. It also means that if you choose PowerShares ETFs to build your portfolio, you are no longer a true index investor, which (judging by historical data) may put you at something of a disadvantage.

The company has been quite innovative in its offerings of market-sector ETFs. Examples of this innovation include the Water Resources ETF (PHO), which allows you to invest in a "group of companies that focus on the provision of potable water," and the WilderHill Clean Energy Fund (PBW), which allows you to invest in "companies that focus on greener and generally renewable sources of energy." Another example is the KBW Property & Casualty Insurance Portfolio (KBWP). If you want to slice and dice your portfolio a gadzillion different ways (or at least 120 ways), this lineup of ETFs will let you do just that.

Russell's review: I'm hesitant to embrace PowerShares' new indexes without a longer track record. But nothing about the PowerShares alternative indexes scares me too much, either. Thus far, the firm has been very good at avoiding capital gains taxes, and with average management expenses of 0.60 percent, the funds are still cheap when compared to actively managed mutual funds. Some of the market segments created by PowerShares, such as those mentioned in the previous paragraph, are intriguing, especially if they prove over time to show limited correlation to the rest of the stock market. Still, Water Resources should not make up the whale's share of anyone's portfolio.

For more information, call 800-983-0903 or visit www.powershares.com.

ProShares

ProShares offers nearly the same number of ETFs as PowerShares. The Short QQQ ProShares (PSQ) allows you to *short* the NASDAQ 100: If the NASDAQ goes down 5 percent tomorrow, your ETF will go up (more or less) 5 percent. Of course, the inverse is true, as well. Other ProShares offerings allow you to short the Dow, the S&P 500, or the S&P MidCap 400, among other indexes.

The Ultra ProShares lineup of ETFs allow you to move with the market at double the speed. Ultra QQQ ProShares (QLD), for example, is designed to rise 10 percent when the NASDAQ 100 goes up 5 percent (and, of course, to fall 10 percent when the NASDAQ 100 goes down 5 percent). All these percentages are rough approximations. In the real world, you're going to profit less and risk more than you hoped for.

Russell's review: I'm not too hot on shorting and leveraging strategies, especially as these ETFs employ them, which is to say on a daily returns basis. In short, selling short is akin to market timing, and market timing, while loads of fun, isn't often profitable. As for the less-than-double-your-money, more-than-double-your-risk ProShares Ultra ETFs, well . . . excuse me while I take a minute to scratch my head and try to figure out the logic in that. See my discussion of both strategies in Chapter 11.

For more information, call 866-776-5125 or visit www.proshares.com.

Van Eck (Market Vectors ETFs)

Nothing boring here. There isn't a single investment offered by Van Eck that your grandfather ever heard of, never mind invested in! All 35 Market Vectors ETFs offered by Van Eck Global are in "alternative" asset classes. You won't be investing in Procter & Gamble or McDonalds, but rather in, well, the names of a few of the ETFs will give it away . . . There's the Market Vectors Uranium & Nuclear Energy ETF (NLR), and the Market Vectors Brazil Small-Cap ETF (BRF), for example. Van Eck's niche seems to be finding small segments of the market, be they small industry sectors or out-of-the-way foreign markets, that no other providers thought to capitalize on. In other words, if you can't slice and dice the market into enough fragments using Invesco PowerShares, you always have Van Eck.

Russell's review: There's a reason to use alternative investments, for sure, but they should not be used haphazardly. I do not suggest Van Eck ETFs for the core of your portfolio, but perhaps for the periphery. Just make sure you have a good reason for sending your money to such exotic places.

For more information, call 800-826-5444 or visit www.vaneck.com.

WisdomTree

WisdomTree Investments out of New York, with some fairly big-gun backers, issued 20 ETFs in June 2006. It has since launched 30 more but has closed

10 of the original lot. Just as I was writing this chapter, WisdomTree announced plans to change the investment objectives, strategies, and fund names of eight international equity ETFs in the next few months. (These big guns are busy, turning every which way!)

Like Invesco PowerShares, WisdomTree does not like conventional cap-weighted indexes but prefers to create its own, using weightings based on earnings or dividends. Dividends, in fact, are something of a fetish of WisdomTree's. You can buy the WisdomTree LargeCap Dividend Fund (DLN), the WisdomTree SmallCap Dividend Fund (DES), or the WisdomTree International Dividend Top 100 Fund (DOO).

Russell's review: DOO? WisdomTree? It sounds like a remedial reading course for middle-school students. WisdomTree seems to be still finding itself. I'm seek maturity in my financial associations. And where does this dividend fetish come from? I hope for this company's sake that dividend investing proves profitable moving forward, but I'm not certain that it will. More on that subject in Chapter 11.

For more information, call 866-909-9473 or visit www.wisdomtree.com.

Guggenheim

With its takeover of Rydex SGI in 2011, Guggenheim became eighth among U.S.-based ETF providers, with about $11 billion in assets. It is an interesting company with an unusual mix of products. Many of its ETFs are largely designed for people who are unhappy buying the usual indexes and want to take something of a gamble on a particular equity style, such as large growth stocks. For such an investor, Guggenheim offers its customized S&P 500/ Citigroup Pure Growth ETF. Using a proprietary seven factors to determine which stocks among the S&P 500 are the most "growthy," the firm bundles them into a package that promises purity for the gung-ho growth investor. The company does the same for you on the other side if you are a gung-ho value investor. Yeeeehaaaaa!

If you want to gamble that the Euro is about to go on a tear, you can buy the firm's Euro Currency Trust exchange-traded *product* — not quite an ETF, but almost. And perhaps most intriguing of all of Guggenheim's investment products, the firm offers an innovative S&P Equal Weight ETF (RSP), which, just like it sounds, offers you an opportunity to invest in the S&P 500 with all company stocks represented in equal allocations (as opposed to the more traditional market capitalization–weighted method of allocation).

Russell's review: With an average annual management fee of about 0.50 percent, Guggenheim funds are a bit pricey. As for the currency funds, I don't like gambling in currencies; there is simply no way to know which way the Euro is going *vis-à-vis* the dollar. As for the "pure" funds, I find them intriguing, but in their first few years of existence, they haven't exactly lit the world on fire. The S&P 500 Pure Value ETF (RPV), for example, has a one-star rating from Morningstar . . . and can you blame Morningstar for the trash review? The fund lost nearly 48 percent of its value in 2008 — that's 11 percentage points worse than the Russell 1000 Value Index. The S&P Equal Weight ETF (RSP) is worth some consideration, especially for smaller investors.

For more information, call 800-345-7999 or visit www.guggenheimfunds.com.

Other suppliers

Fidelity Investments is the number one or number two U.S. brokerage house, running neck-and-neck with Vanguard the past couple of years. However, it produces only one ETF, the Fidelity NASDAQ Composite ETF (ONEQ), which tracks companies listed on the NASDAQ Stock Market. For more information, visit www.fidelity.com.

Two of the larger brokerage houses introduced their own ETFs in recent years: Charles Schwab, evidently going after the iShares/SPDRs/Vanguard market, now has 13 very low-cost, broad-market ETFs; and Scottrade has introduced a similar lineup of low-cost ETFs (although more industry-sector oriented) called FocusShares. There are now 15 of those. Also, PIMCO, the mutual fund leader (especially in fixed-income investments), has launched 13 bond ETFs, with talk of launching more soon. Visit www.schwab.com, www.focusshares.com, and www.pimcoetfs.com respectively.

Almost 40 other suppliers of ETFs exist, mostly smaller companies with only a handful of offerings. Many will be gone in the years to come.

Familiarizing Yourself with the Indexers

At the core of every ETF is an index. The index is the blueprint on which the ETF is based. Some ETF providers use old, established indexes. Others create their own, often in conjunction with seasoned indexers. (That association helps them get approval from the SEC.) As a rule, for an ETF to be any good, it has to be based on a solid index. On the other hand, a solid index doesn't guarantee a good ETF because other things, like costs and tax efficiency, matter as well. That being said, I turn now to the five indexers that create and re-create the indexes on which most ETFs are based.

Standard & Poor's

Owned by publishing powerhouse McGraw-Hill, Standard & Poor's is perhaps best known for its credit-rating services. The company also maintains hundreds of indexes, including the S&P 500 (the one you're most likely to see flashed across your television screen on the business channel). Over $1 trillion in investors' assets are directly tied to S&P indexes — more than all other indexes combined.

More ETFs are based on S&P indexes than any other, by far. Those include the iShares broad-based domestic and international ETFs, the Sector SPDRs that track various market segments, most Vanguard U.S. ETFs, the Invesco PowerShares industry-sector funds, and the Guggenheim equal-weight ETFs. For more information, visit www.standardandpoors.com.

Dow Jones

If there were an index for the price of unsalted peanuts in Portugal, Dow Jones would be its purveyor. The company, aside from publishing *The Wall Street Journal* and *Barron's,* develops, maintains, and licenses more than 3,000 market indexes. Those indexes include the world's best-known stock indicator, the Dow Jones Industrial Average, which, in my opinion, should have long ago gone the way of the Edsel. (I explain why in Chapter 5.)

The iShares industry and sector ETFs are based on Dow Jones indexes, as are at least some of the ETFs issued by State Street, ProShares, Deutsche Bank, and Charles Schwab. For more information, visit www.djindexes.com.

MSCI

With indexes of all kinds — stocks, bonds, hedge funds, U.S. and international securities — MSCI (formerly Morgan Stanley Capital International), although not quite a household name, has been gaining ground as the indexer of choice for many ETF providers.

MSCI indexes are the backbone of the international Vanguard ETFs, as well as many of the iShares global-industry funds and single-country ETFs. For more information, visit www.msci.com.

Russell

The largest 1,000 U.S. stocks make up the Russell 1000 index, although it remains relatively obscure because the Dow Industrial and the S&P 500 hog the spotlight when it comes to measuring large cap performance. The next 2,000 largest stocks on the U.S. market are in the Russell 2000. And the Russell 1000 plus the Russell 2000 make up the Russell 3000. Those are Russell's more popular indexes, but it has plenty of others as well.

A dozen of the iShares domestic ETFs are based on Russell indexes, as are seven of Vanguard's U.S. offerings. ProShares and Direxion also use Russell indexes. For more information, visit www.russell.com.

Barclays

Lehman Brothers for years was the leading indexer in the world of fixed income investments. The firm was acquired by Barclays Capital in 2008 (just as Barclays was leaving the ETF business), and thus the long-famous Lehman Brothers Aggregate Bond Index, the closest thing the fixed-income world has to the S&P 500, is now called the Barclays Capital Aggregate Bond Index.

BlackRock's iShares, SPDRs, Vanguard, and Van Eck all use Barclays Capital indexes for their fixed-income ETFs. Considering that the implosion of Lehman Brothers prior to its takeover by Barclays signaled the beginning of the financial crisis in 2008, a name change for these indexes seems understandable. For more information, visit https://ecommerce.barcap.com/indices/index.dxml.

Meeting the Middlemen

In the beginning, most ETFs were traded on the American Stock Exchange. In July 2005, however, iShares decided to move its primary listings for 81 of its ETFs to the New York Stock Exchange, citing superior technology. Then, in 2008, the American Stock Exchange was gobbled up by the New York Stock

Exchange, which today goes by the name NYSE Arca. As a result, more than 90 percent of all U.S.-based ETFs today are listed on the NYSE Arca, with the remainder listed on the NASDAQ.

Note that there is a difference between an ETF being *listed* on, say, the NYSE Arca, and an ETF being *traded* on the NYSE Arca. Long ago, the terms were more or less synonymous. Today, an ETF or stock that is listed on the NYSE Arca can trade on any number of exchanges simultaneously. In fact, the Securities Exchange Act of 1934 permits securities listed on any national securities exchange to be traded by all other such exchanges.

Does it matter to you on which exchange your ETF is listed? No, not really, except to the extent that the stock exchanges love ETFs, and if you are an ETF investor, they will love *you*. The reason is fairly obvious: The stock exchanges make their money on, uh, exchanges of stocks. Mutual funds, per se, are not exchanged. ETFs are. And to promote ETFs, the stock exchanges offer some fairly cool stuff on their websites that you should know about.

NYSE Arca

Tracing its origins to 1792, the New York Stock Exchange (NYSE) Arca today lists about 8,000 securities, has about 3,000 member companies, and trades about 3.5 billion shares a day. Almost all ETFs are listed on the NYSE Arca. I list the exceptions in the next section on the NASDAQ. The website for NYSE Arca is www.nyse.com.

NASDAQ

No bricks and mortar here — the NASDAQ is a uniquely electronic exchange. ETFs listed on the NASDAQ include a handful or two of the foreign iShares ETFs, a dozen of the PowerShares industry-sector ETFs, and the PowerShares QQQ Trust, which tracks the 100 biggest stocks on the NASDAQ and is one of the most beloved ETFs among day-traders.

The acronym NASDAQ, by the way, stands for National Association of Securities Dealers Automatic Quotation. If you go to www.nasdaq.com and click on "ETFs," you'll find a number of very useful tools, including the ETF screener and (awesome, indeed) the ETF "Heatmap," which allows you to see how 100 of the largest ETFs are faring on that particular day. I wouldn't say that the feature has great practical value, but for an investment-world junkie like me, it offers a good rush.

Meeting the Wannabe Middlemen

On January 24, 1848, James Marshall found gold at Sutter's Mill, touching off the California gold rush. About 150 years later, ETFs were the hottest investment product in the land, and so began the ETF rush. Everyone wants in on the game. So we have our ETF providers, the brokerage houses where ETFs are bought and sold, the exchanges where they are listed, and the indexes on which they are based. Who else is there? Ah, the wannabe middlemen: They are about as necessary as forks in a soup kitchen, but be assured that they will continue to try to muscle in on the money.

Commissioned brokers

Most often they call themselves "financial planners," and some may actually do some financial planning. Many, however, are merely salesmen in poor disguise, marketing pricey and otherwise inferior investment products and living off the "load." The *load* — or entrance fee — to buying certain investment products, such as some mutual funds, most annuities, and virtually all life insurance products, can be ridiculously high. Thank goodness they don't exist in the world of ETFs — yet.

When first introduced, the PowerShares lineup of ETFs was designed to be sold through commissioned brokers at 2 percent a pop. The Securities and Exchange Commission killed the idea. But in time, the commissioned brokers will likely return to the world of ETFs, with their lobbyists in tow.

Separately managed accounts (SMAs)

SMAs have traditionally been aimed at the well-to-do. Instead of buying into mutual funds, the wealthy hire a private manager with Persian rugs in his lobby to do essentially what a mutual fund manager does: pick stocks. But now many SMAs are billing themselves as "ETF SMAs." Instead of picking stocks, they pick ETFs — at a price.

ETF SMAs that promise to beat the market through exceptional ETF selection or market timing are unlikely to do any better than stock SMAs. You should not hold your breath waiting for these guys to make you rich. Some SMA managers may be very good at what they do, but much of what they do can be learned in this book. If you want to hire someone to manage your ETFs, that's fine, but if they start talking about skimming 2 percent a year off your assets . . . heck, you'll do better on your own. Trust me.

Annuities and life insurance products

I've seen ads lately from a variable annuity company that features ETFs in its portfolio. Great! That's better than high-priced mutual funds. But still, most variable annuities are way overpriced, carry nasty penalties for early withdrawal, and prove to be lousy investments. The same is true for many life insurance products other than simple term life. Investments in ETFs can make these products better, but that's a relative thing. As a rule, it's best to keep your investment products apart from your insurance products. And never buy an annuity unless you are absolutely sure you know what you are buying.

Mutual funds of ETFs

The term is "closet index funds," and there's an increasing number of them out there, just eager to take your money and invest it in "hand-picked" portfolios of stocks that strangely resemble the entire stock market. In the old days, closet index fund managers would actually have to wake up on Monday morning to make sure their high-priced portfolios were in line with the indexes. Today, they can sleep late because they've socked an indexed ETF or two into their portfolios. You, the investor, get to invest in the ETF or two, and the alleged manager of the mutual fund gets to milk you for much more than you would be charged as a direct ETF shareholder.

Question the purchase of any mutual fund that features ETFs among its top holdings. Ask yourself if there's a good reason for you to be paying two layers of management fees. And if those two layers add up to, say, more than a percentage point, you need to *really* start to question your purchase. Any mutual fund — such as the Seligman TargETFund (cute, eh?) Core A (SHVAX) — that charges a 4.75 percent load along with a gross expense ratio of 1.93 percent to hold a bunch of ETFs for you is worthy of . . . Well, the Seligman fund is dead. But others will come to take its place, for sure.

Part II

Building the Stock (Equity) Side of Your Portfolio

The 5th Wave   By Rich Tennant

"He's proposing a Texas-style ETF — energy, cattle, and hairspray futures."

In this part . . .

Over the past 80 years, the S&P 500 (an index of large U.S. stocks) has enjoyed an average annual return of nearly 10 percent before inflation, and 7 percent after inflation — a substantially greater return rate than bonds, CDs, gold, silver, or even real estate. Most foreign stocks have done equally as well. Small stocks have done even better. Although history doesn't always repeat, it does often echo. And for that reason, most investment advisors, including me, would recommend that a good parcel of your long-term investments be put into stocks.

As fate would have it, the majority of ETFs represent stock holdings. So it's appropriate that I now ask you to turn your attention to how to use ETFs to invest in the stock market. In the first chapter of this section, I look at some basic concepts of equity investing, most notably diversification and risk control. In the seven chapters that follow, I guide you through a step-by-step exploration of the world of stock ETFs. We examine which ETFs may belong in your portfolio and how to best mix and match them.

Chapter 4

Risk Control, Diversification, and Some Other Things You Need to Know

. . . .

In This Chapter

▶ Understanding the relationship between risk and return

▶ Measuring risk

▶ Introducing Modern Portfolio Theory

▶ Addressing the assertion that "MPT is dead"

▶ Seeking a balanced portfolio

. . . .

> *October. This is one of the peculiarly dangerous months to speculate in stocks. The others are July, January, September, April, November, May, March, June, December, August, and February.*
>
> Mark Twain

A peculiarly good writer, but also a peculiarly bad money manager, Twain sent his entire fortune down the river on a few bad investments. A century and a half later, investing, especially in stocks, can still be a peculiarly dangerous game. But today we have low-cost indexed ETFs and a lot more knowledge about the power of diversification. Together, these two things can help lessen the dangers and heighten the rewards of the stock market. In this chapter, I hope to make you a better stock investor — at least better than Mark Twain.

Risk Is Not Just a Board Game

Well, okay, actually Risk *is* a board game, but I'm not talking here about *that* Risk. Rather, I'm talking about investment risk. And in the world of investments, risk means but one thing: volatility. Volatility is what takes people's nest eggs, scrambles them, and serves them up with humble pie. Volatility is what causes investors insomnia and heartburn. Volatility is the potential for financially crippling losses.

Ask people who had most of their money invested in stocks in 2008. For five years prior, the stock market had done pretty darned well. Investors were just starting to feel good again. The last market downfall of 2000–2002 was thankfully fading into memory. And then . . . *POW* . . . the U.S. stock market tanked by nearly 40 percent over the course of the year. Foreign markets fell just as much. Billions and billions were lost. Some portfolios (which may have dipped more than 40 percent, depending on what kind of stocks they held) were crushed. Many who had planned for retirement had to readjust their plans.

There was nothing pretty about 2008.

Is risk to be avoided at all costs? Well, no. Not at all. Risk is to be mitigated, for sure, but risk within reason can actually be *a good thing.* That is because risk and return, much like Romeo and Juliet or Coronas and lime, go hand in hand. Volatility means that an investment can go way down or way up . . . You hope it goes way up. Without some volatility, you resign yourself to a portfolio that isn't poised for any great growth. And in the process, you open yourself up to another kind of risk: the risk that your money will slowly be eaten away by inflation.

If you are ever offered the opportunity to partake in any investment scheme that promises you oodles and oodles of money with "absolutely no risk," run! You are in the presence of a con artist or a fool. Such investments do not exist.

The trade-off of all trade-offs (safety versus return)

To get to the Holy Grail — to get a big, fat payoff from our investments — you and I need to take on the Black Knight and the fire-breathing dragon. There simply is no way that either of us is going to make any sizeable amount of money off our investments without accepting some volatility. The Holy Grail is not handed out to people who stuff money in their mattresses or carry their pennies to the local savings bank.

If you look at different investments over the course of time, you find an uncanny correlation between risk (volatility risk, not inflation risk) and return. Safe investments — those that really do carry genuine guarantees, such as U.S. Treasury Bills, FDIC-insured savings accounts, and CDs — tend to offer very modest returns (often negative returns after accounting for inflation). Volatile investments — like stocks and "junk" bonds, the kinds of investments that cause people to lose sleep — tend to offer handsome returns if you give them enough time.

Time, then, is an essential ingredient in determining appropriate levels of risk. You would be wise to keep any cash you are going to need within the next six months to a year in a savings bank, or possibly in an ETF such as the iShares Barclays 1–3 Year Treasury Bond Fund (SHY), a short-term bond fund that yields a modest return but is very unlikely to lose value. You should *not* invest that portion of your money in any ETF that is made up of company stocks, such as the popular SPY or QQQ. True, SPY or QQQ can (and should), over time, yield much more than SHY, but they are also much more susceptible to sharp price swings. Unless you are not going to need your cash for at least a couple of years (and preferably not for six or seven or more years), you are best off avoiding any investment in the stock market, whether it be through ETFs or otherwise.

So just how risky are ETFs?

Asking how risky, or how lucrative, ETFs are is like trying to judge a soup knowing nothing about the soup itself, only that it is served in a blue china bowl. The bowl — or the ETF — doesn't create the risk; what's inside it does. Thus stock and real estate ETFs tend to be more volatile than bond ETFs. Short-term bond ETFs are less volatile than long-term bond ETFs (I explain why in Part III). Small-stock ETFs are more volatile than large-stock ETFs. International ETFs often see more volatility than U.S. ETFs. And international "emerging-market" ETFs see more volatility than international developed-nation ETFs.

Figure 4-1 shows some examples of various ETFs and where they fit on the risk-return continuum. Note that it starts with bond ETFs at the bottom (maximum safety, minimum volatility) and nearer the top features the EAFE (Europe, Australia, Far East) Index and the South Korea Index Fund. (An investment in South Korean stocks involves not only all the normal risks of business but also includes currency risk, as well as the risk that some deranged North Korean dictator may decide he wants to pick a fight. Buyer beware.)

High Risk (and highest return potential)

iShares MSCI South Korea Index Fund (EWY)

iShares MSCI EAFE Index Fund (EFA)

Vanguard Mid Cap ETF (VO)

SPDR S&P 500 (SPY)

iShares Barclays 7-10 Year Treasury Bond Fund (IEF)

iShares Barclays 1-3 Year Treasury Bond Fund (SHY)

Low Risk (with more modest return potential)

Figure 4-1:
The risk
levels of a
sampling
of ETFs.

Keep in mind when looking at Figure 4-1 that I am segregating these ETFs — treating them as stand-alone assets — for illustration purposes. As I discuss later in this chapter (when I discuss something called Modern Portfolio Theory), stand-alone risk measurements are of limited value. The true risk of adding any particular ETF to your portfolio depends on what is already in the portfolio. (That statement will make sense by the end of this chapter. I promise!)

Smart Risk, Foolish Risk

There is safety in numbers, which is why teenage boys and girls huddle together in corners at school dances. In the case of the teenagers, the safety is afforded by anonymity and distance. In the case of indexed ETFs and mutual funds, safety is provided (to a limited degree only!) by diversification in that they represent ownership in many different securities. Owning many stocks, rather than a few, provides some safety by eliminating something that investment professionals, when they're trying to impress, call *nonsystemic risk.*

Nonsystemic risk is involved when you invest in any individual security, such as shares of HP, Martha Stewart Omnimedia, ImClone, (remember Martha and ImClone?), Enron, or General Motors. It's the risk that the CEO of the company will be strangled by his pet python, that the national headquarters will be destroyed by a falling asteroid, or that the company's stock will take a sudden nosedive simply because of some Internet rumor started by an 11th-grader in the suburbs of Des Moines. Those kinds of risks (and more serious ones) can be effectively eliminated by investing not in individual securities but in ETFs or mutual funds.

Nonsystemic risk contrasts with *systemic risk,* which, unfortunately, ETFs and mutual funds cannot eliminate. Systemic risks, as a group, simply can't be avoided, not even by keeping your portfolio in cash. Examples of systemic risk include the following:

- ✔ **Market risk.** The market goes up, the market goes down, and whatever stocks or stock ETFs you own will generally (though not always) move in the same direction.

- ✔ **Interest rate risk.** If interest rates go up, the value of your bonds or bond ETFs (especially long-term bond ETFs such as TLT, the iShares 20-year Treasury ETF) will fall.

- ✔ **Inflation risk.** When inflation picks up, any fixed-income investments that you own (such as any of the conventional bond ETFs) will suffer. And any cash you hold will start to dwindle in value, buying less and less than it used to.

- ✔ **Political risk.** If you invest your money in the United States, England, France, or Japan, there's little chance that revolutionaries will overthrow the government anytime soon. When you invest in the stock or bond ETFs of certain other countries (or when you hold currencies from those countries), you'd better keep a sharp eye on the nightly news.

- ✔ **Grand scale risks.** The government of Japan wasn't overthrown, but that didn't stop an earthquake and ensuing tsunami and nuclear disaster from sending the Tokyo stock market reeling in early 2011.

Although ETFs cannot eliminate systemic risks, don't despair. For while nonsystemic risks are a bad thing, systemic risks are a decidedly mixed bag. Nonsystemic risks, you see, offer no compensation. A company is not bound to pay higher dividends, nor is its stock price bound to rise simply because the CEO has taken up mountain climbing or hang gliding.

Systemic risks, on the other hand, do offer compensation. Invest in small stocks (which are more volatile and therefore incorporate more market risk), and you can expect (over the very long term) higher returns. Invest in a country with a history of political instability, and (especially if that instability doesn't occur) you'll probably be rewarded with high returns in compensation for taking added risk. Invest in long-term bonds (or long-term bond ETFs) rather than short-term bonds (or ETFs), and you are taking on more interest-rate risk. That's why the yield on long-term bonds is almost always greater.

In other words,

> Higher systemic risk = higher historical returns
>
> Higher nonsystemic risk = zilch

That's the way markets tend to work. Segments of the market with higher risks *must* offer higher returns or else they wouldn't be able to attract capital. If the potential returns on emerging-market stocks (or ETFs) were no higher than the potential returns on short-term bond ETFs or FDIC-insured savings accounts, would anyone but a complete nutcase invest in emerging-market stocks?

How Risk Is Measured

In the world of investments, risk means volatility, and volatility (unlike angels or love) can be seen, measured, and plotted. People in the investment world use different tools to measure volatility, such as standard deviation, beta, and certain ratios such as the Sharpe ratio. Most of these tools are not very hard to get a handle on, and they can help you better follow discussions on portfolio building that come later in this book. Ready to dig in?

Standard deviation: The king of all risk measurement tools

So, you want to know how much an investment is likely to bounce? The first thing you do is look to see how much it has bounced in the past. Standard deviation measures the degree of past bounce and, from that measurement, gives us some notion of future bounce. To put it another way, standard deviation shows the degree to which a stock/bond/mutual fund/ETF's actual returns vary from its average returns over a certain time period.

Table 4-1 presents two hypothetical ETFs and their returns over the last six years. Note that both portfolios start with $1,000 and end with $1,101. But note, too, the great difference in how much they bounce. ETF A's yearly returns range from –3 percent to 5 percent while ETF B's range from –15 percent to 15 percent. The standard deviation of the six years for ETF A is 3.09. For ETF B, the standard deviation is 10.38.

Table 4-1	Standard Deviation of Two Hypothetical ETFs	
Balance, Beginning of Year	**Return (% Increase or Decrease)**	**Balance, End of Year**
ETF A		
1,000	5	1,050
1,050	−2	1,029
1,029	4	1,070
1,070	−3	1,038
1,038	2	1,059
1,059	4	1,101
ETF B		
1,000	10	1,100
1,100	6	1,166
1,166	−15	991
991	-8	912
912	15	1,048
1,048	5	1,101

Predicting a range of returns

What does the standard deviation number tell us? Let's take ETF A as an example. The standard deviation of 3.09 tells us that in about two-thirds of the months to come, we should expect the return of ETF A to fall within 3.09 percentage points of the mean return, which was 1.66. In other words, about 68 percent of the time returns should fall somewhere between 4.75 percent (1.66 + 3.09) and −1.43 percent (1.66 − 3.09). As for the other one-third of the time, anything can happen.

It also tells us that in about 95 percent of the months to come, the returns should fall within two standard deviations of the mean. In other words, 95 percent of the time you should see a return of between 7.84 percent [1.66 + (3.09 × 2)] and −4.52 percent [1.66 − (3.09 × 2)]. The other 5 percent of the time is anybody's guess.

Making side-by-side comparisons

The ultimate purpose of standard deviation, and the reason I'm describing it, is that it gives you a way to judge the relative risks of two ETFs. If one ETF has a 3-year standard deviation of 12, you know that it is roughly twice as volatile as another ETF with a standard deviation of 6 and half as risky as an ETF with a standard deviation of 24. A real-world example: The standard deviation for most short-term bond funds falls somewhere around 0.7. The standard deviation for most precious-metals funds is somewhere around 26.0.

Important caveat: Don't assume that combining one ETF with a standard deviation of 10 with another that has a standard deviation of 20 will give you a portfolio with an average standard deviation of 15. It doesn't work that way at all, as you will see in a few pages when I introduce Modern Portfolio Theory. The combined standard deviation will not be any greater than 15, but it could (if you do your homework and put together two of the right ETFs) be much less.

Beta: Assessing price swings in relation to the market

Unlike standard deviation, which gives you a stand-alone picture of volatility, beta is a relative measure. It is used to measure the volatility of something in relation to something else. Most commonly that "something else" is the S&P 500. Very simply, beta tells us that if the S&P rises or falls by x percent, then our investment, whatever that investment is, will likely rise or fall by y percent.

The S&P is considered our baseline, and it is assigned a beta of 1. So if you know that Humongous Software Corporation has a beta of 2, and the S&P shoots up 10 percent, Jimmy the Greek (if he were still with us) would bet that shares of Humongous are going to rise 20 percent. If you know that the Sedate Utility Company has a beta of 0.5, and the S&P shoots up 10 percent, Jimmy would bet that shares of Sedate are going to rise by 5 percent. Conversely, shares of Humongous would likely fall four times harder than shares of Sedate in response to a fall in the S&P.

In a way, beta is easier to understand than standard deviation; it's also easier to misinterpret. Beta's usefulness is greater for individual stocks than it is for ETFs, but nonetheless it can be helpful, especially when gauging the volatility of U.S. industry-sector ETFs. It is much less useful for any ETF that has international holdings. For example, an ETF that holds stocks of emerging-market nations is going to be volatile, trust me, yet it may have a low beta. How so? Because its movements, no matter how swooping, don't generally happen in response to movement in the U.S. market. (Emerging-market stocks tend to be more tied to currency flux, commodity prices, interest rates, and political climate.)

Real-life examples of standard deviation and beta

Following are the (three-year) standard deviations and betas of several diverse ETFs. Note that iShares MSCI Hong Kong (EWH) is more volatile than iShares MSCI U.K. Index (EWU) as measured by its standard deviation, but EWH has a lower beta. That tells us that the volatility of the Hong Kong market, however great it is, seems to be less tied to the fortunes of the S&P 500 than is the volatility of the U.K. market.

ETF	Ticker	Standard Deviation	Beta
SPDR S&P 500	SPY	21.8	1.0
Consumer Staples Select Sector SPDR	XLP	14.7	0.59
Health Care Select Sector SPDR	XLV	17.6	0.66
iShares MSCI U.K. Index	EWU	27.1	1.11
PowerShares QQQ Trust Series 1	QQQ	25.1	1.07
iShares MSCI Hong Kong	EWH	28.3	0.55

The Sharpe, Treynor, and Sortino ratios: Measures of what you get for your risk

Back in 1966, a goateed Stanford professor named Bill Sharpe developed a formula that has since become as common in investment-speak as RBIs are in baseball-speak. The formula looks like this:

$$\frac{\text{Total portfolio return} - \text{Risk-free rate of return}}{\text{Portfolio standard deviation}} = \text{Sharpe measure (or Sharpe ratio)}$$

The risk-free rate of return generally refers to the return you could get on a short-term U.S. Treasury bill. If you subtract that from the total portfolio return, it tells you how much your portfolio earned above the rate you could have achieved without risking your principal. You take that number and divide it by the standard deviation (discussed earlier in this section). And what *that* result gives you is the Sharpe ratio, which essentially indicates how much money has been made in relation to how much risk was taken to make that money.

Suppose Portfolio A, under manager Bubba Bucks, returned 7 percent last year, and during that year Treasury bills were paying 5 percent. Portfolio A also had a standard deviation of 8 percent. Okay, applying the formula,

$$\frac{7\% - 5\%}{8\%} = \frac{2\%}{8\%} = 0.25$$

That result wasn't good enough for Bubba's manager, so he fired Bubba and hired Donny Dollar. Donny, who just read *Exchange-Traded Funds For Dummies,* 2nd Edition, takes the portfolio and dumps all its high-cost active mutual funds. In their place, he buys ETFs. In his first year managing the portfolio, Donny achieves a total return of 10 percent with a standard deviation of 7.5. But the interest rate on Treasury bills has gone up to 7 percent. Applying the formula,

$$\frac{10\% - 7\%}{7.5\%} = \frac{3\%}{7.5\%} = 0.40$$

The higher the Sharpe measure, the better. Donny Dollar did his job much better than Bubba Bucks.

The Treynor approach was first used by — you guessed it — a guy named Jack Treynor in 1965. Instead of using standard deviation in the denominator, it uses beta. The Treynor measure shows the amount of money that a portfolio is making in relation to the risk it carries relative to the market. To put that another way, the Treynor measure uses only systemic risk, or beta, while the Sharpe ratio uses total risk.

Suppose that Donny Dollar's portfolio, with its 10 percent return, had a beta of 0.9. In that case, the Treynor measure would be

$$\frac{10\% - 7\%}{0.9} = \frac{3\%}{0.9} = \frac{.03}{0.9} = 0.033$$

Is 0.033 good? That depends. It's a relative number. Suppose that the market, as measured by the S&P 500, also returned 10 percent that same year. It may seem like Donny isn't a very good manager. But when we apply the Treynor measure (recalling that the beta for the market is always 1.0),

$$\frac{10\% - 7\%}{1.0} = \frac{3\%}{1.0} = \frac{.03}{1.0} = 0.03$$

we get a lower number. That result indicates that while Donny earned a return that was similar to the market's, he took on less risk. Put another way, he achieved greater returns per unit of risk. Donny's boss will likely keep him.

Another variation on the Sharpe ratio is the Sortino ratio, which basically uses the same formula:

$$\frac{\text{Total portfolio return} - \text{Risk-free rate of return}}{\text{Portfolio standard deviation (downside only)}} = \text{Sortino ratio}$$

Note that instead of looking at historical ups and downs, it focuses only on the downs. After all, say members of the Sortino-ratio fan club, you don't lose sleep fretting about your portfolio rising in value. You want to know what your downside risk is. The Sortino-ratio fan club has been growing in size, but as yet, it is difficult to find Sortino-ratio calculations for any given security, including ETFs. I'm sure it will get easier over time, as comparing downside risk among various ETFs can be a helpful tool.

Meet Modern Portfolio Theory

For simplicity's sake, I've discussed the choice of one ETF over another (SHY or SPY?) based on risk and potential return. In the real world, however, few people, if any, come to me or to any financial planner asking for a recommendation on a single ETF. More commonly, I'm asked to help build a portfolio of ETFs. And when looking at an entire portfolio, the riskiness of each individual ETF, although important, takes a back seat to the riskiness of the entire portfolio.

In other words, I would rarely recommend or rule out any specific ETF because it is too volatile. How well any specific ETF fits into a portfolio — and to what degree it affects the risk of a portfolio — depends on what else is in the portfolio. What I'm alluding to here is something called *Modern Portfolio Theory*: the tool I use to help determine a proper ETF mix for my clients' portfolios. You and I will use this tool throughout this book to help you determine a proper mix for your portfolio.

Tasting the extreme positivity of negative correlation

Modern Portfolio Theory is to investing what the discovery of gravity was to physics. Almost. What the theory says is that the volatility/risk of a portfolio may differ dramatically from the volatility/risk of the portfolio's components. In other words, you can have two assets with both high standard deviations and high potential returns, but when combined they give you a portfolio with modest standard deviation but the same high potential return. Modern

Portfolio Theory says that you can have a slew of risky ingredients, but if you throw them together into a big bowl, the entire soup may actually splash around very little.

The key to whipping up such pleasant combinations is to find two or more holdings that do not move in synch: One tends to go up while the other goes down (although both holdings, in the long run, will see an upward trajectory). In the figures that follow, I show how you'd create the fantasy ETF portfolio consisting of two high-risk/high-return ETFs with perfect negative correlation. It is a fantasy portfolio because perfect negative correlations don't exist; they simply serve as a target.

Figure 4-2 represents hypothetical ETF A and hypothetical ETF B, each of which has high return and high volatility. Notice that even though both are volatile assets, they move up and down at different times. This fact is crucial because combining them can give you a nonvolatile portfolio.

Figure 4-2:
ETFs A and
B each have
high return
and high
volatility.

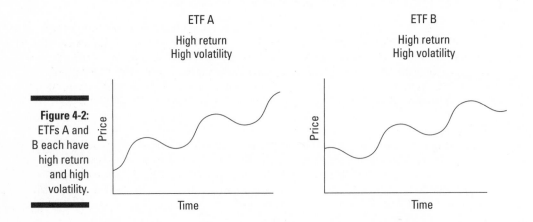

Figure 4-3 shows what happens when you invest in both ETF A and ETF B. You end up with the perfect ETF portfolio — one made up of two ETFs with perfect negative correlation. (If only such a portfolio existed in the real world!)

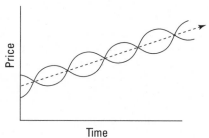

The Perfect Portfolio

High return
Low volatility

Figure 4-3:
The
perfect ETF
portfolio,
with high
return and
no volatility.

Settling for limited correlation

When the U.S. stock market takes a punch, which happens on average every three years or so, most U.S. stocks fall. When the market flies, most stocks fly. Not many investments regularly move in opposite directions. We do, however, find investments that tend to move independently of each other much of the time, or at least they don't move in the same direction all the time. In investment-speak, I'm talking about investments that have *limited* or *low correlation.*

Different kinds of stocks — large, small, value, and growth — tend to have limited correlation. U.S. stocks and foreign stocks tend to have even less correlation; see the sidebar "Investing around the world." But the lowest correlation around is between stocks and bonds, which historically have had almost no correlation.

Say, for example, you had a basket of large U.S. stocks in 1929, at the onset of the Great Depression. You would have seen your portfolio lose nearly a quarter of its value every year for the next four years. Ouch! If, however, you were holding high-quality, long-term bonds during that same period, at least that side of your portfolio would have grown by a respectable 5 percent a year. A portfolio of long-term bonds held throughout the growling bear market in stocks of 2000 through 2003 would have returned a hale and hearty 13 percent a year. (That's an unusually high return for bonds, but at the time the stars were in seemingly perfect alignment.)

Investing around the world

Investing in the U.S. stock market has limited correlation to investing in stock markets outside of the United States, as these five years of returns attest.

	2006	2007	2008	2009	2010
U.S. Stock Market (S&P 500)	15.8	5.5	−37.0	26.5	15.1
Europe (S&P Europe 350)	33.1	15.1	−46.0	35.2	11.8
Japan (MSCI Japan)	6.2	−4.2	−29.2	6.3	15.4
Emerging Markets (MSCI Emerging Markets)	32.3	39.4	−53.3	78.5	18.9

During the market spiral of 2008, there was an unprecedented chorus-line effect in which nearly all stocks — value, growth, large, small, U.S., and foreign — moved in the same direction: down . . . depressingly down. At the same time, all but the highest quality bonds took a beating as well. But once again, portfolio protection came in the form of long-term U.S. government bonds, which rose by about 26 percent in value.

In August 2011, as S&P downgraded U.S. Treasuries, the stock markets again took a tumble, and — guess what? — Treasuries, despite their downgrade by S&P (but none of the other raters), spiked upward!

Reaching for the elusive Efficient Frontier

Correlation is a measurable thing, represented in the world of investments by something called the *correlation coefficient*. This number indicates the degree to which two investments move in the same or different directions. A correlation coefficient can range from –1 to 1.

A correlation of 1 indicates that the two securities are like the Rockettes: When one kicks a leg, so does the other. Having both in your portfolio offers no diversification benefit. On the other hand, if investment A and investment B have a correlation coefficient of –1, that means they have a perfect negative relationship: They always move in the opposite directions. Having both in your portfolio is a wonderful diversifier. Such polar-opposite investments are, alas, very hard to find.

The correlation of various ETFs

The following correlations of several iShares ETFs show to what degree different ETFs moved in the same direction over a recent three-year period. The lower the correlation, the better from a portfolio-building point of view. Low correlations reduce portfolio risk. High correlations do not. Negative correlations are, alas, not that easy to find in the real world, but portfolio managers are forever looking.

ETF 1	ETF 2	Correlation Coefficient	Rating
iShares S&P Small Cap 600 Growth (small growth)	iShares S&P 500 Value (large value)	0.92	Medium to high correlation
iShares S&P 500 Growth (large growth)	iShares Barclays 7–10 Year Treasury (bonds)	−0.19	Negative correlation
iShares MSCI Japan Index (Japanese stocks)	iShares S&P Small Cap 600 Value (small value)	0.74	Modest correlation
iShares S&P Small Cap 600 Growth (small growth)	iShares S&P Small Cap 600 Value (small value)	0.98	High correlation
iShares Dow Jones Utilities Sector	iShares S&P Small Cap 600 Value (small value)	0.61	Modest correlation

A correlation coefficient of zero means that the two investments have no relationship to each other. When one moves, the other may move in the same direction, the opposite direction, or not at all.

As a whole, stocks and bonds (not junk bonds, but high-quality bonds) tend to have little to negative correlation. Finding the perfect mix of stocks and bonds, as well as other investments with low correlation, is known among financial pros as looking for the *Efficient Frontier*. The Frontier represents the mix of investments that offers the greatest promise of return for the least amount of risk.

Fortunately, ETFs allow us to tinker easily with our investments so we can find just that sweet spot.

Accusations that MPT is dead are greatly exaggerated

Since the market swoon of 2008, some pundits have claimed that Modern Portfolio Theory is dead. This claim is nonsense. As I mentioned, U.S.

government bonds more than held their own during this difficult period. And even though all styles of stock moved down in 2008, they moved at different paces. And the degree to which they recovered has differed significantly. You'll see these differences in the charts in the upcoming sections "Filling in your style box" and "Buying by industry sector."

The investors who were hurt terribly in 2008 were those who sold their depressed stocks and moved everything into cash or "safe" bonds. Those bonds, at least long-term government bonds, then lost about 16 percent of their value in 2009. Those who flipped from stocks to bonds would have been doubly wounded. But those who kept the faith in MPT and rebalanced their portfolios, as I discuss fully in Chapter 18, would not have been so badly wounded. These investors would have been buying stock in 2008 instead of selling it. And any investor with a fairly well-balanced portfolio of stocks and bonds would have recouped her losses within two years after the market bottomed in March 2009.

Mixing and Matching Your Stock ETFs

Reaching for the elusive Efficient Frontier means holding both stocks and bonds — domestic and international — in your portfolio. That part is fairly straightforward and not likely to stir much controversy (although, for sure, experts differ on what they consider optimal percentages). But experts definitely don't agree on how best to diversify the domestic-stock portion of a portfolio. Two competing methods predominate:

- ✔ One method calls for the division of a stock portfolio into domestic and foreign, and then into different styles: large cap, small cap, mid cap, value, and growth.

- ✔ The other method calls for allocating percentages of a portfolio to various industry sectors: healthcare, utilities, energy, financials, and so on.

My personal preference for the small to mid-sized investor, especially the ETF investor, is to go primarily with the styles. But there's nothing wrong with dividing up a portfolio by industry sector. And for those of you with good-sized portfolios, a mixture of both, without going crazy, may be optimal.

Filling in your style box

Most savvy investors make certain to have some equity in each of the nine boxes of the grid in Figure 4-4, which is known as the *style box* or *grid* (sometimes called the *Morningstar grid*).

Large cap value	Large cap blend	Large cap growth
Mid cap value	Mid cap blend	Mid cap growth
Small cap value	Small cap blend	Small cap growth

Figure 4-4:
The style
box or grid.

The reason for the style box is simple enough: History shows that companies of differing cap (capitalization) size (in other words, large companies and small companies), and value and growth companies, tend to rise and fall under different economic conditions. I define *cap size, value,* and *growth* in Chapter 5, and I devote the next several chapters to showing the differences among styles, how to choose ETFs to match each one, and how to weight those ETFs for the highest potential return with the lowest possible risk.

Table 4-2 shows how well various investment styles, per Morningstar, have fared in the past several years. Note that a number of ETFs are available to match each style.

Table 4-2   Recent Performance of Various Investment Styles

	2006	*2007*	*2008*	*2009*	*2010*
Large cap growth	5.7	12.3	−41.9	44.4	12.9
Large cap value	25.8	−0.4	−36.1	11.4	14.7
Small cap growth	10.0	11.1	−39.9	33.0	31.3
Small cap value	20.0	−8.1	−31.7	40.3	26.0

Buying by industry sector

The advent of ETFs has largely brought forth the use of sector investing as an alternative to the grid. Examining the two models toe-to-toe yields some interesting comparisons — and much food for thought.

One study on industry-sector investing, by Chicago-based Ibbotson Associates, came to the very favorable conclusion that sector investing is a potentially superior diversifier to grid investing because times have changed since the 1960s when style investing first became popular. "Globalization has led to a rise in correlation between domestic and international stocks; large, mid, and small cap stocks have high correlation to each other. A company's performance is tied more to its industry than to the country where it's based, or the size of its market cap," concluded Ibbotson.

The jury is still out, but I give an overview of the controversy in Chapter 10. For now, I invite you to do a little comparison of your own by comparing Tables 4-2 and 4-3. Note that by using either method of diversification, some of your investments should smell like roses in years when others stink. Also, recall what I stated earlier about how all stocks crashed in 2008 but recovered at significantly different paces; this is true of various styles and sectors. And it is certainly true for various geographic regions. Modern Portfolio Theory is not dead!

Table 4-3 shows how well various industry sectors (as measured by their respective Dow Jones indexes) fared in recent years. Yes, there are ETFs that track each of these industry sectors — and many more.

Table 4-3	Recent Performance of Various Market Sectors				
	2006	*2007*	*2008*	*2009*	*2010*
Healthcare	6.9	8.4	−22.8	21.7	4.5
Real Estate	35.3	−18.1	−40.1	30.8	26.9
Basic Materials	17.6	32.9	−50.8	65.5	31.7
Telecommunications	36.0	−0.8	−42.5	27.1	21.3

What creates returns, and what kind of returns will the future bring?

In the world of stock markets, with their by-and-large juicy long-term returns, the juice comes from three sources:

- ✔ Dividends

- ✔ Earnings growth

- ✔ Price/earnings multiples (the measure of market expectations), otherwise known as P/E

Dividends, it may surprise you to learn, account for the lion's share of stock market returns over the past two centuries. The stock market has given us roughly a 7 percent post-inflation rise during that period. Perhaps three-quarters of that 7 percent is attributable to dividends. That's history, of course. Today's dividend yield on the S&P 500, although it has grown in the past several years, is only about 1.7 percent and is very unlikely to exceed 5 percent ever again. Instead of paying dividends, companies today funnel much of their profits into internal growth, repurchasing shares of their own stock, and dishing out astronomical compensation for top executives.

In the future, we may be looking at a 2 percent dividend yield, tops, plus whatever good fortune brings us in the way of earnings growth. The price/earnings multiple — the factor by which investors are willing to invest in stocks in hopes of future earnings — soared wildly in the bull market of the 1990s but has since shrunk to a level that's pretty close to its historical norm. (The true historical average is about 15, but when interest rates are very low, as they are while I'm writing these words, the average tends to rise to about 20, which is right about where we are now.). It may grow again, or it may shrink. Who knows? And whether earnings growth can pick up where dividend yield left off and provide investors with 7 percent returns after inflation is a big unknown.

When I look into my crystal ball (I really try not to do that very often), I can't see what returns will be, but I do know for sure that the stock market will continue to be volatile, perhaps even more so than it has been in the past. Many investors may end up jumping overboard long before they get to any port where they'll find the Holy Grail. Fortunately, with a well-balanced portfolio of ETFs, you will be in a position to complete the voyage.

But don't presume that you can avoid all risk or that the future will mirror the past, and don't put everything you have into stocks.

Don't slice and dice your portfolio to death

One reason I tend to prefer the traditional style grid to industry-sector investing, at least for the nonwealthy investor, is that there are simply fewer styles to contend with. You can build yourself, at least on the domestic side of your stock holdings, a pretty well-diversified portfolio with but four ETFs: one small value, one small growth, one large value, and one large growth. With industry-sector investing, you would need a dozen or so ETFs to have a well-balanced portfolio, and that may be too many.

I hold a similar philosophy when it comes to global investing. Yes, you can, thanks largely to the iShares lineup of ETFs, invest in about 50 individual countries. (And in many of these countries, you can furthermore choose between large cap and small cap stocks, and in some cases, value and growth.) Too much! I prefer to see most investors go with larger geographic regions: U.S., Europe, Asia, emerging markets . . .

You don't want to chop up your portfolio into too many holdings, or the transaction costs (especially with ETFs that require trading costs) can start to bite into your returns. Rebalancing gets to be a headache. Tax filing can become a nightmare. And, as many investors learned in 2008 — okay, I'll admit it, as *I* learned in 2008 — having a very small position in your portfolio, say less than 2 percent of your assets, in any one kind of investment isn't going to have much effect on your overall returns anyway.

As a rough rule, if you have $50,000 to invest, consider something in the ballpark of a 5- to 10-ETF portfolio, and if you have $250,000 or more, perhaps look at a 15- to 25-ETF portfolio. Many more ETFs than this won't enhance the benefits of diversification but will entail additional trading costs every time you rebalance your holdings. (See my sample ETF portfolios for all sizes of nest eggs in Part IV.)

Chapter 5

Large Growth: Muscular Money Makers

*P*ick up a typical business magazine and look at the face adorning the cover. He's Mr. CEO. Tough and ambitious and looking for acquisitions under every rock, his pedigree is Harvard, his wife is the former Miss Missouri, his salary (not to mention other perks) exceeds the gross national product of Peru, and his house has 14 bathrooms. (Yeah, I know this seems like a stereotype, but U.S. CEOs do tend to be a rather homogenous lot.) The title of the cover story emblazoned across Mr. CEO's chest suggests that buying stock in his company will make you rich. Without knowing anything more, you can assume that Mr. CEO heads a large growth company.

In other words, Mr. CEO's company has a *total market capitalization* (the value of all its outstanding stock) of at least $5 billion, earnings have been growing and growing fast, the company has a secure niche within its industry, and many people envision the Borg-like corporation eventually taking over the universe. Think Microsoft, Apple, Chevron, and Exxon Mobil. Think General Electric, IBM, and — even though its CEO may not exactly fit the stereotype — Google.

In this chapter, I explain what role such behemoths should play in your portfolio. But before getting into the meat of the matter, take a quick glance at Figures 5-1 and 5-2. Figure 5-1 shows where large growth stocks fit into a well-diversified stock portfolio. (I introduce this style box or grid, which divides a stock portfolio into large cap and small cap, value and growth, in Chapter 4.) Figure 5-2 shows their historical returns.

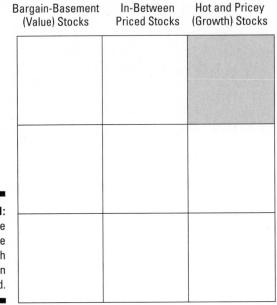

	Bargain-Basement (Value) Stocks	In-Between Priced Stocks	Hot and Pricey (Growth) Stocks
Big Companies			
In-Between Sized Companies			
Little Companies			

Figure 5-1:
The place of large growth stocks in the grid.

U.S. Large Cap Value Stocks
1927-2010: Total Returns

GROWTH OF $1

$4,228

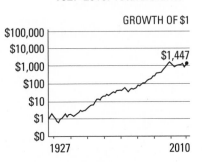

U.S. Large Cap Growth Stocks
1927-2010: Total Returns

GROWTH OF $1

$1,447

Figure 5-2:
Large growth stocks have given investors ample returns over the decades.

U.S. Small Cap Value Stocks
1927-2010: Total Returns

GROWTH OF $1

$52,892

U.S. Small Cap Growth Stocks
1927-2010: Total Returns

GROWTH OF $1

$1,359

Source: Fama/French data provided by Eugene F. Fama and Kenneth R. French

Style Review

In Chapter 4, I note that one approach to building a portfolio involves investing in different styles of stocks: large cap, mid cap, small cap, value, and growth. How did the whole business of style investing get started? Hard to say. Benjamin Graham, the "Dean of Wall Street," the "Father of Value Investing," who wrote several oft-quoted books in the 1930s and 1940s, didn't give us the popular style grid that you see in Figure 5-1. But Mr. Graham certainly helped provide the tools of fundamental analysis whereby more contemporary brains could figure things out.

In the early 1980s, studies out of the University of Chicago began to quantify the differences between large caps and small caps, and in 1992, two economists named Eugene Fama and Kenneth French delivered the seminal paper on the differences between value and growth stocks.

What makes large cap large?

Capitalization or *cap* refers to the combined value of all shares of a company's stock. The lines dividing large cap, mid cap, and small cap are sometimes as blurry as the line between, say, *Rubenesque* and *fat*. The distinction is largely in the eyes of the beholder. If you took a poll, however, I think you would find that the following divisions are generally accepted:

- ✓ **Large caps:** Companies with more than $5 billion in capitalization
- ✓ **Mid caps:** Companies with $1 billion to $5 billion in capitalization
- ✓ **Small caps:** Companies with $250 million to $1 billion in capitalization

Anything from $50 million to $250 million would usually be deemed a *micro cap.* And your local pizza shop, if it were to go public, might be called a *nano cap (con aglio).* There are no nano cap ETFs. For all the other categories, there are ETFs to your heart's content.

How does growth differ from value?

Many different criteria are used to determine whether a stock or basket of stocks (such as an ETF) qualifies as *growth* or *value.* (In Chapter 6, I list "Six Ways to Recognize Value.") But perhaps the most important measure is the ratio of price to earnings: the *P/E ratio,* sometimes referred to as the *multiple.*

The P/E ratio is the price of a stock divided by its earnings per share. For example, suppose McDummy Corporation stock is currently selling for $40 a share. And suppose that the company earned $2 last year for every share of stock outstanding. McDummy's P/E ratio would be 20. (The S&P 500 currently has a P/E of about 15, but that ratio changes frequently.)

The higher the P/E, the more investors have been willing to pay for the company's earnings. Or to put it in terms of growth and value:

- ✔ The higher the P/E, the more *growthy* the company: Either the company is growing fast, or investors have high hopes (realistic or foolish) for future growth.
- ✔ The lower the P/E, the more *valuey* the company. The business world doesn't see this company as a mover and shaker.

Each ETF carries a P/E reflecting the collective P/E of its holdings and giving you an indication of just how growthy or valuey that ETF is. A growth ETF is filled with companies that look like they are taking over the planet. A value ETF is filled with companies that seem to be meandering along but whose stock can be purchased for what looks like a bargain price.

Putting these terms to use

Today, most investment pros develop their portfolios with at least some consideration given to the cap size and growth or value orientation of their stock holdings. Why? Because study after study shows that, in fact, a portfolio's performance is inexorably linked to where that portfolio falls in the style grid. A mutual fund that holds all large growth stocks, for example, will generally (but certainly not always) rise or fall with the rise or fall of that asset class.

Some research shows that perhaps 90 to 95 percent of a mutual fund's or ETF's performance may be attributable to its asset class alone. In other words, any large cap growth fund will tend to perform similarly to other large cap growth funds. Any small cap value fund will tend to perform similarly to other small cap value funds. And so on. That's why the financial press's weekly wrap-ups of top-performing funds will typically list a bunch of funds that mirror each other very closely. (That being the case, why not enjoy the low cost and tax efficiency of the ETF or index mutual fund?)

Big and Brawny

Large growth companies grab nearly all the headlines, for sure. The pundits are forever singing their praises — or trumpeting their faults when the growth trajectory starts to level off. Either way, you'll hear about it; the northeast corner of the style grid includes the most recognizable names in the corporate world. If you're seeking employment, I strongly urge you to latch on to one of these companies; your future will likely be bright. But do large growth stocks necessarily make the best investments?

Er, no.

Contrary to all appearances . . .

According to Fama and French (who are still operating as a research duo), over the course of the last 83 years, large growth stocks have seen an annualized return rate (not accounting for inflation) of about 8.8 percent. Not too bad. But that compares to 11.1 percent for large value stocks, with no greater volatility. Theories abound as to why large growth stocks haven't done as well as value stocks. Value stocks pay greater dividends, say some. Value stocks really *are* riskier; they just don't look it, argue others.

The theory that makes the most sense, in my opinion, is that growth stocks are simply hampered by their own immense popularity. Because growth companies grab all the headlines, because investors *think* they must be the best investments, the large growth stocks tend to get overpriced by the time you buy them. In the past few months, for example, everyone I know seems to be talking about Baidu.com, a company that is connecting hundreds of millions of Chinese citizens to the Internet. Yes, the company is growing faster than crabgrass. And it probably will continue to grow. But with a price-to-earnings ratio of 75, your stock investment in Baidu is dependent on continued supersonic growth . . . anything less than supersonic growth, and the stock is not going to shine. If people expected the stock to tank (in which case, the P/E would be much lower), value investors might jump in and make a profit even if the company didn't grow at all — but merely didn't tank!

Let history serve as only a rough guide

So given that large value stocks historically have done better than large growth stocks, and given (as I discuss in Chapters 7 and 8) that small caps historically have knocked the socks off large, does it still make sense to sink some of your investment dollars into large growth? Oh yes, it does. The past is only an indication of what the future may bring. No one knows whether value stocks will continue to outshine. In the past 10 years or so especially, large growth stocks have lagged behind value and have fallen behind smaller stocks by a wide margin. But this trend was itself a reversal of what happened during much of the 1990s when growth trumped value. So perhaps we're going to see yet another reversal.

(Please don't accuse me of market timing! I'm not saying that just because large growth stocks have been depressed they are due for a big comeback. I have no idea. But to a small and limited degree, a little timely *tactical* tilting, I feel, is an okay thing. That is, it may make some sense to tilt a portfolio *gently* toward whatever sectors seem to be sagging and away from sectors that have been blazing. If you do that subtly, and regularly, and don't let emotions sway you — and if you watch out carefully for tax ramifications and trading costs — history shows that you may eke out some modest added return. More on tactical tilting in Chapter 18.)

Stocks of large companies — value and growth combined — should make up between 50 and 70 percent of your total domestic stock portfolio. The higher your risk tolerance, the closer you'll want to be to the lower end of that range.

Whatever your allocation to domestic large cap stocks, I recommend that you invest anywhere from 40 to 50 percent of that amount in large growth. Take a tilt toward value, if you wish, but don't tilt so far that you risk tipping over.

ETF Options Galore

The roster of ETFs on the market now includes about 100 broad-based domestic large cap funds, of which 20 or so are acceptable large growth options. The remainder of the broad-based (as opposed to industry sector or other specialized) large cap funds are either *blend* (a growth-and-value cocktail) or strictly large value. As I emphasize throughout this book, each and every investment you make should be evaluated in the context of your entire portfolio.

In this chapter, I'm focusing on large growth ETFs. But before you start shopping for a large growth ETF, you need to ask yourself whether one belongs in your portfolio at all. In a nutshell, it does, but only if your portfolio is large enough to be divided into various styles.

Strictly large cap or blend?

All things being equal, I'd like to see you invest in large growth and large value stocks — separately. That approach gives you the opportunity to rebalance once a year and, by so doing, juice out added return while reducing risk. (More on rebalancing in Chapter 18.) But the profit you expect to reap from that tweak must exceed the transaction costs of making two trades (generally selling shares of the outperforming ETF for the year and adding to the underperformer).

If your portfolio isn't big enough for the profit of the tweaking to outweigh the cost of the trading, you're better off with a blend of value and growth. If your portfolio is so small that any tweaking is unlikely to be profitable, I would suggest not only a blend of large value and growth, but a blend of *everything.* Keep these parameters in mind as you read on.

"Everything" investment options

I don't know where you park your money, and I don't know exactly how much you spend per trade, but I would say that if you have a portfolio of $10,000 or less, you should either be thinking mutual funds (not ETFs), or you should seek to invest at a brokerage that will not charge you for trading ETFs. Otherwise, the trading costs could eat you alive. If, however, you are unlikely to do any trading in the next several years, an ETF portfolio may make sense. In that case, consider a simple and all-encompassing "everything" (total ball of wax) ETF for your domestic stock holdings.

Good options in the "everything" domestic stock category include the iShares Dow Jones U.S. Total Market ETF (IYY), the Vanguard Total Stock Market ETF (VTI), and the Schwab U.S. Broad Market ETF (SCHB). Of the three, I have a slight preference for the Schwab and the Vanguard choices because of their ultra-low costs (0.06 and 0.07 percent respectively, versus 0.20 percent for the iShares offering).

(**Note:** There are several "everything" ETFs where you can tap into even broader investments than the entire U.S. stock market; I discuss a few of these options in Chapter 11.)

Large and small cap blends

If you have more than $10,000 but less than $20,000 or so, and you're able to invest it and keep it put for a good while, consider splitting up your domestic stock portfolio into large and small cap. In this case, I'd recommend a diversified small cap blend and a diversified large cap blend. Good options among the large cap blends would include the Vanguard Large Cap ETF (VV), the Vanguard Mega Cap 300 ETF (MGC), the iShares Russell 1000 ETF (IWB), and the Schwab U.S. Large-Cap ETF (SCHX). I discuss these options in detail in the upcoming section "Blended options for large cap exposure."

Large cap growth and value options

If you have a portfolio of more than $20,000, you should split up the large caps into growth and value. Good large growth options would include the Vanguard Growth ETF (VUG), Vanguard Mega Cap Growth ETF (MGK), iShares Morningstar Large Growth ETF (JKE), and the Schwab U.S. Large-Cap Growth ETF (SCHG). See the upcoming section "Strictly large growth" for details on these ETFs.

Blended options for large cap exposure

Among the *blended* (large cap value and growth) options for smaller portfolios ($10,000 to $20,000), I feel comfortable recommending any of the ETFs discussed in this section.

Please keep in mind that all the expense ratios, average cap sizes, price/earnings ratios, and top five holdings for the ETFs I list here and elsewhere in the book are true as of a certain date and are subject to change. You should verify all key details before making any purchase.

Vanguard Large Cap ETF (VV)

Indexed to: MSCI U.S. Prime Market 750 Index (750 corporate biggies from both the value and growth sides of the grid)

Expense ratio: 0.12 percent

Average cap size: $43.2 billion

P/E ratio: 16.7

Top five holdings: Exxon Mobil, Apple, Chevron, General Electric, International Business Machines

Russell's review: The low cost, as with nearly all Vanguard offerings, makes me want to stand up and cheer. The MSCI U.S. Prime Market 750, as the name implies, encompasses a larger universe of stocks than the more popular S&P 500, which translates to holdings with a somewhat smaller average cap size than you'll find with some other large cap options. The MSCI index is also more "indexy" than the S&P 500: The choice of companies is purely quantitative, whereas with the S&P, some human judgment is applied. Personally, I like the hands-off approach. This ETF is an excellent choice for people with smaller portfolios trying to limit the number of ETFs they have to manage. Shares trade free of commissions if held at Vanguard.

Vanguard Mega Cap 300 ETF (MGC)

Indexed to: MSCI U.S. Large Cap 300 Index (the biggest 300 U.S. companies, regardless of type)

Expense ratio: 0.13 percent

Average cap size: $62.9 billion (whooeeee!)

P/E ratio: 15.9

Top five holdings: Exxon Mobil, Apple, Chevron, General Electric, International Business Machines

Russell's review: What the heck? If you're going to go big, why not go all the way? Note that the top five holdings are the very same that you'll find with the other Vanguard blended option, the Vanguard Large Cap ETF (VV). But in the case of this ETF, you won't be getting the lesser sized of the large cap companies. That's less than optimal from a diversification standpoint, and for that reason, I wouldn't recommend MGC over VV as a stand-alone investment. But if you are combining either of these funds with a blended small cap fund, then MGC will give you somewhat lower correlation (in other words, greater simultaneous zig and zag potential), which is a good thing. For most investors' portfolios, either Vanguard option would be an excellent choice. Shares trade free of commissions if held at Vanguard.

Schwab U.S. Large-Cap ETF (SCHX)

Indexed to: Dow Jones U.S. Large-Cap Total Stock Market Index (approximately 750 of America's largest corporations)

Expense ratio: 0.08 percent

Average cap size: $40.65 billion

P/E ratio: 16.2

Top five holdings: Apple, AT&T, Chevron, Exxon Mobil, General Electric

Russell's review: For frugality's sake alone, this fund makes a good option. The management fee is one of the lowest in the industry. And, like all Schwab ETFs, you can trade this baby for free if held at Schwab. Most importantly, the index is a good one. I expect Schwab to do a good job of tracking the index, even though its ETFs were introduced only in late 2009.

iShares Russell 1000 ETF (IWB)

Indexed to: Russell 1000 (the largest 1,000 publicly traded companies in the land)

Expense ratio: 0.15 percent

Average cap size: $38.8 billion

P/E ratio: 20.2

Top five holdings: Exxon Mobil, Apple, Chevron, General Electric, International Business Machines

Russell's review: The cost isn't high, but it is higher than the comparable Vanguard and Schwab funds . On the other hand, this ETF offers somewhat greater diversification — only a potential plus, really, if this is going to be a major part of your portfolio. Given the exposure to smaller companies, which tend to see greater price flux than large companies, this fund may prove over the long run to be slightly more volatile but slightly more rewarding than the comparable Vanguard or Schwab or other iShares options. Like a number of other broad-based iShares ETFs, IWB trades are free if held at Fidelity.

Strictly large growth

For large growth and large growth alone (complemented by large value, of course) — a position I much prefer for people with adequate assets ($20,000+) — the four options I list here all provide good exposure to the asset class at very reasonable cost.

Vanguard Growth ETF (VUG)

Indexed to: MSCI U.S. Prime Market Growth Index (400 or so of the nation's largest growth stocks)

Expense ratio: 0.12 percent

Average cap size: $35.6 billion

P/E ratio: 19.2

Top five holdings: Apple, International Business Machines, Microsoft, Google, Oracle

Russell's review: The price is right. The index makes sense. There's good diversification. The companies represented are certainly large, even though they could be a bit more growthy. This ETF is certainly a very good option. There's also "The Vanguard edge" (see Chapter 3), which gives this fund another advantage for those who may already own the Vanguard Growth Index mutual fund. Shares trade free of commissions if held at Vanguard.

Vanguard Mega Cap 300 Growth ETF (MGK)

Indexed to: MSCI U.S. Large Cap Growth Index (300 of the largest growth companies in the United States)

Expense ratio: 0.13 percent

Average cap size: $46.7 billion

P/E ratio: 17.9

Top five holdings: Apple, International Business Machines, Microsoft, Google, Oracle

Russell's review: Bigger is better . . . sometimes. If you have small caps in your portfolio, this mega cap fund will give you slightly better diversification than the Vanguard Growth ETF (VUG), but this fund is also a tad less growthy than VUG, so you'll get a bit less divergence from your large value holdings. Nothing to sweat. Either fund, given Vanguard's low expenses and reasonable indexes, would make for a fine holding. Shares trade free of commissions if held at Vanguard.

iShares Morningstar Large Growth ETF (JKE)

Indexed to: Morningstar Large Growth Index (90 of the largest and most growthy U.S. companies)

Expense ratio: 0.25 percent

Average cap size: $45.3 billion

P/E ratio: 23.3

Top five holdings: Apple, Microsoft, Coca-Cola, Oracle, Google

Russell's review: Nothing in life is perfect. This ETF offers the growthiness that the Vanguard ETFs lack, but the flip side is that the diversification leaves something to be desired. Apple and Microsoft together make up a tad more than 16 percent of the index; that's a little more than I would like to see for two companies that happen to be in the same industry, especially when the fourth and fifth largest holdings are also in that industry. And perhaps because Morningstar indexes aren't nearly as popular as S&P indexes, this ETF is thinly traded, which could result in a larger spread when you buy or sell. What tips the scales for me, however, and makes this one a contender, is that Morningstar indexes are crisp and distinct: Any company that appears in the growth index is not going to be popping up in the value index. Even though that crispness could lead to slightly higher turnover, I like it.

Schwab U.S. Large-Cap Growth ETF (SCHG)

Indexed to: Dow Jones U.S. Large-Cap Growth Total Stock Market Index (450 or so of the largest and presumably fastest-growing U.S. firms)

Expense ratio: 0.13 percent

Average cap size: $29.4 billion

P/E ratio: 19.2

Top five holdings: Apple, Berkshire Hathaway, Cisco Systems, Google, Microsoft

Russell's review: For the sake of economy alone, this fund, like all Schwab ETFs, makes a good option. The management fee is one of the lowest in the industry. And, like all Schwab ETFs, you can trade this fund for free if held at Schwab. Most importantly, the index is a good one. You can expect Schwab to do a reasonable or better job of tracking the index, even though its ETFs were introduced only in late 2009.

ETFs I wouldn't go out of my way to own

None of the ETFs listed below is horrible — far from it. But given the plethora of choices, barring very special circumstances, I would not recommend these:

- **DIAMONDS Trust Series 1 (DIA):** Based on the index on which this ETF is based, I basically don't like it. The Dow Jones Industrial Average is an antiquated and somewhat arbitrary index of 30 large companies that look good to the editors of *The Wall Street Journal*. That isn't enough on which to build a portfolio.

- **SPDR S&P 500 (SPY):** It's the oldest and largest and among the cheapest (0.09 percent), but it's not the best thing on the ETF market. The S&P 500, which the fund tracks, isn't the greatest of indexes. The legal structure of SPY — unlike the vast majority of ETFs — does not allow for the immediate reinvestment of dividends, which can create a cash drag. Its popularity alone may also create extra drag, for as new companies are admitted into the 500 club, their stock prices tend to pop a bit, requiring fund managers to pay premium prices.

- **PowerShares Dynamic Large Cap Growth (PWB):** This ETF doesn't make me recoil in horror; you could do somewhat worse. But the high-by-ETF-standards expense ratio (0.61 percent) is something of a turn-off. And the "enhanced" index reminds me too much of active investing, which has a less than gleaming track record. I may change my mind if this new fund still shines after many more years on the market, but for right now — with a five-year track record that lags the Russell 1000 Growth Index by a full 3 percent a year! — I'd shy away.

Chapter 6

Large Value: Counterintuitive Cash Cows

*W*hy do American suburbanites gingerly cultivate their daisies, yet go nuts swinging spades or spraying poison chemicals at their dandelions? Why is a second cup of coffee in a diner free, but a second cup of tea isn't? Some things in this world just don't make a lot of sense. Why, for example, would slower-growing companies (the dandelions of the corporate world) historically reward investors better than faster-growing (daisy) companies? Welcome to the shoulder-shrugging world of value investing.

I'm talking about companies you've probably heard of, yes, but they aren't nearly as glamorous as Google or as exciting as Cisco. I'm talking about companies that usually ply their trade in older, slow-growing industries, like insurance, petroleum, and transportation. I'm talking about companies such as Chevron, Procter & Gamble, Wells Fargo, and Exelon (providing electricity and gas to customers in Illinois and Pennsylvania).

I see you yawning! But before you fall asleep, consider this: In the past 83 years, large value stocks have enjoyed an annualized growth rate of 11.1 percent, versus 8.8 percent for large growth stocks — with roughly the same standard deviation (volatility). And thanks to ETFs, investing in value has never been easier.

In this chapter, I explain not only the role that large value stocks play in a portfolio but why you may want them to be the largest single asset class in your portfolio. Take a gander at Figures 6-1 and 6-2. They show where large value stocks fit into the investment style grid (which I introduce in Chapter 4) and the impressive return of large value stocks over the past eight or so decades.

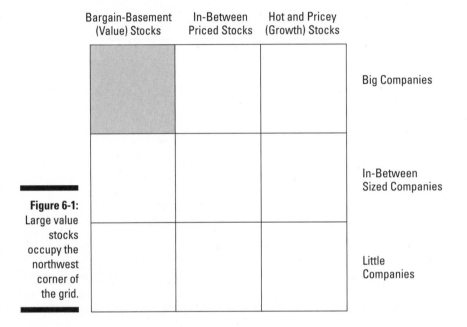

Figure 6-1: Large value stocks occupy the northwest corner of the grid.

Pass the dandelion fertilizer, will ya?

Six Ways to Recognize Value

Warren Buffett knows a value stock when he sees one. Do you? Different investment pros and different indexes (upon which ETFs are fashioned) may define "value" differently, but here are some of the most common criteria:

✔ **P/E ratio:** As early as 1934, Benjamin Graham and David Dodd (in their book with the blockbuster title *Security Analysis*) suggested that investors should pay heavy consideration to the ratio of a stock's market price (P) to its earnings per share (E). Sometimes called the *multiple,* this venerable ratio sheds light on how much the market is willing to cough up for a company's earning power. The lower the ratio, the more "valuey" the stock. (The P/E ratio as it relates to growth stocks is addressed in the previous chapter.)

U.S. Large Cap Value Stocks
1927-2010: Total Returns

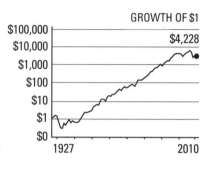

GROWTH OF $1

$4,228

U.S. Large Cap Growth Stocks
1927-2010: Total Returns

GROWTH OF $1

$1,447

U.S. Small Cap Value Stocks
1927-2010: Total Returns

GROWTH OF $1

$52,892

U.S. Small Cap Growth Stocks
1927-2010: Total Returns

GROWTH OF $1

$1,359

Figure 6-2:
This chart shows the growth of $1 invested in a basket of large value stocks from 1927 to the present.

Source: Fama/French data provided by Eugene F. Fama and Kenneth R. French

- ✔ **P/B ratio:** Graham and Dodd also advised that the ratio of market price to book value (B) should be given at least "a fleeting glance." Many of today's investment gurus have awarded the P/B ratio the chief role in defining value versus growth. A ratio well below sea level is what floats a value investor's boat. *Book value* refers to the guesstimated value of a corporation's total assets, both tangible (factories, inventory, and so on) and intangible (goodwill, patents, and so on), minus any liabilities.

- ✔ **Dividend distributions:** You like dividends? Value stocks are the ones that pay them.

- ✔ **The cover of *Forbes*:** Magazine covers are rarely adorned with photos of the CEOs of value companies. While growth companies receive broad exposure, value companies tend to wallow in obscurity.

- ✔ **Earnings growth:** Growth companies' earnings tend to impress, while you can expect value companies to have less than awe-inspiring earnings growth.

- ✔ **The industry sector:** Growth stocks are typically found in high-flying industries, such as computers, wireless, and biotechnology. Value stocks are more often found in older-than-the-hills sectors, such as energy, banking, transportation, and toiletries.

Looking for the Best Value Buys

Many academic types have looked at the so-called *value premium* and have tried to explain it. No one can agree on why value stocks have historically outperformed growth stocks. (A joke I remember from my college days: Put any three economists in a room, and you'll get at least five opinions.)

Some people say there is hidden risk in value investing that warrants greater returns. They explain that although the standard deviation for the two asset classes is about the same, value stocks tend to plummet at the worst economic times. This argument is not very persuasive. Although value was hit harder than growth in the market plunge of 2008, the reverse held true in the prior market nosedive of 2000–2002. In the late summer of 2011, after S&P decided to downgrade U.S. Treasuries, U.S. value and growth stocks fell at about the same pace.

Others say that value stocks outperform growth stocks because of the greater dividends paid by value companies. Growth companies tend to plow their cash into acquisitions and new product development rather than issuing dividends to those pesky shareholders.

Here's the best explanation for the value premium, if you ask this humble author: Value stocks simply tend to be ignored by the market — or have been in the past — and therefore come relatively cheap. When value stocks do receive attention, it's usually negative. And studies show that investors tend to overreact to bad news. Such overreactions end up being reflected in a discounted price.

Taking the index route

Famous value investors like Warren Buffett make their money finding stocks that come at an especially discounted price. They recognize that companies making lackluster profits, and even sometimes companies bleeding money, can turn around (especially when Mr. Buffett sends in his team of whip-cracking consultants). When a lackluster company turns around, the stock that was formerly seen as a financial turd (that's a technical term) can suddenly turn into 14-karat gold. It's a formula that has worked well for the Oracle of Omaha.

Good luck making it work for you.

Unlike Warren Buffett, many or most value stock pickers repeatedly take gambles on failing companies that continue to fail. I say the best way to invest in large value is to buy the index. There is no better way of doing that than through ETFs.

Making an ETF selection

Of the 100 or so diversified large cap ETFs on the market, perhaps 20 or so are worth particular attention for tapping into the value market. The following five offer good large value indexes at reasonable prices: the Vanguard Value ETF (VTV), Vanguard Mega Cap 300 Value Index ETF (MGV), iShares Russell 1000 Value ETF (IWD), iShares Morningstar Large Value ETF (JKF), and the Schwab U.S. Large-Cap Value ETF (SCHV).

I suggest that you read through my descriptions that follow and make the choice that you think is best for you. Whatever your allocation to domestic large cap stocks (see Chapter 16 if you aren't sure), your allocation to value should be somewhere in the ballpark of 50 to 60 percent of that amount. In other words, I suggest that you tilt toward value, but don't go overboard.

The criteria you use in picking the best large cap value ETF should include expense ratios, appropriateness of the index, and tax efficiency (if you're investing in a taxable account). If you have a modest portfolio, or if you are making regular contributions, the trading costs need to be factored in as well. Note that the expense ratios, average cap sizes, price/earning ratios, and top five holdings are all subject to change; you should definitely check for updated figures before investing.

Vanguard Value Index ETF (VTV)

Indexed to: MSCI U.S. Prime Market Value Index (400 or so of the nation's largest value stocks)

Expense ratio: 0.12 percent

Average cap size: $50.7 billion

P/E ratio: 14.9

Top five holdings: Exxon Mobil, Chevron, General Electric, AT&T, Procter & Gamble

Russell's review: The price is right. The index makes sense. There's good diversification. The companies represented are certainly large. This ETF is a very good option, although I'd like it even more if it were a tad more valuey. (On the other hand, making it more valuey could increase turnover, which might increase costs and taxation.) All told, I like the VTV. I like it a lot. If you already own the Vanguard Value Index mutual fund and you're considering moving to ETFs, this fund would clearly be your choice (see "The Vanguard edge" sidebar in Chapter 3). If held at Vanguard, this ETF, like all Vanguard ETFs, trades for free.

Vanguard Mega Cap 300 Value Index ETF (MGV)

Indexed to: The MSCI U.S. Large Cap Value Index (150 or so of the largest U.S. stocks with value characteristics)

Expense ratio: 0.13 percent

Average cap size: $84.8 billion

P/E ratio: 14.4

Top five holdings: Exxon Mobil, Chevron, General Electric, AT&T, Procter & Gamble

Russell's review: This fund offers exposure to larger companies than does the more popular VTV featured above. Is bigger better? Could be. If you have small caps in your portfolio (which you should!), this mega cap fund will give you slightly less correlation than you'll get with VTV. As a stand-alone investment, however, I would expect that the very long-term returns on this fund will lag VTV, given that giant caps historically have lagged large caps. Given Vanguard's low expenses and reasonable indexes, either fund would make a fine holding. MGV also trades free of commission if held at Vanguard.

iShares Russell 1000 Value ETF (IWD)

Indexed to: The 600 or so more-valuey stocks in the Russell 1000 Index (the largest 1,000 publicly traded companies in the land)

Expense ratio: 0.20 percent

Average cap size: $74.9 billion

P/E ratio: 13.0

Top five holdings: Chevron, AT&T, Procter & Gamble, JPMorgan Chase, Pfizer

Russell's review: The cost isn't high, but it is higher than the comparable Vanguard and Schwab funds. On the other hand, this ETF offers a slightly more valuey lean than the others. Like a number of other broad-based iShares ETFs, IWD trades free if held at Fidelity.

iShares Morningstar Large Value ETF (JKF)

Indexed to: Morningstar Large Value Index (76 of the largest U.S. value stocks, "value" being determined by Morningstar's proprietary formula)

Expense ratio: 0.25 percent

Average cap size: $101.7 billion

P/E ratio: 15.9

Top five holdings: Exxon Mobil, Chevron, AT&T, JPMorgan Chase, Pfizer

Russell's review: Exxon Mobil alone makes up more than 12 percent of this ETF, and that, in my mind, is less than ideal. Add the 6.5 percent held in Chevron, and you have nearly one-fifth of the fund in two stocks, both in the same oily industry. (That concentration in the giants explains why the average cap size of this fund is even greater than Vanguard's Mega Cap ETF.) To boot, Morningstar indexes aren't nearly as popular as S&P indexes, so this ETF is thinly traded, which could result in a larger spread when you buy or sell. On the positive side, however, Morningstar indexes are neat boxes: Any company that appears in the value index is not going to pop up in the growth index. I think that's worth something, for sure.

Schwab U.S. Large-Cap Value ETF (SCHV)

Indexed to: Dow Jones U.S. Large-Cap Value Total Stock Market Index (made up of the more valuey half of the 600 or so stocks that comprise the DJ U.S. Large Cap Stock Market Index)

Expense ratio: 0.13 percent

Average cap size: $75.9 billion

P/E ratio: 14.1

Top five holdings: Exxon Mobil, General Electric, Chevron, International Business Machines, Procter & Gamble

Russell's review: For the sake of economy alone, this fund, like all Schwab ETFs, is a good option. The management fee is one of the lowest in the industry. And, like all Schwab ETFs, you can trade this fund for free if held at Schwab. Most importantly, the index is a good one. I expect Schwab to do a reasonable or better job of tracking the index, even though its ETFs were introduced only in late 2009.

Chapter 7

Small Growth: Sweet Sounding Start-ups

*O*nce upon a time in the kingdom of Redmond, there was a young company called Microsoft. It was a very small company with very big ideas, and it grew and grew and grew. Its founder and its original investors became very, very rich and lived happily ever after.

Oh, you've heard that story? Then you understand the appeal of small growth companies. These are companies that typically have *market capitalization* (the market value of total outstanding stock) of about $300 million to $1 billion. They frequently boast a hot product or patent, often fall into the high tech arena, and always seem to be on their way to stardom. Some of them make it, and along with them, their investors take a joy ride all the way to early retirement.

Unfortunately, for every Microsoft, there are a dozen, or two or three dozen, small companies that go belly up long before their prime. For every investor who gambles on a small company stock and takes early retirement, 100 others still drive their cars to work every Monday morning.

Beep beep.

In this chapter, I ask you to take a ride with me through the world of small cap growth stocks. I explain what role, if any, they should play in your ETF portfolio. First stop along the ride: Figure 7-1, where you can see how small growth fits into the investment style grid I introduce in Chapter 4. Second stop: Figure 7-2, which shows that small growth stocks, at least over the past eight decades, haven't exactly lit the world on fire.

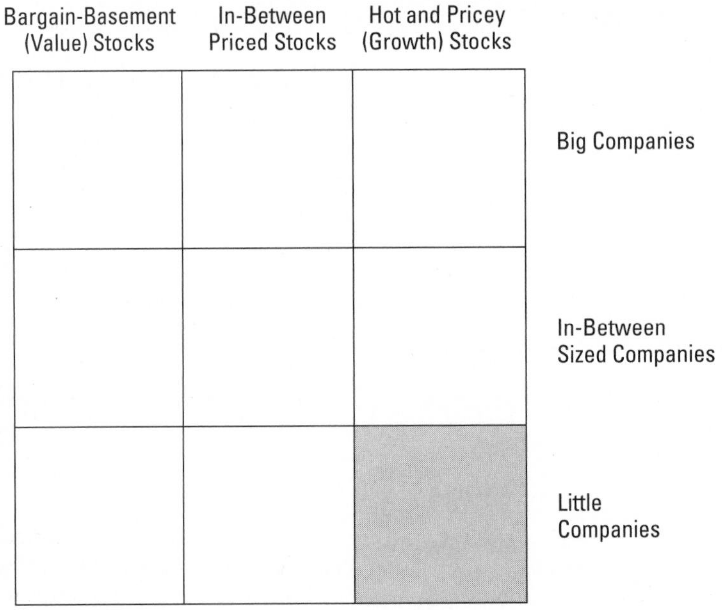

Bargain-Basement (Value) Stocks   In-Between Priced Stocks   Hot and Pricey (Growth) Stocks

Big Companies

Figure 7-1: The shaded area is the portion of the investment grid represented by small growth stocks.

In-Between Sized Companies

Little Companies

Getting Real about Small Cap Investments

In the past century, small cap stocks have outperformed large cap stocks just as assuredly as Honduras has produced more Hondurans than the United States. The volatility of small cap stocks has also been greater, just as assuredly as the United States has more roller coasters than Honduras. In terms of return per unit of risk (risk-adjusted rate of return), however, small caps are clearly winners. And so it would seem that investing in small caps is a pretty smart thing to do. But please know that not all small caps are created equal.

As it happens, the true stars of the small cap world have been small cap *value* stocks rather than small cap *growth* stocks. (Take a look at Chapters 5 and 6 if you aren't sure what I mean by these terms.) How slow-growing, often ailing companies have beat out their hot-to-trot cousins remains one of the great unresolved mysteries of the investing world. But the numbers don't lie.

U.S. Large Cap Value Stocks
1927-2010: Total Returns

U.S. Large Cap Growth Stocks
1927-2010: Total Returns

Figure 7-2:
Historically,
the growth
of a basket
of small
growth
stocks
hasn't been
anything to
write home
about.

U.S. Small Cap Value Stocks
1927-2010: Total Returns

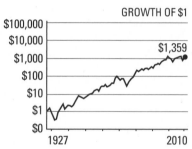

U.S. Small Cap Growth Stocks
1927-2010: Total Returns

Source: Fama/French data provided by Eugene F. Fama and Kenneth R. French

In fact, if you look at the numbers, such as those in Figure 7-2, you may be inclined to treat small growth stocks as a pariah. Please don't. They belong in a well-diversified portfolio. Some years are clearly small growth years. The best example is rather recent: As I'm writing this chapter, about midway through 2011, small cap growth stocks have seen a 12-month return of more than 30 percent, beating both small value and large caps by a very wide margin. Back in 2003, small growth was the undisputed King of Returns, clocking in at an astounding 50.37 percent. Who is to say that the long-term past wasn't a fluke and that small growth may actually go on to outperform all other asset classes in the next 20 years?

Your Choices for Small Growth

If you have a portfolio of under $20,000 or so, I recommend that you consider a small cap *blend* fund, which combines small value and small growth stocks. Small cap domestic stocks shouldn't occupy more than 20 percent or so of your portfolio (more on that topic in Chapter 16), and if you divide up 20 percent of less than $20,000, the trading costs (some you'll see, and some that may be hidden) could seriously impact your returns. So keep it simple until your portfolio grows to the point that you can start slicing and dicing a bit more economically.

If you have a portfolio of more than $20,000 and you are a buy-and-hold kind of guy or gal, I suggest that you break up your small cap holdings into a growth ETF and a value ETF. Given the dramatic outperformance of value in the past, you might tilt in that direction — more so than you do with large caps. A reasonable tilt may call for somewhere between 60 and 75 of your small cap exposure going to value, and 25 to 40 percent going to growth.

Small cap blend funds

A bit of growth, a bit of value, your choice in small cap blend funds should take into consideration such things as expense ratios, average cap size, and P/E ratio (explained in Chapter 5). Keep in mind that these numbers are subject to change, so I recommend checking them before you act.

Some good ETF options for people with limited-size portfolios include the Vanguard Small Cap (VB), iShares Morningstar Small Core (JKJ), iShares S&P Small Cap 600 (IJR), and Schwab U.S. Small-Cap (SCHA) ETFs.

Vanguard Small Cap ETF (VB)

Indexed to: MSCI U.S. Small Cap 1750 Index (1,750 broadly diversified smaller U.S. companies)

Expense ratio: 0.17 percent

Average cap size: $1.8 billion

P/E ratio: 27.3

Top five holdings: Informatica Corp., Polycom Inc., TIBCO Software Inc., SM Energy Company, WABCO Holdings Inc.

Russell's review: The expense ratio is quite low, especially when compared to most other offerings in the small cap arena. The diversification is lovely. And Vanguard's ETFs — largely because they are pegged to indexes with little turnover — are arguably the most tax-efficient of all ETFs. Those are the three positives. On the downside, the P/E ratio is higher than that of competing ETFs (an indication of a greater orientation toward growth and away from value). And the average cap size is larger than some others. On balance, this is a very good selection, but (as with all blend funds) I'd scrap it for something more refined — a growth and value split — as soon as your portfolio is large enough to allow for such refinement. There are no commissions for trading this ETF if it's held at Vanguard.

iShares Morningstar Small Core ETF (JKJ)

Indexed to: 260 companies from the Morningstar Small Core Index that fall somewhere between extreme growth and value

Expense ratio: 0.25 percent

Average cap size: $1.9 billion

P/E ratio: 24.6

Top five holdings: SandRidge Energy Inc., Cypress Semiconductor Corp., Polaris Industries Inc., Amerigroup Corp., The Cooper Companies Inc.

Russell's review: The diversification isn't quite what you get with Vanguard, but it's adequate. The somewhat lower P/E could translate into slightly higher returns over the next few years, but that may be offset by the higher expense ratio. These Morningstar iShares aren't heavily traded, so you could get zonked with a larger spread when you buy and sell.

iShares S&P Small Cap 600 ETF (IJR)

Indexed to: Roughly 600 companies that make up the S&P Small Cap 600 Index

Expense ratio: 0.20

Average cap size: $1.2 billion

P/E ratio: 25.3

Top five holdings: Regeneron Pharmaceuticals Inc., Amerigroup Corp., HealthSpring Inc., Holly Corp., BioMed Realty Trust Inc.

Russell's review: This is a perfectly acceptable ETF for small cap exposure at a fair price. Vanguard's price, however, is even more fair. If you already own this ETF, that's not reason enough to switch unless you're holding a rather large position and capital gains are not an issue. But if you're starting from scratch, I don't know if paying the higher fee would be warranted. This ETF trades free of commission if held at Fidelity, so it may be an optimal selection in smaller portfolios where trading costs can make a more serious dent.

Schwab U.S. Small-Cap ETF (SCHA)

Indexed to: Dow Jones U.S. Small-Cap Total Stock Market Index (1,750 of America's most modest-sized publicly traded companies)

Expense ratio: 0.13 percent

Average cap size: $1.8 billion

P/E ratio: 19.1

Top five holdings: Atmel Corp., Riverbed Technology Inc., Skyworks Solutions Inc., Chimera Investment Corp., Gentex Corp.

Russell's review: The low P/E ratio indicates something of a value lean, which isn't a bad thing to have if this one fund is your only exposure to U.S. small caps. The number of stocks represented is large, and (all other things being equal) a larger number of stocks in an index is better. The expense ratio of this ETF is the lowest in the category, and the fund trades free of commissions if held at Schwab. All in all, it isn't a bad package. In fact, I find it quite attractive.

Strictly small cap growth funds

If you have enough assets to warrant splitting up small value and small growth, go for it, by all means. Following are some good small growth options from iShares and Vanguard. I also review the Guggenheim small cap "pure growth," fund, even though I have some mixed feelings about that one. In the next chapter, I present small value options to complement the funds presented here.

Vanguard Small Cap Growth ETF (VBK)

Indexed to: MSCI U.S. Small Cap Growth Index (approximately 970 small cap growth companies in the United States)

Expense ratio: 0.12 percent

Average cap size: $1.9 billion

P/E ratio: 34.5

Top five holdings: Informatica Corp., Polycom Inc., TIBCO Software Inc., VeriFone Systems Inc., JDS Uniphase Corp.

Russell's review: I don't know why Vanguard charges 0.05 less for this fund than it does for its small cap blend ETF, but hey — let's not question a bargain. Add to that economy the wide diversification, tax efficiency beyond compare, and a very definite growth exposure, and I really have no complaints. The Vanguard Small Cap Growth ETF offers an excellent way to tap into this asset class. And that's especially true if you happen to hold your portfolio at Vanguard, where trading Vanguard ETFs incurs no commissions.

iShares Morningstar Small Growth Index ETF (JKK)

Indexed to: Approximately 370 companies from the Morningstar Small Growth Index

Expense ratio: 0.30 percent

Average cap size: $1.8 billion

P/E ratio: 34.1

Top five holdings: Biomarin Pharmaceutical, Interdigital Inc., Techne Corp., Equity Lifestyle Properties, Coeur D'Alene Mines Corp.

Russell's review: My only beef with the Morningstar indexes is that they tend to be a bit too concentrated, at least in the large cap arena. In their small caps, however, concentration isn't a problem. The largest holding here, Biomarin Pharmaceutical, gets an acceptably small 1.2 percent allocation. The expense ratio, too, is acceptable, although higher than some others in this category. I like that Morningstar promises no crossover between growth and value. If you own this ETF along with the iShares Morningstar Small Value Index, you should get pleasantly limited correlation.

iShares S&P Small Cap 600 Growth ETF (IJT)

Indexed to: Despite the "600" in its name, this ETF tracks the 350 or so holdings that make up the S&P Small Cap 600/Citigroup Growth Index

Expense ratio: 0.25 percent

Average cap size: $1.3 billion

P/E ratio: 26.7

Top five holdings: Regeneron Pharmaceuticals Inc., HealthSpring Inc., American Medical Systems Holdings Inc., Salix Pharmaceuticals Ltd., Signature Bank

Russell's review: S&P indexes are a bit too subjective for me to really love them. I'm also a bit baffled that the current P/E ratio of this fund is so similar to that of the iShares S&P Small Cap Value 600 Index fund (IJS), which I review in the next chapter. In fact, the P/E ratios are practically the same. Growth fund P/Es are generally much higher than value P/Es. Of course, this number could just be an aberration; all ratios can fluctuate greatly from week to week, especially with small cap funds. In any event, the fund's price is reasonable, and there's no reason to snub this iShares offering. Apparently, Fidelity likes it because it allows you to buy and sell this ETF without paying any commission. (Of course, Fidelity gets some remuneration from iShares.)

Guggenheim S&P 600 Small Cap Pure Growth ETF (RZG)

Indexed to: Approximately 150 of the smallest and most growthy of the S&P 600 companies

Expense ratio: 0.35

Average cap size: $1.2 billion

P/E ratio: 20.0

Top five holdings: Sturm Ruger & Co., Hi-Tech Pharmacal Co., BJ's Restaurants, Regeneron Pharmaceuticals Inc., Jos. A Bank Clothiers

Russell's review: The price is higher than others in this category, and the promise of "purity" is a bit murky — especially if the quest for purity leads to high turnover, which could reduce tax efficiency. Guggenheim also seems to cater mostly to traders rather than to buy-and-hold investors, and that makes me uncomfortable. Traders usually trade themselves into losses. *Caveat:* More than one-third of the holdings in this fund are tech stocks.

Smaller than Small: Meet the Micro Caps

If you want to invest your money in companies that are smaller than small, you're going to be investing in micro caps. These companies are larger than the corner delicatessen, but sometimes not by much. In general, micro caps are publicly held companies with less than $300 million in outstanding stock. Micro caps, as you can imagine, are volatile little suckers, but as a group they offer impressive long-term performance. In terms of diversification, micro caps — in conservative quantity — could be a nice addition to your portfolio, although I wouldn't call them a necessity. Take note that micro cap funds, even index ETFs, tend to charge considerably more in management fees than you'll pay for most funds.

Micros move at a modestly different pace from other equity asset classes. The theory is that because micro caps are heavy borrowers, their performance is more tied to interest rates than the performance of larger cap stocks is. (Lower interest rates would be good for these stocks; higher interest rates would not.) Micro caps also tend to be more tied to the vicissitudes of the U.S. economy and less to the world economy than, say, the fortunes of General Electric or McDonald's.

Given the high risk of owning any individual micro cap stock, it makes sense to work micro caps into your portfolio in fund form, despite the management fees, rather than trying to pick individual companies. To date, a handful of micro cap ETFs have been introduced. They differ from one another to a much greater extent than do the larger cap ETFs. Notice that the top five holdings of each ETF are completely different; you don't find Exxon Mobil and Apple in every list, as you do with large cap growth funds.

Despite the differences, all three funds discussed next have seen rather lackluster performance since their inception. It may be possible that microcaps are a particular kind of asset class (commodities would be another) where indexed ETFs may be less than the ideal vehicle. The performance may have something to do with the illiquidity of microcaps (it's not always easy to buy and sell shares on the open market). Time will tell. In the meantime, proceed with caution, and if you want to invest in any of these funds, do so with only a modest percent of your portfolio.

iShares Russell Microcap Index ETF (IWC)

Indexed to: 1,300 of the smallest publicly traded companies, all culled from the Russell 3000 Index

Expense ratio: 0.60 percent

Average cap size: $400 million

P/E ratio: 29.1

Top five holdings: Acacia Research–Acacia Tec, ARIAD Pharmaceuticals Inc., Kodiak Oil & Gas Corp., Buckeye Technologies Inc., Dollar Financial Corp.

Russell's review: There aren't a lot of choices in this field, so I'm glad this is one of them. I'm not crazy about paying 0.60 percent, which is high for an ETF, but there seems to be price collusion in the micro cap area, so what are you going to do? (Personal note to ETF firms' attorneys: Hey, I'm only kidding about the price collusion, guys! It just *seems* that way.) ***Caveat:*** One-quarter of the stocks held in this fund are financial stocks.

PowerShares Zacks Micro Cap Portfolio ETF (PZI)

Indexed to: The proprietary Zacks Micro Cap Index, which includes roughly 400 micro cap stocks chosen for "investment merit criteria, including fundamental growth, stock valuation, investment timeliness . . . ." In other words, someone behind the scenes is stock picking.

Expense ratio: 0.60 percent

Average cap size: $400 million

P/E ratio: 15.2

Top five holdings: TravelCenters of America LLC, Hercules Offshore Inc., Gramercy Capital Corp., Mercer International Inc., Web.com Group Inc.

Russell's review: I don't like stock picking, and I don't generally trust any manager to know what qualifies as "investment timeliness." Still, this ETF's selections yield an average cap size that makes it, in my mind, a contender if you want eensy-weensy company exposure, despite the active management. There is also a bit less industry concentration than exists with the iShares option — only one-fifth, as compared to one-fourth, of this fund's portfolio is in financial stocks.

First Trust Dow Jones Select MicroCap ETF (FDM)

Indexed to: Dow Jones Select MicroCap Index, which contains about 200 of the smallest stocks listed on the New York Stock Exchange and the NASDAQ

Expense ratio: 0.60

Average cap size: $390 million

P/E ratio: 17.5

Top five holdings: Buckeye Technologies Inc., Lindsay Corporation, Strategic Hotels & Resorts Inc., iStar Financial Inc., First Industrial Realty Trust Inc.

Russell's review: The expense ratio is the same as the others, and the average cap size is not much different. All in all, everything else looks okay, but this fund offers less diversification. In fact, there's a lot of industry concentration — at last glance, more than 27 percent in financials. For that reason, I'd give this fund the bronze metal, and award gold and silver to the iShares and PowerShares options.

Chapter 8

Small Value: Diminutive Dazzlers

*L*ook at the list of some of the top companies represented in the Vanguard Small Cap Value ETF: First Niagara Financial Group, Camden Property Trust, Beazer Homes USA, Corn Products International . . . These are not household names. Nor are they especially fast-growing companies. Nor are they industry leaders. Nor is there much excitement to be seen in companies such as Corn Products International. ("Our starches, sweeteners and other ingredients are used by our customers to provide everything from sweetness, taste and texture to immune system support, fat replacement and adhesive strength.") As you go farther down the list of holdings, you'll likely find some companies in financial distress. Others may be facing serious lawsuits, expiration of patents, or labor unrest. If you wanted to pick one of these companies to sink a wad of cash into, I would tell you that you're crazy.

But if you wanted to sink that cash into the entire small value index, well, that's another matter altogether. Assuming you could handle some risk, I'd tell you to go for it. By all means. Your odds of making money are pretty darned good — at least if history is our guide.

Don't take my word for it; see Figure 8-2, which shows the enormous growth of value stocks over the past eight decades. On the way there, see Figure 8-1, which shows where small value fits into the investment style grid I introduce in Chapter 4. And then, follow me as I explain the importance of small value stocks in a poised-for-performance ETF portfolio.

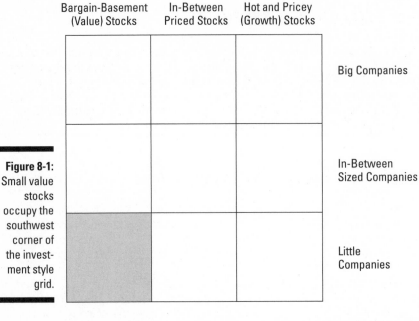

	Bargain-Basement (Value) Stocks	In-Between Priced Stocks	Hot and Pricey (Growth) Stocks
Big Companies			
In-Between Sized Companies			
Little Companies			

Figure 8-1: Small value stocks occupy the southwest corner of the investment style grid.

U.S. Large Cap Value Stocks
1927-2010: Total Returns

GROWTH OF $1
$4,228

U.S. Large Cap Growth Stocks
1927-2010: Total Returns

GROWTH OF $1
$1,447

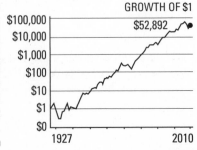

U.S. Small Cap Value Stocks
1927-2010: Total Returns

GROWTH OF $1
$52,892

Figure 8-2: As you can see, small value has truly shined in the past eight decades.

U.S. Small Cap Growth Stocks
1927-2010: Total Returns

GROWTH OF $1
$1,359

Source: Fama/French data provided by Eugene F. Fama and Kenneth R. French

It's Been Quite a Ride

Small value stocks collectively have returned more to investors than have large value stocks or any kind of growth stocks. In fact, the difference in returns has been somewhat staggering: I'm talking about an annualized return of about 14.2 percent over the past 83 years for small value versus 11.1 percent for large value, 8.8 for large growth, and 9.2 for small growth. Compounded over time, the outperformance of small value stocks has been HUGE.

Latching on for fun and profit

To be sure, small value stocks are risky little suckers. Even the entire index (available to you in neat ETF form) is more volatile than any conservative investor may feel comfortable with. But as part — a very handsome part — of a diversified portfolio, a small value ETF can be a beautiful thing indeed.

If we knew the past was going to repeat, such as it did in the movie *Groundhog Day,* there'd be no reason to have anything but small value in your portfolio. But, of course, we don't know that the past will repeat. Bill Murray's radio alarm clock may not go off at sunrise. And the small value premium, like Bill Murray's hairline, may start to seriously recede. Still, the outperformance of small value has historically been so much greater than that of small growth that I favor a good tilt in the direction of value.

But keeping your balance

Whatever your total allocation to domestic small cap stocks (see Chapter 16 for advice), I recommend that anywhere from 60 to 75 percent of that amount be allocated to small value. But no more than that, please. If the value premium disappears or becomes a value discount, I don't want you left holding the bag. And even if small value continues to outperform, having both small value and small growth (along with their bigger cousins, all of which tend to rise and fall in different cycles) will help smooth out some of the inevitable volatility of holding stocks.

The best choices among small value ETFs include offerings from Vanguard and iShares. I also review an option from Guggenheim, which isn't terrible.

Vanguard Small Cap Value ETF (VBR)

Indexed to: MSCI U.S. Small Cap Value Index (about 1,000 small value domestic companies)

Expense ratio: 0.23 percent

Average cap size: $1.8 billion

P/E ratio: 19.1

Top five holdings: American Capital Agency, Camden Property Trust, Essex Property Trust, BE Aerospace, Corn Products International

Russell's review: Low cost, wide diversification, tax efficiency beyond compare, and a very definite value bias — what's not to like? The Vanguard Small Cap Value ETF offers an excellent way to tap into this asset class. If you hold this fund at Vanguard, you get a bonus: You can trade with no commission.

iShares Morningstar Small Value Index (JKL)

Indexed to: Morningstar's Small Value Index (about 230 companies of modest size and modest stock price)

Expense ratio: 0.30 percent

Average cap size: $1.9 billion

P/E ratio: 14.1

Top five holdings: Rock-Tenn Company, Temple-Inland, GenOn Energy, Ryder System, Complete Production Services

Russell's review: My only complaint with the Morningstar indexes is that they tend to be a bit too concentrated, at least in the large cap arena where a company like Exxon Mobil can hold too much sway. In the Morningstar small cap indexes, that isn't a problem. The largest holding here, Rock-Tenn Company, gets only a 1.24 percent allocation, which is fine and dandy. The expense ratio, too, is acceptable although higher than some others in this category. I like that Morningstar promises no crossover between growth and value. If you own this ETF along with the iShares Morningstar Small Growth Index, you should get pleasantly modest correlation. (In lay terms, if one fund gets slammed, the other may not.)

iShares S&P Small Cap 600 Value Index (IJS)

Indexed to: 457 of the S&P SmallCap 600 Value Index

Expense ratio: 0.25 percent

Average cap size: $1.2 billion

P/E ratio: 22.4

Top five holdings: World Fuel Services, ProAssurance Corp., Teledyne Technologies, New Jersey Resources, Moog-Inc.–Class A

Russell's review: S&P indexes are a bit too subjective for me to want to marry them. I'm also a slight bit baffled that the current P/E ratio of this fund, which is supposed to be a value fund, is so similar to the iShares S&P Small Cap 600 Growth Index (IJT). It shouldn't be that way. Of course, P/E ratios can change from week to week, especially with small cap funds, but I've been checking this one out for a while. Nonetheless, this fund's price is reasonable, and there's no reason to entirely snub this iShares offering. (Marry it, but have a pre-nup. You may later decide that you'll do better elsewhere.) Oh, this fund also trades commission-free on the Fidelity platform.

Guggenheim S&P 600 Small Cap Pure Value (RZV)

Indexed to: S&P SmallCap Pure Value Index (approximately 150 of the most valuey and small of the S&P 600 companies)

Expense ratio: 0.35

Average cap size: $350 million

P/E ratio: 15.8

Top five holdings: Agilysys, Red Robin Gourmet Burgers, Ciber Inc., Lithia Motors, Audiovox Corp.

Russell's review: The price is higher than others in this category, and the promise of "purity" is a bit murky, especially if that quest for purity leads to high turnover, which blows the tax efficiency. Guggenheim also seems to cater mostly to traders rather than buy-and-hold investors, which gives me something of a feeling of discomfort. Traders usually trade themselves into hamburger-eating misery. In addition, although the low P/E ratio is tantalizing, the smaller-than-small cap size makes me concerned. When cap size gets too small (and small caps start looking like micro caps), liquidity becomes an issue, and index funds can sometimes get hurt.

What About the Mid Caps?

In a word, my take on mid cap ETFs is . . . *why*? Yes, for the past several years mid cap stocks — investments in companies with roughly $5 to $20 billion in outstanding stock — have performed especially well. They've done better than large caps and have even given small cap stocks a run for their money. But such outperformance of mid cap stocks is a fluke. So, too, is any underperformance.

If you look at the risk/return profile of mid caps over many years, you find that it generally falls right where you would expect it to fall: smack dab in between large and small cap. Owning both a large cap and small cap ETF, therefore, will give you an average return very similar to mid caps but with considerably less volatility because large and small cap stocks tend to move up and down at different times.

Other investment pros may disagree, but I really don't see the point of shopping for mid cap ETFs, even though there are many mid cap offerings. Keep in mind, too, that most large cap and small cap funds are rather fluid: You will get some mid cap exposure from both. Many sector funds — including real estate, materials, and utilities — are also chock-full of mid caps (see Chapter 10).

Chapter 9

Going Global: ETFs without Borders

*I*f you were standing on a ship in the middle of the ocean (doesn't matter whether it's the Atlantic or Pacific), and you looked up and squinted real hard, you might see investment dollars sailing overhead. For at least a decade now, U.S. fund investors have been steadily adding money to the international side of their stock portfolios. According to figures from the Investment Company Institute, the average U.S. investor in 2001 had but 13 percent of his or her equity portfolio allocated to foreign stocks; today, that figure is 27 percent.

Just to be clear: The terms *foreign* and *international* are used interchangeably to refer to stocks of companies outside of the United States. The word *global* refers to stocks of companies based anywhere in the whole world, including the United States.

Many investors have been moving to foreign stocks for the same reason that they move, moth-into-light style, into any other kind of investment: They've been lured by recent high returns, especially the returns of emerging market nation stocks.

As of mid-2011, the 10-year annualized return of the U.S. stock market stood at about 4 percent. In sharp contrast, stocks of the world's emerging market nations clocked in with a rather astounding 16 percent per year for the past decade. Developed nations in the Pacific Rim (Japan, Australia, Singapore) more or less matched the United States for the decade. European stocks (including the United Kingdom), despite some sharp recent losses due largely to a debt mess in Greece and Portugal, showed an average return of about 6 percent.

In the past, most Americans were woefully under-invested abroad, so I see the recent turn as a decidedly good thing. I'm *glad* most investors have finally started to send their dollars abroad — even if some of them are doing it, by and large, for the wrong reason. In this chapter, I explain my love for global diversification and reveal how you can accomplish it easily with ETFs.

The Ups and Downs of Different Markets around the World

If you expect emerging market stocks to continue to clock such phenomenal returns, you are sure to be disappointed. If you expect European stock markets to do half again as much as the U.S. markets, I think you are similarly in for a sad surprise. I do think you can expect that foreign stocks overall may do better than U.S. stocks in the coming decade or two. (If you want the nitty-gritty of my reasoning, see the section, "Why ETFs are a great tool for international investing.") But I certainly wouldn't bet the farm on international stocks outperforming U.S. stocks — or underperforming them either, for that matter. The difference in returns in the future, as it has been in the long-term past, is not likely to be all that extreme.

In all likelihood, international stocks as a whole will have their day. U.S. stocks will then come up from behind. Then international stocks will have their day again. And then U.S. stocks will get the jump. This type of horse race has been going on since, oh, long before *Mr. Ed* was on the air. Take a look at Figure 9-1. Note (as depicted by the peaks and valleys in the chart) that over a 35-year period, outperformance by U.S. stocks versus non-U.S. stocks has been followed quite regularly by years of underperformance.

The reason to invest abroad isn't primarily to try to outperform the Joneses . . . or the LeBlancs, or the Yamashitas. Rather, the purpose is to diversify your portfolio so as to capture overall stock market gains while tempering risk. You reduce risk whenever you own two or more asset classes that move up and down at different times. Stocks of different geographic regions tend to do exactly that.

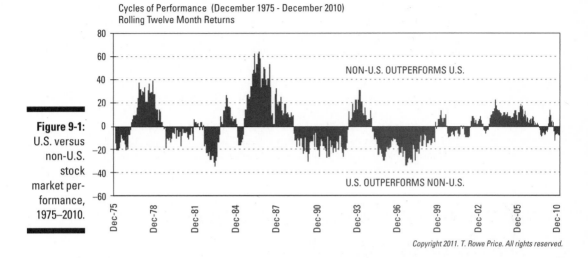

Cycles of Performance (December 1975 - December 2010)
Rolling Twelve Month Returns

NON-U.S. OUTPERFORMS U.S.

U.S. OUTPERFORMS NON-U.S.

Figure 9-1:
U.S. versus
non-U.S.
stock
market per-
formance,
1975–2010.

Low correlation is the name of the game

Why, you may ask, do you need European and Japanese stocks when you already have all the lovely diversification discussed in past chapters: large, small, value, and growth stocks, and a good mix of industries? (See Chapter 5 if you need a reminder of what these terms mean.) The answer, *mon ami, mi amigo,* is quite simple: You get better diversification when you diversify across borders.

I'll use several iShares ETFs to illustrate my point. Suppose you have a wad of money invested in the iShares S&P 500 Growth Index fund (IVW), and you want to diversify:

✔ If you combine IVW with its large value counterpart, the iShares S&P 500 Value Index Fund (IVE), you find that your two investments have a five-year correlation of 0.92. In other words, over the past five years, the funds have had a tendency to move in the same direction 92 percent of the time. Only 8 percent of the time have they tended to move in opposite directions.

✔ If you combine IVW with the iShares S&P Small Cap 600 Growth Index Fund (IJT), you find that your two investments have tended to move up and down together roughly 91 percent of the time.

✔ If you combine IVW with the iShares S&P Small Cap 600 Value Index Fund (IJS), your investments tend to move north or south at the same time 86 percent of time. Not bad. But not great.

Now consider adding some Japanese stock to your original portfolio of large growth stocks. The iShares MSCI Japan Index Fund (EWJ) has tended to move in synch with large U.S. growth stocks only about 76 percent of the time. And the ETF that tracks the FTSE China 25 Index (FXI) has moved in the same direction as large cap U.S. growth stocks only 65 percent of the time. There's clearly more zig and zag when you cross oceans to invest, and that's what makes international investing a must for a well-balanced portfolio.

The increasing inter-dependence of the world's markets wrought by globalization may cause these correlation numbers to rise over time. Indeed, we saw in 2008 that in a global financial crisis, stocks markets around the world will suffer. The trend toward rising correlations has led some pundits to make the claim that diversification is dead. Sorry, those pundits are wrong. In down times, yes, stocks of different colors, here and abroad, tend to turn a depressing shade of gray together. When investors are nervous in New York, they are often nervous in Berlin. And Sydney. And Cape Town. That's been true for years. The great apple-cart-turnover of 2008 was a particular case in point. But even in 2008, it still paid to be diversified, as U.S. and foreign stocks recovered, and are still recovering, at very different rates.

Diversification lowers, but does not eliminate, stock-market risk. Never did. Never will. Your portfolio, in addition to being well-diversified, should also have some components, such as cash and bonds, that are less volatile than stocks.

Remember what happened to Japan

To just "stay home" on the stock side of your portfolio would be to exhibit the very same conceit seen among Japanese investors in 1990. If you recall, that's when the dynamic and seemingly all-powerful rising sun slipped and then sank. Japanese investors, holding domestically-stuffed portfolios, bid *sayonara* to two-thirds of their wealth, which, more than two decades later, they have yet to fully recapture. (By year-end 2010, a basket of large-company Japanese stocks purchased in 1989 would have returned a very sad –1.3 percent a year over two full decades. Ouch.) It could happen here. Or worse.

Finding Your Best Mix of Domestic and International

About 65 percent of the entire world stock market is now outside of the United States. Should you invest that much of your stock portfolio in foreign ETFs? No, I think that may be overdoing it. Many financial experts say 15 to 25 percent of your stock holdings should be international, but that was also their recommendation back when the United States represented more than half of the world's stock value. I think that percentage may be under-doing it today. I say that 40 to 50 percent of your stock portfolio should be international, and this section explains why.

Why putting two-thirds of your portfolio in foreign stocks is too much

I see six distinct reasons to avoid overloading your portfolio to the tune of 65 percent foreign stocks:

✔ **Currency volatility:** When you invest abroad, you are usually investing in stocks that are denominated in other currencies. Because your foreign ETFs are denominated in Euros, Yen, or Pounds, they tend to be more volatile than the markets they represent. In other words, if European stock markets fall and the dollar rises (*vis-à-vis* the Euro) on the same day, your European ETF will fall doubly hard. If, however, the dollar falls on a day when the sun is shining on European stocks, your European ETF will soar.

Over the long run, individual currencies tend to go up and down. Although it could happen, it is unlikely that the dollar (or Euro) would permanently rise or fall to such a degree that it would seriously affect your nest egg. In the short term, however, such currency fluctuations can be a bit nauseating. See more on currencies in the sidebar "Pure (and purely silly) currency plays."

Pure (and purely silly) currency plays

If you would like to bet that the dollar is going to fall and the Euro is going to rise, you can purchase shares of the WisdomTree Dreyfus Euro Fund (EU). You may turn out to be right, in which case you'll make money. But I wouldn't call that successful investing; you made a lucky bet, not an investment. Currencies can move like a trash-can top in a hurricane, and you never know what direction they'll follow. This fund (and dozens of other currency ETFs and exchange-traded notes) may indeed serve a purpose in the world of commerce (such as a manufacturer's need to hedge against currency losses), but for the average investor's portfolio, EU deserves no allocation. Nor do the other funds that allow you speculate on the exchange rate of the Swiss Franc, the Chinese Yuan, or the Indian Rupee. If you follow my advice and invest in international stocks (and perhaps bonds, too, as I discuss in Chapter 12), you will get plenty of exposure to Euros (and Yen and Pounds) already — perhaps too much. You don't need any more.

✔ **Inflation issues:** Another risk with going whole hog for foreign stock ETFs is that to a certain extent, your fortunes are tied to those of your home economy. Stocks tend to do best in a heated economy. But in a heated economy, we also tend to see inflation. Because of that correlation between general price inflation and stock inflation, stock investors are generally able to stay ahead of the inflation game. If you were to invest all your money in, say, England, and should the economy here take off while the economy there sits idly on the launch pad, you could potentially be rocketed into a Dickensian kind of poverty.

✔ **Higher fees for foreign ETFs:** In the world of ETFs, the really good buys are to be had on the domestic side of the offerings. For whatever reason, global and international ETFs are about twice the price of broadly diversified U.S. ETFs. For example, while many Vanguard, Schwab, and Fidelity domestic ETFs carry management expenses of 0.10 percent or less, no foreign funds go nearly that low.

✔ **An overheated market:** It's possible that international stocks now account for about two-thirds of the world stock market simply because they are overheated. The timing to delve deeply abroad could be all wrong. As you see in the hills and valleys of Figure 9-1, periods in which foreign stocks beat the pants off U.S. stocks are often followed by periods in which those foreign-made pants fall to the ground. We may be on the verge of a U.S. comeback. (And, let me add, when emerging market stocks fall, they have been known to fall exceptionally hard.)

✔ **Lower correlation with homegrown options:** Certain kinds of stock funds in the United States offer even lower correlation to the rest of the U.S. market than do many international stock funds, and I suggest leaving room in your portfolio for some of those. I discuss some of these industry-sector funds in Chapter 10. You may also want to make room for *market-neutral* funds, which I discuss in Chapter 15.

✔ **A double tax hit:** Finally, foreign governments almost always hit you up for taxes on any dividends paid by stocks of companies in their countries. You don't pay this tax directly, but it is taken from your fund holdings. If your funds are held in certain accounts, Uncle Sam may want your money, too, and you wind up taking a double tax hit. This is a relatively minor reason not to go overboard when sailing overseas. (Specifics on this tax, and how to avoid getting double-whammied, are at the very end of this chapter.)

Why putting one-fifth of your portfolio in foreign stocks is insufficient

Some well-publicized research indicates that an 80-percent-or-so domestic stock/20-percent-or-so foreign stock portfolio is optimal for maximizing return and minimizing risk. But almost all that research defines *domestic stock* as the S&P 500 and *foreign stock* as the MSCI EAFE. The MSCI EAFE is an index of mostly large companies in the developed world. (*MSCI* stands for Morgan Stanley Capital International, and *EAFE* stands for Europe, Australasia, and Far East.) This analysis takes little account of the fact that you are not limiting yourself to the S&P 500 or to the MSCI EAFE. In the real world, you have the option of adding many asset classes to your portfolio of U.S. stocks. And among your international holdings, you can include developed world stocks in Europe, Australia, and Japan; emerging market stocks in China, India, and elsewhere; and foreign stocks in any and all flavors of large, small, value, and growth.

Many investment pros know well — and several have even told me — that they favor a much larger international position than they publicly advocate. Some may be afraid of seeming unpatriotic. Much more prevalent is a certain lemming-over-the-cliff-cover-my-ass mentality. If I, as your financial advisor, suggest a portfolio that resembles the S&P 500 and your portfolio tanks, you'll feel a bit peeved but you won't hate me. That's because all your friends' and neighbors' portfolios will have sunk as well. Should I give you a portfolio that's 50 percent foreign, and should foreign stocks have a bad year, you'll compare your portfolio to your friends' and neighbors' portfolios, and you may hate me. You may even sue me.

I wouldn't want that. Neither would most investment professionals. So most err on the side of caution and give you a portfolio that's more S&P 500 and less foreign — for their own protection, and not in the pursuit of your best interests.

Why ETFs are a great tool for international investing

By mixing and matching your domestic stock funds with 40 to 50 percent international, you will find your investment sweet spot. In Chapter 16, I pull together sample portfolios that use this methodology. Time and time again, I've run the numbers through the most sophisticated (and perhaps most expensive) professional portfolio analysis software available, and time and time again, 40-to-50-percent foreign is where I find the highest returns per unit of risk. And yes, this range has worked very well in the real world, too.

Although I try not to make forecasts because the markets are so incredibly unpredictable, I will say that if you had to err on the side of either U.S. or foreign stock investment, I would err on the side of too much foreign. The world economic and political climate is telling me that the U.S. stock market may be on relatively shakier ground. I could give you a long list of reasons (raging federal deficit and debt, trade deficit, aging population, military overextension, healthcare crisis), but what's most troubling about the United States is the extent to which it is becoming a nation of haves and have-nots. If history tells us anything, it is that great inequality leads to great dissension and upheaval.

As for me, personally, I eat my own international cooking: I have fully half of my own stock portfolio in foreign stocks — the vast majority of it held in ETFs.

Not All Foreign Nations — or Stocks — Are Created Equal

At present, you have more than 300 global and international ETFs from which to choose. (Once again, *global* ETFs hold U.S. as well as international stocks; *international* or *foreign* ETFs hold purely non-U.S. stocks.) I'd like you to consider the following half dozen factors when deciding which ones to invest in:

- ✔ **What's the correlation?** Certain economies are more closely linked to the U.S. economy than others, and the behavior of their stock markets reflects that. Canada, for example, offers limited diversification. Western Europe offers a bit more. For the least amount of correlation among developed nations, you want Japan (the world's second-largest stock market) or emerging market nations like Russia, Brazil, India, and China.

- ✔ **How large is the home market?** Although you can invest in individual countries, I generally wouldn't recommend it. Oh, I suppose you could slice and dice your portfolio to include 50 or so ETFs that represent individual countries (from Belgium to Austria and Singapore to Spain and, more recently, Vietnam to Poland), but that is going to be an awfully hard portfolio to manage. So why do it? Choose large regions in which to invest. (The only exceptions might be Japan and the United Kingdom, which have such large stock markets that they each qualify, in my mind, as a region.)

- ✔ **Think style.** If you have a large enough portfolio, consider dividing your international holdings into value and growth, large and small, just as you do with your domestic holdings. You can also divvy up your portfolio into global industry groupings. I discuss this strategy in Chapter 10. I generally prefer style diversification to sector diversification, but using both together can be truly powerful. You'll note that I take the combined approach in my sample portfolios in Part IV of this book.

- ✔ **Consider your risk tolerance.** Developed countries (United Kingdom, France, Japan) tend to have less volatile stock markets than do emerging market nations (such as those of Latin America, the Middle East, China, Russia, or India). You want both types of investments in your portfolio, but if you are inclined to invest in one much more than the other, know what you're getting into.

A boom economy doesn't necessarily mean a robust stock market

You would think that a fast-growing economy would be the best of places to invest. And yet there is more to stock returns than the growth of a national economy. (Just ask those investors who poured money into China several years ago.) In fact, the mind-blowing conclusion of a handful of recent studies is that the reverse is true: If you look at the stock returns of various national markets over the past 100 years, you actually find an *inverse* relationship. *Slow-growing* economies (such as India's, whose stock market has lately left China's in the dust) generally make for better stock investments!

There are several possible explanations for this anomaly. Some say that rapid economic growth is attributable more to small, entrepreneurial businesses rather than to larger, publicly held corporations. Others have suggested that the fruits of economic growth often don't go to shareholders. Instead, those fruits may go to labor or consumers or (with the United States being a prime example) top executives and option-holders. Another possible explanation is that the prices of stocks in fast-growing economies (just like domestic growth stocks) often start off overpriced due to higher-than-reasonable expectations. Stocks of slow-growing economies (just like value stocks) may tend to be underpriced.

The moral of the story is to spread your investment dollars around the world. Don't think you can pick countries that will outperform by using projected growth rates as your crystal ball.

✔ **What's the bounce factor?** As with any other kind of investment, you can pretty safely assume that risk and return will have a close relationship over many years. Emerging market ETFs will likely be more volatile but, over the long run, more rewarding than ETFs that track the stock markets of developed nations. ***One caveat:*** Don't assume that countries with fast-growing economies will necessarily be the most profitable investments; see the sidebar "A boom economy doesn't necessarily mean a robust stock market."

✔ **Look to P/E ratios.** How expensive is the stock compared to the earnings you're buying? You may ask yourself this question when buying a company stock, and it's just as valid a question when buying a nation's or a region's stocks. In general, a lower P/E ratio is more indicative of promising returns than is a high P/E ratio. (See Chapter 5 for a reminder of how to calculate a P/E ratio.)

Using ETFs as our proxies for world markets, we find that the Vanguard Total (U.S.) Stock Market ETF (VTI) currently has a P/E of about 18; the Vanguard European ETF (VGK) has a P/E of about 13; the Vanguard Pacific ETF (VPL) has a P/E of approximately 14; and the Vanguard Emerging

Market ETF (VWO) also has a P/E of roughly 14. So it seems as if foreign stocks — led by Europe — are currently the "value stocks" of the world.

You want your portfolio to include U.S., European, Pacific, and emerging market stocks, but if you are going to overweight any particular area, you may want to consider the relative P/E ratios, among other factors.

Choosing the Best International ETFs for Your Portfolio

Although I'm (obviously) a huge fan of international investing, and I believe that ETFs are the best way to achieve that end, there are only a dozen or so foreign ETFs that I think really fit the bill for most portfolios. This section introduces my favorites, complete with explanations of why I like them.

Note that I've split them up into three major categories: European, Pacific region, and emerging markets. For most portfolios, a reasonable split of foreign stock holdings would be something in the neighborhood of 40/40/20, with 40 percent going to Europe (England, France, Germany, Switzerland), 40 percent to the developed Pacific region (mostly Japan, with a smattering of Australia, New Zealand, and Singapore), and 20 percent to the emerging market nations (Brazil, Russia, Turkey, South Africa, Mexico, and a host of countries where the entire value of all outstanding stock may be less than that of any S&P 500 company).

Four brands to choose from

The ETFs I discuss here by and large belong to four ETF families: Vanguard, BlackRock (iShares); Schwab; and BLDRS (pronounced "builders"), a small product line issued by Invesco PowerShares. Yes, there are other global and international ETFs from which to choose. I discuss some of your other options in the next chapter, where I turn to global stocks divvied up by industry sector. As for global stocks that fit into a regional- or style-based portfolio, those mentioned in this section are among your best bets.

BLDRS stands for "Baskets of Listed Depositary Receipts," which is a very fancy way of saying "foreign stocks that trade on American stock exchanges." Vanguard and iShares foreign ETFs also include some Depositary Receipts (often referred to as *ADRs* — the *A* is for "American") but are made up more of true foreign stocks. That is to say that they own mostly foreign stocks only traded on foreign exchanges. For you, the investor, these nuances don't matter much, if at all, if you are holding your stock ETFs for the long haul (which, of course, you are!). In the short run, however, "true" foreign stocks and ADRs may diverge somewhat in performance.

A special word on BLDRS

The BLDRS indexes, when these funds first appeared, were restricted to American Depository Receipts that traded on the NASDAQ. Today the indexes include ADRs traded mostly on the NASDAQ, but also on the New York Stock Exchange. The indexes have attracted some criticism for their apparent randomness. In a way, the critics are right. Building a European ETF out of only ADRs that trade mostly on the NASDAQ is a little like putting together a football team of players whose first names all start with *R*. But my feeling is that all indexes are somewhat random. Some are weighted according to cap size; others are equally weighted; still others are weighted by number of shares outstanding. In point of fact, a team of football players named Robert, Rick, and Raul are not necessarily going to be any better or worse than a team with Clay, Dave, and Sam. And so it is with BLDRS: Their performance has been pretty much on a par with the other ETF options of the same regions.

For more information on any of the international ETFs I discuss next, keep the following contact information handy:

- ✔ **Vanguard:** www.vanguard.com; 1-877-662-7447
- ✔ **BlackRock iShares:** www.ishares.com; 1-800-474-2737
- ✔ **BLDRS:** www.invescopowershares.com; 1-800-983-0903
- ✔ **Schwab:** www.schwab.com; 1-866-232-9890

All the world's your apple: ETFs that cover the planet

If you have a portfolio of under $10,000, or if you have a strong desire to keep your investment management simple, you may be best off combining one of the total-market U.S. funds I discuss in Chapter 5 with a total international fund, the best of which are the Vanguard FTSE All-World ex-US ETF (VEU) and the Schwab International Equity ETF (SCHF). Both of these funds give you instant exposure to everything in the world of stocks, minus U.S. investments. Both ETFs are ultra low-cost (0.13 percent for Schwab, and 0.22 percent for Vanguard), well-diversified, and tax-efficient. The iShares MSCI ACWI (All Country World Index) ex US Index (ACWX) is also a perfectly acceptable option, although it will cost you 0.35 percent a year.

If you *really* want to keep things simple, you can buy a single ETF that tracks an index of all stocks everywhere, U.S. and foreign. That one fund would be the Vanguard Total World Stock ETF (VT), with an expense ratio of 0.25 percent, or the iShares MSCI ACWI Index Fund ETF (ACWI), with an expense ratio of 0.35 percent. Both are perfectly fine options. These indexed ETFs, like practically all others, are self-adjusting. That is, if your goal is to own a single global fund that reflects each country's percentage of the global economy, as that percentage grows or shrinks, so will its representation in these ETFs. Easy!

And if you *really, really* want simplicity — stocks and bonds and the kitchen sink, all in one package — see the end of Chapter 11 for suggestions.

If you have a portfolio larger than $10,000 and you are okay with adjusting its alignment (via rebalancing) once a year or so, I suggest that you keep your stocks and bonds in separate funds and that you furthermore break down your stock holdings into U.S. and non-U.S. Then, just as I have advised for your domestic stocks, assign your foreign holdings to each of at least three categories.

If you've read the preceding Part II chapters, you know that my preferred way to split up your U.S. stock holdings is by style: large growth, large value, small growth, and small value. On the international side, alas, such a break-down is difficult to achieve. I'm not sure why the ETF purveyors have not given us international stocks in four neat styles, but they haven't. That's okay. You can slice the pie into regions: European, Pacific, and emerging markets. Or slice it into large value, large growth, and small cap.

I help you weigh the options in the pages that follow. In Part IV, you'll see how both means of diversification can be used to build sample portfolios.

European stock ETFs: From the North Sea to the shores of the Mediterranean

Europe boasts the oldest, most established stock markets in the world: the Netherlands, 1611; Germany, 1685; and the United Kingdom, 1698. Relative to the stocks of most other nations, European stocks, as a whole, are seemingly low-priced (going by their P/E ratios, anyway).

Europe's strengths include political stability (well, for the most part . . .), an educated workforce, and a confederation of national economies making for the world's largest single market. Germany, the largest economy in Europe, has been growing its export industry faster than any nation on the planet.

Europe's great weaknesses include a persistently high rate of unemployment (outside of Germany); a rapidly aging population; and a few member nations, most notably Greece and Portugal (and to a lesser extent Spain, Italy, and Ireland), whose governments have racked up some very serious debt. These nations are collectively — and none too flatteringly — known as the "PIGS" (**P**ortugal, **I**reland, **G**reece, **S**pain) or sometimes "PIIGS" (with **I**taly thrown in).

Even with its weaknesses on full display, the European market definitely deserves a piece of your portfolio. The ETFs I present here are good options to consider when you make that investment.

Vanguard MSCI Europe ETF (VGK)

Indexed to: MSCI Europe Index, which tracks approximately 465 companies in 16 European nations

Expense ratio: 0.14 percent

Top five country holdings: United Kingdom, France, Germany, Switzerland, Spain

Russell's review: This ETF has everything going for it: low cost, good diversification, and tax efficiency. You can't go wrong (unless the European stock market falters, which, of course, could happen). The mix of many nations and currencies (Euro, British Pound, Swiss Franc, Swedish Krona) gives this fund an especially good balance and an especially good way to help protect your portfolio from any single-country (or currency) collapse. Like all Vanguard ETFs, VGK trades free of commission if held at Vanguard.

BLDRS Europe 100 ADR (ADRU)

Indexed to: The Bank of New York Mellon Europe 100 ADR Index, a market-weighted basket of 100 European market-based ADRs (American Depositary Receipts) representing the United Kingdom (about half the money pot) and major nations of the European continent, in addition to, for some unknown reason, Israel

Expense ratio: 0.30 percent

Top five country holdings: United Kingdom, Switzerland, France, Spain, Germany

Russell's review: Not as diverse as the Vanguard European ETF, but with 100 stocks, it's plenty diverse enough. The yearly expense ratio is about midway between the Vanguard European offering and the iShares Europe offering. All told, the BLDRS Europe is a good choice, although it may not be the best. (That, as usual, would be Vanguard.)

iShares S&P Europe 350 (IEV)

Indexed to: Standard & Poor's Europe 350 Index, a collection of 350 large cap companies in 16 European countries

Expense ratio: 0.60 percent

Top five country holdings: United Kingdom, France, Germany, Switzerland, Spain

Make wheat, not war

In the stock market Olympics of the last century (1900–2000), the overall winner in terms of real stock market return (return *after* inflation — the kind of return that really counts) was . . . drum roll . . . the socialist, Volvo-producing, snow-covered nation of Sweden. Sweden's overall rate of return for the century was 7.6 percent. In second place was Australia with 7.5 percent. In third place was South Africa with 6.8 percent. The United States came in fourth with 6.7 percent, and Canada was fifth with 6.4 percent. At the bottom of the world barrel, the Belgian equity market returned only 2.5 percent, with Italy, Germany, Spain, and France dragging closely behind with respective 100-year annualized post-inflation returns of 2.7, 3.6, 3.6, and 3.8 percent.

Here's the conclusion of the authors who pulled these numbers together, a group of distinguished professors from the London Business School: "Generally speaking, the worst performing equity markets were associated with countries which either lost major wars, or were most ravaged by international or civil wars." The best performers, point out professors Elroy Dimson, Paul Marsh, and Mike Staunton, were "resource rich countries."

An updated listing of the long-term stock-market winners appears in the Credit Suisse Global Investment Returns Sourcebook 2011, using return data from 1900 through 2010. Australia has now taken the lead with 7.4 percent, South Africa is in second place with 7.3 percent, and Sweden now holds third place (tied with the United States) with a 6.3 percent real stock market return over the past 110 years.

Russell's review: I really like iShares domestic offerings, and their foreign ETFs aren't bad products — not at all. The diversification is excellent. The indexes make sense. The tax efficiency is top notch. I only wish the darned things didn't cost so much. At roughly 3.3 times the cost of the Vanguard European offering, IEV just isn't anything to write home about.

Pacific region stock ETFs: From Mt. Fuji to that big island with the kangaroos

The nations of the Pacific have evidenced a good comeback in recent years. With the rapid growth of China as the world's apparent soon-to-be largest consumer, surrounding nations may bask in economic glory. Australia, in particular, has benefited greatly from the recent run-up in prices for natural resources caused in part by Chinese demand. And Japan still leads the world in labor productivity, despite some obvious economic challenges (such as a serious real-estate collapse and a level of debt greater than that of any other major nation). On the other hand, the threat posed by North Korea, the tensions between China and Taiwan, and the presence of nuclear weapons in unfriendly neighbors India and Pakistan loom like black clouds over the region.

But black clouds and all, the Pacific region merits a chunk of any balanced portfolio. Investing that chunk can be fairly easy; start by considering the ETF options laid out here.

Vanguard Pacific ETF (VPL)

Indexed to: MSCI Pacific Index, which follows roughly 500 companies in five Pacific region nations

Expense ratio: 0.14 percent

Top five country holdings: Japan, Australia, Hong Kong, Singapore, New Zealand

Russell's review: The cost can't be beat. And 500 companies certainly allows for good diversification. As with all Vanguard funds, tax efficiency is tops. Japan — the world's second-largest stock market — makes up 64 percent of this fund, considerably more than the BLDRS Asia 50. I have a preference for VPL over all other Pacific options. If you hold this ETF at Vanguard, you'll pay no commission to buy or sell.

BLDRS Asia 50 ADR (ADRA)

Indexed to: The Bank of New York Mellon Asia 50 ADR Index, a market-weighted basket of 50 Asian market-based ADRs representing a total of 8 countries. (Japan accounts for 44 percent of the pie.)

Expense ratio: 0.30 percent

Top five country holdings: Japan, Australia, China, Taiwan, India

Russell's review: The cost is higher than Vanguard's Pacific ETF, and you're tapping into fewer companies. Still, 50 companies isn't bad diversification. This fund also gives a bit more weight to non-Japan stock markets, which may be a good thing — although note that some of the countries represented are clearly emerging market nations. If you use ADRA, you'll want to factor that fact into your overall portfolio analysis. All in all, ADRA is a good investment, although if you bent my arm to choose between it and VPL, I'd probably choose the Vanguard ETF.

iShares MSCI Japan (EWJ)

Indexed to: MSCI Japan Index, representing approximately 340 of Japan's largest companies

Expense ratio: 0.54 percent

Top five country holdings: Just Japan here

Russell's review: For the life of me, I can't understand why iShares doesn't offer a Pacific region ETF. If you want the equivalent of either the BLDRS or Vanguard Pacific ETFs, you need to buy at least two iShares ETFs: the MSCI Japan and the MSCI Pacific ex-Japan (EPP). That's a doable option for larger portfolios, but with a cost ratio several times greater than Vanguard's, I'm not sure I see the point.

Emerging-market stock ETFs: Well, we hope that they're emerging

When economists feel optimistic, they call them "emerging market" nations. But these same countries are also sometimes referred to as the Third World or, even more to the point, "poor countries." As I write these words, the recent astonishing returns of emerging market stocks are due in good part to sharp increases in the prices of commodities, such as oil, which come largely from these nations. But commodity prices fluctuate greatly. And political unrest, corruption, and overpopulation, as well as serious environmental challenges, plague many of these countries.

On the other hand, emerging market stocks are perhaps still (despite their recent rise) underpriced. Many emerging economies seem especially strong. And — perhaps most importantly — these countries have young populations. Children tend to grow up to be workers, consumers, and perhaps even investors. Future growth seems almost assured.

Vanguard MSCI Emerging Market ETF (VWO)

Indexed to: The MSCI Emerging Markets Index, which tracks roughly 900 companies in 23 emerging market nations

Expense ratio: 0.22 percent

Top five country holdings: China, Brazil, Korea, Taiwan, South Africa

Russell's review: There's no better way that I know to capture the potential growth of emerging market stocks than through VWO. The cost is the lowest in the pack, and the diversity of investments is more than adequate.

Frontier markets: Nations that may emerge to become emerging markets

Of late, a number of ETFs, including the PowerShares MENA Frontier Countries Portfolio (PMNA), the Guggenheim Frontier Markets ETF (FRN), and the Market Vectors Gulf States ETF (MES), have cropped up to allow you to invest in so-called frontier markets. These markets feature economies even smaller, stock markets even newer and potentially less regulated, and governments perhaps even shakier than in emerging market nations.

Do you really want to invest in Bangladesh, Oman, Kuwait, Sri Lanka, and Trinidad and Tobago? Well, maybe . . . the payoff could be big. And the lack of correlation to other markets could be quite sweet.

But before you invest, realize how volatile these holdings are. Please do not invest too much, and diversify. The PMNA and FRN options are probably your best bets for now, but I'm sure other frontier market ETFs will appear on the market soon.

If you do want to throw a few dollars into a frontier market ETF (stand advised that they tend to be costly), go for it. I suggest you use money that you otherwise would have allocated to emerging market stocks. But I wouldn't consider frontier markets a necessary part of a diversified portfolio.

BLDRS Emerging Markets 50 ADR (ADRE)

Indexed to: The Bank of New York Mellon Emerging Markets 50 ADR Index, a market-weighted basket of 50 emerging market–based ADRs

Expense ratio: 0.30 percent

Top five country holdings: Brazil, China, Taiwan, South Korea, India

Russell's review: Yeah, 50 companies falls way short of Vanguard's 900, but 50 companies is still enough to give you pretty good diversification. I have no problem whatsoever recommending this ETF as a way to tap into emerging markets, although I do have a wee preference, once again, for Vanguard. Note that there is some overlap in the countries represented by this fund and the BLDRS Asia fund.

iShares MSCI Emerging Markets (EEM)

Indexed to: MSCI Emerging Markets Index, a basket of approximately 800 companies in 20 emerging market nations

Expense ratio: 0.69 percent

Top five country holdings: China, Brazil, South Korea, Taiwan, South Africa

Russell's review: Good fund. Good company. Good index. If it weren't more than twice the price of the other options in this area, I'd jump to recommend it.

iShares value and growth: Two special ETFs for style investing abroad

Studies show that the same *value premium* — the tendency for value stocks to outperform growth stocks — that seemingly exists here in the United States can be found around the world. (See the full value premium discussion in Chapters 6 and 8.) Therefore, I suggest a mild tilt toward value in your international stock portfolio, just as I recommend for your domestic portfolio.

You can accomplish this tilt easily by using the iShares MSCI EAFE Value Index (EFV) along with the iShares MSCI EAFE Growth Index (EFG).

Using these two funds together — allotting perhaps 55 to 60 percent to the value fund and 40 to 45 percent to growth — will give you full exposure to large cap, developed nation stocks. You still want to allocate some of your portfolio to emerging markets and to small cap international stocks.

Or, if you've already decided to split your international stocks up by regions — Europe, Pacific, emerging market — then adding a bit of EFV can give you the value lean you seek.

iShares MSCI EAFE Value Index (EFV)

Indexed to: MSCI EAFE Value Index, which is made up of approximately 520 large value companies of developed world nations, with about 40 percent of the fund's net assets in either Japan or the United Kingdom, the second and third largest equity markets on the planet

Expense ratio: 0.40 percent

Top five country holdings: Japan, United Kingdom, Switzerland, Germany, France

Russell's review: It's the only fund of its kind, and I'm greatly appreciative that it exists. It's a bit costly when compared to the Vanguard funds but still considerably less than most of the other international iShares options.

A word on foreign taxes

If you are buying both a foreign and a domestic ETF, with one going into a taxable account and the other into your IRA, Roth IRA, or other tax-deferred retirement plan, choose the foreign fund for the taxable account and plug the domestic fund into your tax-deferred account. That's because many foreign countries will slap you with a withholding tax on your dividends, which you can write off only in a taxable account. Typically, such a tax may be 15 percent. (If you invest, say, $30,000 in a foreign fund with a dividend yield of 3 percent, you'll be losing $135 a year to foreign taxes.) If the foreign ETF is in a non-retirement account, your brokerage house will likely supply you with a year-end statement noting the foreign tax paid. You can then write that amount off in full against your U.S. taxes. (See line 43 of your friendly IRS Form 1040.) If the foreign fund is held in your retirement account, however, no year-end statement, no write-off; you eat the loss.

iShares MSCI EAFE Growth Index (EFG)

Indexed to: MSCI EAFE Growth Index, which is made up of approximately 570 large growth companies of the developed world nations, with about 44 percent of the fund's money invested in the United Kingdom and Japan, the second and third largest stock markets

Expense ratio: 0.40 percent

Top five country holdings: United Kingdom, Japan, Switzerland, Australia, Germany

Russell's review: Like EFV, this international growth fund is the only one of its kind. I'm grateful for its existence, and I'm grateful that iShares has kept the expense ratio lower than what it charges for most of its other international funds.

Small cap international: Yes, you want it

Small cap international stocks have even less correlation to the U.S. stock market than larger foreign stocks. The reason is simple: If the U.S. economy takes a swan dive, it will seriously hurt conglomerates — Nestle, Toyota, and

British Petroleum, for example — that serve the U.S. market, regardless of where their corporate headquarters are located. A fall in the U.S. economy and U.S. stock market is less likely to affect smaller foreign corporations that sell mostly within their national borders.

Regardless of the investment vehicle you choose, I suggest that a good chunk of your international stock holdings — perhaps as much as 50 percent, if you can stomach the volatility — go to small cap holdings. The two ETFs I'd like you to consider are from Vanguard and iShares. Note that there are considerable differences between the two.

Vanguard FTSE All-World ex-US Small Cap Index (VSS)

Indexed to: The FTSE Global Small Cap ex-US Index, which tracks more than 3,000 small cap company stocks in both developed nations (76 percent of the stocks) and emerging markets (24 percent)

Expense ratio: 0.33 percent

Top five country holdings: Canada, United Kingdom, Japan, Taiwan, Australia

Russell's review: For exposure to small cap international, you aren't going to find a less expensive or more diversified avenue. This fund trades commission-free if held at Vanguard.

iShares MSCI EAFE Small Cap Index (SCZ)

Indexed to: The MSCI EAFE Small Cap Index, which tracks more than 2,300 stocks from developed market nations other than the United States

Expense ratio: 0.40 percent

Top five country holdings: Japan, United Kingdom, Australia, Germany, Switzerland

Russell's review: Although a little more expensive than the Vanguard offering, this fund is still an excellent choice for international small cap exposure. Note, however, that unlike the Vanguard ETF, SCZ does not allocate any portion of its portfolio to emerging markets. If you own SCZ and you want that exposure, you might consider a modest position in one of a handful of small cap emerging market ETFs, such as the SPDR S&P Emerging Markets Small Cap (EWX) or the WisdomTree Emerging Markets SmallCap Dividend ETF (DGS).

Chapter 10

Sector Investing: ETFs According to Industry

- -

- -

*A*ny *Star Trek* fan (yeah, beam me up) knows that matter and antimatter, should they ever meet, would result in an explosion so violent as to possibly destroy the entire universe or, at the very least, mess up Donald Trump's hair. Despite the firm convictions of zealots on both sides, style investing (large/small/growth/value) and sector investing (technology/ utilities/healthcare/energy) are not matter and antimatter. They can, and sometimes do, exist very peacefully side-by-side.

In this chapter, I present the nuts and bolts of sector investing: how it can function alone, or in conjunction with style investing, to provide diversity both on the domestic and international sides of your portfolio (or overlapping the two). However you decide to slice the pie (whether by style and/or sector), using ETFs as building blocks makes for an excellent strategy. (Hmm, am I starting to sound like a zealot myself?)

Selecting Stocks by Sector, not Style

As of this writing, there are about 200 U.S. industry-sector ETFs. You can find a fund to mirror each of the major industry sectors in the U.S. economy: energy, basic materials, financial services, consumer goods, and so on. See Figure 10-1 for a bird's-eye view of the U.S. economy split into its major industry sectors, each accorded its proper allotment.

Percentage of Total
U.S. Stock Market

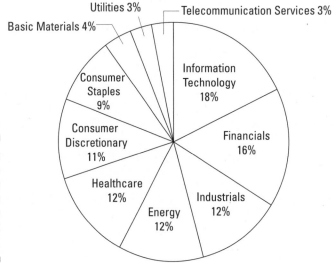

Figure 10-1:
The industry sector map for the United States.

Based on the breakdown of the MSCI U.S. Broad Market Index, this chart reveals the size of ten major industry sectors of the U.S. economy. What you're seeing is the total *capitalization* (value of stock) of all public companies within each industry group. ***Note:*** No standard methodology exists for breaking up the U.S. industry into sectors; MSCI does it one way, and S&P does it a slightly different way.

Some ETFs mirror subsections of the economy, such as semiconductors (a subset of information technology) and biotechnology (a subset of health-care). In some cases, subsectors of the economy you may not even know exist — such as nanotech, cloud computing, and water resources — are represented with ETFs!

A good number of newer ETFs allow you to invest in industry sectors in foreign countries (which are not represented in Figure 10-1) or in *global* industries (which is to say U.S. and foreign countries together; see Figure 10-2). About 150 international and global sector ETFs are available.

(As you look at Figures 10-1 and 10-2, note that one of the biggest differences between the U.S. chart and the global chart is the portion of the pie that goes to healthcare. Only in the United States does a trip to the dermatologist affect the national economy!)

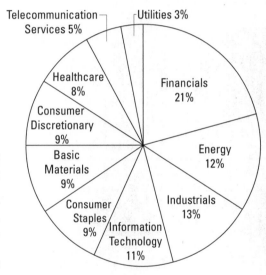

Percentage of Total Worldwide Stock Market

Figure 10-2: The industry sector map for the entire world.

Certain newer ETFs — such as the PowerShares S&P SmallCap Industrials Portfolio ETF (PSCI) or the PowerShares S&P SmallCap Health Care Portfolio ETF (PSCH) — allow you to invest in industry sectors *and* styles at the same time.

And finally, the living proof that you can, if you so wish, slice and dice a portfolio to ultimate death: You can even find some ETFs that allow you to buy into a particular industry within a particular country. Examples include the Global X Brazil Financials ETF (BRAF) and Global X China Technology ETF (CHIB). Unless you have a really compelling reason to purchase such a specialized fund (and pay the hefty expenses and subject your portfolio to excess concentration), I suggest you don't.

Speculating on the Next Hot Industry

Is there a God? Does he have a long, white beard, and does he wear sandals? Why do sector investors tend to be speculators, while style investors tend to be buy-and-hold kinds of people? These are questions that sometimes keep me awake at night. I won't attempt to address the first two here. As for the third . . . heck, I have no idea. But there's little question that people who divide their portfolios into large/small/value/growth are much more likely to be long-term investors with long-term strategies than are people who buy into sectors (often through ETFs). That's just the way it is.

Sizzling and sinking

Sector funds are often purchased by investors who think they know which sectors (or sectors within specific countries, such as financials in Brazil) are going to shine, and goshdarnit, they're going to profit by it. Unfortunately, they are often wrong.

I'm old enough to recall a day when environmental service companies, by dint of the realization that pollution was becoming a serious problem, were going to be a sure bet. But then, lo and behold, environmental service companies seriously lagged the overall market for years. Then it was information technology that couldn't possibly fail to outperform, yet for three brutal years (2000–2002), the technology sector fell like hail. At the time of this writing, materials is the sector that people are pouring money into. Information technology is also hot (once again) with the entire world, it seems, waiting for Facebook to go public. By the time this book comes out, who knows what everyone will be panting after?

Momentum riders and bottom feeders

Interestingly, while most investors are *momentum investors* — they tend to buy what's hot — other investors look for what's not, on the theory that everything reverts to the mean. The two camps are forever trading sector funds back and forth. Right now, the momentum investors are buying materials and energy; the bottom feeders (who prefer to see themselves as value investors) are buying financials and housing construction. Fortunately (or unfortunately), there is no dearth of ETFs to please both crowds.

(**Note:** I'm not saying that neither momentum investing nor buying up down-and-out industries has value. Both strategies have been known to make money. But such strategies can't be done helter-skelter. Like any other kind of investing, they require careful thought and study. Many rapid sector traders are not such deep thinkers.)

You can tell from my tone, no doubt, that I'm no big fan of sector speculation — or speculation of any sort. But what about using sector ETFs as buy-and-hold instruments? Even though few people do it, can a buy-and-hold portfolio be just as easily and effectively divided up by industry sector as it can by investment style? Keep reading.

Doing Sector Investing Right

An in-depth study on industry-sector investing, done several years ago by Chicago-based Ibbotson Associates (now part of Morningstar), came to the very favorable conclusion that sector investing — because times have allegedly changed — is potentially a superior diversifier to grid (style) investing. (I discuss the style grid in Chapters 4 and 5.) Globalization has led to a rise in correlation between domestic and international stocks; large, mid, and small cap stocks have high correlation to each other. A company's performance is tied more to its industry than to the country where it's based or its market capitalization, concluded Ibbotson.

The Ibbotson report didn't end there. It also ballyhooed sector investing as a superior instrument for fine-tuning a portfolio to match an individual investor's risk tolerance. A conservative investor might overweight utilities (a less volatile sector); a more aggressive investor might tilt toward technology (whooeee).

That sounds like a good plan, although the lead author of that study once confided to me that he has the bulk of his personal portfolio still broken up into value, growth, large cap, and small cap — as do I. However, we both have some industry-sector ETFs (for fine-tuning), as well.

Calculating your optimal sector mix

If you are going to go the sector route and build your entire stock portfolio, or a good part of it, out of industry-sector ETFs, I suggest that before you do anything, take a look at Figures 10-1 and 10-2. Make sure you are able to have allocations to all or most major sectors of the economy.

Some advisors would tell you to keep your allocations roughly proportionate to each sector's share of the broad market. I think that's decent advice, with just a bit of caution: Had you taken that approach in 1999, your portfolio would have been chocked to the top with technology, given the gross overpricing of the sector at that point. (And you would have taken a bath the following year.) I'd suggest that no matter what sectors are hot at the moment, no single sector should ever make up more than 20 percent of your stock portfolio.

(If you've read Chapter 9, you may recall I noted that single-country and especially small single-country ETFs are not something I go out of my way to own. One reason is that a smaller country's economy can be dominated by one or two industries, making its markets especially volatile.)

Start perhaps with roughly allocating your sector-based portfolio according to the market cap of each sector, and then tweak from there — based not on crystal ball predictions of the future but on the unique characteristics of each sector. What do I mean? Read on.

Seeking risk adjustment with high and low volatility sectors

Some industry sectors have historically evidenced greater return and greater risk. (Return and risk tend to go hand-in-hand, as I discuss in Chapter 4.) The same rules that apply to style investing apply to sector investing. Know how much volatility you can stomach, and then, and only then, build your portfolio in tune with your risk tolerance.

As for historical risk and return, Figure 10-3 shows an approximation of how the major sectors rank. Keep in mind that *any* single sector — even utilities, the least volatile of all — will tend to be more volatile than the entire market because there is little diversification. Don't overindulge!

Finally, keep in mind that your allocation between bonds and stocks will almost certainly have much more bearing on your overall level of risk and return than will your mix of stocks. In Part III of this book, I introduce bonds and discuss how an ETF investor should hold them.

The Most Volatile Sector ETFs (with highest return potential)

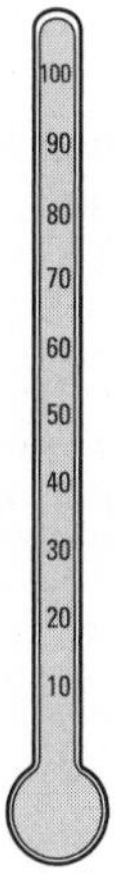

Technology

Financial (includes REITs)

Healthcare

Consumer Discretionary

Industrial

Materials

Energy

Consumer Staples

Utilities

The Least Volatile Sector ETFs (with lowest return potential)

Figure 10-3:
Industry
sectors,
from most
to least
volatile.

Knowing where the style grid comes through

There is nothing wrong with dividing up a stock portfolio into industry sectors, but please don't be hasty in scrapping style investing. I really believe that if you're going to pick one strategy over the other, the edge goes to style investing. For one thing, we know that it works. Style investing helps to diffuse (but certainly not eliminate) risk. Scads of data show that.

In addition, style investing allows you to take advantage of years of other data that indicate you can goose returns without raising your risk, or raising it by much, by leaning your portfolio toward value and small cap (see Chapters 6, 7, and 8). When you invest in industry sectors through ETFs, you are most often investing the vast majority of your funds in large caps, and you're usually splitting growth and value evenly. That approach may limit your investment success.

Another reason ETF investors shouldn't scrap style investing: Style ETFs are the cheaper choice. For whatever reason — yes, another one of those eternal mysteries that keeps me awake at night — style ETFs tend to cost much less than industry-sector ETFs. On average, they're about half the cost. Go figure.

And one final reason to prefer style to sector for the core of your portfolio: You will require fewer funds. With large growth, large value, small growth, and small value, you pretty much can capture the entire stock market. With sector funds, you need nearly a dozen funds to achieve the same effect. Each sector fund offers minimal diversification because the price movements of companies in the same industry sector tend to be closely correlated.

Combining strategies to optimize your portfolio

There's no point to having dozens of ETFs in your portfolio if they are only going to duplicate each other's holdings. So if you already own the entire market through diversified ETFs in all corner quadrants of the style grid — large, small, value, and growth — why add any industry sectors that are obviously already represented?

It would make sense to add a peppering of semiconductor stocks or utility stocks if you knew that semiconductors or utilities were going to blast off. (Of course, a rational investor would never say he or she knew anything about the future, other than that the sun will probably rise tomorrow.) And yet, taking on an added dose of semiconductors or utilities may still make sense if that added dose of either industry sector somehow were to raise your performance potential without raising risk. That could happen only if you chose an industry sector that is not closely correlated to the broader market.

Seeking low correlations for added diversification

Some sectors, or industry subsectors, even though they are part of the stock market, tend to move out of lockstep with the rest of the market. By way of example, consider REITs: real estate investment trusts. (If you look for REITs in Figure 10-1, you will find them buried under "Financials.") I devote Chapter 13 almost entirely to REITs, and especially REIT ETFs.

Another sector that fits the bill, at least of late, is energy. Yes, Exxon Mobil and Chevron are part of the entire market, but they tend to zig when everything else zags (in part because when the price of oil rises, these companies profit more, while the rest of the economy, at least outside of Texas, suffers).

Newness is a red flag

At about 350 and counting (roughly one-third of all ETFs), you can find an ETF to mirror just about any sector or subsector of the U.S. or global economy. The latest arrivals include a host of commodity funds . . . dozens and dozens of them. And new ones are sure to arrive shortly.

Proceed with caution. New sector offerings occur most often after recent run-ups in price. The sector is hot. The public is buying. The financial industry is accommodating. Everyone is happy, for the moment. But maybe a bubble is about to burst.

For example, consider that in 2002, when the total U.S. stock market tanked by almost 11 percent, REITs were up 31 percent. The year 2005 was pretty lackluster for the total stock market, yet energy stocks were up 31 percent.

Of late, the basic materials (sometimes called "natural resources") sector has shown a delightful lack of correlation with the rest of the market. As I write these words, this sector — comprised of companies involved in the mining and refining of precious and industrial metals, and the manufacture of chemical and fertilizer products — has thus far in 2011 shown the greatest one-year return of all major industry sectors.

Of course, there are years when it works the other way, and these sectors may fall way short of the overall market.

In Chapter 16, where I draw up some sample portfolios, you'll see more of REITs, energy, and basic materials.

If you decide to build your portfolio around industry sector funds, I urge you at the very least to dip into the style funds to give yourself the value/small cap tilt that I discuss in Chapters 6, 7, and 8. That's especially true if you use SPDRs to build your sector portfolio. This fund group is especially weighted toward large cap. Again, in Chapter 16, I offer a few sample portfolios to illustrate workable allocations.

Sector Choices by the Dozen

After you decide which industry sectors you wish to invest in, you need to pick and choose among ETFs. Blackrock's iShares offers about 40 U.S. selections and 40 global or international selections. PowerShares has about 50 domestic and a dozen international sector funds. State Street Global Advisors offers about two dozen SPDRs that cover U.S. industry sectors and nearly as many that cover international and global markets. Vanguard has 11 U.S. sector funds and one international. And there are other players, too.

Begin your sector selection here:

✔ **Do you want representation in large industry sectors (healthcare, technology, utilities)?** Your options include Vanguard ETFs, Blackrock's iShares, and State Street Global Advisors Select Sector SPDRs, as well as funds from FocusShares, Guggenheim, Jefferies, and WisdomTree.

✔ **Do you want to zero in on narrow industry niches (insurance, oil service, nanotech)?** Consider PowerShares, First Trust, or Market Vectors ETFs. You can also choose State Street Global Advisors (non-Select Sector) SPDRs.

✔ **Are you looking for sometimes ridiculously narrow industry niches (aluminum) or sectors within sectors within small countries?** You should look at EG Shares, Global X, and Guggenheim ETFs.

✔ **Do you want to keep your expense ratios to a minimum?** Vanguard's ETFs, the State Street Global Advisors Select Sector SPDRs, and FocusShares from Scottrade tend to cost the least.

In the following sections, I give you a more in-depth view of the sector offerings available to you.

Vanguard ETFs

The Vanguard industry sector offerings include the following:

U.S. Sector Fund Name	Ticker
Vanguard Consumer Discretionary ETF	VCR
Vanguard Consumer Staples ETF	VDC
Vanguard Energy ETF	VDE
Vanguard Financials ETF	VFH
Vanguard Health Care ETF	VHT
Vanguard Industrials ETF	VIS
Vanguard Information Technology ETF	VGT
Vanguard Materials ETF	VAW
Vanguard REIT Index ETF	VNQ
Vanguard Telecommunications Services ETF	VOX
Vanguard Utilities ETF	VPU

Vanguard's International sector fund is the Global ex-U.S. Real Estate ETF (VNQI).

Fill your domestic stock portfolio with Vanguard's 11 U.S. industry-sector ETFs, and presto! You've captured just about the entire universe of Yankee stocks. Granted, that universe will be weighted in such a manner that you'll have only token representation of mid and small caps (although you'll have more small cap exposure than you would with SPDRs).

The one exception is the Vanguard REIT Index ETF (VNQ). Principally a mid cap fund, VNQ is a prince among ETFs. With an expense ratio of 0.12 percent, it is the least expensive of all industry-sector ETFs. It is also well diversified within its own real estate universe. If you're going to own a U.S. REIT ETF, Vanguard's selection is an excellent choice. (See Chapter 13 for more on REITs.) The other Vanguard U.S. sector ETFs carry an expense ratio of 0.24 percent — a real bargain among sector funds, although a bit more expensive than the Select Sector SPDRs.

In general, Vanguard ETFs, based on MSCI indexes, and the Select Sector SPDRs, based on S&P indexes, are your best building blocks for a U.S. stock portfolio sliced and diced by industry sectors. They are also excellent options for peppering a style grid–based portfolio with sector funds.

If you want a more globally-based sector approach, then the more expensive iShares options may be your best bet. In Part IV, where I build sample portfolios, you'll see how some of these funds can be incorporated into an optimally diversified investment strategy.

Select Sector SPDRs: State Street Global Advisors (Part 1)

In this section, I focus on *Select* Sector SPDRS. In the next, I introduce just plain old SPDRs representing industry sectors. What's the difference? Keep reading because I explain in the next section. First, let me acquaint you with some fund names.

Select Sector SPDR offerings include the following:

U.S. Sector Fund Name	*Ticker*
Biotech Select Sector SPDR	XBI
Consumer Discretionary Select Sector SPDR	XLY
Consumer Staples Select Sector SPDR	XLP
Energy Select Sector SPDR	XLE
Financial Select Sector SPDR	XLF
Health Care Select Sector SPDR	XLV
Industrial Select Sector SPDR	XLI
Materials Select Sector SPDR	XLB
Technology Select Sector SPDR	XLK
Utilities Select Sector SPDR	XLU

Overall, I put the Select Sector SPDRs on a par with the Vanguard sector ETFs. Like the Vanguard funds, they represent large U.S. industry groupings. They follow reasonable indexes, and they will cost you a tad less than the Vanguard ETFs — 0.20 versus 0.24 percent a year in management fees.

Because the S&P indexes upon which the Select Sector SPDRs are built tend to represent mostly large cap companies, I urge anyone building a Select Sector SPDR portfolio to tap into small caps through some other means, such as buying into one of the small cap ETFs discussed in Chapters 7 and 8.

SPDRs: State Street Global Advisors (Part II)

SPDRs industry sector offerings are as follows:

U.S. Sector Fund Name	*Ticker*
SPDR KBW Bank	KBE
SPDR KBW Capital Markets	KCE
SPDR KBW Insurance	KIE
SPDR S&P Oil & Gas Exploration & Production	XOP
SPDR S&P Oil & Gas Equipment & Services	XES
SPDR S&P Health Care Equipment	XHE

International Sector Fund Name	*Ticker*
SPDR S&P International Consumer Staples Sector ETF	IPS
SPDR S&P International Materials Sector ETF	IRV
SPDR S&P International Energy Sector ETF	IPW
SPDR S&P International Technology Sector ETF	IPK
SPDR S&P International Utilities Sector ETF	IPU
SPDR Dow Jones International Real Estate ETF	RWX

Global Sector Fund Name	*Ticker*
SPDR Dow Jones Global Real Estate ETF	RWO
SDPR S&P Global Natural Resources ETF	GNR

Ready to find out what distinguishes a Select Sector SPDR from a plain old industry sector SPDR? Both are industry sector funds. Both are owned and run by megabank State Street Global Advisors. But the two ETF lineups are somewhat different. Retailers and car manufacturers call the differentiation *product-line extension.* So just as Honda has its Acura line of cars as well as plain old Hondas, and Toyota has its Lexus line in addition to the plain old Toyotas, State Street has both SPDRS and Select Sector SPDRS.

A big difference between the two lineups (just as with Hondas and Acuras, and Toyotas and Lexuses) is price, but if you assume that the "Select" names will cost you more, surprise! Whereas the Select Sector SPDRs charge 0.20 percent in management fees, the non-Select Sector SPDRs charge 0.35 percent for the domestic options and 0.50 percent for the international.

Another difference is the exposure. Select Sector SPDRs track large sectors of the economy, such as healthcare and energy. The plain old SPDRs, which happen to be darlings among day traders, track more narrow segments of the market. Instead of energy, you're looking at Oil & Gas Exploration & Production or Oil & Gas Equipment & Services, for example. Instead of healthcare, you're looking at just healthcare equipment. Because I prefer larger segments of the market, and I certainly prefer lower prices, I tend to prefer the Select Sector SPDRs over the SPDRs for any kind of domestic stock exposure.

As for the international side of things, I'm not wild about the SPDRs lineup. The management fee is a tad higher than you would pay for the iShares global sector ETFs, and the funds are, by and large, not global. I tend to recommend global sector funds over international (*global* refers to the whole planet, whereas *international* is the planet minus the United States) for the sake of keeping the total number of holdings in the portfolio manageable.

However, State Street recently issued a handful of global sector funds, and in this handful are two funds that I like quite a bit: The SPDR Dow Jones Global Real Estate ETF (RWO) and, even more impressive, the SDPR S&P Global Natural Resources ETF (GNR). These global selections offer reasonable management fees of 0.50 and 0.40 respectively.

The SPDRs website — www.sectorspdr.com — is full of fabulous tools. Check out especially the Correlation Tracker, SPDR Map of the Market, and the Sector Tracker. (You don't have to be a SPDRs investor to use the tools.)

BlackRock's iShares

The iShares industry sector offerings include the following:

U.S. Sector Fund Name	*Ticker*
iShares Dow Jones U.S. Basic Materials Index	IYM
iShares Dow Jones U.S. Consumer Goods Index	IYK
iShares Dow Jones U.S. Consumer Services Index	IYC
iShares Dow Jones U.S. Energy Index	IYE
iShares Dow Jones U.S. Financial Sector Index	IYF
iShares Dow Jones U.S. Financial Services Index	IYG
iShares Dow Jones U.S. Healthcare Index	IYH
iShares Dow Jones U.S. Industrial Index	IYJ
iShares Dow Jones U.S. Real Estate Index	IYR
iShares Dow Jones U.S. Technology Index	IYW
iShares Dow Jones U.S. Telecommunications Index	IYZ
iShares Dow Jones Transportation Average Index	IYT
iShares Dow Jones U.S. Utilities Index	IDU
iShares Cohen & Steers Realty Majors Index	ICF

International Sector Fund Name	*Ticker*
iShares MSCI ACWI ex-US Energy Sector Index Fund	AXEN
iShares MSCI ACWI ex-US Consumer Staples Sector Index Fund	AXSL
iShares MSCI ACWI ex-US Materials Sector Index Fund	AXMT
iShares MSCI ACWI ex-US Industrials Sector Index Fund	AXID
iShares MSCI ACWI ex-US Telecommunication Services Sector Index Fund	AXTE

Global Sector Fund Name	*Ticker*
iShares S&P Global Energy	IXC
iShares S&P Global Materials	MXI
iShares S&P Global Technology	IXN
iShares S&P Global Timber & Forestry	WOOD
iShares S&P Global Utilities	JXI

As you may be aware by now, I like iShares just fine. I like their style funds. As I discuss in Chapter 9, I like many of their international funds. As for domestic industry-sector funds, however, BlackRock, Inc. (sponsor of iShares) simply charges too much. With the exception of the iShares Cohen & Steers Realty Majors Index (REIT) ETF, which carries an expense ratio of 0.35 percent, all the other iShares sector options are 0.47 or (in most cases) 0.48 percent. That's about double the cost of either the Vanguard ETFs or Select Sector SPDRs.

On the international and global front, however, the iShares ETFs are competitive with SPDRs: Most charge 0.48 percent in management fees. And the iShares lineup offers more global sector funds than any other ETF provider. (The ones I list here are just a representative sampling.) If you want to divide your portfolio into global sectors, iShares is the place to go.

PowerShares

PowerShares industry sector offerings include the following:

U.S. Sector Fund Name	*Ticker*
PowerShares Dynamic Biotechnology & Genome	PBE
PowerShares Dynamic Building & Construction	PKB
PowerShares Dynamic Energy & Exploration	PXE
PowerShares Dynamic Food & Beverage	PBJ
PowerShares Dynamic Hardware & Consumer Electronics	PHW
PowerShares Dynamic Insurance	PIC
PowerShares Dynamic Leisure & Entertainment	PEJ
PowerShares Dynamic Media	PBS
PowerShares Dynamic Networking	PXQ
PowerShares Dynamic Oil & Gas Services	PXJ
PowerShares Dynamic Pharmaceuticals	PJP
PowerShares Dynamic Retail	PMR

U.S. Sector Fund Name	*Ticker*
PowerShares Dynamic Semiconductors	PSI
PowerShares Dynamic Software	PSJ
PowerShares Dynamic Telecommunications & Wireless	PTE
PowerShares Dynamic Utilities	PUI
PowerShares Lux Nanotech	PXN
PowerShares Aerospace & Defense	PPA
PowerShares WilderHill Clean Energy	PBW
PowerShares Water Resources	PHO

Global Sector Fund Name	*Ticker*
PowerShares Global Coal Portfolio	PKOL
PowerShares Global Nuclear Energy	PKN
Powershares Global Steel Portfolio	PSTL
PowerShares Global Wind Energy Portfolio	PWND

On the down side, PowerShares charges 0.60 percent for its domestic offerings and 0.75 percent for its global funds: That's a whole lot more than most of the competition is charging or would dare charge. The funds are also "dynamic," which means that the indexes they track are actively managed (someone somewhere is picking stocks). Many investors would see that as a plus; I don't. It means added expense (both up front and behind the scenes) and a possible loss of tax efficiency. On the upside, however, PowerShares' selection of industry groupings, in both their U.S. and global offerings, has been innovative, to say the least.

Although I wouldn't suggest building an entire portfolio of PowerShares sector ETFs, if you're looking to sprinkle some noncorrelating holdings into an otherwise well-diversified portfolio, PowerShares may have something to offer. I'm especially intrigued with the WilderHill Clean Energy ETF (PBW) and the Water Resources ETF (PHO). Investing in companies that provide alternative fuels and the filtration and delivery of drinking water respectively, these two ETFs, so far, seem to have sweetly low correlations to the broad market. I'm keeping an eye on them.

Unhealthy investments

Just as I was writing the first edition of this book, the first truly loony ETFs were hitting the market. At that time, I alerted readers to the advent of a dozen ETFs that invested in companies involved in treating specific diseases. You could have invested in the Ferghana-Wellspring (FW) Derma and Wound Care Index Fund, or the FW Metabolic-Endocrine Disorders Index Fund, or the FW Respiratory/Pulmonary Index Fund. As I stated at the time, "I can think of no good reason to take a gamble on such small market niches. Should a cure to cancer be found, the company that nails it will see its stock skyrocket, for sure. The other however-many companies? Their stocks may well plummet. If you're holding the entire basket, it's a flip of the coin to say which way your investment may head. If you like flipping coins, fine, but please don't bet your retirement money on such foolishness." Well, the market saw thorough the craziness of these funds, few people bought them, and the funds have since folded. But I'm sorry to say that many more crazy ETFs have taken their place . . . and many of them, if not most, track industry sectors.

Because commodities have been hot (and investors just love what's hot), we've seen lately the arrival of funds that allow you to invest in every conceivable individual commodity, from aluminum and potash to uranium and jelly beans. (I'm kidding about the jelly beans; alas, serious about the rest.) Many sector funds are leveraged, promising to generate — for better or worse — some multiple of their underlying index's returns; they bear names like the Direxion Daily Natural Gas Related Bull 2X Shares (GASL). Or they are inverse funds, moving opposite to their index, such as the PowerShares DB Crude Oil Short ETN (SZO). Or they are inverse *and* leveraged, such as the Direxion Daily Gold Miners Bear 2x Shares ETF (DUST — a ticker symbol that could end up being an apt description of the fate of invested capital). Other exotic sector funds represent narrow sectors within small stock markets, such as the Global X Brazil Financials ETF (BRAF).

Most of these inverse/leveraged/tiny-sliver-of-some-market funds are not only crazy to begin with (unless perhaps you are a very seasoned trader with vastly superior information . . . and if you're reading this book, chances are you're not one), but they charge ongoing fees that are three, four, or five times what most ETFs charge. Keep your portfolio healthy, and avoid these gimmicky funds. Please.

Chapter 11

Specialized Stock ETFs

• •

In This Chapter

▶ Unearthing some facts about socially responsible investing

▶ Determining the potential payoff of dividend funds

▶ Introducing an opportunity to invest in initial public offerings

▶ Assessing funds that thrive (allegedly) when the market falters

▶ Considering a leveraged fund (woooeeee!)

▶ Examining lifecycle and asset-allocation options

• •

*I*n this chapter, I introduce a few stock ETFs that don't fit into any of the categories I discuss in previous chapters. They are neither growth nor value, large nor small. They are not industry sector funds, nor are they international. If ETFs were ice cream, the funds presented here would not represent chocolate and vanilla, but rather, the outliers on the Baskin Robbins menu: Turtle Cheesecake, Tiramisu, No Sugar Added Chocolate Chip, Pink Bubblegum, and Wild 'N Reckless (a swirl of green apple, blue raspberry, and fruit punch sherbets).

Wild 'N Reckless? I wouldn't say that these funds are necessarily wild or reckless, but nonetheless, they are stock funds, by and large, and anything related to stocks — trust me on this — carries risk. That being said, I present you with a few ETFs that bill themselves as socially responsible, a slew of funds that focus on companies paying high dividends (they're especially hot at the moment I'm writing this chapter), one that invests only in corporations that have relatively recently begun selling shares to the public, and a few funds that go up when everything else is going down (don't get too excited; it isn't as good as it sounds). I also describe a few all-in-one funds for the ultimate couch-potato approach to investing. And I describe one hypothetical specialized stock ETF (see the sidebar "The author's pipedream") that I wish someone would introduce.

Investing for a Better World

An increasing number of people — both individuals and institutions — are investing using some kind of moral compass. The investments chosen are screened not only for potential profitability but for social, environmental, and even biblical factors as well. Some screens, for example, attempt to eliminate all companies that profit from tobacco or weapons of mass destruction. Others try to block out the worst-polluting companies, or companies that use child labor in countries that have no effective child labor laws.

The total amount of money invested in socially screened portfolios (which include more than 100 mutual funds, certain state and city pension funds, union and church monies, some university endowments, and, as of recently, two dozen or so ETFs) has grown from about $1 trillion in 1997 to an estimated $3 trillion or so today.

Many of the funds that call themselves socially responsible (otherwise known as *SRI funds* – the *I* stands for "investment") not only invest with a purpose but also use their financial muscle to lobby companies to become better world citizens. The movement's greatest victory to date may have been the role it played in ending apartheid in South Africa. SRI seems to have had some impact on corporate America as well, most notably by pushing certain auto, oil, and utility companies to research ways to reduce emissions of greenhouse gasses. Other victories include a nationwide ban on mercury thermometers and commitments from various corporations to start recycling programs, reduce toxic waste emissions, and end discrimination against employees based on their sexual orientation.

In this section, I discuss how SRI funds have performed in their relatively short history, the social aims of various types of funds, and some specific options available for your portfolio.

Tracking the history of SRI performance

Whereas investing in a socially responsible mutual fund or ETF may do the world some good, the question remains whether it will do your portfolio any good. Proponents believe that nice companies, like nice salespeople, will naturally be more successful over time. Skeptics of investing with a social screen not only scoff at the notion of good karma but also say that limiting a fund manager's investment choices could lead to *lower* performance.

So far, no solid evidence exists that either side is right — or wrong. Over the past decade or so, the collective performance of socially responsible mutual funds has been very similar to that of all other mutual funds. It could be argued that a tie should be resolved in favor of socially responsible investing. If one can achieve market returns while at the same time prodding companies to improve their behavior, why not do that?

What about the specific performance of the socially responsible ETFs? To be blunt, they haven't been around long enough for their collective performance record to count for much. And, of course, performance is only one factor I look at when deciding whether to recommend an ETF. But if it matters to you, consider the performance of the oldest socially responsible ETF, the iShares MSCI USA ESG Select Index (KLD), founded in January 2005. KLD has a five-year annualized return of about 3.5 percent — pretty much on a par with the average large cap blend fund. And (perhaps ironically) this performance is also on a par with USA Mutuals' VICE mutual fund (VICEX), which seeks to invest in socially *irresponsible* companies! (No, you will not find VICEX included in any of my sample portfolios presented later in this book. Invest in sin on your own!)

Your growing number of choices for social investing

If you decide that you want to be a socially responsible investor, you have many choices: About 110 mutual funds and two dozen ETFs now invest with some social screen. The growing number of ETFs designed to appeal to your conscience spans the spectrum from U.S. to foreign to *global* (foreign and U.S. combined). There are ETFs that emphasize environmental awareness, social responsibility, clean energy, religious values, and more. Here are just a hand-ful of examples:

✔ **ETFs focused on social issues:** Among domestic ETFs aiming to show commitment to broad social issues are these:

- iShares KLD 400 Social Index ETF (DSI)

- Pax MSCI North America ESG Index ETF (NASI)

For the same kind of stock exposure on the international side, you find:

- Pax MSCI EAFE ESG Index ETF (EAPS)

Funds that invest in global stocks focused on clean energy include:

- Market Vectors Global Alternative Energy ETF(GEX)

- Guggenheim Solar ETF (TAN)

✔ **ETFs focused on religious values:** If your social conscience is tied to the New Testament, then FaithShares has an ETF for you: the FaithShares Christian Values ETF (FOC). No gambling. No pornography. No stem cell research. Until recently, FaithShares had individual ETFs that attempted to allow you to invest according to your specific brand of Christianity, whether you were a Baptist, Catholic, Methodist, or Lutheran; these funds have all closed shop.

In June 2009, a company called Javelin introduced the Javelin Dow Jones Islamic Market International Index Fund, which avoided investing in companies involved in alcohol, gaming, weapons production, and pork products. The ETF failed to attract much in the way of investor dollars and so closed down a little more than a year later. Anyone seeking investments that conform to Islamic principles can still pursue that objective via mutual funds offered by Amana Mutual Funds Trust (www.amanafunds.com).

Reasonable people can sometimes disagree on the specifics of what is and is not socially responsible corporate behavior. If you decide to invest in an SRI fund, I urge you to review a fund's statement of values before investing. Otherwise, you could end up investing at cross purposes with your own values.

A close-up look at your SRI options

The two oldest and most popular ETFs that use social screens are as different as night and day. The iShares MSCI USA ESG Select Index ETF (KLD) is a broad-based large cap *blend* (both value and growth) fund. The PowerShares WilderHill Clean Energy Fund (PBW) is a narrow industry sector fund *and* a style fund (overwhelmingly small growth) and — whew — something of a global fund as well. (Approximately 25 percent of the holdings are non-U.S.)

Unlike my reviews of other kinds of ETFs (found in Chapters 5 through 10), I review these two funds together. That way, I avoid repeating myself because my feelings about both — and, in fact, about most of the socially conscious ETFs — are the same: I'm absolutely, positively, conclusively ambivalent. My double-shot-plus review follows a brief synopsis of the two most-popular SRI funds.

iShares MSCI USA ESG Select Index ETF (KLD)

Indexed to: The MSCI USA ESG Select Social Index (*ESG* stands for environment, social, and governance). The index starts with 250 or so fairly large U.S. corporations. Based on each company's record for social justice and environmental performance, it overweights purportedly ethical companies and underweights supposedly unethical ones while making sure that all industries other than tobacco are represented. (Tobacco is totally snuffed.)

Expense ratio: 0.50 percent

Top five companies: Eaton Corp.; International Business Machines; Starbucks; Johnson & Johnson; Becton, Dickinson and Company

Top five industries: Information technology, healthcare, consumer discretionary, consumer staples, financials

PowerShares WilderHill Clean Energy Fund (PBW)

Indexed to: The WilderHill Clean Energy Index, which tracks three dozen companies that invest in solar energy, windmills, hydrogen fuel cells, rechargeable batteries, and other forms of environmentally friendly power

Expense ratio: 0.70 percent

Top five companies (most of which you've probably never heard of): GT Solar, Tesla Motors, Sociedad Qumica y Minera de Chile, OM Group, SunPower Corp.

Top five countries: United States, China, Canada, Brazil, Germany

Russell's double-shot-plus review: These two funds are very different from each other. KLD covers a large swath of the market, while PBW is more narrowly focused. Both funds cost less than half of what the average socially conscious mutual fund would cost; that is certainly a good thing. On the other hand, SRI ETFs charge considerably more than many other ETFs. (The average expense ratio for the entire SRI category is about 0.70 percent, whereas many ETFs carry expense ratios of 0.20 percent or less.)

Keep in mind that SRI ETF providers don't offer or promise the same kind of shareholder activism that you get with some of the more aggressive mutual fund companies. That's because most mutual funds are more actively managed than ETFs. As I explain in Chapter 2, passive management is part of what makes ETFs so appealing because it leads to lower management fees and greater transparency. However, active management — such as that found with many mutual funds — may help keep an SRI fund more closely aligned with its stated values. Depending on the level of activism you'd like to see in your SRI fund company, this fact may lessen the appeal of pursuing socially responsible investing via ETFs.

KLD is quite liberal in its definition of "socially responsible." (I mean *liberal* not in the political sense but in the ease with which a stock can survive its screen — although some people may deem social responsibility itself to be a political statement). The fund makes many compromises in its selection of stocks. Certain socially conscious mutual funds have much tougher screening criteria than KLD does.

In terms of diversification, I like to see large cap stocks split distinctly into value and growth. With the SRI ETFs, however, you get a mushier exposure to these large cap categories. Looking through the lens of diversification, PBW offers up a small sliver of the economy and, as such, can involve considerable risk. On the other hand, all energy stocks — both clean and dirty — have lately shown a delightful lack of correlation to the market as a whole.

If you want to invest for a better world and a better portfolio, I suggest you do additional research. One person's idea of socially responsible may be very different than another's. What works for one portfolio may not work for another. There's a ton of information on the website of the Forum for Sustainable and Responsible Investment: www.ussif.org.

Dividend Funds: The Search for Steady Money

The check is in the mail. When you know it's true (it isn't always), there are perhaps no sweeter words in the English language. To many investors, the thought of regular cash payments is a definite turn-on. Always willing to oblige, the financial industry of late has been churning out "high dividend" funds — both mutual funds and ETFs — like there's no tomorrow.

The idea behind these funds is simple enough: They attempt to cobble together the stocks of companies that are issuing high dividends, have high dividend growth rates, or promise future high dividends. In this section, I spell out some of the high dividend ETF options and then debate the value of investing in them.

Your high dividend ETF options

The oldest and largest of the ETF dividend funds is the iShares Dow Jones Select Dividend Index Fund (DVY). For U.S. domestic investments, here are some other options:

- ✔ SPDR Dividend ETF (SDY)
- ✔ Vanguard Dividend Appreciation ETF (VIG)
- ✔ First Trust Morningstar Dividend Leaders Index Fund (FDL)
- ✔ PowerShares Dividend Achievers Portfolio (PFM)
- ✔ PowerShares High Yield Equity Dividend Achievers Portfolio (PEY)

Why *two* PowerShares domestic dividend ETFs? The first one (PFM) "seeks to identify a diversified group of dividend paying companies." The second one (PEY) "seeks to deliver high current dividend income and capital appreciation." (A third, the PowerShares High Growth Rate Dividend Achievers Portfolios [PHJ] sought "to identify companies with the highest ten-year annual dividend growth rate," but that ETF has been closed.) If you're having a hard time telling these dividend funds apart based on their descriptions, you aren't alone. I'm confused as heck!

And if your choices on the U.S. front aren't enough — or aren't confusing enough — you could also go with the PowerShares International Dividend Achievers Portfolio (PID), which "seeks international companies that have increased their annual dividend for five or more consecutive fiscal years."

And if *that* weren't enough choice (or confusion), the newest kids on the ETF block, WisdomTree and Guggenheim, offer about 20 *other* high dividend funds . . . with every wrinkle or subwrinkle imaginable.

In a way, seeking dividends makes sense. In another, larger way, the logic is a bit loopy, just as the marketing (sort of like toilet paper and breakfast cereal marketing) is a bit intense and sometimes silly. Let me explain.

Promise of riches or smoke and mirrors?

Dividends! Dividends! On the face of it, they look like free money. But nothing in life is quite so simple. Here are the typical arguments for buying a high dividend fund, along with my retort to each:

> ✔ **Argument for dividends #1: Steady money is just like honey.** Huh? Are you crazy, Russell? Who in his right mind wouldn't want dividends? A stock that pays dividends is *obviously* more valuable than a stock that doesn't pay dividends. If I buy a high dividend ETF, my account balance will grow every month.
>
>
>
> **Retort:** Suppose you own an individual share of stock in the McDummy Corporation (ticker MCDM), and MCDM issues a dividend of $1. The market price of your one share of MCDM, as a rule, will fall by $1 as soon as the McDummy Corporation sends out the dividend. That's because the dividend comes from the company's cash reserves, and as those cash reserves diminish, the value of the McDummy Corporation diminishes (just as it would if it gave away, say, 100 plastic pink flamingoes from the front lawn of its corporate headquarters, or any other asset for that matter). As the value of the company diminishes, so too does the value of its shares. And the very same holds true for every stock held in an ETF.

✔ **Argument for dividends #2: They lower my tax hit.** But . . . but . . . Suppose I need a steady stream of income? Isn't it better that I rely on dividends, which are generally taxed at 15 percent, instead of interest from bonds or CDs, which is taxed at my higher income tax rate?

First retort: First, if you need a steady stream of income, nothing is stopping you from creating *artificial dividends* by selling off any security you like. You may pay capital gains tax, but that will be no higher than the tax on dividends. In the end, whether you pull $1,000 from your account in the form of recently issued dividends or $1,000 from the sale of a security, you are withdrawing the same amount. And what if one month you find you don't need the income? You can sell nothing and pay no tax, whereas with a high dividend ETF, you'll pay the tax regardless.

Second retort: The special dividend tax break is set to expire at the end of 2012. Unless Congress extends it, dividends will be taxed at ordinary income rates.

Third retort: If you're really concerned about taxes, maybe you should be investing in tax-free municipal bonds.

✔ **Argument for dividends #3: Taxes, what taxes?** Russell, what gives? If I invest in an ETF, I won't have to worry about taxes because, as you've told us all along, ETFs are incredibly tax efficient.

Retort: ETFs are head-and-shoulders above most mutual funds when it comes to tax efficiency, but that tax efficiency is aimed at reducing taxable capital gains, not dividends. An ETF can't do a whole lot to lessen the tax hit from dividends. ETF or mutual fund, you'll pay.

✔ **Argument for dividends #4: It's a new world!** Russell, you sound like a stick in the mud. This is an exciting new development in the world of investments.

Retort: New development? Really? Equity income funds have been around for years and years, and they haven't exactly set the world on fire. And consider the age-old *Dogs of the Dow* strategy. Many people have believed that if every year you purchase the ten highest-paying dividend stocks in the Dow (the so-called *Dogs*), you can rack up serious returns. The strategy has been well-studied, and it clearly isn't as powerful as the hype. The Dogs do seem to have some bark, but no more so than any other similarly sized and similarly volatile stocks. In other words, put a value lean on your portfolio, as I suggest in numerous places throughout this book (see especially Chapters 6 and 8), and you'll be getting plenty of dividends and much of the edge that high dividend investors seek.

✔ **Argument for dividends #5: Don't you read history?** Over the course of history, Russell, much of the stock market's returns have come from dividends. You should know that.

First retort: Yeah, so? During the longest bull market in history — the 1990s — stock market returns were running double digits a year, and very little was being shelled out in dividends. A company that isn't paying dividends is either investing its cash in operations or buying back its own stock. Either way, shareholders stand to gain. Just because much of the stock market's past returns have come from dividends doesn't mean that future returns must or will come from the same source.

Second retort: If you look at high-dividend-paying sectors of the economy, you don't necessarily find that those sectors beat the broader market over long periods of time. The utilities sector is a perfect example. If the power of dividends were as great as the dividend hawks say they are, wouldn't the historical return of the utilities industry and financial stocks clobber the S&P 500? That isn't the case.

✔ **Argument for dividends #6: Dividends offer protection.** Stocks that pay high dividends are going to be less risky than stocks that don't. Those dividends create a floor, even if only psychologically. High-dividend-paying stocks cannot become worthless.

Retort: You would think that high-dividend-paying stock ETFs would be less likely to fall precipitously should there be a major downturn in the stock market. On the face of it, the argument seems logical. In the real world, however, studies of high-dividend-paying stocks reveal that they actually tend to be somewhat *more* volatile than the broad market. Go figure. Besides, if your main goal is to temper risk, you have other, more effective, ways of doing that. (See Chapter 12 on bonds.)

✔ **Argument for dividends #7: But still, it can't hurt.** All right, I concede, maybe these funds aren't the greatest thing since sliced bread. Still, can it hurt to buy one?

Retort: Look, I don't *despise* these funds. Far from it. If you want to buy one, buy one. Put it into your retirement account, if there's room in there, and you won't even have to worry about any tax on the dividends. But don't assume that you're going to beat the broad market over the long haul. And know that you are buying a fund that is mostly large value stocks, typically within just a handful of industries (notably pharmaceuticals, utilities, and consumer staples). Your risk may be greater than you think. And if dividend-paying stocks are incredibly hot at the moment (as they are while I write these words), be aware that their prices may be inflated.

✔ **Final argument: I want my dividends!** I don't care what you say. I'm going to buy a high dividend ETF.

Final retort: Fine. Consider the Vanguard option (VIG) or the SPDR (SDY). With expense ratios of 0.18 percent and 0.35 percent respectively, they are considerably less costly than the competition. The iShares option (DVY) isn't too bad, either, with expenses of 0.40 percent.

I'd steer clear of the PowerShares options. Their 0.60 percent expense ratios are problematic enough. And quite frankly, having to choose between "high dividend paying companies" and "high current dividend income and capital appreciation" is enough to give me a big, fat headache. WisdomTree's many, many dividend offerings, which tend to be just as pricey as (and in some cases even pricier than) PowerShares, threaten to make my head explode.

By the way, for income, consider Real Estate Investment Trusts (REITs); several ETF REIT options exist, and they tend to yield *double* the dividends paid by so-called "high dividend" stock ETFs. (For info on REITs, see Chapter 13.)

Last but not least, if you're not going to be using that dividend money right away, make sure your ETF is held in an account at a brokerage house that will reinvest your dividends without charging you a commission. The vast majority will do so, but not all.

Investing in Initial Public Offerings

Want to take a real joyride? In April 2006, First Trust Advisors introduced the First Trust IPOX-100 Index Fund (FPX). You can invest in an ETF that, according to the prospectus, tracks the 100 "largest, typically best performing, and most liquid initial public offerings" in the United States.

Just prior to the introduction of the fund, the index on which it is based clocked a three-year annualized return of 33.74 percent. Needless to say, with that kind of return, this new ETF got the attention of a good number of investors. Those who jumped on board didn't exactly have a smooth ride. When the market tanked in 2008, FPX lost 43.79 percent — almost 7 percentage points more than the S&P 500 lost. Oooo, the pain. But in 2009, this fund gained 44.56 percent, and as of this writing, it has continued to outperform the broad market.

Thinking about plunking some cash into FPX? I may not have a crystal ball, but I do have an inkling of what the future will bring for this fund: more extreme volatility. Keep reading to find out why.

The rollercoaster of recent IPO performance

When times are good for small and mid cap stocks, as they were in the three years prior to the launch of FPX, times are typically very good for IPOs. But when times are bad, you can guess what happens. The index on which this ETF is based suffered terribly during the bear market of 2000, 2001, and 2002, with respective annual dips of –24.55 percent, –22.77 percent, and –21.64 percent. (If you started with $10,000 in 2000, you would have been left at the end of 2002 with a rather pathetic $4,566.04.) And I've already addressed the more recent recession of 2008.

Taking a broader look at IPOs

But what about the very long-term performance of IPOs? Jay Ritter, a professor of Finance at the University of Florida, keeps copious records on the returns of IPOs. Dr. Ritter asserts that, collectively, they haven't done all that well *vis-à-vis* the broad market. But he hastens to add that long-term performance is dragged down by the smaller IPOs, and that larger IPOs — the ones included in the IPOX ETF — as a group have modestly outperformed the market, albeit with greater volatility.

Indeed. As the IPOX Index now stands, tech stocks, volatile as heck in their own right, make up slightly more than 25 percent of the roster. The top three companies together represent nearly one-third of the index's value. Do you really want that kind of swing in your portfolio, on top of an expense ratio of 0.60 percent?

Maybe you do. But if you are inclined to take such a gamble, please don't do it with any more money than you can afford to lose. Of course, that's true of all stocks, but especially of these youngsters.

Funds That (Supposedly) Thrive When the Market Takes a Dive

In June 2006, an outfit called ProShares introduced the first ETFs designed to *short* the market. That means these *inverse* ETFs are designed to go up as their market benchmark goes down, and vice versa. The four original ProShares ETFs are the Short QQQ fund (PSQ), which is betting against the NASDAQ-100; the Short S&P500 (SH); the Short MidCap400 (MYY); and the Short Dow30 (DOG).

DOG, indeed. If I were to devise a ticker for the entire lot, it would be "HUH?"

As it happens, this HUH? category of ETFs and exchanged-traded notes (ETNs) has proliferated like no other. You can now find well over 100 exchange-traded products, from ProShares, PowerShares, Direxion,

Guggenheim, and iPath, allowing you to short anything and everything, including the kitchen sink (see the ProShares UltraShort Consumer Goods ETF [SZK]). From the U.S. stock market, to various industry sectors, to the stock markets of other countries, to Treasury bonds, to gold and oil, it is now easy to bet that prices are heading south.

And for the truly pessimistic investor, many of these short ETFs now allow you to bet in *multiples*. In other words, if the market falls, these funds promise to rise on a leveraged basis. For example, the Direxion Daily Natural Gas Related Bear 2X Shares (FCGS) is designed to rise 10 percent if the market in natural gas falls 5 percent. And the Direxion Daily Semiconductor Bear 3x Shares (SOXS) is designed to rise 30 percent if the market for semiconductor stocks falls 10 percent.

From where I sit, these funds look an awful lot like legalized gambling. If you're considering putting your bag of nickels in any of these slots, keep reading for my two cents.

Entering an upside-down world

In other parts of this book, I talk about correlation and how wonderful it is when you can find two asset classes that go up and down at different times. Heck, it would seem that funds that short the stock and bond markets would be ideal additions to a portfolio. Talk about diversification! Ah, but there are hitches. For example, when you diversify, you want to find various asset classes that move out of synch but that are all expected to move upward over time, making money for you. Funds that short the stock and bond markets fail to meet the long-term test.

Sure, sometimes stocks decline. But over the long run (granted, the very long run), they rise. If they didn't, we wouldn't have a stock market. Who would invest? So over the long run, you would expect the short funds to lose money. Just about the only way to make money with these funds is to time the market just right: to jump in just as the market is about to dive and then pull out before the market goes up. Good luck! Market timing, I'm not the first to say, is a fool's game.

Here's another hitch: These short ETFs are designed to move against the market on a *daily* basis. That means if the market goes down 5 percent on Wednesday, your fund should go up 5 percent (or, if your fund is leveraged, 10 percent or 15 percent) on Wednesday. But the mathematics of this, as I show you in the upcoming section "Funds That Double the Thrill of Investing (for Better or Worse)," is very tricky. This tricky math means that if you invest in these funds for more than a very brief spell, you are destined to lose money, regardless of which way the market moves!

Boasting a track record like none other

Don't take my word for anything I stated in the previous section. Just check the long-term performance records of these beasts. All of the original ProShares ETFs introduced in 2006 have lost a bundle. The ProShares Short QQQ (PSQ), for example, has lost 12.51 percent annually since inception. But to truly appreciate the losing power of these funds, you need to look at ProFunds, the mutual funds produced by the very same people who produce ProShares ETFs. The company's so-called *inverse* mutual funds and the company's short ETFs are very similar. Ready for some depressing numbers? See `www.profunds.com/pricesperformance/performancedata.html`.

Here, for example, are the annualized returns for the UltraShort NASDAQ-100 ProFund mutual fund, which has been proudly torturing investors since June 2, 1998:

- ✔ One year: –39.45 percent
- ✔ Five years: –25.81 percent
- ✔ Ten years: –25.47 percent
- ✔ Since inception: –33.46 percent

Sure, the stock market could tumble at any time, and you could profit by buying inverse or short funds. But you will need to time that stock market tumble just right, and the odds of doing so are very slim. Moreover, to play this stacked game will cost you dearly: None of the short ETFs charge less than 0.75 percent, and most carry an expense ratio of 0.95 percent, making them just about the most expensive ETFs on the market.

Funds That Double the Thrill of Investing (for Better or Worse)

ProShares introduced four other ETFs in 2006, targeting investors at the other end of the sentiment spectrum: extreme optimists. These are leveraged funds that include the Ultra QQQ (QLD), which "seeks daily investment results, before fees and expenses, that correspond to twice (200%) the daily performance of the NASDAQ-100 Index," and the similarly designed Ultra S&P500 (SSO), Ultra MidCap400 (MVV), and Ultra Dow30 (DDM).

You think the market is going to rock? These funds, which use futures and other derivatives to magnify market returns, promise to make you twice the money you would make by simply investing in the NASDAQ-100, the S&P 500, the S&P MidCap 400, or the Dow. Of course, you'll have to accept twice the volatility. It seems like it might be a fair bet. But it really isn't.

Crazy math: Comparing leveraged funds to traditional ETFs

Suppose you invest in the Ultra S&P500 (SSO), as opposed to, say, the SPDR S&P 500 (SPY). On a daily basis, if the underlying index goes up, your investment will go up twice as much. If the underlying index goes down, your investment will go down twice as much. Clearly the volatility is double. But let's look at the potential returns, as well.

The SPY is going to cost you 0.10 percent in operating expenses. The SSO is going to cost you 0.95 percent. That's a difference of 0.85 percent a year, or $425 on a $50,000 investment. You can expect about 1.8 percent in annualized dividends on SPY. Because SSO invests largely in futures, you aren't going to get much in dividends — probably less than half. On a $50,000 investment, that's a difference of an additional $450 or more. Already you've lost $875 ($425 + $450), regardless of which way the market goes.

But it isn't actually the loss of dividends or the high operating expenses that will hurt you the most with leveraged funds. It's more the added volatility — daily volatility — that will eat up and spit out your principal regardless of which way the market goes.

Follow closely:

Suppose you invest $1,000 in the ProShares Ultra QQQ ETF (QLD), which seeks a return of 200 percent of the return of the NASDAQ-100 index (the 100 largest over-the-counter stocks in the land). Now suppose that the index goes up 10 percent tomorrow but then drops 10 percent the day after tomorrow. You think you're back to $1,000? Guess again. The math of compounding is such that, even if you had invested in the index itself — unleveraged — you'd be in the hole after Day Two. Run the numbers: your 10 percent gain on Day One would take you up to $1,100, but your loss of 10 percent of $1,100 the next day equals $110. Subtract that amount from $1,100, and you're left with $990 on Day Two, or an overall loss of 1 percent.

With QLD, you're going to get double socked. On Day One, you'll happily be up 20 percent to $1,200. But on Day Two, you'll lose 20 percent of that amount and find yourself with $960. You didn't lose the promised *double* (2 percent); you just lost *quadruple* (4 percent). Pull out your calculator if you don't believe me.

In a classic illustration of the principle that life is not fair, you are not helped if the market goes down and then up, instead of the other way around. Lose

10 percent of $1,000 and you've got $900. Gain 10 percent the next day, and what do you have? $990 ($900 + $90). The situation is magnified with QLD: You would lose 20 percent on Day One for a balance of $800 and gain 20 percent on Day Two to bring you right back to the same $960 you were left with in the first example.

And THAT, dear reader, is how these funds eat up your hard-earned savings, and why I strongly suggest that you do not use them.

Examining a rather pathetic track record

I encourage you to look at the performance records of these funds carefully before considering them. Take the ProShares Ultra QQQ ETF (QLD). The NASDAQ-100 index returned 3.28 percent a year in the three years prior to May 31, 2011. And QLD, which promises twice the performance of the NASDAQ-100? That fund has returned 0.73 percent annually during the same period — with a boatload more volatility. (The fund lost about 73 percent in 2008!)

But to really, really appreciate the dangers of these leveraged funds, you need to look at their longer-term track record. ProShares Ultra ETFs, like their short counterparts, have mutual fund equivalents (issued by the very same company) that have been in existence for many years. The UltraBull ProFund, for example, has been around since November 1997. Just like its ETF cousin SSO, it promises you twice the punch of the S&P 500 and operates in much the same way. Let's see how well it has done.

Annualized return figures for the UltraBull ProFund are as follows:

- ✔ One year: 25.13 percent
- ✔ Five years: –5.61 percent
- ✔ Ten years: –3.10 percent
- ✔ Since inception: –2.21 percent

How does this compare to the SPDR S&P 500 (SPY)? Annualized return figures for SPY are as follows:

- ✔ One year: 25.71 percent
- ✔ Five years: 3.24 percent
- ✔ Ten years: 2.57 percent
- ✔ Since UltraBull's inception: 4.3 percent

The "twice the punch" leveraged fund offers twice the volatility with much, much lower long-term returns. Sign me up!

The author's pipe dream

I would love to see someone create a "Reasonably-Paid-Top-Executives ETF." I might buy into it if it did exist. It stands to reason that when corporations pay astronomical salaries to their CEOs, shareholders may stand to lose. After all, those millions and millions (indeed, sometimes billions) have to come from *somewhere.*

According to compensation researchers Lucian Bebchuk of Harvard University and Jesse Fried of the University of California at Berkeley, the pay of top executives at America's largest corporations eats seriously into U.S. corporate profits. Not too surprisingly (at least in my mind), one study by the Institute for Policy Studies and United for a Fair Economy found that those reduced profits are indeed hurting shareholders. The study looked at stock market returns for major U.S. corporations between 1991 and the end of 2004. Sure enough, the "Greedy CEO Portfolio" — a portfolio of those corporations that pay their CEOs the most — severely underperformed the S&P 500. Hence, an ETF comprised of stocks in companies that curb executive pay just might be expected to outperform the market.

All-In-One ETFs: For the Ultimate Lazy Portfolio

The rest of this chapter has introduced you to ETFs that tend to focus fairly narrowly in order to meet your investing needs (or, in the case of short and leveraged funds, your gambling needs). In this section, I introduce you to funds that cast a much wider net, allowing you to invest in enormous pools of stocks and bonds without having to focus at all. First I present a handful of ETF options that fit the bill, and then I explain why you probably don't want them.

Getting worldwide exposure to stocks and bonds

Even the laziest investor has to make choices: Do you want worldwide exposure to stocks only? Or to stocks and bonds? Do you want the allocation between stocks and bonds to remain the same for the life of your investment? Or do you want that allocation to adjust as you get closer to retirement? In this section, I lay out your options.

Buying into the world's stock markets

If you want instant exposure to the broadest possible index of stocks, including U.S. and all sorts of foreign stocks (from both developed and emerging market countries), here are your options as of this writing:

- ✔ iShares MSCI ACWI Index Fund (ACWI), with 2,467 stock holdings and management fees of 0.35 percent

- ✔ Vanguard Total World Stock ETF (VT), with 2,894 holdings and management fees that are slightly lower at 0.25 percent

Adding bonds to the mix

Not enough diversity for you? Never fear: You can go even broader than the worldwide stock funds, buying one ETF that will give you exposure not only to the entire world of stocks but to bonds as well. (I discuss bond ETFs in Chapter 12.)

These all-in-one ETFs are referred to as *asset allocation funds* when they are *static,* meaning the division between stocks and bonds stays more or less the same for the life of the fund (for example, 50 percent stock and 50 percent bonds). The folks from iShares offer a dozen of these babies, including these:

- ✔ iShares S&P Aggressive Allocation Fund (AOA)

- ✔ iShares S&P Conservative Allocation Fund (AOK)

- ✔ iShares S&P Moderate Allocation Fund (AOM)

These three funds, which carry total management expenses of about 0.46 percent, offer varying exposure to stocks and bonds depending on how aggressive a portfolio you want.

Picking a retirement date and investing accordingly

If a fund seeks to change its asset allocation over time, growing more conservative as you get older and less able or willing to handle market risk, it may be called a *lifecycle* or *target-date* fund (rather than an asset allocation fund). The iShares people also offer a bevy of these funds, including these three:

- ✔ iShares S&P Target Date 2020 Index Fund (TZG)

- ✔ iShares S&P Target Date 2025 Index Fund (TZI)

- ✔ iShares S&P Target Date 2030 Index Fund (TZL)

The dates refer to anticipated retirement dates. These funds start off more aggressive (stressing stocks over bonds) and wind up, by your expected retirement date, holding a more conservative portfolio. The expense ratio for each is about 0.43 percent.

Both the iShares asset allocation funds and the target-date funds are actually funds of funds (mostly other iShares ETFs). The expenses you see include the fees for both the component funds and the all-in-one fund wrapper.

Deutsche Bank DBX Strategic Advisors offers five funds of similar nature to the iShares. These funds, which include the db-X 2030 Target Date Fund (TDN) and the db-X 2040 Target Date Fund (TDV), carry expense ratios of 0.65 percent.

Russell's average review for the average reader on an average day

"For every complex problem," said H. L. Mencken, "there is an answer that is clear, simple — and wrong." Certainly, finding the optimal portfolio is a complex problem. The all-in-one ETFs I introduce in this section provide an answer that is clear, simple — and usually wrong. Never mind the high expense ratios; what's wrong is that there is no one-size-fits-all portfolio that makes sense for most people. Oh, I suppose if you were the average 50-year-old, with the average amount of money, looking to work an average number of years, expecting to die at the average age, and you were willing to take on an average amount of risk . . . Well, if you were all those things and planned on remaining forever average, these funds might make sense for you.

But if you are anything other than perfectly average, I urge you to move on to Part IV of this book whenever you feel ready. Take a look at my model portfolios, and craft an ETF portfolio that makes sense for *you*.

Part III

Adding Bonds, REITs, and Other ETFs to Your Portfolio

The 5th Wave   By Rich Tennant

"I've brought in Tom, Denise, and Kyle, to talk about our REIT, Bond, and metal ETFs respectively."

In this part . . .

The majority of ETFs — all those I discuss in Part II — represent common stock holdings. In this part, I introduce you to the minority: those ETFs that represent bonds, real estate investment trusts (REITs), and commodities such as gold, silver, and oil. Such holdings (especially bonds) have enormous diversification power: the power to protect you when the stock market takes a big roll, as it inevitably does from time to time. (I probably don't need to tell you that!)

For sure, you have various means of owning such holdings. You can buy individual bonds, investment properties from foreclosure sales in Nevada (be careful not to step on a cactus), gold coins, and silver bullion. Heck, you can fill your garage with barrels of oil. But no method is as easy, efficient, and frugal as holding them as ETFs.

Chapter 12

For Your Interest: The World of Bond ETFs

I love inline skating. Sometimes, I admit, I take to the Pennsylvania hills a bit too fast. There's just something about the trees racing by and the wind in my face that I can't resist. Whoosh!

On occasion, I hit a bump, or some tiny woman in a monster SUV who can barely see over the steering wheel (they're all over my neighborhood) cuts me off and I crash to the pavement. But thanks to the heavy black plastic armor that covers my knees, elbows, wrists, and head (just call me the Black Knight of Wealth Management), I've never been seriously injured.

Bonds are your portfolio's knee and elbow pads. When the going gets rough, and you hit the big bump (by any chance, do you remember 2008?), you'll be very, very glad to have bonds in your portfolio.

Plain and simple, there is no time-honored diversification tool for your portfolio that even comes close to bonds. They are as good as gold . . . even better than gold when you look at the long-term returns. Bonds are what may have saved your grandparents from selling apples on the street following the stock market crash of 1929.

The one thing that grandpa and grandma never had — but you do — is the ability to invest in bond ETFs. Like stock ETFs, most bond ETFs (at least the ones I'm going to suggest) are inexpensive, transparent (you know exactly what you're investing in), and highly liquid (you can sell them in a flash). Like individual bonds or bond mutual funds, bond ETFs can also be used to produce a reliable flow of cash in the form of interest payments, making them especially popular among grandparent types of any generation.

Throughout this chapter, I discuss a few things about bond investing in general. Then, without knowing the intimate particulars of your individual economics, I try my best to help you decide if bond ETFs belong in your portfolio, and if so, which ones. I also address that all-important and highly controversial question of how to achieve an optimal mix of stocks and bonds.

The single most important investment decision you ever make may occur when you determine the split between stocks and bonds in your portfolio. No pressure.

Tracing the Track Record of Bonds

Bonds, more or less in their present form, have been used as financial instruments since the Middle Ages. Then, as now, bonds of varying risk existed. (See the sidebar "The three risks of bond investing.") Then, as now, risks and returns were highly correlated.

For the most part, bonds are less volatile than stocks, and their returns over time tend to be less. Over the past 80 years, the average annualized nominal return of the S&P 500 has been around 9.9 percent, while the return of long-term U.S. government bonds has been approximately 5.5 percent.

Comparing the *real* returns of stocks versus bonds (the return *after* inflation, which happens to be the return that really counts), stocks over the past 80 years clock in at about 6.7 percent and bonds at 2.4 percent — a huge difference. A dollar invested in the stock market in 1926 (ignoring all taxes, investment fees, and so on) would today be worth $243.00. That same dollar invested in bonds would be worth about $7.65.

These numbers may lead you to look at bonds and say to yourself, "Why bother?" Well, in fact, there's good reason to bother. Please read on before you decide to forsake this all-important asset class.

The three risks of bond investing

When you buy a stock, your risks are plenty: The company you're investing in may go belly up; the public may simply lose interest in the stock, sending its price tumbling; or the entire economy may falter, in which case, your stock, like most others, may start to freefall. In the world of bonds, the risks aren't quite so high, and they tend to differ. Here are the three major risks of investing in bonds or a bond ETF:

✔ **Risk of default:** A bond is a promissory note. The note is only as good as the government, agency, or company that makes the promise to repay. If you buy a bond from ABC Corporation, and ABC Corporation can't pay, you lose. This risk of default is mostly an issue with high-yield ("junk") bonds. Don't invest in high-yield corporate bonds unless you're willing to shoulder some serious risk. Keep in mind when buying a high-yield bond ETF that if the economy tanks and shaky companies start to sink, you'll possibly lose both the income from the bonds and the principal. And that could hurt. High-yield bonds, for example, were little comfort to those who lost money in the stock market in 2008. The SPDR Barclays Capital High Yield Bond ETF (JNK), for example, saw returns in 2008 of –24.68 percent.

✔ **Interest-rate risk:** Suppose you are holding a bond with a 5 percent coupon rate, bought at a time when interest rates in general were 5 percent. Now suppose that the prevailing interest rate jumps to 10 percent. Are you going to be happy that you're holding a bond that is paying 5 percent? Of course not. If you hold the bond to maturity, there's a great opportunity cost. If you try to sell the bond before maturity, no one will give you full price; you'll need to sell it at a deep discount and take a loss. The longer the maturity of the bond, the greater the interest-rate risk. For that reason, the iShares Barclays 20+ Year Treasury Bond Fund (TLT) carries substantial interest-rate risk, while the iShares Barclays 1–3 Year Treasury Bond Fund (SHY) carries very little. Most of the other funds are somewhere in between. (There's a flip side to interest-rate risk: If you are holding a bond with a 5 percent coupon rate, and the prevailing interest rate drops to 3 percent, your bond will suddenly become a very hot ticket, selling at a juicy premium.)

✔ **Inflation risk:** Plain and simple, if you are holding a bond that pays 5 percent, and the inflation rate is 8 percent, you are in trouble. This is perhaps the biggest risk with bonds, especially low-yielding bonds, such as short-term and intermediate-term Treasurys. (The iShares Barclays 1–3 Year Treasury Bond Fund could very easily fall behind the inflation rate.) The only bonds immune to this risk are inflation-protected bonds, which is why part of your bond portfolio should be invested in a fund such as the iShares Barclays TIPS Bond Fund (TIP). Such bonds do, however, carry interest-rate risk, and another risk that's unique to them: *deflation* risk. If consumer prices start to drop, your inflation adjustment will be worth zero, and you'll be left holding the lowest yielding bond in the land.

Portfolio protection when you need it most

When determining the attractiveness of bonds, you need to look not only at historical return but also at volatility: Long-term U.S. government bonds (which tend, like all long-term bonds, to be rather volatile) in their worst year *ever* (2009) returned –17.2 percent. In their second worst year ever (1980) they returned –14.6 percent. Those are big moves but still a walk in the park compared to the worst stock market years of 1931 (–43.3 percent), 1937 (–35 percent), 1974 (–26.5 percent), and 2008 (–36.7 percent).

As I note in the introduction to this chapter, during the Great Depression years, bonds may have saved your grandma and grandpa from destitution. The annualized real return of the S&P 500 from 1930–1932 was –20 percent. The annualized real return of long-term U.S. government bonds during the same three years was 14.9 percent.

There are two reasons that U.S. government bonds (and other high-quality bonds) often do well in the roughest economic times:

✔ People flock to them for safety, raising demand.

✔ Interest rates often (not always, but often) drop during tough economic times. Interest rates and bond prices have an inverse relationship. When interest rates fall, already-issued bonds (carrying older, relatively high coupon rates) shoot up in price.

As in the past, bonds may similarly spare your hide should the upcoming years prove disastrous for Wall Street. (You never know.) Whereas international stocks and certain industry sectors, like energy and real estate, have limited correlation to the broad U.S. stock market, bonds (not U.S. junk bonds, but most others) actually have a slight *negative* correlation to stocks. In other words, when the bear market is at its growliest, the complicated labyrinth of economic factors that typically coincide with that situation — lower inflation (possible deflation), lower interest rates — can bode quite well for fixed income. They certainly have done so in the past.

The way in which bonds tend to zig when stocks zag (and vice versa) is beautifully illustrated in Figure 12-1, provided by Vanguard Investments.

And also consider Figure 12-2, which shows how stocks and bonds have fared in some of the most exciting (read: volatile) investment years in the past eight decades.

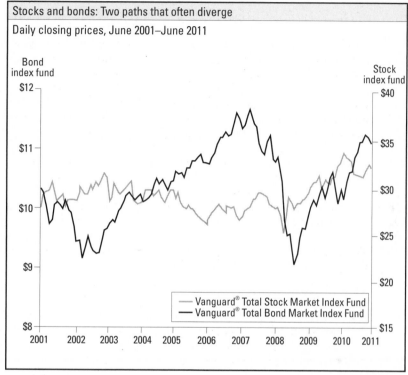

Stocks and bonds: Two paths that often diverge

Daily closing prices, June 2001–June 2011

Bond index fund

Stock index fund

— Vanguard® Total Stock Market Index Fund
— Vanguard® Total Bond Market Index Fund

Figure 12-1: The performance of stocks and bonds from June 2001 to June 2011.

Source: Vanguard, with permission.

History may or may not repeat

Of course, as investment experts say again and again (although few people listen), historical returns are only mildly indicative of what will happen in the future; they are merely reference points. Despite all the crystal balls, tea leaves, and CNBC commentators in the world, we simply don't know what the future will bring.

Although the vast majority of financial professionals use the past century as pretty much their sole reference point, some point out that in the 19th century, stocks and bonds actually had more similar — nearly equal, in fact — rates of return. And perhaps that may be true for the 21st century as well. Time will tell. In the meantime, given all this uncertainty, it would be most prudent to have both stocks and bonds represented in your portfolio.

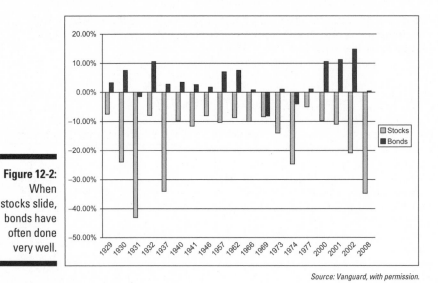

Figure 12-2:
When
stocks slide,
bonds have
often done
very well.

Source: Vanguard, with permission.

Tapping into Bonds in Various Ways

Like stocks, bonds can be bought individually, or you can invest in any of hundreds of bond mutual funds or about 150 bond ETFs. The primary reason for picking a bond fund over individual bonds is the same reason you might pick a stock fund over individual stocks: diversification.

Sure, you have to pay to get your bonds in fund form, but the management fees on bond ETFs tend to be very low, as you'll see later in this chapter. Conversely, the cost to trade individual bonds can be quite high. That's especially true of corporate and municipal bonds.

I'm not saying that you should not consider ever buying individual bonds. Doing so may make sense, provided that you know how to get a good price on an individual bond (if not, please read my book on that topic, *Bond Investing For Dummies,* published by Wiley) and provided that you are buying a bond with little default risk (such as a Treasury bond). That's especially true when you know that you will be needing x amount of money on y date. But for the most part, investors do better with low-cost, indexed bond funds.

Like stocks, bonds can (and should, if your portfolio is large enough) be broken up into different categories. Instead of U.S. and international, large, small, value, and growth (the way stocks are often broken up), bond categories may include U.S. government (both conventional and inflation-adjusted), corporate, international, and municipal bonds — all of varying maturity dates and credit ratings. Unless you're a billionaire, you simply can't effectively own enough individual bonds to tap into each and every fixed income class.

Finding strength in numbers

To be honest, diversification in bonds, while important, isn't quite as crucial as diversification in stocks. If you own high-quality U.S. government bonds (as long as they aren't terribly long-term) and you own a bevy of bonds from the most financially secure corporations, you are very unlikely to lose a whole lot of your principal, as you can with any stock. But the benefits of diversification are more than protecting principal. There's also much to be said for smoothing out returns and moderating risk.

Bond returns from one category of bonds to another can vary greatly, especially in the short run. In 2008, for example, high-yield corporate bonds, as represented by the SPDR Barclays Capital High Yield Bond ETF (JNK), saw a return of –24.68 percent. That same year, U.S. Treasury bonds, as represented by the iShares Barclays 7–10 Year Treasury Bond ETF (IEF), returned 17.9 percent. But the very next year, 2009, was a terrible year for Treasurys; IEF sagged –6.56 percent and JNK shot up 37.65 percent.

By owning a handful of bond funds, you can effectively diversify across the map. You can have Treasurys of varying maturities, corporate bonds of varying credit worthiness, international bonds of varying continents and currencies, and municipal bonds from across the nation. As you'll see throughout the rest of this chapter, I urge investors primarily to seek safety in bonds. If you're looking for high returns, go to stocks. The purpose of bonds, as far as I'm concerned, is to provide ballast to a portfolio.

The purposes served by bond funds are to make your bond investing easy, help you to diversity, and keep your costs low. Just as in the world of stock funds, all bond funds are not created equal. Some Treasury funds are better than others. Some corporate bond funds are better than others. Ditto for funds holding municipal bonds and foreign bonds.

Considering bond fund costs

Low costs are even more essential in picking a bond fund than they are in picking a stock fund. When (historically, at least over the past century) you're looking at maybe earning 2.4 percent above inflation, paying a manager even 1.2 percent a year is going to cut your profits in half . . . more than half if you are paying taxes on the bond dividends. Do you really care to do that?

As I write these words, interest rates are very low, which means that real interest rates (factoring in inflation) for most bonds are considerably less than 2.4 percent. That fact means paying attention to the cost of your bond funds is more essential than ever.

The most economical bond funds are index funds, and you have a number of excellent index bond mutual funds to choose from. The index bond ETFs I highlight in this chapter include some of the cheapest funds on the planet, which is a reason to like them.

Although I'm a big proponent of ETFs, I must tell you that the ETF edge in the fixed income arena isn't nearly as sharp as it is in stocks. The tax efficiency of a bond index mutual fund and a bond ETF are just about the same. The wonderful structure of ETFs that I discuss in Chapter 2 simply doesn't matter much when it comes to bonds. Bonds pay interest — that's how you make money with bonds — and they rarely see any substantial capital gains. To the extent that they do have capital gains, however, ETFs may have an edge over mutual funds. But that's generally not going to be any big deal.

Casting a wide net

In the next section, I provide a menu of bond ETFs. These are, by and large, very good options for the fixed income side of your portfolio.

You may also wish to consider various bond mutual funds to complement your bond ETF selections, especially if you have a large portfolio and are in the northern tax brackets. I discuss a number of these mutual funds in Chapter 15 and include them in some of the sample portfolios created in Chapter 16.

Sampling Your Basic Bond-ETF Menu

At the time of this writing there are about 150 bond ETFs, most of them introduced in the past five years. They are issued by iShares, Market Vectors, PIMCO, PowerShares, State Street SPDRs, Vanguard, iPath, Guggenheim, and WisdomTree.

The U.S. Securities and Exchange Commission, I happen to know, is sitting on applications for many other fixed-income ETFs, including a dozen or so additional funds from PIMCO (a mutual fund company famous for its bond management) and another two dozen or so from State Street SPDRs. So not only do you have many choices today, but also many more choices are coming. In this section, I present some of my favorites.

Please note that with the discussion of each bond ETF, I include the *current yield:* how much each share is paying as a percentage of your investment on the day I'm writing this chapter. I do so only to give you a flavor of how the yields differ among the funds. Current yields on a bond or bond fund, especially a long-term bond or bond fund, can change dramatically from week to week. So, too, can the difference in yields between short- and long-term bonds (known as the yield *curve*). You can check the current yield of any bond fund, as well as the yield curve, on the sites of the ETF providers themselves (see Appendix A) or on general investing sites such as www.morningstar.com. One great site for all sorts of information on bonds, including yields for all bond categories, is www.investinginbonds.com.

Note that several different kinds of bond yield exist. (For detailed information, once again I refer you to my book *Bond Investing For Dummies.*) For the sake of consistency, the bond yield I refer to throughout the rest of this chapter is the "SEC 30-Day Yield." (Here's the formula for you techno-heads: $2[\{(a-b)/cd+1\}^6-1\}!]$.)

For you non-techno-heads, here's what this yield essentially means: If you (or the fund manager) were to hold to maturity each and every one of the bonds in a fund's portfolio, as it stood over the past 30 days, and reinvest all interest payments (that is, you plow those interest payments right back into your bond portfolio), your SEC yield is what you'd get over the course of a year. It takes into account all fund fees and expenses. The formula was created, and the methodology is enforced, by the U.S. Securities and Exchange Commission, which is where the "SEC" in the formula's name comes from.

Bonus technical stuff: One added advantage of bond funds over individual bonds — very often overlooked by fans of individual bonds — is that you have the option of automatically reinvesting your interest payments. You can't do so with individual bonds, where your interest payments (if you don't spend the money right away) wind up going into your cash position (typically a money market fund). I've encountered numerous investors who buy individual bonds and allow their interest payments to accumulate into humongous piles of very low-interest-paying cash. These people would likely have done considerably better in bond funds.

Tapping the Treasurys: Uncle Sam's IOUs

If the creator/issuer of a bond is a national government, the issue is called a *sovereign* bond. The vast majority of sovereign bonds sold in the United States are Uncle Sam's own Treasurys. (Yeah, that's how they're typically spelled. I don't know why.) Treasury bonds' claim to fame is the allegedly absolute assuredness that you'll get your principal back if you hold a bond to maturity. The United States government guarantees it. For that reason, Treasurys are sometimes called "risk-free."

Treasury bond ETFs come in short-term, intermediate-term, and long-term varieties, depending on the average maturity date of the bonds in the ETF's portfolio. In general, the longer the term, the higher the interest rate but the greater the volatility. Note that interest paid on Treasurys — including Treasury ETFs — is federally taxable but not taxed by the states. As it happens, bonds issued by state and local governments in the United States, known as *municipal bonds,* are not taxed by the federal government. This reciprocal deal was orchestrated by the Supremes (those judges in Washington, not the singing group) back in 1895.

Following are detailed descriptions of three popular iShares Treasury ETFs, along with my reviews. I also identify some other options, although I don't think you're going to do much better than iShares in this particular category.

iShares Barclays 1–3 Year Treasury Bond Fund (SHY)

Indexed to: The Barclays Capital U.S. 1–3 Year Treasury Bond Index, an index tracking the short-term sector of the U.S. Treasury Bond Index. The fund uses a representative sampling — typically around 35 individual bond issues.

Expense ratio: 0.15 percent

Current yield: 0.25 percent

Average weighted maturity: 1.9 years

Russell's review: This ETF and others of its ilk (such as the Vanguard Short-Term Government Bond ETF [VGSH]) are fine for what they are, but the asset class they represent is not among my favorite asset classes. Sure, very short-term Treasurys are ultra-safe investments with little — almost no — volatility. And the yield may be better than you can get in your local savings bank. Maybe. As I write this, with yields on short-term Treasurys so low, that may not be the case. But even if the yield were a wee bit higher than a savings account, is this really where you want to stash your cash? Keep in mind that every time you make a deposit or withdrawal, unless you hold VGSH at Vanguard, you'll very likely pay a commission. You may do better keeping your short-term money in a three- to six-month CD or in an Internet bank like EmigrantDirect or Ally Bank. The latter two options generally pay just as much as SHY; they are FDIC insured (making them just as safe); and you won't pay for each and every transaction.

iShares Barclays 7–10 Year Treasury Bond Fund (IEF)

Indexed to: The Barclays Capital U.S. 7–10 Year Treasury Bond Index, an index tracking the intermediate-term sector of the U.S. Treasury market. The fund uses a representative sampling — typically around 15 individual bond issues.

Expense ratio: 0.15 percent

Current yield: 2.58 percent

Average weighted maturity: 8.6 years

Russell's review: Expect modest returns and modest volatility. Of the three kinds of Treasurys, the intermediate-term bonds make the most sense for most people's portfolios, and IEF is an excellent way to invest in them. Vanguard's Intermediate-Term Government Bond Index ETF (VGIT) would be another good option; it is a very similar fund with just about the same components and costs. Whatever your total allocation to fixed income, IEF (or VGIT) deserves an allotment of perhaps one-fifth to one-third of that amount. See how I work these ETFs into several model portfolios in Chapter 16.

iShares Barclays 20+ Year Treasury Bond Fund (TLT)

Indexed to: The Barclays Capital U.S. 20+ Year Treasury Bond Index, an index tracking the long-term sector of the U.S. Treasury market. The fund uses a representative sampling — typically around 15 individual bond issues.

Expense ratio: 0.15 percent

Current yield: 4.3 percent

Average weighted maturity: 28.1 years

Russell's review: Hmmm. I believe that Treasurys are perhaps the safest investment in the land, but not *entirely* risk-free. I don't mean to sound unpatriotic. I don't mean to sound alarmist. But the size of our nation's debt and deficit makes the hills of Pennsylvania look flat by comparison. Honestly, this issue scares me, and only recently has the U.S. electorate (thanks to a debt stalemate in Congress in 2011) seemed to take notice. I may consider a short-term Treasury bill to be risk-free, but a 20+ year Treasury? Wave your flag all you like, but you take on *some* risk of principal loss here. And given the maturity of the bond, you're certainly going to encounter a heck of a lot of volatility.

Understand the risk here: The U.S. government doesn't need to go "bankrupt" before Treasury bonds take a hit. Interest rates are set by the marketplace and, in part, reflect creditworthiness. The more indebted our nation becomes, the more closely it begins to resemble a deadbeat. Deadbeats pay higher interest rates than others. If the market starts to demand deadbeat rates of interest on U.S. sovereign debt, interest rates will shoot up and the value of this fund will shoot down. Long-term Treasurys may deserve a modest allocation in your portfolio, and this ETF — or the very similar Vanguard Long-Term Government Bond Index ETF (VGLT) — is a fine way to get it. Either way, make sure that any money allocated to this fund is money that you aren't going to need to touch for a number of years.

Gas at $5.00 a gallon? Getting inflation protection in a flash

Technically, U.S. Treasury Inflation-Protected Securities are Treasurys, but they are usually referred to as *TIPS*. I discuss them separately from the other Treasury obligations here because they play a distinctly different role in your portfolio.

The gig with TIPS is this: They pay you only a nominal amount of interest (currently long-term TIPS are paying about 2 percent), but they also kick in an adjustment for inflation. So, for example, if inflation is running at 3 percent, all things being equal, your long-term TIPs will yield 5 percent.

If you want to know what the rate of inflation is going to be over the next few years, I can't tell you, but I can tell you what rate of inflation the bond market expects. That would be the difference between conventional Treasury bonds and TIPS. If, for example, a 10-year conventional Treasury bond were paying 5 percent and the 10-year TIP security were paying 2 percent, the difference (3 percent) would be the rate of inflation that bond buyers collectively expect to see.

Either the iShares Barclays TIPS Bond Fund ETF (TIP) or the very similar SPDR Barclays Capital TIPS ETF (IPE) is a fabulous way to tap into this almost essential ingredient in a well-balanced portfolio.

iShares Barclays TIPS Bond Fund (TIP)

Indexed to: The Barclays Capital U.S. Treasury Inflation-Protected Securities Index. The fund uses a representative sampling of roughly 30 bond issues.

Expense ratio: 0.20 percent

Current yield: 2.01 percent + adjustment for inflation

Average weighted maturity: 8.9 years

Russell's review: TIPS belong in your portfolio, and this fund may be the best way to hold them. You won't get rich off this fund, and the volatility may be more than you like. But if inflation goes on a tear, you are protected. Not so with other bonds. Of course, if inflation doesn't go on a tear, your money will earn sub-par returns. But that's okay — you can think of any lost interest as the premium on an insurance policy that you know you should have.

Note that TIPS are notoriously tax inefficient, even when held in an ETF. Ideally, you would hold your shares of TIP in a tax-advantaged retirement account. In general, whatever your overall allocation is to fixed income (excluding short-term cash needs), perhaps one-quarter to one-third of that amount could be put into a fund such as TIP or IPE. Err more toward one-quarter if you have a fairly aggressive portfolio. Err more toward one-third if you have a more conservative portfolio. Rationale: Your stocks are also, historically speaking at least, a good hedge against inflation. The more stocks you own, the less important the role of TIPS.

Banking on business: Corporate bond ETFs

Logically enough, corporations issue bonds called *corporate* bonds, and you can buy a dizzying array of them with varying maturities, yields, and ratings. Or you can buy a representative sampling through the iShares iBoxx $ Investment Grade Corporate Bond Fund (LQD). Corporate bonds typically pay higher rates than government bonds (historically about 1 percent a year higher), so you would expect the long-term payout from this ETF to be higher than any government bond ETF, except perhaps for the longest of the long-term government bond ETFs.

In the area of corporate bonds, credit ratings are essential. Know that the average bond rating of the iShares iBoxx $ Investment Grade Corporate Bond Fund is A, which means, more or less, that the bonds are issued by companies that are fairly solvent (although certainly not on a par with the U.S. government — yet, anyway). See the sidebar "Understanding bond ratings" if you wish to know more.

iBoxx $ Investment Grade Corporate Bond Fund (LQD)

Indexed to: The iBoxx $ Liquid Investment Grade Index — an index of bond issues sponsored by a chorus line of companies rated "investment grade" (which means highly unlikely to go bankrupt any time soon) or above. Technically, we're speaking of bonds rated BBB or better by S&P. About 600 bonds are typically used to create a representative sampling of this universe.

Expense ratio: 0.15 percent

Current yield: 3.99 percent

Average credit quality: A

Average weighted maturity: 11.8 years

Understanding bond ratings

In August 2011, the credit rating agency Standard & Poor's (S&P) downgraded U.S. Treasury bonds from the highest rating (AAA) to a smidgeon below (AA+). Other bond raters did not follow suit. Despite S&P's dramatic announcement, U.S. Treasury bonds are still considered by nearly all to be the safest bonds in the land because they are backed by the full faith and credit of the U.S. government. And even though that government has a huge debt, it does have the ability to raise taxes. Bonds issued by federal government agencies (such as the Government National Mortgage Association, commonly known as Ginnie Mae) are typically seen as one tiny step below Treasury bonds in terms of safety.

Bonds issued by corporations and municipalities (cities, counties, and their agencies) can vary in safety from quite high to very low, depending on the financial strength of the issuer. (Corporations tend to default more often than do municipalities.) The financial strength of the issuer is judged by credit rating agencies such as S&P and Moody's. Following are the most common ratings.

S&P Rating	Moody's Rating	Quality	What It Means
AAA	Aaa	Highest grade	Your money is safe; there's no risk of default.
AA	Aa	High grade	Your money is safe; there's almost no risk of default.
A	A	Medium grade	Your money is likely safe.
BBB	Baa	A little shaky	Your money is probably safe.
BB	Ba	Somewhat speculative	With a little luck, you'll get your money back.
B	B	Very speculative	With a lotta luck, you'll get your money back.
CCC	Caa	Possibly in default	Pray!
CC	Ca	Toilet paper	Pray harder!

Russell's review: Investment-grade corporate bonds have done a pretty good job of holding their own in bad times. You get a bit more return than you do with Treasurys of equal maturity, although unlike Treasurys, with corporate bonds you pay state taxes on the dividends. If your portfolio is large enough, you want LQD, as well as one of the conventional Treasury and inflation-adjusted Treasury ETFs. See how I include all three of these winners in the sample portfolios presented in Chapter 16.

Vanguard Short-Term Corporate Bond Index (VCSH)

Indexed to: The Barclays U.S. 1–5 Year Corporate Index, a pot of about 1,400 bonds from corporations that the raters think have little chance of going belly up

Expense ratio: 0.15 percent

Current yield: 1.76 percent

Average credit quality: A

Average weighted maturity: 3.0 years

Russell's review: In normal times, I would encourage most investors to stick with intermediate-term bonds and forget about short-term bonds that typically yield considerably less. However, when interest rates are as low as they have been in decades (as they are while I'm writing this chapter), I tend to lean my client portfolios more to the short-term. Reason: When interest rates rise, as eventually they will, longer-term bonds are going to get hit. For more conservative investors especially, VCSH, during times of very low interest rates, may warrant half your allocation to corporate bonds. When interest rates start to climb back up to more normal historical levels, you may then want to move some or all of the money in VCSH to LQD.

The whole shebang: Investing in the entire U.S. bond market

The broadest fixed income ETFs are all-around good bets, especially for more modest sized portfolios. Note that these bonds use a total bond market approach, which means about two-thirds government bonds and one-third corporate. These funds also make the most sense for investors with lots of room in their tax-advantaged retirement accounts. If you have to stick your bonds in a taxable account, you're probably better off separating your Treasury bonds and your corporate bonds. Reason: You get a tax break on Treasury bond interest, in that you do not have to pay state income tax. If, however, your Treasury bonds are buried in an aggregate fund, such as these, you have to pay state income tax on the interest. Dem's da rules.

Vanguard Total Bond Market (BND)

Indexed to: The Barclays Capital U.S. Aggregate Float Adjusted Index, which is made up of about 8,000 bonds, two-thirds of which are U.S. government bonds and one-third of which are higher quality corporate bonds. The average credit quality indicates that there is very little chance any of the bonds in the index will default. (Even if a few did, with about 8,000 holdings, the entire apple cart wouldn't turn over.)

Expense ratio: 0.11 percent

Current yield: 2.67 percent

Average credit quality: AA

Average weighted maturity: 7.4 years

Russell's review: How can you go wrong with the world's largest provider of index funds tracking the entire bond market for you and charging you only 0.11 percent (that's 11 percent of 1 percent)? BND makes an excellent building block in smaller portfolios or for any investor seeking the ultimate in simplicity, especially where there's lots of room in tax-advantaged accounts. For larger portfolios, however, where you can afford to mix and match other bond funds of different flavors, the need for BND becomes less clear.

iShares Barclays Aggregate Bond Fund (AGG)

Indexed to: The Barclays Capital U.S. Aggregate Bond Index, which tracks the performance of the total U.S. investment grade bond market, including both government bonds and the highest quality corporate bonds

Expense ratio: 0.20 percent

Current yield: 2.44 percent

Average credit quality: AA

Average weighted maturity: 6.9 years

Russell's review: AGG is a good fund, and I used it until BND came along. The two funds are awfully similar, but the Vanguard offering charges about half as much.

The ultimate in investment simplicity

Want *real* simple investing? Combine the Vanguard Total Bond Market ETF (BND) with the Vanguard Total Stock Market ETF (VTI) and the Vanguard FTSE All-World ex-US ETF (VEU). Presto! These three ETFs give you the whole enchilada — filled with virtually all of the world's stocks and bonds — at an incredibly low price.

Vanguard Short-Term Bond (BSV)

Indexed to: The Barclays Capital U.S.1–5 Year Government/Credit Float Adjusted Index, which is about 2,300 bonds, two-thirds of which are short-term U.S. government and one-third of which are higher quality corporate bonds, also of short-term maturity

Expense ratio: 0.11 percent

Current yield: 0.89 percent

Average credit quality: AA

Average weighted maturity: 2.7 years

Russell's review: In normal times, I encourage most investors to stick with intermediate-term bonds and forget about short-term bonds that typically yield considerably less. Recently, however, with interest rates so low, low, low, I've been leaning my client portfolios more to the short-term. Reason: When interest rates pop, as eventually they will, longer-term bonds are going to suffer. For more conservative investors especially, BSV may warrant half of your allocation to U.S. bonds. When interest rates start to climb back up to historical norms, you may then want to move some or all of your BSV assets to BND.

Moving Beyond Basics into Municipal and Foreign Bonds

Every investor needs bonds. Not every investor needs municipal bonds or foreign bonds. But for higher-income investors who find themselves in the northern tax zones, municipal bonds, which pay interest exempt from federal income tax (and possibly state income tax as well) can make enormous sense. For those with larger bond portfolios, the added diversification of foreign bonds is something to consider very seriously.

Municipals for mostly tax-free income

Historically, municipal bonds have yielded about 80 percent of what Treasury bonds of similar maturity yield. As I write these words, the two kinds of bonds have yielded about the same recently — mostly due to Treasurys paying less and less. But that's on a before-tax basis. After taxes, you do better with munis, even if you're in a low tax bracket. In a higher tax bracket, you do *much* better with munis . . . assuming the munis you buy don't default.

In fact, munis rarely do default. And the diversification offered by certain municipal ETFs makes any loss of principal due to defaults even less likely (but not impossible, by any means). Still, muni ETFs are more risky than Treasurys. You don't want your entire portfolio in munis.

To figure out the tax-equivalent yield on a muni or muni fund, you may want to visit one of the gazillion tax-equivalent yield calculators on the Internet. One of my faves is to be found on www.dinkytown.com. Click *Investments* in the column on the far left of your screen. Then click on *Municipal Bond Tax Equivalent Yield.* You'll figure it out from there.

Note that I'm about to highlight a few *national* muni ETFs — that is, funds that offer munis from across the land. If you live in a state with high income taxes, such as New York or California, and you're in a high tax bracket, you may want to investigate state-specific muni mutual funds; plenty of them are out there (try Vanguard, T. Rowe Price, and Fidelity). ETF purveyors iShares and SPDRs also offer a handful of state-specific ETFs. When you buy muni funds that are specific to your home state, you exempt yourself from having to pay state or federal income tax on the interest.

iShares S&P National Municipal Bond Fund (MUB)

Indexed to: The S&P National AMT-Free Municipal Bond Index, which includes investment-grade municipal bonds from all 50 states, as well as Puerto Rico and U.S territories such as Guam and the U.S. Virgin Islands. There are 8,500 constituent bonds in the index.

Expense ratio: 0.25 percent

Current yield: 2.97 percent

Average credit quality: AA

Average weighted maturity: 8.0 years

Russell's review: This fund is the best of the lot to date, with a reasonable expense ratio and excellent diversification. It is also free of the AMT (alternative minimum tax), which is a decidedly good thing if you derive a lot of income from tax-free sources.

SPDR Nuveen Barclays Capital Municipal Bond (TFI)

Indexed to: The Barclays Capital Municipal Managed Money Index, which features about 18,000 bonds from the Atlantic to the Pacific states and everything in between

Expense ratio: 0.30 percent

Current yield: 3.02

Average credit quality: AA

Average weighted maturity: 13.6

Russell's review: This fund is slightly more expensive than MUB, with a bit more volatility given the longer average maturity of the bonds. For example, in 2008 (a fairly bad year for municipal bonds), this fund earned a flat 0 percent versus 1.17 percent for MUB.

Foreign bonds for fixed-income diversification

Over the long haul, bonds of similar default risk and maturity will likely yield about the same percentage. But in the short run, substantial differences can exist in the yields and total returns of U.S. versus foreign bonds. The big difference is often due to currency exchange rates. If you are holding foreign bonds and the dollar drops *vis-à-vis* your foreign currencies, your foreign bond funds tend to do better. If the dollar rises, you'll likely be disappointed in your foreign bond fund returns.

If you follow my advice on the stock side of the portfolio and allocate roughly half your equities to overseas positions, you'll have plenty of exposure to foreign currencies. But still, if you have a fairly large portfolio and half or more of it is in bonds, allocating perhaps 10 to 25 percent of your bonds to overseas ETFs such as the ones I discuss next would enhance the benefits you can achieve from diversification. At the same time, you should understand that because of their exposure to foreign currencies, these bond funds tend to be more volatile than U.S. bond funds.

Note that as is the case with U.S. bonds, international bonds can be of the conventional type or inflation-adjusted. Whereas I believe strongly that U.S. inflation-protected bonds deserve an allotment in most portfolios, foreign inflation-protected bonds just don't make as much sense (unless you plan to retire abroad or take a lot of senior world cruises). Nevertheless, for the sake of added diversification, if you want to add a small dose of inflation-adjusted foreign bonds to your portfolio, I won't object.

As you can see in my recommendations, I have a preference for the iShares offerings in the foreign bond arena.

iShares S&P/Citigroup International Treasury Bond Fund (IGOV)

Indexed to: The S&P/Citigroup International Treasury Bond Index Ex-US, which holds about 100 bonds that, collectively, track the sovereign debt of developed foreign nations, mostly in Western Europe and Japan

Expense ratio: 0.35

Current yield: 3.3 percent

Average credit quality: AA

Average weighted maturity: 8.5 years

Top five countries: Japan, Italy, France, Germany, Netherlands

Russell's review: This may be your best option for one-shot foreign bond exposure. Be aware that about half of the fund's holdings are denominated in Euros. Your returns will therefore be very dependent on the Euro-Greenback exchange rate. (You want the Euro to fly.) This fund is very, very similar to the SPDR Barclays Capital International Treasury Bond (BWX), but BWX carries an expense ratio of 0.50 percent. Go with the iShares fund.

iShares International Inflation-Linked Bond Fund (ITIP)

Indexed to: The BofA Merrill Lynch Global ex-US Diversified Inflation-Linked Index, which compiles about 40 inflation-linked bonds of both developed and emerging-market nations

Expense ratio: 0.40 percent

Current yield: 1.2 percent + inflation bump

Average credit quality: AA

Average weighted maturity: 11.4 years

Top five countries: United Kingdom, France, Turkey, Israel, Brazil

Russell's review: This fund is awfully similar to the SPDR DB International Government Inflation-Protected Bond ETF (WIP), which carries an expense ratio of 0.50 percent. I therefore prefer the iShares brand for this category of bond, which I consider strictly optional for most portfolios.

Emerging-market bonds: High risk, high return

I don't like U.S. high-yield ("junk") bonds. They tend to be highly volatile, and they tend to move up and down with the stock market. In other words, they don't provide much of the diversification power or soft cushion that bonds are famous for. Foreign junk bonds are different. These bonds, issued by the governments of countries that may not be entirely stable, are just as volatile as bonds issued by unstable U.S. corporations, but they do not tend to go up and down with the U.S. stock market (although they certainly may at times . . . and did so in 2008).

For reasons of diversification, investors with fairly good sized portfolios may want to consider allocating a modest part of their portfolios to emerging-market debt. In my personal portfolio, I have allocated 5 percent of the total to this asset class. Note that I'm not referring to "my bond portfolio" but to my "portfolio." I actually think of my holdings in emerging-market debt as more of a stock-like investment than a true bond investment. After all, you're likely to see stock-like volatility and long-term stock-like returns with these investments.

Although these ETFs have been around for only a few years, emerging-market bond mutual funds have been in existence for much longer. The T. Rowe Price Emerging Markets Bond Fund (PREMX), for example, has a 15-year average annual return of 11.45 percent. But there has been volatility, for sure: In 2008, the fund lost nearly 18 percent of its value.

iShares JP Morgan USD Emerging Markets Bond Fund (EMB)

Indexed to: The JPMorgan EMBI Global Core Index, which is made up of about 80 bond issues, all U.S. dollar denominated, from various emerging-market nations

Expense ratio: 0.60

Current yield: 4.57 percent

Average credit quality: BBB

Average weighted maturity: 11.5 years

Top five countries: Russia, Brazil, Turkey, Philippines, Mexico

Russell's review: The expense ratio is a bit high for my liking, but there isn't a lot of choice in this arena. The iShares fund is a perfectly good way to tap into this asset class.

PowerShares Emerging Markets Sovereign Debt Portfolio (PCY)

Indexed to: The DB Emerging Market USD Liquid Balanced Index, which tracks the returns of approximately 22 emerging-market sovereign bonds

Expense ratio: 0.50

Current yield: 5.53 percent

Average credit quality: BB–BBB

Average weighted maturity: 14.7 years

Top five countries: Turkey, Columbia, Qatar, Bulgaria, Indonesia

Russell's review: This fund is slightly cheaper than the iShares emerging-market fund, and I like that. And I certainly like the higher yield. But the dicey mix of nations and lengthy average maturity also make this fund considerably more volatile. (Ah, that old risk and return thing again!) In 2008, this fund lost 18.79 percent; EMB, in contrast, lost 2.09 percent in that sorry year.

Determining the Optimal Fixed Income Allocation

Okay, now that I've discussed which bonds to buy, it's time to tackle the really tough question: How much of your portfolio should you allocate to (non-emerging-market) bonds? The common thinking on the subject — and I'm not above common thinking, especially when it is right on the mark — is that a portfolio becomes more conservative as its percentage allocation to bonds increases.

Of course, that doesn't answer the $64,000 question (or however much that question would now be worth with inflation factored in): Just how conservative do you want your portfolio to be? Different financial planners use different approaches to arrive at an answer to this question. I feel confident that my approach is best (otherwise I wouldn't use it); in the interest of brevity, let me present it in the simplest terms.

Here's my take: I reckon that stocks are very likely — but by no means certain — to outperform bonds over the next decade or two. But as in the past, we will see up years and down years in both markets. The down years in the stock market are the far more dangerous. Bear stock markets, historically, don't last for more than a few years, although some have been particularly brutal and have lasted a decade or more. (Think about the 1930s, the late 1960s to mid 1970s, and 2000 to 2009.)

Yet for most investors over the past 100 years, stocks have paid off handsomely. So it's a balancing act. Too much in the way of stocks and, should the markets go sour, you risk quick poverty. Too much in the way of bonds and, should consumer prices rise too much, you risk slow poverty as the interest you collect just barely stays ahead of inflation, or not even that, and you are forced to eat into your capital to pay the bills. In this section, I show you how to begin thinking about your own balancing act.

60/40? 50/50? Finding a split that makes sense

The balance between stocks and bonds is usually expressed as "[% stocks]/ [% bonds]," so a 60/40 portfolio means 60 percent stocks and 40 percent bonds. The optimal balance for any given person depends on many factors: age, size of portfolio, income stream, financial responsibilities, economic safety net, and emotional tolerance for risk.

In general, I like to see working investors hold three to six months of living expenses in cash (money markets or Internet savings accounts) or near-cash (very short-term bond funds or short-term CDs). Non-working investors living largely off their portfolios should set aside much more, perhaps one to two years of living expenses. Beyond that, most people's portfolios, whether they're working or not, should be allocated to stocks (including REITs, which I discuss in Chapter 13), intermediate-term bonds, and perhaps a few alternative investments, such as market-neutral funds and commodities (including precious metals).

In determining an optimal split, I would first ask you to pick a date when you think you may need to start withdrawing money from your nest egg. How much do you anticipate needing to withdraw? Maybe $30,000 a year? Or $40,000? If you haven't given this question much thought, please do! Start with your current job income. Subtract what you believe you'll be getting in Social Security payments or other pension income. The difference is what you would need to pull from your portfolio to replicate your current income. But most retirees find they need perhaps 80 to 90 percent of their working-days income to live comfortably. (You likely put less in the gas tank, buy fewer lunches out, have lower wardrobe expenses, and pay lower taxes.)

Take a minute, please. Come up with a rough number of how much you're going to need to take from your nest egg each year.

Got it?

Whatever the number, multiply it by 10. That amount, ideally, is what I'd like to see you have in your bond portfolio, at a minimum, on the day you retire. In other words, if you think you'll need to pull $30,000 a year from your portfolio, I'd like to see you have at least $30,000 in cash and about $300,000 ($30,000 × 10) in bonds. That's regardless of how much you have in stocks — and, with the assumptions outlined above, you should have at least an equal amount in stocks. (See more on building an adequate nest egg in Chapter 19.)

So here's the rough rule I'm suggesting (keeping in mind, please, that all rough rules can get you into trouble sometimes): If you are still in your 20s or 30s and want to keep the vast lion's share of your portfolio in stocks, fine. But as you get older and start to think about quitting your day job, begin to increase your bond allocation with the aim of getting to your retirement date with at least ten times your anticipated post-retirement withdrawals in bonds. Most people (who aren't rich) should have roughly one year's income in cash and the rest in a 50/50 (stock/bond) portfolio on retirement day.

With at least one year's living expenses in cash and ten years of living expenses in bonds, you can live off the non-stock side of your portfolio for a good amount of time if the stock market goes into a swoon. (You then hope that the stock market recovers.)

If my rule seems too complex, you can always go with an even rougher rule that has appeared in countless magazines. It says you should subtract your age from 110, and that's what you should have, more or less, in stocks, with the rest in bonds. So a 50-year-old should have (110 − 50) 60 percent in stocks and 40 percent in bonds. A 60-year-old would want a portfolio of about (110 − 60) 50 percent stocks and 50 percent bonds. And so on and so on. This rough rule — even rougher than mine! — may not be bad, assuming that you are of average wealth, are going to retire at the average age, will live the average life expectancy, and expect that the markets will see roughly average performance!

Meet Joe, age 67, with a little more than $600,000 in the bank

So let's consider Joe. He's a single guy with no kids who figures he's going to retire in one year. His salary is $45,000 a year ($35,000 after taxes). He has $600,000 in investments. He also has about $35,000 in cash and short-term CDs. He estimates that after Social Security and his very decent government pension, he needs to pull another $24,000 a year out of savings to pay all the bills. It seems to me that Joe can do that and have a very good chance that his money will last as long as he lives. (Chapter 19 explains why.) How much should Joe invest in bonds and how much in stocks?

As a ballpark figure, without knowing much more about Joe (and ignoring for the moment such sticky things as present value and future taxes and Joe's expected longevity), I'd start by urging Joe to keep the amount he has in cash and short-term CDs ("near cash") exactly where it is. Then I'd take about $240,000 ($24,000 × 10) of the $600,000 and plunk it into a handful of fixed income funds that would almost certainly include a conventional Treasury fund (such as the iShares Barclays 7–10 Year Treasury Bond Fund [IEF]); an inflation-protected bond fund (perhaps the iShares Barclays TIPS Bond Fund [TIP]); and a high-quality corporate bond fund (such as the iShares iBoxx $ Investment Grade Corporate Bond fund [LQD] or the Vanguard Short-Term Corporate Bond Index [VCSH]).

Depending on Joe's home state and his tax bracket (I didn't specify how much he'll be collecting in Social Security and pension benefits), I might also include some municipal bonds. The rest of Joe's money I would invest in a widely diversified portfolio made up mostly of stock ETFs.

Thus, Joe might be looking at an allocation of $360,000 stocks/$240,000 bonds, or a 60/40 allocation. Joe also might be a good candidate for an immediate fixed annuity that would guarantee him the $24,000 a year he needs, or a good portion of it. (***Important note:*** Many annuities are financial dogs, and even the best annuities aren't for everyone. Please see my discussion in Chapter 15.)

A 60/40 allocation might be considered too risky for a 67-year-old. Many retirement models would allocate more to the tune of 50/50 or even be less aggressive than that. I would opt for a more conservative route, too, if Joe didn't have his secure government pension. Note, too, that I would use 60/40 only as my starting point. After taking all aspects of Joe's personal circumstances into consideration, including his guaranteed income stream, expected longevity, risk tolerance, and legacy desires (would he be okay with the idea of dying broke?), I might end up suggesting a 50/50 portfolio or perhaps even 40/60.

Meet Betsy and Mike, age 36, with $30,000 in the bank

Betsy and Mike are happily married. (Yes, happy is important, both from a financial and non-financial point of view!) They both work and make decent incomes — enough so that if they needed to, they could live on one income. Betsy works in academia. Mike is a self-employed landscaper and a piano teacher. They have no children. They have no debt. They would like to retire by age 62 and do a lot of traveling.

Betsy and Mike obviously need to accumulate a lot more than $30,000 if they want to retire by their early 60s and travel to anyplace other than nearby Cincinnati. Their situation, I feel, warrants taking about as much risk as any investor should take. I might suggest a 75/25 portfolio or even (if Betsy and Mike were the type of people who could emotionally handle the volatility) an 80/20 portfolio. The 25 or 20 percent in bonds — $7,500 or $6,000 — I might allocate to the Vanguard Total Bond Market ETF (BND), provided they had room in their retirement plans.

I can hardly imagine any investor for whom I would want to see any portfolio more aggressive than 80/20 (80 percent stock, 20 percent bonds) or more sedate than 20/80. Here's why:

✔ Studies show that 20 percent in bonds doesn't really lessen a portfolio's long-term performance all that much. Reason: When the market crashes, as it does every once in a while, you want some "dry powder" (such as bonds) that you can use to take advantage of the opportunity to purchase stock at fire-sale prices.

✔ Conversely, 20 percent in stocks doesn't really raise a portfolio's volatility all that much (and it may even lessen the volatility). Reason: Bond prices tend to drop the most when interest rates rise sharply. Interest rates tend to rise sharply when the economy is humming and stocks are doing well. Zig and zag. When you have no zig, you are more susceptible to heavy zag. And you can quote me on that!

Chapter 13

Real Estate Investment Trusts (REITs): Becoming a Virtual Landlord

> *Why, land is the only thing in the world worth workin' for, worth fightin' for, worth dyin' for, because it's the only thing that lasts.*

— Spoken by the character Gerald O'Hara in Gone with the Wind

*S*carlett's father said those words long before the U.S. real estate crash at the onset of the 21st century. Unless you happen to have bought into real estate just prior to that crash, you've probably done quite well with any investments you've made in land.

The value of commercial real estate — just about anywhere in the nation — softened right along with the housing market. But again, unless you bought just prior to the decline that began its serious fall in 2006, any investment in commercial property has probably done well. In fact, if you happen to own some commercial property, perhaps through a real estate investment trust (REIT), you likely made out very well in more recent years after the dust from the crash had at least partially settled.

In a nutshell, *real estate investment trusts,* popularly known as *REITs* (rhymes with "beets"), are companies that hold portfolios of properties, such as shopping malls, office buildings, hotels, amusement parks, or timberland. Or they may hold certain real estate–related assets, such as commercial mortgages. More than 150 REITs in the United States are publicly held, and their stock trades on the open market just like any other stock.

Via dozens of mutual funds, you can buy into a collection of REITs at one time. Via about 30 or so ETFs, you can similarly buy a bevy of REITs. And that may not be a bad idea. For the 20 years that ended December 2010, the so-called Dow Jones U.S. Select REIT Index has enjoyed an average annual return of 9.5 percent. That outshines by a full percentage point per year the S&P 500's 8.5 percent return during the same period. In the last two years of that period, REITs really shined, with the index return clocking 28.5 percent in 2009 and 28.1 percent in 2010.

Some holders of REITs and REIT funds believe (and fervently hope) that such performance will continue. Others argue that the glory of REITs may already be gone with the wind. In this chapter, I provide you with several reasons (in addition to those offered by Scarlett's dad) why REITs deserve a permanent allocation in most portfolios.

Considering Five Distinguishing Characteristics of REITs

You may wonder why an entire chapter of this book is devoted to REIT ETFs. Why, you may ask, didn't I merely include them in Chapter 11 with the other specialized stock ETFs, like high dividend and socially responsible funds? Or in Chapter 10 where I talk about industry sector ETFs? Good question!

I have *five* reasons. Any one alone probably wouldn't justify giving REITs a chapter of their very own. All five together do, however. The first three reasons explain why REITs deserve some special status in the world of investments. The last two reasons are less compelling than the first three, but I include them in the interest of completeness.

Limited correlation to the broad markets

An index of U.S. REITs (similar to the Dow Jones U.S. Select REIT Index) has evidenced a correlation of 0.38 with the S&P 500 over the past 20 years. That means the price of an S&P 500 index fund and the share price of a REIT index fund have tended to move in the same direction considerably less than half the time. The REIT index has practically no correlation to bonds.

Holding 20 percent REITs in your portfolio over the past 20 years — regardless of whether your portfolio was made up of mostly stocks or bonds — would have both raised your returns and lowered your volatility. It's the Efficient Frontier (as I discuss in Chapter 4) in action.

Will REITs continue to work their magic? Their correlation with the broad market has been increasing; undoubtedly REITs are becoming somewhat the victims of their own success. As they have become more mainstream investments, they have come to act more like other equities. Years ago, practically no one held REITS in their portfolios. Nowadays, according to one recent poll, fully two-thirds of professional money managers are using them.

But as I write these words, and for the next few years, I believe we can expect continued positive returns and limited correlation — albeit on a lesser scale on both fronts. Therefore, REITs will still help to diversify a portfolio.

Unusually high dividends

REITs typically deliver annual dividend yields significantly higher than even the highest dividend-paying non-REIT stocks, and twice that of the average stock. (Many stocks, of course, pay no dividends.) At the time of this writing, the Vanguard Total Stock Market Index ETF (VTI) is producing a yield of 1.7 percent, versus 3.1 percent for the Vanguard REIT Index ETF (VNQ).

So the cash usually keeps flowing regardless of whether a particular REIT's share price rises or falls, just as long as the REIT is pulling in some money. That's because REITs, which get special tax status, are required by law to pay out 90 percent of their income as dividends to shareholders. Cool, huh?

Still, REITs, like other stocks, can be expected also to see growth in share prices. Since 1972, about one-third of the total return of REIT stocks has come from capital appreciation.

Different taxation of dividends

Because REITs are blessed in that they don't have to pay income taxes, their dividends are usually fully taxable to shareholders as ordinary income. In other words, whatever dividends you get will be taxed at year-end according to your income tax bracket. Few, if any, REIT dividends you receive will qualify for the special 15 percent dividend tax rate. For that reason, your accountant will undoubtedly urge you to handle your REITs a bit carefully. I urge you to do so, as well.

Special status among financial pros

The vast majority of wealth advisors — whether they primarily use style investing, sector investing, or astrology charts and tea leaves — recognize REITs as a separate asset class and tend to include it in most people's portfolios. Is that distinction logical and just? Yes, but . . . I've asked myself this question: If REITs deserve that distinction of honor, what about some other industry sectors, such as utilities and energy? After all, both utilities and energy have lately shown less correlation to the S&P 500 than have REITs. Don't they deserve their own slice of the portfolio pie?

I don't mean to slam REITs; I like REITs. But one possible reason they are seen as a separate asset class (in addition to the three reasons I explain in the previous sections) may be that the REIT marketers are savvier than the marketers of utility stocks (which, in addition to having low correlation to the broad market, *also* pay exceptionally high dividends).

Connection to tangible property

Some people argue that REITs are different than other stocks because they represent tangible property. Well yeah, REITs do represent stores filled with useless junk and condos filled with single people desperately looking for dates, and I suppose that makes them different from, say, stock in Microsoft or Procter & Gamble. (Isn't toothpaste tangible?) But the reality is that REITs are stocks. And to a great degree, they behave like stocks. If REITs are different than other stocks, dividends and lack of market correlation are the likely distinctions — not their tangibility.

Calculating a Proper REIT Allocation

You don't really need REITs for the income they provide. Some people have this notion that withdrawing dividends from savings is somehow okay but withdrawing principal is not. Don't make that mistake. The reality is that if you withdraw $100 from your account, it doesn't matter whether it came from cash dividends or the sale of stock.

If you need cash, you can always create your own "artificial dividend" by selling any security you like (preferably one that has appreciated). Not that I have anything against dividends — they're fine — but they shouldn't be your primary reason for purchasing REITs.

Your primary motivations for buying REITs should be diversification and potential growth. In the past, the diversification afforded by REITs has been significant, as has the growth. In this section, I help you consider how much of your portfolio you may want to allot to REITs.

Judging from the past

If we could go back in time 20 years, I'd have you put, heck, *everything* in Apple. But REITs would not have been a bad option either. After all, they've done fabulously well, beating the S&P 500 and most other investments. Looking forward, of course, the picture's a bit less clear. However, I think we can presume fairly safely that REITs will continue to move in somewhat different cycles than other stocks.

Your residence, your portfolio

If you bought your home for, say, $130,000 some 26 years ago, and that home is now worth $1.3 million, I say "Congratulations!" (Yeah, even though it may have been worth $1.8 million in 2005.) But don't let that bounty affect your portfolio decisions very much. After all, you'll always need a place to live. Sell the house today, and you'll presumably need to buy another (made of a similarly overpriced bundle of tiles and plywood).

Of course, someday you may downsize, and at that time you will be able to allot part of the value of your home to your portfolio. For that reason, and that reason alone, you may want to consider that the value of domestic real estate and the value of commercial real estate, while two different animals, are related. If your home represents a big chunk of your net worth, and especially if you are approaching a stage in life when you may consider downsizing, you may want to invest less in REITs than would, say, a renter of similar means. Or you may forget about U.S. REITs altogether and invest only in foreign REITs.

I think we can also presume fairly safely that REITs will continue to produce healthy gains, although people who poured money into them *after* REITs beat the broad stock market so soundly in 2010 will probably be disappointed. You will *not* see annual gains of 28+ percent a year for years to come — I'm sure of that. And you *will* see some bad years, such as 2008, when the collective REIT market fell by 39.2 percent.

Putting all the factors together, I suggest that most investors devote 15 to 20 percent of the equity side of their portfolios to REITs. If your portfolio is 50 percent stock and 50 percent bonds, I might suggest that 7.5 to 10 percent of your entire portfolio be devoted to REITs.

What if, like many people, you're a homeowner whose home represents most of your net worth? You may want to play it a little light on the REITs, but don't let the value of your home affect your portfolio decisions to any great degree. (See the sidebar "Your residence, your portfolio.")

Splitting the baby: Domestic and international REIT funds

International REITs are worth breaking out of your international stock holdings for all the same reasons that U.S. REITs are worth having tucked into a larger portfolio of U.S. stocks. The REIT allotment you give to your portfolio might be evenly split between U.S. and international REITs, in keeping with the 50/50 split between U.S. and non-U.S. stocks that I suggest for your overall portfolio.

As I discuss in Chapter 9, about 65 percent of the world's stocks are non-U.S.; in my mind, it stands to reason that an optimally diversified portfolio will have good exposure to foreign stocks. If you follow my advice, you might have two REIT funds, and each might be given a 4 to 5 percent allocation in your portfolio. If you have a very handsome portfolio ($500,000+), and *only* if you have such a portfolio, you may also want to consider one or two individual timber REITs, which can sometimes zig when other REITs zag.

Lumber over to Chapter 15, where I discuss how to work non-ETFs into your portfolio, and you'll get all the specifics.

Picking REIT ETFs for Your Portfolio

If you want REITs in your portfolio, you won't get a whole lot of them unless you purchase a REIT fund. For all the room they take up, REITs simply don't make up that large a segment of the economy.

If, for example, you were to buy an S&P 500 index fund, only about 1 percent of that fund would be made up of stock from REITs. If you were to buy an S&P mid cap index fund (most REITs would probably qualify as mid caps), you would still be holding an investment that's only about 4 percent REITs.

So if you want the diversification power of this special asset class, you need to go out of your way to get it. But thanks to ETFs, doing so shouldn't be much of a hassle, and you get many of ETFs' other benefits in the bargain, including rock-bottom expenses.

The tax efficiency of ETFs will help cap any capital gains you enjoy on your REIT fund, but it can't do anything to diminish the taxes you'll owe on the dividends. For that reason, all REIT funds — ETFs or otherwise — are best kept in tax-advantaged retirement accounts, such as your IRA or Roth IRA.

Although more than 30 REIT ETFs are currently available to U.S. investors, a handful really stand out for their low costs and reasonable indexes. In fact, making the selection shouldn't be all that hard.

If you're curious to see the whole buffet of REIT ETFs available, visit www. reit.com; click on "Individual Investor," then "List of REIT Funds," and finally "Exchange-Traded Funds." You'll notice that some are leveraged (such as ProShares Ultra Real Estate [URE]), and I'd rather you stay away from the leveraged ETFs for reasons I discuss in Chapter 11. Others are focused on slivers of the REIT market (such as the iShares FTSE NAREIT Industrial/Office Capped Index Fund [FIO]), and I'd rather you steer clear of those, too. (You can slice and dice a portfolio to death, but why do so?) Of what's left, several are quite good. I outline the best of the best below.

U.S. domestic REIT ETFs

The two funds I recommend here are strikingly similar, and either one fits the bill nicely when it comes to investing in the U.S. REIT market.

Vanguard REIT Index ETF (VNQ)

Indexed to: The MSCI U.S. REIT index, which tracks roughly two-thirds of the U.S. REIT market

Expense ratio: 0.12 percent

Number of holdings: 108

Top five holdings: Simon Property Group, Equity Residential, Public Storage, Vornado Realty Trust, Boston Properties

Russell's review: Once again, Vanguard brings to market the most economical investment vehicle. You can't find a better way to invest in the U.S. REIT market than through VNQ. This is a broadly based ETF with an ultra-low expense ratio. Be aware, however, that even with all the advantages of an ETF and the considerable tax-minimizing prowess of Vanguard, this ETF will represent something of a tax burden. For that reason, I recommend that you consider purchasing an ETF as a long-term investment and keeping it in a tax-advantaged retirement account. Like all Vanguard ETFs, this fund trades free of commissions if held in a Vanguard account.

Focus Morningstar Real Estate ETF (FRL)

Indexed to: The Morningstar Real Estate Index, which tracks the market for publicly traded U.S. REITs

Expense ratio: 0.12

Number of holdings: 85

Top five holdings: Simon Property Group, Equity Residential, Vornado Realty Trust, Public Storage, Boston Properties

Russell's review: Focus Morningstar ETFs from FocusShares are the creation of Morningstar and Scottrade. All FocusShares ETFs trade free of commission at Scottrade. Given the similarly in construction to Vanguard's VNQ and the identical expense ratio, this fund could be a viable substitute if for any reason you'd want to use FocusShares instead of Vanguard (such as if you have an account at Scottrade). Vanguard VNQ and FocusShares FRL are both about half the price of any other REIT ETF on the market.

Global REIT funds

If you follow my advice and split your REIT allocation between U.S. and international funds, the next two ETFs come in quite handy. The first fund, VNQI, invests only in markets outside the United States and pairs quite nicely with VNQ in any portfolio. The second fund, RWO, is divided between U.S. and non-U.S. REITs, so it provides one-stop shopping for REIT investments (although at a higher cost than you'd pay for the Vanguard options).

Vanguard Global ex-U.S. Real Estate ETF (VNQI)

Indexed to: The S&P Global ex-U.S. Property Index, which tracks the performance of REITs in both developed and emerging markets outside of the United States

Expense ratio: 0.35 percent

Number of holdings: 424

Top five holdings: Sun Hung Kai Properties, Mitsubishi Estate Company, Cheung Kong Holdings, Unibail-Rodamco, Westfield Group

Top five countries: Hong Kong, Japan, Australia, United Kingdom, Singapore

Russell's review: Go for it. There is no less expensive way to tap into this asset class. This fund trades free if held at Vanguard, and it makes a very nice companion fund to VNQ. Do take note that foreign REITs, like all foreign stocks, are going to be subject to currency flux as well as market volatility. In other words, expect a bit more of a rollercoaster ride with this and all foreign ETFs than you would expect of domestic ETFs.

SPDR Dow Jones Global Real Estate (RWO)

Indexed to: The Dow Jones Global Real Estate Securities Index, an index based on the publicly traded real estate market in both developed and emerging-market nations

Expense ratio: 0.50 percent

Number of holdings: 216

Top five holdings: Simon Property Group, Westfield Group, Unibail-Rodamco, Brookfield Asset Management, Equity Residential

Top five countries: United States (50 percent of the fund), Australia, Japan, United Kingdom, Hong Kong

Russell's review: If you have a smaller portfolio, or if you lust for simplicity, go with this perfectly fine ETF. But for most folks, I suggest that you instead combine the Vanguard domestic REIT ETF (VNQ) with the international REIT fund (VNQI). You'll wind up with pretty much the same mix of REITs, but you'll be spending less than half as much on management expenses.

Chapter 14

All That Glitters: Gold, Silver, and Other Commodities

*O*ne of my childhood passions was collecting coins from around the world. Sometime during the Johnson administration, on my meager allowance of $1 a week, I saved up for three months or so to buy myself a gold coin: an uncirculated 1923 50-kurush piece from Turkey. Maybe you can remember getting a shiny new bicycle for Christmas when you were 5 or 6. Maybe, like Citizen Kane, you remember getting your first sled. My most prized possession from childhood was that gold coin, smaller than a dime but absolutely gorgeous.

I still have it.

I never thought of my piece of gold as an investment. But for many people, gold is just that. Historically, the soft and shiny metal has been seen as the ultimate hedge against both inflation and market turmoil. Most people through the ages have bought gold just as I did: as coins, or sometimes in bricks. Alternatively, in more recent decades, they may have invested in shares of gold-mining companies.

Whether people invested in the physical metal or the stock of companies that mined it, the traditional ways of investing in gold have always been a pain in the neck. With shares of gold-mining companies, factors other than the price of gold come into play. For example, political turbulence in South Africa, or a fall in the value of the Rand, might send your stock down the mines. Buying gold coins entails hefty commissions. Likewise for gold bricks, with possible added expenses for assaying. And both bricks and coins have to be stored and should be insured.

All these hassles became optional for gold investors with the introduction of the first gold ETF in November 2004. Suddenly it became possible to buy gold at its spot price — in an instant — with very little commission and no need to fret about storage or insurance. Thanks to ETFs, you can now also buy silver in the same way. Or platinum.

In fact, you can invest in just about any commodity you please. You can invest in just about any precious or industrial metal: tin, nickel, you name it. Even natural gas, or crude oil, if that's your cup of Texas tea, can be purchased (sort of) with an ETF, as can coffee futures and contracts on wheat, sugar, or corn. Indeed, it seems the only commodity that's not available for purchase by the retail investor is weapons-grade plutonium.

In this chapter, I discuss the whys and wherefores of investing in commodity ETFs, as well as certain commodity pools and exchange-traded notes (products that differ from ETFs). I also explain why investing in ETFs that feature stocks of commodity-producing companies and countries may be a somewhat better long-term play than investing in the commodities themselves.

Oh, by the way, I recently saw that a 50-kurush gold coin just like mine sold online for $219. *But I'm not selling mine!*

Gold, Gold, Gold!

Stocks and bonds rise and fall. Currencies ebb and flow. Economies go boom and then bust. Inflation tears nest eggs apart. And through it all, gold retains its value. Or so we're told.

The primary reason for buying gold, according to the World Gold Council (www.gold.org), is that

> *Market cycles come and go, but gold has maintained its long term value. Jastram [1977] demonstrated that in inflationary and deflationary times, in the very long term, gold kept its purchasing power. The value of gold, in terms of real goods and services that it can buy, has remained remarkably stable.*

Hmm. I'm not sure who Jastram was, and I don't know exactly what is meant by "very long term," but I've done a bit of research on this subject. Although I don't claim that my research is exhaustive or in any way conclusive regarding the investment merits of gold, it does cast *some* doubt on the veracity of the World Gold Council's claim.

Table 14-1 shows the price of gold in a sampling of years between 1980 and 2010; the average price of a basic Hershey chocolate bar in those years (which I found on a website called `www.foodtimeline.org`); and how many Hershey bars you could buy with an ounce of gold. Note that one ounce of gold in 1980 bought 2,460 Hershey bars, while 20 years later, in 2000, it bought a mere 558 bars. At 2010 prices — about $1,500 for an ounce of gold and about 80 cents for a Hershey bar — you'd get 1,875 chocolate bars for the same nugget.

Table 14-1	Trading Gold for Hershey Bars		
Year	*Average price of a Hershey bar*	*Average price of an ounce of gold*	*Hershey bars per ounce of gold*
1980	$0.25	$615	2,460
2000	$0.50	$279	558
2010	$0.80	$1,500	1,875

Midas touch or fool's gold?

Okay, let's give the World Gold Council the benefit of the doubt and assume that gold, in the very long term, does maintain its purchasing power. Maybe Hershey bars are an anomaly. Maybe the years 2000 and 2010 were anomalies. Still, you would hope that your investments would do better than merely keep their purchasing power. If that is all gold can do, why hold it as an investment? (After all, it is an unproductive lump of metal, so what should you really expect?)

Well, if you type "gold" into your favorite search engine, you'll find 10,000 vendors selling it and 10,000 reasons, according to those vendors, why *now* is the time to buy. (Um, excuse me, sirs, but if the price of gold "can only go up," why are you trying so hard to sell it?) Every day I hear one explanation or another as to why gold "must" go up from here on (India's demand for gold . . . dentists' demand for gold . . . the mines are drying up . . . gold demand in the tech industry . . . and so on and so on). These are the very same arguments I've been hearing for years. Only now there's one more: All these ETF investors are demanding gold!

I believe that the best you can expect from gold over the very long term, as the World Gold Council puts it, is that it will maintain its purchasing power. But, hey, that's not a bad thing when every other investment is tanking. Gold, as it happens, does show little long-term correlation to other assets. And when the going gets really tough — or even seems that way — when people run from most investments, they often turn to gold. Then, as a self-fulfilling prophecy, the price rises. Indeed, that seems like a plausible explanation for gold's run-up in the years following 9/11, when we've seen wars in Iraq and Afghanistan, mounting federal deficits and debt, a financial crisis, and growing doubts about the true value of paper currencies.

In the final analysis, it probably wouldn't hurt you to hold gold in your portfolio. But please don't buy the nonsense that gold "must go up." It will go up. It will go down. It will go up again. Have a ball. Just don't bank your retirement on it, okay? (Personally, I don't own shares in a gold ETF, but I haven't ruled it out.)

If you allot a small percentage of your portfolio to gold — no more than, say, 5 percent please (actually make that 5 percent *total* precious metals) — and keep that percentage constant, you'll likely eek out a few dollars over time. Every year, if the price of gold falls, you might buy a bit; if the price rises, perhaps you sell. That strategy is called *rebalancing,* and I recommend it for all your portfolio allocations. (See my discussion of yearly portfolio rebalancing in Chapter 18.)

And if all goes to hell in a hand basket, your gold may offer you some protection.

A vastly improved way to buy the precious metal

When, in November 2004, State Street Global Advisors introduced the first gold ETF, it was a truly revolutionary moment. You buy a share just as you would buy a share of any other security, and each share gives you an ownership interest in one-tenth of an ounce of gold held by the fund. Yes, the gold is actually held in various bank vaults. You can even see pictures of one such vault filled to near capacity (very cool!) on www.spdrgoldshares.com.

If you are going to buy gold, this is far and away the easiest and most sensible way to do it.

You currently have several ETF options for buying gold. Two that would work just fine include the original from State Street — the **SPDR Gold Shares (GLD)** — and a second from iShares introduced months later — the **iShares Gold Trust (IAU).** Both funds are essentially the same. Flip a coin (gold or other), but then go with the iShares fund, simply because it costs less: 0.25 percent versus 0.40 percent.

The tax man cometh

Strange as it seems, the Internal Revenue Service considers gold to be a collectible for tax purposes. A share of a gold ETF is considered the same as, say, a gold Turkish coin from 1923 (don't ask). So what, you ask? As it happens, the long-term capital gains tax rate on collectibles is 28 percent and not the more favorable 15 percent afforded to capital gains on stocks.

Holding the ETF should be no problem from a tax standpoint (gold certainly won't pay dividends), but when you sell, you could get hit hard on any gains. Gold ETFs, therefore, are best kept in tax-advantaged accounts, such as your IRA. (Note that this advice won't serve you well if gold prices tumble and you sell. In that event, you'd rather have held the ETF in a taxable account so that you could write off the capital loss. Life is complicated, isn't it?)

Silver: The Second Metal

Talk about a silver bullet. In early 2006, after years of lackluster performance, the price of silver suddenly, within three short months, shot up 67 percent. Why? Largely, the move served as testimony to the growing power of ETFs!

The price jump anticipated the introduction of the **iShares Silver Trust (SLV)** ETF in April 2006. SLV operates much the same as the iShares COMEX Gold Trust (IAU). When you buy a share of SLV, you obtain virtual ownership of 10 ounces of silver.

To be able to convey that ownership interest, iShares had to buy many ounces of silver (initially 1.5 million), and that pending demand caused the silver market to bubble and fizz. Within several weeks after the introduction of the ETF, the price of silver continued to rise, reaching a 23-year high in May 2006 ($14.69 an ounce) before tumbling in the following weeks. The volatility has continued to this day as the price has darted above and below $40 an ounce.

Quick silver on the move

To say that silver is volatile is a gross understatement. In 1979, the price of an ounce of silver was about $5. It then rose tenfold in less than a year — to as high as $54 an ounce in 1980 — after the infamous Hunt brothers had cornered the silver market (until they were caught, because, y'know, it's illegal to corner the market in just about anything). The price then fell again. Hard.

Fast forward to April 2011. The price of silver, having risen steadily and sharply since the introduction of the first silver ETF, had topped $48 an ounce and seemed headed back to the highs of 1980. And then . . . pop! Within a mere several days, the price fell about 30 percent to slightly under $34. Then it rose back up in the following months to $42, and then, in September 2011 . . . pop! In a mere two days, it fell back down to $30.

If there is any reason to stomach such volatility, it stems from the fact that silver has a very low correlation to other investments. For the three years prior to my writing these words, the price of silver has had very, very little correlation to stocks (except for some modest correlation to the stocks of silver-producing countries, such as Chile); almost no correlation to bonds; and even a decidedly limited correlation (0.75) to the price of gold.

If you must . . .

If you're going to take a position in silver, the iShares ETF is the way to go. The expense ratio of 0.50 percent will eat into your profits or magnify your losses, but it will still likely be cheaper than paying a commission to buy silver bars or coins and then paying for a good-sized lockbox.

In the very long run, I don't think you're likely to do as well with silver as you would with either stocks or bonds. Note, however, that unlike gold, silver has many industrial uses. Demand for silver can come from diverse sources — not just jewelers and collectors — which can cause the metal's price to fluctuate with changing expectations for industrial production. Because the uses for silver effectively "consume" the metal, the laws of supply and demand may influence the future prospects of silver prices in a way that doesn't apply to gold. In the end, silver may prove useful as a hedge, maybe even better than gold. But I would urge you to invest very modestly; no more than 5 percent of your portfolio should be allocated to precious metals. Keep in mind that the same strange tax law pertains to silver as to gold. Any capital gains will be taxed at the "collectibles" rate of 28 percent. You may want to keep your silver shares in a tax-advantaged account.

All-in-one ETF for precious metals

One simple approach to precious-metals investing is worth considering: the ETFS Physical Precious Metals Basket Shares (GLTR), an ETF that was introduced in October 2010. In one fund, you get a basket of four precious metals: gold, silver, platinum, and palladium, each in proportion to its economic footprint. Shares are backed up by the physical metals held in vaults. The fund's cost is 0.60 percent a year.

Oil and Gas: Truly Volatile Commodities

The **United States Oil Fund (USO)** opened on the American Stock Exchange on April 10, 2006. Even though the fund is technically not an ETF but a very close cousin called a *commodity pool,* in my mind that date marks a sort of end to the Age of Innocence for ETFs. The United States Oil Fund, as official as that sounds, is run by a group called Victoria Bay Asset Management, which I will turn to in just a moment.

Don't mistake this fund for something like the Vanguard Energy ETF (VDE) or the Energy Select Sector SPDR (XLE) funds (see Chapter 10), both of which invest in oil companies like Exxon Mobil Corp. and Chevron. Don't mistake this fund for something like the precious metal commodity funds discussed in the preceding sections. Victoria Bay, wherever that is, is not filled with oil. Whereas Barclays and State Street maintain vaults filled with gold and silver, Victoria Bay deals in paper: futures contracts, to be exact.

In other words, this company uses your money to speculate on tomorrow's price of oil. If the price of oil rises in the next several weeks, you should, theoretically, earn a profit commensurate with that rise, minus the fund's costs of trading and its expense ratio of 0.75 percent. When the price of oil and gas go on a tear, this fund promises to give you a piece of that action, perhaps offering warm comfort every time you pull up to the pump and have to yank out your credit card. So should you pump your money into USO? Keep reading for my opinion about this slick investment.

Oily business

If you buy into USO and the price of oil escalates, you stand to make money. But is there reason to believe that the price of oil will always (or even usually) escalate? It has certainly gone up and down over the years, as have oil futures.

The famed economist John Maynard Keynes in 1930 theorized that commodity futures, over time, will offer compensation above and beyond any rise in the price of a commodity. He speculated that speculators will somehow be rewarded for taking the risk of future price uncertainty. Keynes's theory was very controversial for very many years, and in the past few years it has come to look as if Keynes was wrong. Of course, he didn't know that so many investors, largely thanks to ETFs such as USO, were going to pile into the commodity-futures arena. Such piling on has resulted in some ugly discrepancies between commodity future prices and the price of the actual commodity.

But even if Keynes were right, and even if the futures market more accurately tracked the price of the actual commodity (AKA the "spot price"), why pick a single commodity to invest in? Why not diversify your risks with a variety of commodities? A good number of ETFs attempt to do that, and more are on the way. (I discuss these options next in this chapter.) I equate the arrival of USO with the end of ETFs' Age of Innocence because as I see things, USO is clearly pandering to people's disgust over high oil and gas prices.

No experience necessary

The issuer of the USO fund is not a major investment bank. Victoria Bay Asset Management, LLC is "a wholly-owned subsidiary of Wainwright Holdings, Inc., a Delaware Corporation . . . that also owns an insurance company organized under Bermuda law." The fund's prospectus, especially the part about the management of Victoria Bay, makes for *very* interesting reading.

Two of the top people running the fund also manage a mutual fund called Ameristock, and a third, Malcolm R. Fobes III (no relation to Malcolm Forbes), is the founder of the Berkshire Focus Fund (no relation to the fabulously successful Berkshire Hathaway.) Both Ameristock and Berkshire Focus (both with Morningstar one-star ratings) have track records that would make most people cringe.

But the part of the prospectus that really raises an eyebrow is where it explains that "the managing and directing of day-to-day activities and affairs [of the fund] relies heavily on . . . Mr. John Love," who, we later learn, is not only employed by Ameristock but also "holds a BFA in cinema-television from the University of Southern California. Mr. Love does not have any experience running a commodity pool." His experience: "from December 2000 to February 2001, Mr. Love was employed by Digital Boardwalk, Inc."

Even if John Maynard Keynes were right, no one running this fund seems nearly as smart as J.M. Keynes — or Jed Clampett. I would not invest in this fund, and neither should you.

The sad saga of contango

As fate would have it, the promise of the United States Oil Fund has turned out to be nothing like the reality. Consider this: The price of an actual barrel of oil rose from about $40 in January 2009 to nearly $100 in June 2011. In the same time period, USO's share price went from about $35 to $38 — not much of an increase.

That meager return, however, might be considered pure gravy compared to the return suffered by investors in Victoria Bay's United States Natural Gas Fund (UNG) introduced on April 18, 2007. Through mid-2011, this fund's share price, which started at about $90 a share, had fallen to — are you ready? — roughly $11 a share. Investors in UNG have had anything but a gas.

The explanation for USO's stagnant share price and UNG's sink-like-a-rock share price can be found not only in the lackluster résumés of their managers and the dynamics of supply and demand for natural gas but also in something called *contango.* That's a word that nearly all investors in commodity ETFs, at least those that rely on futures contracts, wish to heck they never heard.

Contango refers to a situation where distant futures prices for a particular commodity start to run well ahead of near futures prices. In other words, if you want to maintain a futures position that looks one month out, you buy futures contracts for the next month that expire in 30 days. Then one month later you replace them with contracts that contango has made more expensive. The effect is sort of like holding a fistful of sand and watching the sand sift through your fingers until you are left with nothing but an empty hand.

The actual price of natural gas, for example, dropped precipitously in the several years prior to this writing because new gas drilling technologies and the discovery of new reserves have increased supply beyond demand. But buyers of UNG were not tapping into these falling prices each month. Instead, they were buying future contracts each month that were more expensive than the futures contracts they replaced. Why? The explanation is complicated, but the buying pressure coming from investors themselves helped to fuel the inflated futures' prices. On top of that, speculators, knowing that funds such as UNG had to buy additional futures contracts as the old ones expired, started to front-run the purchases and drove prices higher yet.

As a result of contango, many commodity investors have lost money, and some have lost lots of money, in recent years — even in cases where, as with oil, the price of the commodity itself rose. The illustrious managers at Victoria Bay led their investors to slaughter. But more experienced managers were also caught with their trousers down.

For you, the ETF investor, I would advise much caution before investing in commodities, especially in funds that use futures and other derivatives.

Taxing your tax advisor

ETFs that use futures typically generate special tax forms called *K-1 forms.* If you ask anyone who has ever filed a tax return and needed to account for earnings from K-1 investments, he'll tell you that these forms are a pain in the butt. Not only have investors in UNG been stung by falling share prices, but also they often have found that they were paying their tax advisors considerably more than in previous years, simply to file the dastardly K-1s.

As if that weren't bad enough, any gains on the sale of funds that use futures are taxed largely at short-term capital gains rates, even if the funds were held for more than a year — just another one of those IRS quirks. (Granted, not many people have had this problem recently because gains are hard to come by with these funds.)

(Somewhat) Safer Commodity Plays

Just as diversification works to dampen the risks of stock investing, it can similarly smooth out — to a degree — the ups and downs of investing in commodities. If you're willing to accept contango, the K-1 forms, and the natural volatility of most commodities (other than perhaps clay or granite), I urge you at least to diversify. In this section, I show you how to do so.

If you can handle the volatility but are put off by contango and K-1 forms, consider one of the alternative commodity plays I discuss in the final section of this chapter.

General commodity index funds

In this section, I tell you about three funds that allow you to tap into a broad spectrum of commodities. I begin with a commodity pool offered by PowerShares and then discuss two exchange-traded notes issued by Barclays.

PowerShares DB Commodity Index Tracking Fund (DBC)

Make no mistake, the DBC fund, issued in February 2006, is one volatile investment. (It lost about 32 percent in 2008; is that volatile enough for you?) Not a true ETF, this fund (like USO) is a *commodity pool* that deals in commodities futures.

Unlike USO, or the gold and silver ETFs, the PowerShares offering has a bit of diversity to protect you if one commodity suddenly heads south. That diversity, alas, is limited. The fund entails 14 commodity classes, but the top five are all energy-related: light oil (12.4 percent); heating oil (12.4 percent); Brent crude (12.4 percent); gasoline (12.4 percent); and natural gas (5.5 percent). That adds up to about 55 percent. The remaining 45 percent is allocated to various metals and agricultural products.

DBC's expense ratio — 0.85 percent — is close to outrageous by ETF standards (and mine), but cheap is hard to find in this category. I like the idea of a general commodity fund, but I'm not wild about DBC.

iPath commodity ETNs

In June 2006, Barclays issued two funds that may offer better options for investing directly in commodities . . . or, more specifically, investing in a diversified mix of commodities using futures. They are the **iPath S&P GSCI Total Return Index ETN (GSP)** and the **iPath Dow Jones-USB Commodity Index Total Return ETN (DJP).**

These offerings are *exchange-traded notes* (ETNs) and are very different from iShares ETFs. (Note that the iShares ETFs were originally a product of Barclays and were then purchased by BlackRock, Inc. Barclays held onto its lineup of ETNs.) ETNs are actually debt instruments, more like bonds than anything else. By buying them, you are lending Barclays your money, and you are counting on Barclays to give it back. (If Barclays were to go under, you lose.) That's not the case with iShares or any other ETF, where the ETF provider is acting more as a custodian of your funds than anything else. ETNs are becoming more popular, and I talk more about them in Chapter 15.

Barclays is rated a stable company (AA- by S&P; AA3 by Moody's), so I wouldn't worry too much about its going under (although anything is possible, of course). Your bigger worry is the future direction of commodity prices. Barclays promises to use "any tool necessary" to use your money to track commodity prices. Presumably, it works something like the PowerShares fund in that it uses primarily futures contracts. But Barclays won't say. ETNs are not transparent like ETFs, so you don't know exactly what you're holding.

Why do I like these funds more than the PowerShares fund? It's not because of the expense ratio. At 0.75 percent, the Barclays funds are only a tad less expensive. Here are the three reasons I prefer the Barclays funds:

- ✔ I have faith in the company, which is huge, well-managed, and profitable.

- ✔ The Barclays funds, by promising to curtail capital gains and dividends, are likely much more tax efficient than the PowerShares fund.

- ✔ The Barclays ETNs offer somewhat better diversification. Both ETNs invest in a number of commodities, from oil and natural gas to gold and silver to cocoa and coffee.

Of the two Barclays funds, I prefer the DJP for its well-established index and the balanced weightings of its holdings: energy (34 percent), livestock (6 percent), precious metals (15 percent), industrial metals (17 percent), and agriculture (28 percent). Still, even when diversified, commodities are volatile, and their long-term returns are not as well-established as the long-term returns on stocks and bonds.

If you buy into a Barclays ETN, you should do so for the right reason: lack of correlation to your other investments. Both of the iPath funds have shown almost no correlation to either stocks or bonds. For more information on these funds, Barclays has a special website: www.ipathetn.com.

As with precious metals funds, devoting 5 percent of your portfolio to either of the iPath funds would be plenty. No more than that, please. Oh, one little caveat: The IRS not long ago changed its ruling on certain ETNs, making them much less tax efficient. I talk about this situation in Chapter 15. At the moment, the ruling does not pertain to commodity ETNs, but someday it may. If you're not going to stash them in a tax-advantaged retirement account, you could be in for an unpleasant surprise . . . you just never know.

Actively managed, or quasi-actively managed, commodity funds

In Chapter 15, I discuss actively managed funds and whether and how to work non-ETFs into your portfolio. Given all the challenges with investing in commodities by using exchange-traded vehicles, as discussed so far in this chapter, I'm inclined to believe that active management may be just the place to go if you want to invest in commodities. (And, by the way, you don't need to do so; you can invest indirectly in commodities in ways that may make more sense. More on that topic in just a moment.)

If you want direct commodity exposure, consider that a number of the newest ETFs and ETNs are promising to deal with some of the problems of the first-generation commodity funds. The leader in this brigade is iPath, which in April 2011 introduced a new lineup of ETNs called *Pure Beta* indexes. I wouldn't quite call these funds actively managed, but they aren't quite passively run, either. The Pure Beta ETNs promise to "mitigate the effects of certain distortions in the commodity markets" (this language refers to contango) by rolling over futures contracts in an allegedly more intelligent manner (less mechanically) than the older commodity funds that used futures.

It's too soon to say whether Barclays' strategy will prove successful, but I'm keeping my eye on the **iPath Pure Beta Broad Commodity ETN (BCM),** which uses this newfangled strategy to track a basket of commodities consisting of energy (37 percent), agricultural products (24 percent), precious metals (20 percent), industrial metals (16 percent), and livestock (2.5 percent). The management fee is 0.75 percent. I'm ignoring the rest of the Barclays' Beta lineup that allows you to speculate on individual commodities, such as lead, nickel, and aluminum. (The ticker for that last fund is FOIL — cute, eh?)

Another ETN worth considering for commodity exposure is the **ELEMENTS S&P CTI ETN (LSC).** This fund tracks the S&P Commodity Trends Indicator–Total Return index. The fund tracks 16 different commodities, using futures contracts. Unlike Barclays' funds, LSC uses a momentum strategy, buying "long" those commodities rising in price and selling "short" those commodities falling in price.

Backtesting of the index showed that this strategy, known as a managed futures strategy, has been successful for investing in commodities. (Of course, backtested strategies are notorious for performing less well in real time than their hypothetical numbers suggest.) The fund was born in October 2008, and although I feel that the strategy shows promise, it is far from proven. And just like any other kind of futures investing, but even more so, a managed futures strategy will not necessarily reflect ups and downs in the spot prices of commodities.

Because LSC is an ETN and not an ETF, remember that you get your money back only if the issuer remains solvent. This fund is issued and backed by HSBC Bank USA, which has the very same high credit ratings as Barclays.

Awaiting new developments

Given all the confusion about how best to invest in commodities, I'm certain that other ETF and ETN providers will soon introduce all sorts of new strategies to tap into this asset class. Some will likely be crazy; others may turn out to be golden.

Keep in mind also that many commodity mutual funds exist. If you want to try an actively managed approach, don't want to have to file pesky K-1 forms, and don't want the credit risk that come with ETNs, some of the available funds may be reasonable options. Because this book is not about mutual funds, I won't go into much depth here, but one mutual fund worth considering is the **PIMCO Commodity Real Return Strategy Fund (PCRDX).** It's been around since 2002 and has a rather positive history thus far — better than many of the commodity ETFs. See www.pimco-funds.com.

Playing the Commodity Market Indirectly

In a recent interview with the *Journal of Indexes,* famed investment guru Burton G. Malkiel, professor of economics at Princeton and author of *A*

Random Walk Down Wall Street, had this to say about commodity investing: "I think [commodities] should be in every portfolio, but for individuals, my sense is that the way they should get them is through ensuring that they have in their portfolios companies that mine or manufacture the commodities."

He is not alone. Frustrated with the problems of commodity investing I've outlined in this chapter, and doubtful that commodity investing in the very long run will provide returns commensurate with the risk, many investment advisors of late have turned to Malkiel's solution. The drawback is that stocks in commodity-producing companies are not going to show the same lack of correlation, or offer the same diversification power, as pure commodities do. Investing in commodities this way is a trade-off.

Lately, I have been splitting the difference: Putting perhaps 3 to 4 percent of a portfolio in pure commodities (using one of the funds I identify earlier in the chapter) and perhaps another 3 to 4 percent in one of the funds I outline next.

Tapping into commodity companies

In this section, I introduce you to ETFs that let you invest in the stocks of companies in the oil and gas sector, in mining, and in the broader category of "natural resources" or "materials."

Oil and gas ETFs

More than a dozen ETFs allow you to invest in the stocks of oil and gas companies. Among them are these options:

- ✔ Vanguard Energy ETF (VDE)
- ✔ Energy Select Sector SPDR (XLE)
- ✔ iShares Dow Jones U.S. Energy Index (IYE)
- ✔ PowerShares Dynamic Energy Exploration & Production (PXE)
- ✔ iShares Dow Jones U.S. Oil Equipment & Services Index Fund (IEZ)
- ✔ iShares S&P Global Energy Index Fund (IXC)
- ✔ Global X Oil Equities ETF (XOIL)

The funds all sound different from each other, but when you look at each of their rosters, they are actually quite similar, and I feel equally lukewarm about all of them.

Keep in mind that the energy sector represents a large segment of the U.S. economy. Energy companies make up about 10 percent of the capitalization of the U.S. stock market. So just being invested in the market gives you decent exposure to energy.

Mining ETFs

Several ETFs allow you to invest in mining companies. These include:

- ✔ Global X Pure Gold Miners ETF (GGGG)
- ✔ Market Vectors Gold Miners ETF (GDX)
- ✔ SPDR S&P Metals and Mining ETF (XME)
- ✔ Global X Silver Miners ETF (SIL)

To me, these funds may make more sense in a portfolio than the energy ETFs, but they aren't my preferred way of tapping into commodity-producing companies. For my preference, keep reading.

Materials or natural resources ETFs

To give me extra exposure to companies that mine for gold and silver, produce oil and gas, and either produce or distribute other commodities, I prefer broader natural resource funds. (I say "extra" because I already get exposure in my other stock funds.) If commodity prices pop, the broader natural resource funds generally do well, and I'm not taking on too much risk by banking on any one commodity or commodity group. A natural resources fund may also be called a *materials* fund.

Options in this category include these ETFs:

- ✔ Materials Select Sector SPDR (XLB)
- ✔ iShares Dow Jones U.S. Basic Materials (IYM)
- ✔ Vanguard Materials ETF (VAW)
- ✔ iShares S&P North American Natural Resources (IGE)

One of my favorites in this category is the **SPDR S&P Global Natural Resources ETF (GNR).** This fund has an expense ratio of 0.50 percent. About 45 percent of its holdings are in the United States or Canada, and the remaining 55 percent are spread out through both the developed world and emerging markets. It offers exposure to a good variety of commodity firms: oil and gas, 32 percent; fertilizers and agricultural chemicals, 19 percent; diversified metals and mining, 16 percent; and so on.

Tapping into commodity-rich countries

As commodity prices go, so (often) go the stock markets of countries that supply the world with much of its commodities. By and large, these are the emerging market nations. (Yes, developed nations, such as Canada, Australia, and the United States, also bring the world many commodities. But because their economies are larger and more diverse, commodity prices have a much lesser effect on their stock markets.)

Although country funds can be just as volatile as commodities themselves, you can invest, through Barclays iShares, in the stock markets of nations. For example, you can invest in:

- ✔ Gold-rich South Africa via **iShares MSCI South Africa (EZA)**

- ✔ Timber giant Brazil through **iShares MSCI Brazil (EWZ)**

- ✔ Multi-mineral-laden Malaysia with **iShares MSCI Malaysia (EWM)**

- ✔ Top silver producers Chile and Peru through **iShares MSCI Chile Investable Market (ECH)** and **iShares MSCI All Peru Capped (EPU)**

I would suggest that, instead of needlessly taking on the risks associated with any single country, you diversify any investment in emerging markets through one of several ETFs that allow you to invest in a broad array of emerging market nations. These funds include the **iShares MSCI Emerging Markets Index (EEM),** the **BLDRS Emerging Markets 50 ADR (ADRE),** and the **Vanguard Emerging Market ETF (VWO).** I discuss these funds in some depth in Chapter 9.

Chapter 15

Working Non-ETFs and Active ETFs into Your Investment Mix

· ·

In This Chapter

▶ Incorporating ETFs into an existing portfolio of mutual funds or individual securities

▶ Spotting potential holes in an ETF portfolio

▶ Choosing investments that best complement your ETFs

▶ Understanding the difference between ETFs and ETNs

▶ Taking a chance with active ETFs

· ·

*W*hen I wrote the first edition of this book in 2006, building an entire, optimally diversified portfolio out of ETFs was just about impossible — sort of like trying to paint a landscape with no blues or yellows. There were holes, and many of them. You could not, for example, buy an ETF that gave you exposure to tax-free municipal bonds. Or international bonds. Only one ETF at that time allowed you to tap into international small cap stocks. And none allowed for investing in international REITs.

Back then, when there were but 300 ETFs from which to choose, and many of those tracked the same kinds of investments (such as large cap U.S. stocks), you had to look elsewhere if you wished to invest in certain asset classes. Today, the landscape is quite different. Among the 1,300 or so available ETFs, you have blues, yellows, greens . . . an entire palate from which to compose a very well-diversified portfolio. In fact, you have more than enough. Now, not only can you track just about any conceivable stock, bond, or commodity index with passive ETFs, but also you have actively managed ETFs to consider.

In this chapter, I discuss those active ETFs. But first I identify some non-ETFs, such as certain mutual funds and even a few individual stocks, that still — despite the wide variety of ETFs — just might play a positive role in your portfolio. I also explain the differences between ETFs and exchange-traded notes (ETNs).

This chapter serves as a reference if you already have a non-ETF portfolio in place and, for whatever reason, want to keep it more or less intact. Perhaps you have huge unrealized tax gains and don't care to donate to the IRS just yet. Or the investment options in your employer's 401(k) plan may not include ETFs. Or you may simply be happy with your indexed or active mutual funds, which (depending on which ones you own) may be fine.

For some of you — ah, yes, I know you're out there — no amount of cajoling will ever convince you to index or diversify your investments. You fervently believe that by picking a few individual stocks, and buying and selling at the right times, you can clobber the market. So be it. I fear you are going to lose your shirt, but you and I will simply have to agree to disagree. I can still urge you to consider investing in an ETF here and there — and I will!

So, without further ado, I now give you my take on how indexed ETFs, active ETFs, and non-ETFs can get along in peace, harmony, tax-efficiency, and profitability.

Tinkering with an Existing Stock or Mutual Fund Portfolio

Maybe you're intent on staying put with your existing portfolio. I understand that. But even you can benefit from an occasional ETF holding. (And I'm sure you know that, or else you wouldn't be reading this page right now.)

Improving your diversification

I'll start by assuming that you are invested in individual stocks and bonds, saving mutual funds for the next section.

Unless you are really rich, like Warren Buffett rich, you simply cannot have a truly well-diversified portfolio of individual securities — not nearly as well-diversified as even the simplest ETF or mutual fund portfolio. Where would you even start? To have a portfolio as well-diversified as even a simple ETF portfolio, you'd have to hold a bevy of large company stocks (both growth and value), small company stocks (again, both growth and value), foreign stocks (Asia and Europe and emerging markets, growth and value, large and small), and real estate investment trust (REIT) stocks. And that's just on the equity side!

On the fixed-income side of your portfolio, you would ideally have a mix of short-term and long-term bonds, government and corporate issues, and perhaps (especially if you are Warren Buffett rich and find yourself in the northern tax brackets) some federal-tax-free municipal bonds.

Get real. Examine your portfolio. If you, like so many U.S. investors, have the large majority of your equity holdings in large company U.S. stocks, you can diversify in a flash by adding a small cap ETF or two (see Chapters 7 and 8) and a couple of international ETFs (see Chapter 9). If you, like so many investors who lost their shirts in 2008, are simply too heavily invested in stocks, you may want to tap into some of the more sedate bond ETFs (see Chapter 12).

Minimizing your investment costs

Now, let's assume you're basically a mutual fund kind of guy or gal. You've been reading *Money* magazine and *Kiplinger's* for years. You believe that you have winnowed down the universe of mutual funds to a handful of winners, and goshdarnit, you're going to keep them in your portfolio.

You may or may not have heard the terms *core* and *satellite*. They refer to an investment strategy that has been very much in vogue lately. *Core* refers to a portfolio's foundation, which is basically invested in the entire market, or close to it. Then, you have your *satellites:* smaller investments designed to outdo the market. It isn't such a bad strategy.

Suppose you have four mutual funds that you love: one tech fund, one healthcare fund, one energy fund, and one international growth fund. Each charges you a yearly fee of 1.34 percent (the mutual fund average right now, according to Morningstar). And suppose you have $250,000 invested in all four. You are paying ($250,000 × 1.34 percent) a total of $3,350 a year in management fees, and that's to say nothing of any taxes you're paying on dividends and capital gains.

Consider trimming those investments down and moving half the money into an ETF or two or three. Turn your present core into satellites, and create a new core using broad-market funds, such as the Vanguard Total Stock Market ETF (VTI). It carries an expense ratio of 0.07 percent. Your total management fees are now ($125,000 × 1.34 percent) + ($125,000 × 0.07 percent), or $1,675.00 + $87.50, which totals $1,762.50. You've just saved yourself a very nifty $1,587.50 a year, and you'll likely save a considerable amount on taxes, too.

With the newer generation of actively managed ETFs, it's quite possible that the *Kiplinger's* or *Money* or *Wise Money* or whatever magazine picks-of-the-month (yes, I'm skeptical of such picks) may include ETFs. If you are swapping actively managed mutual funds for actively managed ETFs, you may still save money and lower your tax hit to boot. More on actively managed ETFs later in this chapter.

Using ETFs to tax harvest

Regardless of whether you hold individual stocks or mutual funds, you should hope for nothing but good times ahead but be prepared for something less. Historically, the stock market takes something of a dip in one out of every three years. In the dip years, ETFs can help ease the pain.

Say it's a particularly bad year for tech stocks, and you happen to own a few of the most beaten down of the dogs. Come late December, you can sell your losing tech stocks or mutual funds. As long as you don't buy them back for 31 days, you can claim a tax loss for the year, and Uncle Sam, in a sense, helps foot the bill for your losses. Ah, but do you really want to be out of the market for the entire month of January (typically one of the best months for stocks)? You don't need to be.

Buy yourself a technology ETF, such as the Technology Select Sector SPDR (XLK), and you're covered should the market suddenly take a jump. Although I'd much rather you simply hold onto your ETF as a permanent investment, if you wish, at the end of 31 days, you can always sell your ETF and buy back your beloved individual stocks or active mutual funds.

I believe that tax harvesting has its place, but it has been in the past a by-and-large overvalued and overdone strategy. After all, there are costs involved whenever you make a trade. With ETFs and stocks, you pay a commission when you buy or sell. With any security, there is a spread. You can't just buy and sell without some middleman somewhere taking a small cut. Still, many investors cling to tax harvesting religiously. All I'm saying is please discuss the strategy with your tax adviser (or clergy) before proceeding next year, okay? Especially today, with the tax rate on capital gains expected to go up (perhaps depending on your income bracket), this whole business is trickier than ever.

Looking Beyond the Well-Rounded ETF Portfolio

In this section, I address those of you who are convinced that ETFs are the best thing since the abolition of pay toilets. You're ready to build a portfolio of ETFs but are wondering if other investments may fit into the mix and, if so, what investments those might be. Let me provide you with a few possibilities.

If you are considering investing in mutual funds, I suggest that you read the latest edition of Eric Tyson's *Mutual Funds For Dummies* (Wiley) and investigate mutual fund options on www.morningstar.com or http://finance.yahoo.com. The options I discuss in the following sections are some of the mutual funds that I have used personally or in client portfolios. They are all *no load* (meaning you'll pay no commission), have reasonable management expenses, and are run by mutual fund companies with reputations for honesty and solid management. I include websites and telephone numbers in case you want to go directly to the fund provider. Please read the prospectus before purchasing any mutual fund.

Mutual funds as cheap as ETFs: Vanguard Admiral shares

Indexing leader Vanguard, as low as its fund costs are, has always charged larger investors even less. With a certain amount to invest, which was $100,000 until not long ago, you could qualify for Vanguard's ultra-low-cost Admiral shares. In October 2010, largely due to competition from ETFs (including Vanguard's own ETFs), Vanguard lowered the minimum investment in its Admiral shares to a much smaller amount: $10,000 for most Vanguard index funds, and $50,000 for most actively managed funds.

If you can meet those minimums and would rather invest in any of Vanguard's mutual funds instead of ETFs, your average expense ratio would be 0.18 percent for the Admiral shares versus 0.17 percent for the ETFs. It's pretty much a flip of the coin. In many cases, you can choose the very same fund in either the mutual fund or ETF class. For example, you can purchase the Vanguard Extended Market Index Admiral Shares mutual fund (VEXAX) or the Vanguard Extended Market Index ETF (VXF). Same fund. The mutual fund will cost you 0.16 percent a year in management fees; the ETF will cost you 0.16 percent. (If you were to purchase the Investor class of the mutual fund, however, you'd pay 0.30 percent.)

In some cases, the ETF may be a sliver cheaper than the Admiral class mutual fund; in other cases, it's the other way around. But I've never seen a difference that much matters. We're talking pennies here.

Keep in mind the basic differences between ETFs and mutual funds:

✔ ETFs allow you to trade throughout the day, which can be a good thing or a bad thing, depending on whether you use or abuse that privilege. (Vanguard founder John Bogle has numerous times expressed dismay that ETFs encourage investors to trade frequently.)

✔ ETFs typically involve trading fees and small spreads, and they may be subject to some small tracking error (nothing to worry much about unless you are trading frequently).

✔ Also, Vanguard Admiral shares are not available at all brokerage houses. You can't get them at Fidelity, for example.

On balance, whether you go with a Vanguard ETF or Vanguard Admiral share mutual fund, assuming we're talking about two classes of the same fund, is a decision of no great consequence.

Keep in mind that a few of my favorite Vanguard funds — all in the municipal bond category — have not been issued as ETFs . . . yet. These include the Vanguard Intermediate-Term Tax Exempt Admiral fund (VWIUX), and a number of state-specific municipal funds, such as the Vanguard Pennsylvania Long-Term Tax-Exempt Admiral fund (VPALX) and its New York and Ohio equivalents. In early 2011, Vanguard was all set to issue a lineup of muni ETFs that may have included versions of the funds I list here, but the firm decided to pull the plug given recent turbulence in the municipal markets. Stay tuned.

Where few investors have gone before: DFA funds

Perhaps you've never heard of the mutual fund company called Dimensional Fund Advisors, or DFA. For the ultimate in slicing and dicing a portfolio, no mutual fund company compares. Only through DFA can you, for example, find index funds that allow you to invest in emerging markets small cap, emerging markets value, and U.K. small company. All of DFA's funds are expertly managed funds with reasonable expense ratios (although a bit higher than most ETFs or Vanguard mutual funds).

The only problem with DFA is that you can invest in their funds only if you are an institution with huge bucks, or if you go through a *fee-only* wealth manager (meaning he takes no commissions). The problem with that, of course, is that you have to pay the fee-only wealth manager. Since you are reading this book, you are probably a hands-on, do-it-yourself kind of investor, and you may not want to pay someone to manage your money.

If, however, you have a handsome portfolio, and if you can find a fee-only wealth manager who charges you a reasonable amount (try The National Association of Personal Financial Advisors, www.napfa.org), by all means, do consider DFA (www.dfaus.com). It would be nice if DFA would get into the ETF business, but I doubt that will happen; all those fee-only advisors would stand to lose clientele.

Timber REITs

Real estate comes in many forms, from shopping malls to condos to office buildings. As I explain in Chapter 13, you can invest in these properties through publicly listed real estate investment trusts (REITs), which are companies that buy and develop land and pay their investors largely in handsome dividends. A handful of REITs own timberland — gazillions of acres of trees. The land on which the trees grow tends to rise and fall in value along with the going price for timber. Therefore, these special REITs behave largely as a separate asset class. There are days and weeks when most REITs go one way and timber REITs go another. For that reason, if I have a client with a fairly large portfolio, I may take a percentage of the U.S. REIT allocation and move it into timber.

Technically speaking, two timber REIT ETFs exist: the Guggenheim Timber ETF (CUT) and the iShares S&P Global Timber & Forestry Index ETF (WOOD). I'm not a big fan of either. They both charge fairly high fees (0.65 and 0.48 percent respectively), but my bigger issue is that they invest only in a handful of timber REITs, simply because there *are* only a handful of them. Then, to fill their portfolios (because you can't have an ETF with two or three holdings), these ETFs also invest in companies that make toilet paper and cardboard boxes and stationery and such. These companies are not "timber" companies. They are simply related to timber . . . not the same thing.

For that reason, rather than buy a watered-down ETF, I buy individual stocks to tap into this asset class. I'd rather not, but what's available is what's available. Two of the largest timber REITs (these two together make up about one-fifth of the holdings of WOOD) are the following:

- ✔ **Plum Creek Timber Company (PCL):** 800-254-4961; www.plumcreek.com
- ✔ **Rayonier Timber (RYN):** 904-357-9155; www.rayonier.com

Keep in mind that these are individual company stocks. Throughout this book I say that you really shouldn't invest in individual companies, but I'm making a small exception here for timber. Individual stocks can be volatile and sometimes awfully capricious. I suggest limiting your allocation to absolutely no more than 6 percent of the equity side of your portfolio. Perhaps take that 6 percent and split it between PCL and RYN.

Just like all REITs, timber REITs must distribute 90 percent of their income as dividends. And those dividends will be taxed. Keep your timber REITs, if possible, in a tax-advantaged retirement account. In fact, if you don't have room for them in your tax-advantaged accounts, I'll suggest that you may want to pass. Timber is good to have in your portfolio for diversification purposes, and the stocks may — knock wood — perform very well moving forward, but these holdings are not essential.

I Bonds: An Uncle Sam bond with a twist

Like TIPS (see Chapter 12), I Bonds are inflation indexed. Unlike TIPS, they are available as individual bonds in very small denominations — as small as $25.

On the upside: The interest earned can be greater than TIPS (although that hasn't been the case lately). The correlation to inflation is also more closely matched, as I Bonds change their yield to adjust for inflation every six months. Also, you don't pay tax on the interest on I Bonds until you cash them in, making them often a better option for taxable accounts.

And — a potentially very sweet bonus if you have young ones — if you use the I Bonds for higher education expenses, that interest, along with any inflation adjustments, may be yours to keep and spend tax-free.

On the downside: You must hold I Bonds for at least one year, and you forfeit three months' interest if you redeem them before they mature in five years. Also, Uncle Sam lets you buy only as much as $5,000 a year in I Bonds, and you can hold only $20,000 worth. There's a limit on TIPS, too, but it's so huge ($5 million) that I've never encountered anyone too terribly frustrated by that limit.

You can buy I Bonds (or TIPS) by calling 800-722-2678 or visiting www.treasurydirect.gov.

Market-neutral mutual funds

Market-neutral funds use vastly different strategies to meet their ends. The goal of most is to produce long-term returns that are more similar to bonds than stocks (perhaps a tad higher than bonds) while having no correlation to either the bond or stock market.

Some market-neutral funds use a *long–short* strategy. That is, they buy stocks to enjoy the potential appreciation. They also *short* stocks (often stock ETFs) to make money when the market is going down. Others employ this strategy by buying one stock while simultaneously shorting another — whose prospects look poor by comparison — in the same sector. In general, the two stocks will move in the same direction as their sector and the market, but the hope is that the superior stock will ultimately provide superior returns, allowing fund investors to earn the difference. It's a tricky business, and you want to find an experienced manager who has been doing it for a while.

Another strategy involves investing very short-term in companies that are just on the cusp of getting gobbled up by other companies. Such small-fish-about-to-be-eaten, if they can be identified, tend to be tasty investments.

Some of the newer actively managed ETFs may promote themselves as market-neutral, but if there is any area of investing where you want to see some kind of track record, I'd say this is it.

Here are a few market-neutral funds worthy of investigation. These have all been around for at least a half dozen years, charge reasonable fees, and have so far shown limited volatility with fair returns.

- **Hussman Strategic Total Return (HSTRX)** and (the somewhat more aggressive) **Hussman Strategic Growth fund (HSGFX)**: 800-487-7626; www.hussmanfunds.com
- **Merger Fund (MERFX)**: 800-343-8959; www.mergerfund.com
- **Gabelli ABC (GABCX)**: 800-422-3554; www.gabelli.com

A commodity fund without too much hassle

In Chapter 14, I discuss investing in commodities (gold, silver, oil) as an option for larger portfolios. Commodities don't yield dividends, nor are they likely to see huge capital growth over the years (because a nugget of gold or barrel of oil churns no profits, as a company does). However, they still may be worth holding because of their delightfully low lack of correlation to both stocks and bonds. As I point out in Chapter 14, if you go with a commodity ETF that uses futures (which just about all the non-precious-metals ETFs do), you are going to have to deal with increased tax preparation costs in filing dreaded K-1 forms, among other complications.

You could invest in a commodity exchange-traded note (ETN), which I also discuss in Chapter 14 and return to later in this chapter. However, you'll then have to take on credit risk. It's always something.

There is a third alternative: You could invest in an old-fashioned commodities mutual fund, the best of which may be the **PIMCO Commodity Real Return Strategy Fund (PCRDX)**. No credit risk. And because it is structured as a corporation and not as a partnership (as are the commodity ETFs), no K-1 forms. The fund has been in existence since 2002. It charges 1.24 percent a year. (Alas, that's about double what the commodity ETFs and ETNs tend to charge.) But this may be one of those rare cases where a fund's higher fees are justified by its returns, as PCRDX has returned a fairly healthy 7 percent a year since its inception.

My guess is that the continued competition from commodity ETFs and ETNs will force PIMCO to bring down its management fee on this fund. I'll be staying tuned. So might you.

Fixed immediate annuities

For older people especially, and almost definitely for those with no heirs, an annuity — either fixed or variable — can make enormous sense. With an annuity, you give up your principal, and in return you enjoy a yield typically far greater than you would likely get with any other fixed-income option.

There are many horrible annuities out there. I can't tell you how often a new client has walked into my office, thrown his annuity papers on the table, and said, "*Why* did I ever buy this stupid thing?" Most of the really bad ones are variable annuities, not the fixed kind that I prefer.

If you are interested in an annuity, start with Fidelity or Vanguard. In general, brokerage houses offer much, much better deals than you would get going directly to an insurance company. (Actually, the insurance company usually comes to you, with a heavy sales pitch filled with mind-numbing charts that could confuse even Albert Einstein.) The brokerage house annuity products tend to be cheaper, less complicated, and easier to back out of should you change your mind:

  ✔ **Vanguard:** 800-522-5555; www.vanguard.com

  ✔ **Fidelity:** 800-345-1388; www.fidelity.com

Venturing into exchange-traded notes

Exchange-traded notes (ETNs) sure sound like exchange-traded funds, and the two do have some things in common. But they also have one or two big differences. The commonalities include not only their names but the fact that both ETFs and ETNs trade throughout the day, they both tend to track indexes, and they both can be tax efficient — especially the ETNs.

Given these commonalities, the term *exchange-traded products* or ETPs has been used to describe both ETFs and ETNs, as well as closed-end funds, which I describe in the sidebar "A few odd ducks."

A few odd ducks

In this chapter, I discuss mutual funds, individual securities (stocks or bonds), and annuities as possible alternatives, or complements, to ETFs. But the investment world offers other options as well. Here are a few less commonly known investments, some of which may be worth considering for your portfolio:

- **Closed-end mutual funds:** Just as the word *burger* without any qualifiers is usually understood to mean *ham*burger — not veggie burger or turkey burger — so are the words *mutual fund* usually understood to mean *open-end* mutual fund. The vast majority of mutual funds are open-ended. That means that the fund has no set limit of shares, which are purchased from the fund sponsor. As more investors buy into the fund, the fund grows, acquiring more securities and issuing more shares.

  Closed-end funds, on the other hand, are created with a certain number of shares, and that number typically doesn't change. If any new investors want to buy in, they must buy shares from existing investors. For that reason, closed-end mutual funds, unlike open-end mutual funds, may sell shares at a premium or a discount. (ETFs may also trade at a premium or discount, but it tends to be negligible. Closed-end funds, in contrast, may sometimes be bought or sold for 50 percent more or less than the value of the underlying securities.) Closed-end mutual funds tend to be more volatile than open-end mutual funds, and the management fees tend to be higher.

- **Unit investment trusts:** Some ETFs, especially the older ones such as the QQQ (Qubes), SPDR S&P 500 (SPY), and SPDR S&P Mid Cap 400 (MDY), actually are unit investment trusts (UITs). However, not all UITs are ETFs.

  A *UIT* is a fixed portfolio of stocks or bonds generally sold to investors by brokers. The UIT is usually sold through a one-time public offering. It has a termination date, which could be anywhere from several months to 50 years down the road. Upon termination, the UIT dissolves.

  In the case of ETF/UITs, however, it's a slightly different story. When the first ETFs were created, there was an original termination date of 25 years hence. But as the ETFs grew in popularity, ETF providers petitioned the U.S. Securities and Exchange Commission (SEC) to make an exception, which the SEC did.

- **Hedge funds/Limited partnerships:** *Hedge funds* — funds that promise insurance against bad markets — come in many different flavors and use any number of strategies to achieve (or try to achieve) their objective. Most hedge funds are neither mutual funds nor ETFs; rather, they are organized as limited partnerships. Limited partnerships are largely unregulated, fees tend to be high, and *liquidity* (the ability to get your money out if you want or need to) can be very limited. Proceed with great caution.

The big, big, BIG difference (are you listening?) between ETFs and ETNs is this: An ETN is a debt instrument. In other words, a firm like Barclays, which issues the iPath ETNs, promises to pay holders of its ETNs a rate of return commensurate with some index. For example, the iPath DJ-UBS Tin Subindex Total Return ETN (JJT) promises to pay you according to how much the price of tin goes up (or down), minus fund expenses.

Whether Barclays actually invests your money in tin, or in Treasuries, or in whatever the heck it wants, is up to Barclays. The company simply made you a promise to pay, just as if you held one of its bonds. An ETN is more like a bond, really, than an ETF. Instead of a fixed rate of interest, however, you get paid according to some other measure, often the change in price of a commodity or in a foreign currency relative to the dollar.

If all goes well (and the price of tin or the value of the Euro goes up), you get your money. But if something should happen to Barclays, you could lose everything. Your capital is not guaranteed, regardless of what happens in the commodity or currency markets. So quite clearly, you should buy ETNs only from solid companies, and you should never hold too much of your portfolio in any one ETN or group of ETNs issued by any one company.

The advantage of ETNs is that they can be even more tax efficient than ETFs, especially where commodities are concerned. Many ETNs invest (well, sort of) in either a single commodity or a basket of commodities, and you might consider such a commodity ETN if you want to tap into this asset class. Because commodity ETNs are more tax-efficient than commodity ETFs, you may especially want to choose an ETN over an ETF if you have limited room in your tax-advantaged accounts and need to put commodities into a taxable account. ETNs also spare you the agony of having to file special K-1 tax forms that you generally need to file when you own commodity ETFs. (See Chapter 14 for more on commodity investing.)

As for the currency ETNs, unless you know a whole lot more about currency exchanges than the average person, you're likely to take a bath. Steer clear of these funds. They are expensive. They are volatile. And they are unpredictable. Currency ETNs, alone among ETNs, are not even all that tax efficient; you'll likely pay regular income tax on any gains, should you be so lucky as to have them.

ETNs that are not speculating in currencies and not tracking commodity indexes are typically offering you the "opportunity" to double or triple your money in a hurry with leveraged strategies. Or they are employing leveraged "inverse" strategies, promising you big money in a bear market. Do yourself a big favor and stay away from these. (I explain why in Chapter 11.)

Going Active with ETFs

It was perhaps foreshadowing, and somewhat ironic, that the very first actively managed ETF was issued by Bear Stearns. That was in March 2008. Within several months, the financial collapse of the investment banking industry, led by Bear Stearns, was well on its way to creating the worst bear market (more irony) of our lifetimes. That first ETF died, folding (with money returned to investors) in October 2008, as Bear Stearns, after 85 years in business, collapsed and itself folded.

Since that time, we've seen the arrival of only about three dozen actively managed ETFs and ETNs. And even those active funds that have appeared have failed to accumulate a whole lot in assets. Here's why:

- **Most ETF buyers are indexers by nature.** They know that index funds, as a group, do much, much better over time than actively managed funds. (Read about this topic in Chapter 1, or for much more detail, see my book *Index Investing For Dummies*, also published by Wiley.)

- **Most ETF buyers want transparency.** Active managers, reluctant to reveal their "secret sauce," have not been too keen to comply with the transparency rules of ETFs, and they've been lobbying the authorities to do away with those transparency rules.

- **Many of the active funds are just plain goofy.** Cases in point: the WisdomTree Dreyfus New Zealand Dollar (BNZ), the WisdomTree Dreyfus Indian Rupee ETF (ICN), and a dozen others that deal with currency flux. They are highly speculative and not the kinds of investments into which smarter investors (as most ETF investors tend to be) are going to plunk their money. (Explain to me again why the New Zealand dollar is a good investment? Does it have anything to do with wallabies?)

- **A few of the active funds have been issued by relatively unknown and not terribly well-funded companies.** An example is Columbia Management, which sponsors the Columbia Concentrated Large Cap Value Strategy Fund (GVT). Dent Tactical ETF (DENT), based on the strategies of best-selling author and crystal-ball gazer Harry S. Dent, entered the market in the summer of 2010 with a performance thud. In its first 13 months of existence, DENT showed a return of about 2 percent annualized, versus about 16 percent for the S&P 500.

Oh, and did I mention that the DENT ETF charges 1.5 percent a year in management expenses, which, among ETFs, is sort the equivalent of a $380 pair of jeans? The other actively managed ETFs aren't cheap, either. And that's part of their problem. A big part.

As I write this chapter, a good number of ETFs in registration with the SEC are going to be hitting the market shortly (presuming they get the approval they seek). Of these, some will likely be issued by long-standing and respected companies, such as PIMCO (which has already entered the fray with a handful of both passive and actively managed bond ETFs) and T. Rowe Price.

You may be inclined to choose one of these actively managed funds. Heck, I may do so myself someday (maybe, possibly . . . but not likely). After all, if you're going to go active, there's no reason not to do it with an ETF. The active ETFs will probably wind up being less expensive and more tax efficient than their corresponding mutual funds.

But keep in mind that historically, actively managed funds as a group have not done nearly as well as index funds. That being said, active management may sometimes have an edge, especially in some areas of the investment world (such as commodities and non-Treasury bonds). And much of the advantage of index investing has been in its ultra-low costs — something that actively managed ETFs could possibly emulate. We will see.

If you want to go with an actively managed fund, I would ask you at least to keep in mind the lessons learned from indexing and what has made indexing so effective over time. Basically, you want certain index-like qualities in any actively managed fund you pick:

- ✔ **Choose a fund with low costs.** With so many ETFs allowing you to tap into stocks or bonds for less than one-quarter of a percentage point a year, you do not need or want any fund that charges much more. Any U.S. stock or bond fund that charges more than a percentage point, or any foreign fund or commodity fund that charges more than 1.5 percent, is asking too much, and the odds that such a fund will outperform are very, very slim. Go elsewhere.

- ✔ **Watch your style.** Make sure that any fund you choose fits into your overall portfolio. Studies show that index funds tend to do better than active funds in both large caps and small caps, but you have a better chance in small caps that your active fund will beat the indexes.

- ✔ **Check the manager's track record — carefully.** Make sure that the track record you're buying is long-term. (Any fool can beat the S&P 500 in a year. Doing so for ten years is immensely more difficult.) I'd look at performance in both bull and bear markets, but your emphasis should be on average annual returns over time compared with the performance of the fund's most representative market index over the same period.

- ✔ **Don't go overboard with active management.** Studies show *so* conclusively that index investing kicks butt that I would be very hesitant to build anything but a largely indexed portfolio, using the low-cost indexed ETFs that I suggest throughout this book.

Part IV
Putting It All Together

In this part . . .

Pick up your hammer and grab some nails: It's time now to get your hands dirty actually building an ETF portfolio. In the next four chapters, I walk you through the entire construction process. I then share some important maintenance tips, such as when to tweak your portfolio and when to leave hands off. And finally, I take you into the world of retirement, to see how your ETF portfolio may someday provide you with a steady and secure income.

Chapter 16

Sample ETF Portfolio Menus

*I*f there is such a thing as a personal hell, and if, for whatever reason, I piss off the Big Guy before I die, I'm fairly certain that I will spend eternity in either a Home Depot or a Lowe's. The only real question I have is whether His wrath will place me in plumbing supplies, home décor, or flooring.

I'm not the handyman type. Even the words "home renovation" are enough to send shivers up my spine. The last thing I built out of metal or wood — a car-shaped napkin holder — was in shop class at Lincoln Orens Junior High School. I brought the thing home to my mother, and she said, "Oh, Russell, um, what a lovely birdhouse."

And yet, despite my failed relationship with power tools, there is one kind of construction that I absolutely love: portfolio construction.

I enjoy crafting portfolios not only because it involves multicolored pie charts (I've always had a soft spot for multicolored pie charts) but also because the process involves so much more than running a piece of wood through a jigsaw and hoping not to lose any fingers. Portfolio construction is — or should be — a highly individualized, creative exercise that takes into consideration many factors: economics, history, statistics, and psychology among them.

The ideal portfolio (if such a thing exists) for a 30-year-old who makes $75,000 a year is very different from the portfolio of a 75-year-old whose income is $30,000 a year. The optimal portfolio for a 40-year-old worrywart differs from the optimal portfolio for a 40-year-old devil-may-care type. The portfolio of dreams following a three-year bear market when interest rates are low may look a wee bit different from a prime portfolio following a ten-year bull run when interest rates are high.

Every financial professional I know goes about portfolio construction in a somewhat different way. In this chapter, I walk you through the steps that I take and that have worked well for me. I don't mean to present my way as the only way, so I also mention an alternative strategy (see the sidebar "Dividing up the pie either conservatively or aggressively by industry sector" toward the end of the chapter).

Needless to say (since this is, after all, a book about exchange-traded funds), my primary construction materials are ETFs, as I believe they should be for most, but not all, investors. My portfolio-building tools involve some sophisticated Morningstar software, my HP 12C financial calculator, a premise called *Modern Portfolio Theory,* a statistical phenomenon called *reversion to the mean,* and various measures of risk and return. But rest assured that this isn't brain surgery, or even elbow surgery. You can be a pretty good portfolio builder yourself by the time you finish this chapter.

So please follow along. I promise you that nothing you are about to see will resemble either a napkin holder or a birdhouse!

So, How Much Risk Can You Handle and Still Sleep at Night?

The first questions I ask myself — and the first questions anyone building a portfolio should ask — are these: *How much return does the portfolio-holder need to see? And how much volatility can the portfolio-holder stomach?* So few things in the world of investments are sure bets, but this one is: The amount of risk you take or don't take will have a great bearing on your long-term return. You simply are not going to get rich investing in bank CDs. On the other hand, you aren't going to lose your nest egg in a single week, either. The same cannot be said of a tech stock — or even a bevy of tech stocks wrapped up in an ETF.

A well-built ETF portfolio can help to mitigate risks but not eliminate them. Before you build your portfolio, ask yourself how much risk you need to take to get your desired return . . . and take no more risk than that.

Please forget the dumb old rules about portfolio building and risk. How much risk you can or should take on depends on your wealth, your age, your income, your health, your financial responsibilities, your potential inheritances, and whether you're the kind of person who tosses and turns over life's upsets. If anyone gives you a pat formula — "Take your age, subtract it from 100, and that, dear friend, is how much you should have in stocks" — please take it with a grain of salt. Things just aren't nearly that simple. (Although if you're going to go with ANY formula, the one I just provided is far better than most!)

A few things that just don't matter

Before I lay out what matters most in determining appropriate risk and appropriate allocations to stocks, bonds, and cash (or stock ETFs and bond ETFs), I want to throw out just a few things that really *shouldn't* enter into your thinking, even though they play into many people's portfolio decisions:

- ✔ The portfolio of your best friend, which has done great guns.

- ✔ Your personal feelings on the current administration, where the Fed stands on the prime interest rate, and which way hemlines on women's dresses are moving his fall.

- ✔ The article you clipped out of *Lotsa Dough* magazine that tells you that you can earn 50 percent a year by investing in . . . whatever.

Listen: Your best friend may be in a completely different economic place than you are. His well-polished ETF portfolio, laid out by a first-rate financial planner, may be just perfect for him and all wrong for you.

As far as the state of the nation and where the Dow is headed, you simply don't know. Neither do I. (It was once argued that the stock market moves up and down with the hemlines on women's dresses . . . or whether an NFC or AFC team wins the Super Bowl this year.) The talking heads on TV pretend to know, but they don't know squat. Nor does the author of that article in the glossy magazine (filled with ads from mutual fund companies) that tells you how you can get rich quickly in the markets. The secrets to financial success cannot be had by forking over $4.50 for a magazine.

(Whenever I read about some prognosticator suggesting a handful of stocks or mutual funds for the coming year, I Google him to see what projections he made a year prior. Then I check to see how his picks have done. You should do the same! Invariably, my dog Norman, the killer poodle, could do a better job picking stocks.)

The stock market over the course of the past century has returned an average of about 10 percent annually (7 percent or so after inflation). Bonds have returned about half as much. A well-diversified portfolio, by historical standards, has returned something in between stocks and bonds — maybe 7 to 8 percent (4 to 5 percent after inflation). With some of the advice in this book, even though market performance in the future may fall a bit shy of the past, you could see personal returns roughly approximating these numbers. But don't take inordinate risk with any sizeable chunk of your portfolio in the hope that you are going to earn 50 percent a year after inflation — or even before inflation. It won't happen.

On the other hand, don't pooh-pooh a 7 to 8 percent return. Compound interest is a truly miraculous thing. Invest $20,000 today, add $2,000 each year, and within 20 years, with "only" a 7.5 percent return, you'll have $171,566. (If inflation is running in the 3 percent ballpark, that $171,566 will be worth about $110,000 in today's dollars.)

The irony of risk and return

In a few pages, I provide you with some sample portfolios appropriate for someone who should be taking minimal risk as opposed to someone who should be taking more risk. At this point, I want to digress for a moment to say that in a perfect world, those who need to take the most risk would be the most able to take it on. In the real world, sometimes sadly ironic, those who need to take the most risk really can't afford to.

Specifically, a poor person needs whatever financial cushion he has. He can't afford to risk the farm (not that he has a farm) on a portfolio of mostly stocks. A rich person, in contrast, can easily invest a chunk of discretionary money in the stock market, but he really doesn't need to because he's living comfortably without the potential high return. It just isn't fair. Yet no one is to blame, and nothing can be done about it. It is what it is.

Let's move on.

The 20x rule

Whatever your age, whatever your station in life, you probably wouldn't mind if your investments could support you. But how much do you need in order for your investments to support you? That's actually not very complicated and has been very well studied: You need at least 20 times whatever amount you expect to withdraw each year from your portfolio, assuming you want that portfolio to have a good chance of surviving at least 20 to 25 years.

That is, if you need $30,000 a year — in addition to Social Security and any other income — to live on, you should ideally have $600,000 in your portfolio when you retire, assuming you retire in your mid-60s. You can have less, but you may wind up eating into principal if the market tumbles — in which case you should be prepared to live on less, or get a part-time job.

(Factor in the value or partial value of your home only if it is paid up and if you foresee a day when you can downsize.)

The rationale behind the 20x Rule is this: It allows you to withdraw 5 percent from your portfolio the first year, and then adjust that amount upward each year to keep up with inflation. The studies show that a well-diversified portfolio from which you take such withdrawals has a good chance of lasting at least 20 years, which is how long you may need the cash flow if you retire in your 60s and live to your mid-80s.

If you think you might live beyond your mid-80s, or if you want to retire prior to your mid-60s, then having more than 20 times your anticipated expenses would be an excellent idea. It would also be an excellent idea to limit your initial withdrawal, if you can, to 4 percent a year, just in case you live a long life.

In truth, I'd much rather see you have 25 times your anticipated expenses in your portfolio before you retire at any age. But for many Americans who haven't seen a real pay increase in years, this is indeed a lofty goal. For that reason, I say go with 20 times but be prepared to tighten your belt if you need to.

If you are still far away from that 20 times mark, and you are not in debt, and your income is secure, and you are not burning out at work, and you have enough cash to live on for six months, then with the rest of your loot, you might tilt toward a riskier ETF portfolio (mostly stock ETFs). You need the return.

If you have your 20 times (or better yet, 25 times) annual cash needs already locked up or close to it, and you're thinking of giving up your day job soon, you should probably tilt toward a less risky ETF portfolio (more bond ETFs). After all, you have more to lose than you have to gain. (See the upcoming sidebar "Russell's 'today and tomorrow' portfolio modeling technique" for more on my suggestion that you should have not one but two model portfolios: one for right now, and one for the future.) You do need to be careful, however, that your investments keep up with inflation. Savings accounts are unlikely to do that.

If you have way more than 25 times annual expenses, congratulations! You have many options, and how much risk you take will be a decision that's unrelated to your material needs. You may, for example, want to leave behind a grand legacy, in which case you might shoot for higher returns. Or you may not care what you leave behind, in which case leaving your money in a tired savings account, or "investing" in a high-performance but low-yielding Ferrari, wouldn't make much difference.

Other risk/return considerations

I doubt I can list everything you should consider when determining the proper amount of risk to take with your investments, but here are a few additional things to keep in mind:

- ✔ **What is your safety net?** If worse came to worst, do you have family or friends who would help you if you got in a real financial bind? If the answer is yes, you can add a tablespoon of risk.

- ✔ **What is your family health history? Do you lead a healthy lifestyle?** These are the two greatest predictors of your longevity. If Mom and Dad lived to 100, and you don't smoke and you do eat your vegetables, you may be looking at a long retirement. Add a dollop of risk — you'll need the return.

- ✔ **How secure is your job?** The less secure your employment, the more you should keep in nonvolatile investments (like short-term bonds or bond funds); you may need to draw from them if you get the pink slip next Friday afternoon.

- ✔ **Can you downsize?** Say you are close to retirement, and you live in a McMansion. If you think that sooner or later you will sell it and buy a smaller place, you have some financial cushion. You can afford to take a bit more risk.

The limitations of risk questionnaires

Yes, I give my clients a risk questionnaire. And then I go through it with them to help them interpret their answers. Lots of websites offer investment risk questionnaires, but instead of having anyone interpret the answers, a computer just spits out a few numbers: You should invest x in stocks and y in bonds. Yikes!

Please, please, don't allow a computer-generated questionnaire to determine your financial future! I've tried many of them, and the answers can be wacky.

For example: One question that appears on many web questionnaires is this: *Please rate your previous investment experience and level of satisfaction with the following six asset classes.* And then they list money market funds, bonds, stocks, and so on.

I had a client named Jason who was a 38-year-old with a solid job and no kids. After taking an online questionnaire, he was told he should be invested almost entirely in money market funds and bonds based on his previous "very low" satisfaction with stocks and stock mutual funds. This young man definitely should not invest in any stocks or stock funds, the computer-generated program told him, because of his "very low" satisfaction with the funds he had invested in previously.

Oh, jeesh. The reason Jason had "very low" satisfaction with stocks and stock funds is that he got snookered by some stock broker (posing as a "financial planner") into buying a handful of full load, high expense ratio, actively managed mutual funds that (predictably) lost him money. That experience should have *no* bearing on the development of this young man's portfolio, which should have the lion's share invested in stock ETFs or mutual funds.

What I'm saying is that after reading this book, if you aren't too certain where you belong on the risk/return continuum, perhaps you should hire an experienced and impartial financial advisor — if only for a couple of hours — to review your portfolio with you. I write more about seeking professional help in Chapter 20.

Portfolios to go?

Yet a step beyond the online calculators, the Web has seen of late the birth of "online portfolio managers," the most popular of which may be MarketRiders, which charges about $100 a year. As with the online calculators, you plug in certain factoids about yourself, and in an instant, the site spits out not only how much you should have in stocks and bonds but *an entire portfolio* of recommended ETFs.

Hmm ... Maybe someday computer technology will advance to the point that the instant portfolios make sense, but from what I've seen, that day isn't quite here yet. I've played around with MarketRiders and a few of its competitors, inputting my age, expected retirement date, tolerance for risk, investment experience, and whatever else the form asks for. The portfolios suggested by MarketRiders and its ilk just didn't make a lot of sense much of the time.

Such programs, great in theory, must, by their very nature, be awfully simplistic. Where they have no other information, they assume that you are like every other investor in your age group, making no allowances for the many subtle factors that can indicate very different portfolios for two superficially similar investors.

I don't think you can or should allow a computer to make big financial decisions in your life any more than you would rely on a computer to make your career, parenting, or relationship decisions. That being said, using one of these sites to give you a draft portfolio that you then amend based on the information in this book might be a workable endeavor.

Keys to Optimal Investing

When you have a rough idea of where you should be riskwise, your attention should turn next to fun matters such as Modern Portfolio Theory, reversion to the mean, cost minimization, and tax efficiency. Please allow me to explain.

Incorporating Modern Portfolio Theory into your investment decisions

The subject I'm about to discuss is a theory much in the same way evolution is a theory: The people who don't believe it — and, yes, there are some — are those who decide to disregard all the science. Modern Portfolio Theory (MPT) says that if you diversify your portfolio — putting all kinds of eggs into all kinds of baskets — you reduce risk and optimize return.

You get the most bang for your buck, according to MPT, when you mix and match investments that have little *correlation*. In other words, if you build your portfolio with different ETFs that tend to do well (and not so well) in different kinds of markets, you'll have a lean and mean portfolio.

Lately, MPT has been the source of a lot of controversy. It hasn't been working as well as it did in the past. At times in the past few years, there have been stretches of days, even weeks and months, when different asset classes — U.S. stocks, foreign stocks, bonds, commodities, and real estate — have all moved up and down nearly in lockstep. This was the case, unfortunately, in 2008. Like a flock of geese, just about every investment you could imagine headed south at the same time.

While correlations can change over time — and lately the major asset classes have shown alarmingly high rates of correlation — you shouldn't simply scrap the idea that diversification and the quest for noncorrelation are crucial. However, you may want to be cautious of too much reliance on diversification. Yes, you can diversify away much risk. But you should also have certain low-risk investments in your portfolio, investments that hold their own in any kind of market. Low-risk investments include FDIC-insured savings accounts; money market funds; short-term, high-credit-quality bonds; and bank CDs.

Minimizing your costs

Most ETFs are cheap, which is one of the things I love about them. The difference between a typical mutual fund that charges 1.4 percent and a typical ETF that charges 0.2 percent adds up to a *lot* of money over time. One of my favorite financial websites, www.moneychimp.com, offers a fund-cost calculator. Invest $100,000 for 20 years at 8 percent and deduct 0.2 for expenses; you're left with $449,133. Deduct 1.4 percent, and you're left with $359,041. That's a difference of about $90,000. The after-tax difference, given that most ETFs (or at least the ones I tend to recommend) are highly tax-efficient index funds, would likely be much greater.

Because the vast majority of ETFs fall into the super-cheap to cheap range (generally 0.1 to 0.5 percent), the differences among ETFs won't be quite so huge. Still, in picking and choosing ETFs, cost should always be a factor.

Of course, with ETFs, you often pay a small trading fee every time you buy and sell. That too should be examined and minimized. Do all your trading online, and choose a brokerage house that gives you the best deal. If you're going to make frequent buys and sells, either choose ETFs that you can trade commission-free, or opt instead to build your portfolio with mostly low cost, no-load index mutual funds. See my book *Index Investing For Dummies* (Wiley) for more on index mutual funds.

Striving for tax efficiency

Keeping your investment dollars in your pocket and not lining Uncle Sam's is one big reason to choose ETFs over mutual funds. ETFs are, by and large, much more tax efficient than active mutual funds. But some ETFs are going to be more tax efficient than others. I cover this issue in-depth in Chapter 19 where I talk about tax-advantaged retirement accounts, such as Roth IRAs.

For now, let me say that you must choose wisely which ETFs get put into which baskets. In general, high dividend and interest-paying ETFs (REIT ETFs, bond ETFs) are best kept in tax-advantaged accounts.

Timing your investments (just a touch)

If you've read much of this book already, by now you realize that I'm largely an *efficient market* kind of guy. I believe that the ups and downs of the stock and bond market — and of any individual security — are, in the absence of true inside information, unpredictable. (And trading on true inside information is illegal.) For that reason, among others, I prefer indexed ETFs and mutual funds over actively managed funds.

However, that being said, I also believe in something called *reversion to the mean*. This is a statistical phenomenon that colloquially translates to the following: What goes up must come down; what goes waaaay up, you need to be careful about investing too much money in.

At the time I'm writing this, for example, commodities (especially gold and silver) and natural resource stocks have been flying high for years. Emerging market stocks and bonds have also been outperforming big time. These are good reasons that you may want to be just a wee bit cautious about overstocking your portfolio in these particular asset classes.

I'm *not* suggesting that you go out and buy any ETF that has underperformed the market for years, or sell any ETF that has outperformed. But to a small degree, you should factor in reversion to the mean when constructing a portfolio.

For example, say you decide that your $100,000 portfolio should include a 15 percent allocation in the Vanguard Mega Cap 300 ETF (MGC) and an equal allocation in the Vanguard Small Cap ETF (VB), and you happen to be entering the market after an incredible several-year bull market in large cap stocks, with small caps falling far behind. If anything, I'd be inclined to slightly overweight small cap stocks, putting perhaps 16 or 17 percent in VB and maybe 13 to 14 percent in MCG.

Please don't go overboard. I'm suggesting that you use reversion to the mean to very gently tweak your portfolio percentages — not ignore them! This "going-against-the-crowd" investment style is popularly known as *contrarian investing.* In Chapter 18, I introduce one investment advisor, Neil Stoloff, who has developed a compelling twist on being a contrarian.

Finding the Perfect Portfolio Fit

Time now to peek into my private world, as I reveal some of the ETF-based portfolios I've worked out for clients over the years (and updated, of course, as some newer ETFs proved to be superior to the old). You should look for the client that you most resemble, and that example will give you some *rough* idea of the kind of advice I would give you if you were a client. All names, of course, have been changed to protect privacy. For the sake of brevity, I provide you with only a thumbnail sketch of each client's financial situations.

Considering the simplest of the simple

Before I get into anything complicated or present any actual client portfolios, I want to introduce an easier-than-easy ETF portfolio. What I've constructed is a perfectly fine, workable investment model with decent (although not great) diversification. It may be enough for anyone without a great amount in savings (say less than $50,000), or someone who has more but wants to keep things as simple as simple can be.

I include (in order of appearance) large cap stocks, small cap stocks, international stocks (large and small), and bonds (both conventional and inflation-adjusted).

This portfolio can be tailored to suit the aggressive investor who can deal with some serious ups and downs in the hopes of achieving high long-term returns; the conservative investor who can't stand to lose too much money; or the middle-of-the-road investor. Keep in mind that you should always have three to six months in living expenses sitting in cash or near-cash (money markets, short-term CDs, Internet checking account, or very short-term high-quality bond fund). You should also have all your credit card and other high interest debt paid up. The rest of your money is what you may invest.

	Aggressive	*Middle-of-the-Road*	*Conservative*
Vanguard Mega Cap 300 ETF (MGC)	20 percent	16 percent	12 percent
Vanguard Small Cap ETF (VB)	20 percent	14 percent	8 percent
Vanguard FTSE All-World ex-US ETF (VEU)	20 percent	16 percent	12 percent
Vanguard FTSE All-World ex-US Small Cap Index ETF (VSS)	20 percent	14 percent	8 percent
Vanguard Total Bond Market ETF (BND)	15 percent	30 percent	45 percent
iShares Barclays TIPS Bond Fund (TIP)	5 percent	10 percent	15 percent

Racing toward riches: A portfolio that may require a crash helmet

High-risk/high-return ETF portfolios are made up mostly of stock ETFs. After all, stocks have a very long history of clobbering most other investments — *if* you give them enough time. Any portfolio that is mostly stocks should have both U.S. and international stocks, large cap and small cap, and value and growth, for starters. If the portfolio is diversified into industry sectors (an acceptable strategy, as I discuss in Chapter 10), a high-risk/high-return strategy would emphasize fast-growing sectors such as technology.

Let's consider the case of Jason, a single, 38-year-old pharmaceuticals salesman. You met him earlier in the chapter. Jason came to me after getting burned badly by several high cost, load mutual funds that performed miserably over the years. Still, given his steady income of $120,000 and his minimal living expenses (he rents a one-bedroom apartment in Allentown, Pennsylvania), Jason has managed to sock away $220,000. His job is secure. He has good disability insurance. He anticipates saving $20,000 to $30,000 a year over the next several years. He enjoys his work and intends to work till normal retirement age. He plans to buy a new car (ballpark $30,000) in the next few months but otherwise has no major expenditures earmarked.

Jason can clearly take some risk. Following is the ETF-based portfolio that I designed for him, which is represented in Figure 16-1. Note that I had Jason put four to six months of emergency money, plus the $30,000 for the car, into a money market account, and that amount is not factored into this portfolio.

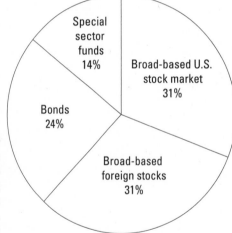

Figure 16-1:
A portfolio that assumes some risk.

Also note that although this portfolio is made up almost entirely of ETFs, I do include one Pennsylvania municipal bond mutual fund to gain access to this asset class that's not yet represented by ETFs. Municipal bonds issued in Jason's home state are exempt from both federal and state taxes, which makes particular sense for Jason because he earns a high income and has no appreciable write-offs. At the time of this writing, New York and California were the only two states with their own municipal bond ETFs. In time, and probably sooner rather than later, I'm quite sure there will be others.

Finally, although this portfolio is technically 76 percent stocks and 24 percent bonds, I include a 4 percent position in emerging market bonds, which can be considerably more volatile than your everyday bond. As such, I don't really think of this as a "76/24" portfolio, but more like an "80/20" portfolio, which is just about as volatile a portfolio as I like to see.

Broad-based U.S. stock market: 31 percent

Vanguard Value ETF (VTV)	9 percent
Vanguard Growth ETF (VUG)	7 percent
Vanguard Small Cap Value ETF (VBR)	9 percent
Vanguard Small Cap Growth ETF (VBK)	6 percent

Broad-based foreign stocks: 31 percent

iShares MSCI EAFE Value Index (EFV)	8 percent
iShares MSCI EAFE Growth Index (EFG)	6 percent
iShares MSCI EAFE Small Cap Index (SCZ)	10 percent
Vanguard Emerging Markets ETF (VWO)	7 percent

Special sector funds: 14 percent

Vanguard REIT ETF (VNQ)	4 percent
Vanguard International Real Estate ETF (VNQI)	4 percent
SPDR S&P Global Natural Resources ETF (GNR)	6 percent

Bonds: 24 percent

iShares Barclays TIPS Bond Fund (TIP)	5 percent
Vanguard Total Bond Market ETF (BND)	10 percent
iShares JPMorgan USD Emerging Markets Bond Fund (EMB)	4 percent
Fidelity Pennsylvania Municipal Income Fund (FPXTX)	5 percent

Sticking to the middle of the road

Next, I present Jay and Racquel, who are ages 63 and 59, married, and have successful careers. Even though they are old enough to be Jason's parents, their economic situation actually warrants a quite similar high-risk/high-return portfolio. Both husband and wife, however, are risk-averse.

Russell's "today and tomorrow" portfolio modeling technique

Career coaches constantly tout the importance of having a career plan; I'm going to tout the importance of having a portfolio plan. Times change; circumstances change. Your portfolio needs to keep up with the times. Suppose you are 45 years old and saving for retirement. Using the 20x rule I discuss in this chapter, you decide that your goal is someday to have a portfolio worth $1.0 million. Your current portfolio has $300,000, so you have a good ways to go. To get where you want, you realize you need to take some risk, but when you start to approach your goal, you want to lower your risk. After all, at that point, you'll have more to lose than gain with any market swings. You should model your portfolio today but also have a picture of what your portfolio may look like when you reach, say, $700,000 . . . whenever that is.

Your picture may look something like this:

Today's $300,000 portfolio

Vanguard Large Cap ETF (VV)	20 percent
Vanguard Small Cap ETF (VB)	20 percent
iShares MSCI EAFE Index Fund (EFA)	30 percent
Vanguard Total Bond Market Fund (BND)	20 percent
iShares Barclays TIPS Bond Fund (TIP)	10 percent

Tomorrow's $700,000 million portfolio

Vanguard Large Cap ETF (VV)	15 percent
Vanguard Small Cap ETF (VB)	15 percent
iShares MSCI EAFE Index Fund (EFA)	25 percent
Vanguard Total Bond Market (BND)	30 percent
iShares Barclays TIPS Bond Fund (TIP)	15 percent

By having your portfolio model for today and your picture of what it may look like tomorrow, you'll always know where you're heading. Trust me, it makes sense. Or trust Yogi Berra, who said, "If you don't know where you're going, you may wind up someplace else."

Jay is an independent businessman with several retail properties (valued at roughly $1.6 million); Racquel is a vice president at a major publishing house. Their portfolio: $800,000 and growing. Within several years, the couple will qualify for combined Social Security benefits of roughly $42,000. Racquel also will receive a fixed pension annuity of about $30,000. The couple's goal is to retire within five to seven years, and they have no dreams of living too lavishly; they should have more than enough money. The fruits of their investments, by and large, should pass to their three grown children and any charities named in their wills.

Being risk-averse, Jay and Racquel keep 30 percent of their portfolio in high quality municipal bonds. They handed me the other 70 percent ($560,000) and told me to invest it as I saw fit. My feeling was that 30 percent high quality bonds was quite enough ballast, so I didn't need to add to their bond position by very much. I therefore constructed a portfolio of largely domestic and foreign stock ETFs. The size of their portfolio (versus Jason's) warranted the addition of a few more asset classes, such as a couple of market-neutral mutual funds and holdings in two large timber REITs. At the couple's request, I also invested a small amount in two commodity ETFs.

I did not include any U.S. REITs other than the timber REITs, given that so much of the couple's wealth is already tied up in commercial real estate. Figure 16-2 presents the portfolio breakdown.

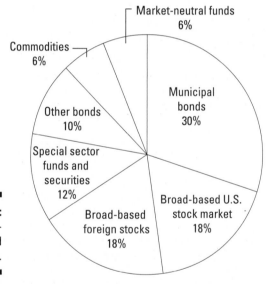

Figure 16-2:
A middle-of-the-road portfolio.

Broad-based U.S. stock market: 18 percent

Vanguard Value ETF (VTV)	6 percent
Vanguard Growth ETF (VUG)	4 percent
Vanguard Small Cap Value ETF (VBR)	5 percent
Vanguard Small Cap Growth ETF (VBK)	3 percent

Broad-based foreign stocks: 18 percent

iShares MSCI EAFE Value Index (EFV)	5 percent
iShares MSCI EAFE Growth Index (EFG)	4 percent
iShares MSCI EAFE Small Cap Index (SCZ)	5 percent
Vanguard Emerging Markets ETF (VWO)	4 percent

Special sector funds and securities: 12 percent

Vanguard International Real Estate ETF (VNQI)	3.5 percent
SPDR S&P Global Natural Resources ETF (GNR)	3.5 percent
Plum Creek Timber Company (PCL)	2.5 percent
Rayonier Timber (RYN)	2.5 percent

Municipal bonds: 30 percent

Various individual high quality tax-exempt municipal bonds

Other bonds: 10 percent

Vanguard Total Bond Market Fund (BND)	7 percent
iShares Barclays TIPS Bond Fund (TIP)	3 percent

Market-neutral funds: 6 percent

Hussman Strategic Growth (HSGFX)	3 percent
Merger Fund (MERFX)	3 percent

Commodities: 6 percent

iPath Dow Jones-UBS Commodity Index Total Return ETN (DJP)	4 percent
SPDR Gold Trust (GLD)	2 percent

Taking the safer road: Less oomph, less swing

We financial professional types hate to admit it, but no matter how much we tinker with our investment strategies, no matter how fancy our portfolio software, we can't entirely remove the luck factor. When you invest in anything, there's always a bit of a gamble involved. (Even when you decide *not* to invest, by, say, keeping all your money in cash, stuffed under the proverbial mattress, you're gambling that inflation won't eat it away or a house fire won't consume it.) Thus, the best investment advice ever given probably comes from Kenny Rogers:

> *You got to know when to hold 'em, know when to fold 'em*
>
> *Know when to walk away and know when to run.*

The time to hold 'em is when you have just enough — when you've pretty much met, or have come close to meeting, your financial goals.

I now present Richard and Maria, who are just about the same age as Jay and Racquel. They are 65 and 58, married, and nearing retirement. Richard, who sank in his chair when I asked about his employment, told me that he was in a job he detests in the ever-changing (and not necessarily changing for the better) newspaper business. Maria was doing part-time public relations work. I added up Richard's Social Security, a small pension from the newspaper, Maria's part-time income, and income from their investments, and I told Richard that he didn't have to stay at a job he hates. There was enough money for him to retire, provided the couple agreed to live somewhat frugally, and provided the investments — $700,000 — could keep up with inflation and not sag too badly in the next bear market.

I should add that the couple owned a home, completely paid for, worth approximately $350,000. They both agreed that they could downsize, if necessary.

For a couple like Richard and Maria, portfolio construction is a tricky matter. Go too conservative, and the couple may run out of money before they die. Go too aggressive, and the couple may run out of money tomorrow. It's a delicate balancing act. In this case, I took Richard and Maria's $700,000 and allocated 25 percent — $175,500 — to a Vanguard immediate fixed annuity. (The annuity was put in Richard's name, with 50 percent survivorship benefit for Maria. It was agreed that should Richard die before Maria, she would sell the home, and buy or rent something more economical.) The rest of the money — $525,000 — I allocated to a broadly diversified portfolio largely constructed using ETFs. Figure 16-3 shows the portfolio breakdown.

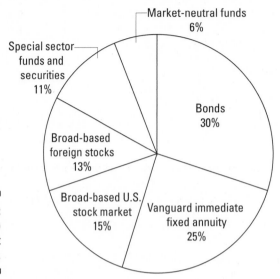

Figure 16-3:
A portfolio
aimed at
safety.

Broad-based U.S. stock market: 15 percent

Vanguard Mega Cap 300 ETF (MGC)	8 percent
Vanguard Small Cap ETF (VB)	7 percent

Broad-based foreign stocks: 13 percent

Vanguard FTSE All-World ex-US ETF (VEU)	7 percent
Vanguard FTSE All-World ex-US Small Cap Index ETF (VSS)	6 percent

Special sector funds and securities: 11 percent

Vanguard International Real Estate ETF (VNQI)	3 percent
SPDR S&P Global Natural Resources ETF (GNR)	3 percent
Plum Creek Timber Company (PCL)	2.5 percent
Rayonier Timber (RYN)	2.5 percent

Bonds: 30 percent

Vanguard Intermediate-Term Corporate Bond Index ETF (VCIT)	15 percent
iShares Barclay TIPS Bond Fund (TIP)	15 percent

Vanguard immediate fixed annuity: 25 percent

With 50 percent survivorship benefit

Market-neutral funds: 6 percent

Hussman Strategic Total Return (HSTRX)   3 percent

Merger Fund (MERFX)   3 percent

Dividing up the pie either conservatively or aggressively by industry sector

In Chapter 10, I talk about *sector* investing (investing by industry sector), as opposed to *grid* investing (splitting your equity into large/small/value/growth). If you want to use sector investing (I have no major problem with that), know that various sectors fall in different places along the risk/return continuum.

According to the people at State Street Global Advisors (SSgA), purveyors of Select Sector SPDR ETFs, with input from Ibbotson Associates, the following sector allocations are the most appropriate for the U.S. equity portion of your portfolio.

Conservative portfolio (15 percent U.S. stocks)

Consumer Discretionary Select Sector SPDR (XLY)	5 percent
Consumer Staples Select Sector SPDR (XLP)	16 percent
Energy Select Sector SPDR (XLE)	14 percent
Financial Select Sector SPDR (XLF)	15 percent
Health Care Select Sector SPDR (XLV)	10 percent
Industrial Select Sector SPDR (XLI)	15 percent
Materials Select Sector SPDR (XLB)	10 percent
Technology Select Sector SPDR (XLK)	14 percent
Utilities Select Sector SPDR (XLU)	15 percent

Aggressive portfolio (63 percent U.S. stocks)

Consumer Discretionary Select Sector SPDR (XLY)	15 percent
Consumer Staples Select Sector SPDR (XLP)	8 percent
Energy Select Sector SPDR (XLE)	6 percent
Financial Select Sector SPDR (XLF)	23 percent
Health Care Select Sector SPDR (XLV)	16 percent
Industrial Select Sector SPDR (XLI)	9 percent
Materials Select Sector SPDR (XLB)	5 percent
Technology Select Sector SPDR (XLK)	18 percent
Utilities Select Sector SPDR (XLU)	6 percent

Chapter 17

Exercising Patience: The Key to Any Investment Success

*N*ow, dear reader, we get to the part of this book you've been waiting for: How to get rich quick using ETFs! The trick is understanding charting patterns.

Let me explain what I mean.

The chart in Figure 17-1 captures a hypothetical daily pricing pattern for a hypothetical ETF that we will give the hypothetical ticker symbol UGH. What you see at point A is a major reversal pattern known to technical analysts as the "Head-and-Shoulders." Notice that as the price dips below the "Neckline" and then rises with simultaneous "Increased Volume" that the "Reversal" of the "Trend" begins to manifest. Buy! Buy!! Within a short time, however, as you can clearly see at point B, a "Minor Top" forms indicating an "Upward Trend" reinforced by the classic "Inverted Triangle." Sell! Sell!! Two minutes later, at point C, where volume increases yet again and the price again rises a point, we see a "Breakaway Gap." Buy! Buy! Buy!

In the next chart (see Figure 17-2), we examine the daily pricing patterns of a hypothetical ETF that we will hypothetically call DUM. You can make millions overnight if you truly understand this charting pattern!

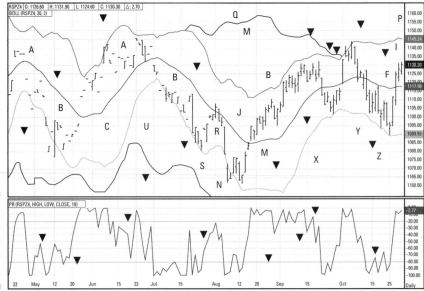

Figure 17-1:
The daily pricing pattern for UGH.

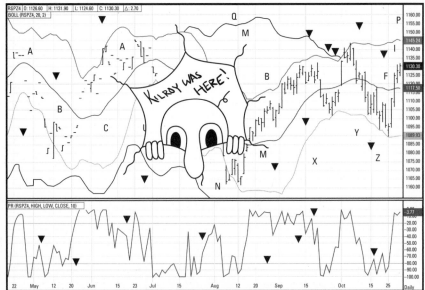

Figure 17-2:
The daily pricing pattern for DUM.

Unless you are totally humor challenged, by now you see that I'm not being entirely serious. Many, if not most, day-traders (who just *love* ETFs, especially the really kooky ones) believe in something called *technical analysis*: the use of charts and graphs to predict movements in securities. Much of the language I used to explain Figure 17-1, as well as the basic idea behind the charts, comes from a best-selling book on technical analysis.

I once had the honor of interviewing one of the biggest names in technical analysis. This guy writes books, gives seminars, and tells everyone that he makes oodles and oodles of money by following charting patterns and buying and selling securities accordingly. At the time I interviewed him, I had been a journalist for 20 years, writing for many of the top U.S. magazines, covering many topics. If you develop one thing being a journalist for two decades, it is a very well-honed bullshit radar. I can tell you after spending an hour on the phone with this "expert" that he is perhaps making of oodles and oodles of money with his books and seminars, but he is *not* making oodles and oodles of money with his charts.

And neither will you.

The key to success in investing isn't to do a lot of trading based on secret formulas every bit as fruitless as alchemy. The key is to keep your investment costs low (ETFs will do that for you), diversify your portfolio (ETFs can do that, too), lose as little as possible to taxes (ETFs can help there, too), and exercise patience (that part's up to you).

In this chapter, I present the evidence to back up my contention that buying and holding, more or less, with regular rebalancing, is the thing to do. Yes, that's true even in today's uber-turbulent markets. You will see that the true champions of the investing world are those with the most patience. Here's a great quote that you may want to post next to your computer to look at the next time you contemplate swapping one ETF for another. It's from someone I admire quite a bit — someone who, I've heard, knows a little bit about investing.

> *The stock market is a method for transferring money from the impatient to the patient.*

> — Warren Buffet

In this chapter, you also discover the difference between hypothetical investing (the kind of investing where you allegedly get rich overnight) and investing in the real world in which Warren Buffet invests. The difference is huge.

The Tale of the Average Investor (A Tragicomedy in One Act)

I talk a bit in this book about *correlation,* the tendency for two things (such as two ETFs or other investments) to move in the same direction. A correlation of 1.0 indicates a *perfect* correlation: think Lucille Ball in the mirror imitating Harpo Marx. Another perfect correlation is the correlation between stock prices and the public's willingness to purchase those stocks.

For some strange reason, the market for stocks (and stock funds, such as ETFs) does not work the same way as, say, the market for cars, shoes, or pineapples. With most products, if the seller drops the price, the public is likely to increase consumption. With stocks and stock funds, when the price *rises,* the public increases consumption.

For example, after tech stocks had their fabulous run in the 1990s, only then — in the latter part of the decade — did money start pouring into tech stocks. After the bubble had burst and tech stocks were selling cheaper than tarnished dirt, people were selling right and left, and no one was buying. As I write these words, the same kind of buying frenzy has been seen more recently with small-growth, gold-mining, and China and India stocks. As soon as the bubble bursts on these, well, it'll be red-tag-sale day once again.

Returns that fall way short of the indexes

Every year, the investment research group Dalbar compares the returns of indexes to the returns that mutual fund investors see in the real world. In their 2010 study, the Dalbar research crew found that the average stock mutual fund investor for the 20 years prior to December 31, 2009 earned a little more than 3 percent a year. This compares to the more than 8 percent that someone would have earned just plunking his money in an S&P 500 index fund for those two decades and leaving it put. Bond fund investors did just as poorly in relation to the bond indexes.

How to explain such lackluster investor returns? In part, the culprit is the average investor's inclination to invest in pricey and poor-performing mutual funds. Another problem is that the average investor jumps ship too often, constantly buying when the market is hot, selling when it chills, and hopping back on board when the market heats up again. He is forever buying high and selling low — not a winning strategy, by any means.

ETFs can solve the first part of the problem. They are, as long as you pick the right ones, not pricey. In fact, they cost very little. Most ETFs are also guaranteed not to underperform the major indexes because they mirror those indexes. As for the jumping-ship problem, however, I fear that ETFs can actually _exacerbate_ the problem.

ETFs can make failure even easier!

ETFs were brought into being by marketing people from the Toronto Stock Exchange who saw a way to beef up trading volume. Unlike mutual funds, which can be bought and sold only at day's end, ETFs trade throughout the day. In a flash, you can plunk a million in the stock market. A few seconds later, you can sell it all.

Yipeee!

In other words, the next time Dalbar does a 20-year return study, after ETFs have really caught on with the average investor, I fear that their findings, if they include ETFs, may be even more dismal. Remember: Just because ETFs can be traded throughout the day doesn't mean you _have_ to or that you _should_ trade them!

The vast majority of ETF trades are made by institutional investors: managers of mutual funds or hedge funds, multibillion-dollar endowments, pension funds, and investment banks. These are highly trained, incredibly well-paid professionals who do nothing all day but study the markets.

When you go to buy, say, the Financial Select Sector SPDR ETF (XLF) which represents stocks in the financial sector , you are betting that the price is going to go up. If you are day-trading, you are betting that the price will go up that day. If you are selling, you are betting that the price will fall that day. Someone, most likely a highly educated financial professional with an army of researchers and computers more powerful than the FBI's, someone who does nothing but study financial stocks 80 hours a week (for which reason his wife is about to leave him) is on the other end of your transaction. As you sell, he — we'll call him Chad — is buying. Or, as you buy, he is selling. Obviously, Chad's vision of the next few hours and days is different from yours. Chad may not know that his wife Barbie is about to leave him for a professional hockey player, but if either of you has any idea which way financial stocks are headed, well . . . Do you really think that you know something Chad doesn't? Do you really think that you're going to get the better end of this deal?

Obviously, lots of ETF traders think they are pretty smart because ETFs are among the most frequently traded of all securities — see the sidebar "The ten ETFs that day-traders love the most." Also see the sidebar "The author's confession (and a few rules if you are going to day-trade)" later in the chapter for an inside view of a repentant day-trader's mind.

The lure of quick riches

If you jump onto the Internet, as I just did, and type in the words "Market timing success," you will see all kinds of websites and newsletters offering you all kinds of advice (much of it having to do with reading charts) that's sure to make you rich. Add the initials "ETF" to your search, and you'll quickly see that an entire cottage industry has formed to sell advice to wannabe ETF day-traders.

According to these websites and newsletters, following their advice has yielded phenomenal returns in the past (and they'll give you specific BIG numbers proving it). And following their advice in the future (after you've paid your hefty subscription fee) will likewise yield phenomenal returns.

If you're wondering, by the way, who regulates investment websites and newsletters and the performance figures they publish, wonder no more. No one does. The U.S. Supreme Court decided in 1985 that, just as long as a newsletter is providing general and not personal advice, the publisher is protected by the free-speech provisions of the First Amendment.

John Rekenthaler, a VP at Morningstar, once told me (and I love how he put it): "Investment newsletter publishers have the same rights as tabloid publishers. There's nothing illegal about a headline that reads 'Martian Baby Born with Three Heads!' and there's nothing illegal about a headline that reads 'We Beat the Market Year In and Year Out!'" Both should be read with equal skepticism.

The ten ETFs that day-traders love the most

They are volatile. They are *liquid* (meaning that they trade easily). And the following ten ETFs are flipped more often than all other ETFs:

- ✔ SPDR S&P 500 (SPY)
- ✔ Financial Select Sector SPDR (XLF)
- ✔ iShares Russell 2000 (IWM)
- ✔ PowerShares QQQ Trust Series 1 (QQQ)
- ✔ iShares MSCI Emerging Markets Index Fund (EEM)
- ✔ iShares Silver Trust (SLV)
- ✔ iShares MSCI Japan Index Fund (EWJ)
- ✔ ProShares UltraShort S&P 500 (SDS)
- ✔ Energy Select Sector SPDR (XLE)
- ✔ Industrial Select Sector SPDR (XLI)

The Value Line Paradox

Throughout the years, one of the most popular purveyors of market-timing and stock-picking advice — though not the worst offender, by far — is Value Line. It's not as popular as it was years ago, but it is still a household name. Not only are the Value Line people now offering advice on picking ETFs as well as stocks, but also they had their own ETF until recently — the Value Line Timeliness Selection ETF — that actually mirrored the advice given by the famed Value Line newsletter. The fund was administered by PowerShares, which pulled the plug on it after four years of lackluster returns.

Some things — Robert E. Lee's march into Pennsylvania, the *Titanic* — look fabulous on paper but, when translated into reality, reveal some rather tremendous flaws.

Paper versus practice

Using a proprietary system more secretly guarded than the recipe for Coke, the Value Line newsletter's performance track record has been nothing short of eye-popping. On paper, at least. From the Value Line website:

> *Value Line's exclusive Timeliness™ ranking system—an "at-a-glance" prognosticator of 6-12 month relative price performance for approximately 1,700 actively traded U.S. stocks, ranging from 1 (highest) to 5 (lowest). Since 1965, higher-ranked stocks that have repeatedly outperformed market indices.*

Each and every year that I've checked the website, lo and behold, Value Line's picks are kicking serious butt. The last time I checked, a banner headline read,

> *The 2010 Results Are Clear. . . Value Line's #1 Ranked Stocks: 29.7% . . . S&P 500: 12.8%.*

It's unclear what timeframe they are talking about, but the message is certainly clear that if you buy Value Line's picks, you'll get rich by "repeatedly outperform[ing] market indices." Hmm. Possibly. On paper. But what about in the real world, where real dollars would be invested in those picks?

Ah, there's the rub.

The company, you see, offers not only a newsletter but a few mutual funds — *ergo,* real investors in the real world. The flagship Value Line mutual fund (VLIFX), which, according to its prospectus, taps into the very same wisdom that guides the newsletter, has not exactly set the world on fire. The fund, which has a Morningstar rating of one star, calls itself a "mid-cap growth fund." According to Morningstar Principia, the fund's ten-year annual return as of June 30, 2011 was –0.07, compared to 5.52 for the Russell Midcap Growth Index and 2.72 for the S&P 500. Going back 15 years, the fund's annual return averaged 2.97 percent compared to 7.73 percent for the Midcap Growth Index and 6.5 percent for the S&P 500. Not only would you have earned terrible returns, but VLIFX's volatility was substantially greater than that of the S&P 500!

The lesson to be learned

How can a mutual fund that tracks the allegedly super-successful newsletter be such a flaming dud? There are a number of possible explanations. One is that the return numbers given by Value Line are a bit, um, off. (In fact, independent research has come up with far, far lower return figures.) Or perhaps the managers of the mutual fund were unable to follow the advice given in their own newsletter. Perhaps trading costs ate up all profits — and then some. Whatever the explanation, investors lost money.

But my point in sharing the Value Line paradox isn't so much to steer you away from any single mutual fund or ETF. My point is to steer you away from thinking that you — or anyone else — can trade in and out of ETFs, stocks, bonds, or anything else successfully. It's not nearly as easy as many people (such as the Value Line editors) make it seem.

"Investment Pornography" in Your Mailbox (and Mine)

Investment websites and newsletters are part of a phenomenon that financial journalist Jane Bryant Quinn once called "investment pornography." Many newsletters, magazines, newspaper columns, books, and television shows exist to titillate and tease you with the promise of riches. Achieving those riches with ETFs is only the latest gimmick.

One glossy consumer finance magazine that arrived in my mailbox caught my attention. A very attractive woman is walking along the beach. She holds a purse in her hand. (Why is she carrying a purse on the beach?) I am told by the caption under her left foot that the attractive woman earned a 40 percent return in one year.

I turn to page 65 of the magazine, and there she is: a single woman! She earned her 40 percent by investing ("on the advice of a friend") in the Hodges mid cap mutual fund. Mid caps happened to have kicked serious butt in the

12 months prior to this issue's release. What the article doesn't tell you is that the Hodges fund has a fairly hefty expense ratio and — no big surprise here — a 15-year return that trails the S&P MidCap 400 index by 3.54 percent annually.

No wonder that poor woman carries her purse on the beach. She has determined that someone is out to steal her money.

Welcome to the wild, wacky world of investment advice

In 1999, a very popular book entitled *Dow 36,000: The New Strategy for Profiting from the Coming Rise in the Stock Market* gave readers 300 pages of in-depth explanation why the Dow Jones Industrial average, at that time riding around 10,000, was destined to more than triple in value. "The case is compelling that 36,000 is a fair value for the Dow today. And stocks should rise to such heights very quickly," wrote James K. Glassman and co-author Kevin A. Hassett. Of course, as soon as the book came out, advising people to pour money into stocks, the Dow proceeded to tumble to less than 8,000 in a three-year bear market.

Where do you suppose James K. Glassman is today? Why, he's writing an investment advice column, of course. And he's writing more books. And he's making more predictions.

Before Glassman, there were the Beardstown Ladies. In 1983, 16 women in Beardstown, Illinois, started an investment club. In 1994, claiming a 23.4 percent annualized ten-year return, they wrote a book called *The Beardstown Ladies' Common-Sense Investment Guide*. It became a huge bestseller. Oops. It turns out, upon further inspection, that the Beardstown Ladies overstated their returns. Their actual return was 9.1 percent a year, considerably less than the stock market.

What happened to the good Ladies of Beardstown? Why, they went on to write five more investment books, of course.

Don't even get me started on Jim "Mad Money" Cramer. If you haven't taken his screaming advice and lost money on your own, simply search his name on the Internet, along with the words "actual performance" or "flip of the coin," and you will be very disinclined ever to buy based on one of Mr. Mad Money's tips. My fellow *For Dummies* author Eric Tyson (see http://EricTyson.com) has made something of a sport of tracking Cramer's actual performance, and it isn't pretty.

Caveat emptor: ETF-trading websites for suckers

I share these investment horror stories of the past and present so that you won't wind up as a player in any future ones. One way to make sure you don't is to be on the lookout for ridiculous claims. Market timing services are popping up all over the Internet. Why not? ETFs are hot. They are in the news. They sound so impressive. And there is a sucker born every minute.

Please, please, don't fork over your money assuming that you're going to get the secrets to instant wealth by trading ETFs. It won't happen.

Following are just a few examples of the countless websites hoping to lure you in with big promises. I can't possibly list them all, so be wary:

✔ www.stockmarkettiming.com

Cost: $359/year for the "Platinum Plan"

Direct from the website: *StockMarketTiming.com, LLC is a financial service for investors and traders who want to increase their portfolios in the most non-stressful and effective way possible in both bullish and bearish markets! We have developed a market timing system that uses technical analysis for trading the popular Exchange Traded Funds (ETFs) — DIA, SPY, and QQQ, which has produced outstanding gains!*

Russell says: Outstanding gains for whom?

We are the home of the most honest, concise, credible (unbiased and zero-hype), low-risk, and one of the most effective financial Web sites on the Internet today!

Russell says: I'm glad that the hype is unbiased. I hate biased hype.

✔ www.marketpolygraph.com

Cost: $816.65/month for investment professionals, but "only" $52.30/month for U.S. private investors.

Direct from the website: *Marketpolygraph provides proprietary market timing research to private and professional investors who receive decisive trading signals for specific exchange traded funds (ETFs). Our simple and direct market timing research entails only minutes of follow-up effort every month and represents the singular requirement for realizing exceptional investment returns.*

Russell says: Only minutes a month, eh? It takes me longer than that each day just to boot up my computer.

✔ www.kt-timing.com/rydex

Cost (from the website): *The yearly subscription fee is $250 for Combo MID term and short term OPEN. $250 for Combo MID term and short term CLOSE. And for $350, you get the Combo MID term and short term OPEN + CLOSE.*

Russell says: Don't ask me what any of the above means; I have no idea, and I refuse to risk hurting my brain by trying to find out.

Direct from the website: *The objective of all our short term trading models is to achieve unsurpassed all weather performance.*

Russell says: Good objective.

Patience Pays, Literally

The flip side of flipping ETFs is buying and holding them, which is almost certain, in the long run, to bring results far superior to market timing. It's the corollary to choosing ETFs over stocks. Study after study shows that the markets are, by and large, *efficient*. What does that mean? So many smart players are constantly buying and selling securities, always on the lookout for any good deals, that your chances of beating the indexes, whether by market timing or stock picking, are very slim.

One of but many studies on the subject, "The Difficulty of Selecting Superior Mutual Fund Performance" by Thomas P. McGuigan, appeared in the *Journal of Financial Planning*. McGuigan found that only 10 to 11 percent of actively managed mutual funds outperform index funds over a 20-year period. (*Active managers* are professionals who try to pick stocks and time the market.)

We can probably safely assume that the professionals do better than the amateurs, and even the professionals fail to beat the market 90 percent of the time.

Talk about unpredictability

Timing doesn't work because markets are largely random. The unpredictability of the stock market (and the bond market, for that matter) never ceases to amaze me. Just when things seem certain to take off, they sink. Just when they seem certain to sink, they fly.

I had one client, a 52-year-old allergist in Allentown, Pennsylvania, who several years ago read up on avian flu and became so concerned about what a pandemic might do to the stock market that he urged me to take his $500,000 portfolio and put everything in cash. We set up a meeting in his office, and I was able to temper his desire to cash out. (However, we did move his portfolio to a somewhat more conservative position.)

Prior to our meeting, I sent the client the following e-mail, which I would like to share with you:

> *Dear Tom,*
>
> *Since your initial e-mail on this topic, I've done a fair amount of reading, and you have reason to be concerned, for sure. I am, too. (Author's note: I was being truthful here, although my concern was more a health concern than a financial one.)*
>
> *Holding some cash and gold wouldn't be a bad idea. (If we had a real economic crisis, you would want small gold coins . . . 1/10 ounce.)*
>
> *But don't assume that pandemics, or any other crisis, necessarily result in stock market crashes.*
>
> *Keep in mind that 1918, the year of the worst pandemic in world history, was a good year for stocks:* `http://www.econ.yale.edu/~shiller/data/chapt26.html`.
>
> *1962 (Cuban Missile Crisis) was a very good year. 1942 (Japan attacked Pearl Harbor; Hitler marched across Europe) wasn't too bad, either.*
>
> *In contrast, let's look at the worst years for the stock market. In 1929, nothing catastrophic was going on. Ditto for 1987. Ditto for 2000.*
>
> *I can't explain the incredible unpredictability of the markets. I can only share these historical truths.*
>
> *Yours,*
>
> *Russell*

Since I wrote that note, we've been though yet another of history's worst years for the stock market. That was 2008. While there was something of a banking crisis going on, I'm not sure that the demise of Lehman Brothers compares to Hitler's blitzkrieg of Europe. But more on 2008 in just a moment.

A short history of the market's resiliency

As I write this chapter, in August 2011, news of the S&P's downgrade of U.S. Treasuries has sent the stock market way down . . . and up . . . and down. More down than up. Nearly all of my stock ETFs have lost serious money in recent months. (Paradoxically and ironically, U.S. Treasury prices have soared. Go figure.) Am I happy? No, of course not. Am I panicking? Nope.

The author's confession (and a few rules if you are going to day-trade)

Um . . . er . . . I don't know quite how to say this, but, despite all of my talk in this chapter and throughout this book about buying and holding, and the futility of day-trading, yes — YES! YES! — I've done it. I admit it! I've bought and sold ETFs within the same day in the hope of making a quick gain! I've done it with the QQQ (an ETF that tracks the NASDAQ) and with EEM (an emerging markets ETF).

What can I say? Gambling (and that is what such short-term forays into the market are) can be fun. Not only that, but the odds of making money by gambling on an ETF are much greater than they are by, say, playing the horses, shooting craps, or standing in line at 7-11 on a Friday afternoon to buy lottery tickets. After all, the "house" takes only a small cut when you play the markets. And time is on your side.

Have I made any short-terms gains? Sure. I've also lost some money. On balance, over the years, I've probably just about broken even . . . or maybe earned ten cents an hour for all my efforts. But it has been fun!

I am sharing this with you because I know that some of you are going to occasionally have that feeling in your gut that you "know" some security is going to go up (or down, if you're into short selling), and you may take a stab.

Okay, go ahead if you must; I'll just ask you to play by a few rules.

Rule #1

Separate gambling from investing; have a (small) fixed amount of money to gamble with. Take it from cash. Don't sell your buy-and-hold investments to finance your gambling.

Rule #2

If you find that you are getting fixated on your wins and losses, quit. If it isn't fun, don't do it.

If you find that you are spending an inordinate amount of time playing the markets, quit. There is more to life.

Rule #3

Don't buy on margin. If you are borrowing money from the brokerage house to trade, that could spell big trouble. Margin money usually costs much more than you think. I hold Fidelity Investments in high regard, but I really don't like their recent full-page magazine advertisements offering low rates for margin borrowing. If you read the very small print at the bottom of the page, it explains that the advertised rate pertains only to margin loans over $500,000. Small players — like you and me — pay much more.

Rule #4

Ask yourself what you're going to do if you get stuck. Have an exit plan. What if you buy EEM on an exceptionally volatile day, and you expect it to rise 3 percent, but instead it falls 4 percent? Are you going to hold it until it climbs back up? Are you going to cash out and take the hit? Have a plan in place before you make the trade, and stick to it. Consider placing a stop-loss order going in, at a price that reflects how much you're willing to lose. That way, if the trade goes against you, your plan will be implemented automatically without requiring you to make a gut-wrenching decision in the heat of the moment.

Rule #5

If you think that you have a superhuman ability to time the markets, ask yourself if that is really what you want to do for a living. Day-trading isn't exactly a career that benefits the community or grows your consciousness. I've known a good number of day-traders; they tend not to be the happiest or most enlightened people on the planet.

When I look over the market year-to-date, at least today, U.S. stocks have lost about 3 percent. Recent history has seen much, much bigger losses, and somehow, eventually, the market has always recovered.

Remember September 11, 2001? Following the destruction of the World Trade Center towers, the Dow immediately dropped more than 7 percent. Six months later, the Dow was up by 10.5 percent. On September 24, 1955, President Eisenhower's heart attack led to a one-day drop of 6.5 percent. Six months later, the Dow was up 12.5 percent. I could give example after example.

In 2008, the market had its worst dip since the Great Depression; the S&P 500 tumbled nearly 37 percent for the year. But it came back, gaining 26 percent in 2009 and about 15 percent in 2010. Had you rebalanced in 2008, shaving off bonds and buying up stock at rock-bottom prices, your portfolio (provided it was well-diversified) would likely have fully recovered in just two years.

That's not to say that the market will *always* come back. One of these days . . . well, even Rome eventually fell. But history shows that the stock market is a mighty resilient beast. I suggest that you build a portfolio of ETFs — including stock and bond ETFs — and hang tight. Sooner or later (barring some truly major economic upheaval), you will very likely be rewarded.

Chapter 18

Exceptions to the Rule (Ain't There Always)

*W*hen I was a kid, long before there was such a thing as online banking, I would often pedal my metallic blue three-speed Schwinn bicycle to one of the local savings banks on Long Island to deposit my allowance money. In those days, if you opened a new account, you were often given a free gift: a toaster, clock radio, leather wallet, crystal candlesticks, or such. This was a great incentive to switch banks, and I did so with some regularity.

Today, I don't generally ride my bicycle to the bank. I don't think they even make three-speeds anymore. And most neighborhood banks no longer give away toasters or clock radios. Times change! Yet sometimes it still makes sense to switch your investments around.

In the previous chapter, I discuss the virtues of a buy-and-hold approach to ETF investing. But that doesn't mean that you should purchase a bunch of ETFs and *never* touch them. Switching from one ETF to another won't get you a clock radio or a leather wallet, but there can be other benefits to making some occasional moves, for sure.

In this chapter, I discuss certain circumstances where it makes sense to trade ETFs rather than buy and hold. For example, you need to rebalance your portfolio, typically on an annual basis, to keep risk in check, and on occasion you may want to swap ETFs to harvest taxes at year end. I also discuss the ways in which life changes may warrant tweaking a portfolio. And finally, I introduce you to the world of ETF options, where frequent trading is a way of life.

Rebalancing to Keep Your Portfolio Fit

Few investors walked away from 2008 smelling like a rose. But those who were slammed, truly slammed, were those who had more on the stock side of their portfolios than they should have. It happens, and it happens especially after bull markets, such as we saw in the several years prior to 2008.

Let's take the case of Samantha. In 2003, when she was 50 years old, she sat down and looked at her financial situation and goals. She determined that she warranted a 60/40 (60 percent stock/40 percent bond) portfolio and duly crafted a darned good one. But then she got lazy. She held that portfolio without touching it through the stock market boom years of 2003 through 2007. As a result, her portfolio morphed from a 60/40 mix to a 70/30 mix by the start of 2008.

Uh oh.

In other words, just when the market tanked, just when she could have really used the ballast that bonds provide, her lopsided portfolio, due to neglect, was primed for disaster. The stock market fell by about 37 percent, and her 70 percent stock portfolio fell by about a quarter. That's a big fall. And to add insult to injury, just when stocks hit rock bottom, she had no "dry powder" (cash) with which to reload her stock portfolio.

It is in large part to prevent such big falls, and lack of "dry powder," that you need to rebalance. That is, on a regular basis, you need to do exactly the opposite of what most investors do: You need to sell off some of your winners and buy up the losers.

By doing so, not only do you cap your risk, but studies show that you will juice your returns. By systematically buying low and selling high, you may, over the long run, increase your average annual returns by as much as 1.5 percent. That's not a bad return at all for an exercise that shouldn't take you more than a couple hours! (***Note:*** I say "as much as 1.5 percent" because the profitability of rebalancing will depend on how many asset classes you own and the correlations they have to each other.)

How rebalancing works

Samantha actually hurt herself in two ways. In 2008, she was 55 years old: five years closer to retirement than she was when she established her "ideal" 60/40 portfolio. It would have been reasonable at that point for Samantha to adjust her mix to, say, 50/50 to reflect the need for a bit more protection against market losses as retirement neared. Had Samantha started off 2008 with a proper portfolio, whether it was 60/40 after rebalancing or 50/50 after reassessing and then rebalancing, she would have been in a much better position to weather the storm that was coming.

Prepare yourself for the next market storm! How? The answer is fairly simple: Don't allow any one slice of your portfolio to overtake the rest. Periodically pull your portfolio back into balance.

To illustrate, I'll use the simple middle-of-the-road ETF portfolio that I introduce in Chapter 16. At the start of the year, the portfolio is just where you want it to be: 60 percent diversified stocks, 40 percent bonds. But it turns out to be a banner year for stocks, and especially for small cap U.S. stocks. At the end of the year, as you can see in Table 18-1, the portfolio looks quite different.

Table 18-1	A Shifting Portfolio Balance
Beginning of Year One (In Balance)	
ETF	**Percent of Portfolio**
Vanguard Mega Cap 300 ETF (MGC)	16 percent
Vanguard Small Cap ETF (VB)	14 percent
Vanguard FTSE All-World ex-US ETF (VEU)	16 percent
Vanguard FTSE All-World ex-US Small Cap Index ETF (VSS)	14 percent
Vanguard Total Bond Market ETF (BND)	30 percent
iShares Barclays TIPS Bond Fund (TIP)	10 percent
End of Year One (Out of Balance)	
ETF	**Percent of Portfolio**
Vanguard Mega Cap 300 ETF (MGC)	17 percent
Vanguard Small Cap ETF (VB)	19 percent
Vanguard FTSE All-World ex-US ETF (VEU)	18 percent
Vanguard FTSE All-World ex-US Small Cap Index ETF (VSS)	15 percent
Vanguard Total Bond Market ETF (BND)	22 percent
iShares Barclays TIPS Bond Fund (TIP)	9 percent

What to do? Bring things back into balance, starting with the bond position. That's because the split between stocks and bonds has the greatest impact on portfolio risk. In this example, you need to increase the bond allocation from 31 percent back up to 40 percent. If you have a year-end portfolio of $100,000, that means you'll buy $9,000 of BND and TIP to bring up your bond allocation by 9 percentage points.

Where will the $9,000 come from? That depends. You could sell off part of your stock position, which may be necessary given that things are pretty seriously out of balance. But do keep in mind that selling off winning positions in a taxable account will require you to pay capital gains — and possibly a small commission on the ETF trades. So to the extent possible, try to rebalance by shoring up your losing positions with fresh deposits or with dividends and interest earned on your portfolio.

How often to rebalance

The question of how often to rebalance has been studied and restudied, and most financial professionals agree that once a year is a good timeframe, at least for those still in the accumulation phase of their investing careers. Anything less frequent than that increases your risk as positions get more and more out of whack. Anything more frequent than annually, and you may lower your returns by interrupting rallies too often and increasing your "friction" costs (trading commissions, spreads, and possible taxes).

Keep these costs in mind as you rebalance. Tweaking a portfolio by a few dollars here and there to achieve "perfect" balance may not make financial sense.

A rule I give myself is never to pay more than one-half of 1 percent to make a trade for rebalancing purposes. In the example in the previous section, if a trade of $8,000 for BND will cost you $10, you are forking out only 0.125 percent to make the trade . . . so, by all means, make the trade.

If, however, to get your portfolio in perfect balance, you were faced with making a $1,000 trade that would cost you $10 (1 percent of the amount you're trading), I don't think I'd opt to spend the $10. I'd rather wait another year (or perhaps less if I sensed that a major shift had occurred) before acting.

Another way to approach rebalancing is to seek to address any allocations that are off by more than 10 percent, and don't sweat anything that's off by less. In other words, if BND is given an allocation in the portfolio of 30 percent, I wouldn't worry too much about rebalancing unless that percentage falls to 27 percent, or rises to 33 percent.

Rebalancing for retirees

If you are in the *decumulation* phase of your investing career (that's a fancy way of saying that you are living off of your savings), you may want to rebalance every 6 months instead of 12. The reason: Rebalancing has a third purpose for you, in addition to risk-reduction and performance-juicing. For you, rebalancing is a good time to raise whatever cash you anticipate needing in the upcoming months. In times of super-low interest rates on money market and saving accounts, such as we've seen in recent years, it can be profitable to rebalance more often so that you don't need to keep as much cash sitting around earning squat. I provide more information on raising cash for living expenses in retirement in Chapter 19.

Contemplating Tactical Asset Allocation

Astute readers — such as you — now may be wondering this: If you can juice your returns by rebalancing (systematically buying low and selling high), can you perhaps juice your returns even more by *over*-rebalancing? In other words, suppose you design a 60/40 portfolio, and suddenly stocks tank. Now you have a 50/50 portfolio. Might you consider not only buying enough stock to get yourself back to a 60/40 portfolio, but also (because stocks are so apparently cheap) buying even *more* stocks than you need for simple rebalancing purposes?

Investment professionals call this kind of maneuver "tactical asset allocation." It is the art of tilting a portfolio given certain economic conditions. Tactical asset allocation is different than market timing only in the degree to which action is required. With tactical asset allocation, you make a gentle and unhurried shift in one direction or another, whereas market timing entails a more radical and swift shifting of assets. While tactical asset allocation, done right, may add to your bottom line, market timing will almost always cost you. The division between the two can be a fine line, so proceed with caution.

Understanding the all-important P/E ratio

I talk about reversion to the mean in Chapter 16. If a certain asset class has been seeing returns much, much lower than its historical average, you may want to very slightly overweight that asset class. If, for example, you are considering overweighting U.S. stocks, it makes more sense to do it when U.S. stocks are selling relatively cheaply. Typically, but not always, an asset class may be "selling cheap" after several years of underperforming its historical returns.

But is there any way to find a more objective measure of "selling cheap"? Investment legend Benjamin Graham liked to use something called the P/E ratio. The P stands for price. The E stands for earnings. When the market price of a stock (or all stocks) is high, and the earnings (or profits for a company or companies) are low, then you have a high P/E ratio; conversely, when the market price is down but earnings are up, you have a low P/E ratio. Graham, as well as his student Warren Buffett, preferred to buy when the P/E ratio was low.

Throughout Part I of this book, I urge you to consider tilting your entire stock portfolio, on a permanent basis, toward lower P/E stocks, otherwise known as *value stocks*. Here, I'm talking not about a permanent tilt but a mild, temporary one. It stands to reason that if value stocks outperform other stocks — and historically they have done just that — if the entire stock market appears to be a value market, then that market may outperform in the foreseeable future.

Recent work by Yale University economist Robert J. Shiller has lent credence to the notion that buying when the P/E ratio is low raises your expected returns. In fact, Shiller has tinkered with the way the P/E ratio is defined so that the earnings part of the equation looks back over a decade (rather than the typical one year) and then factors in inflation. Shiller's research, based on tracking market returns with varying P/E ratios over the decades, indicates that when his adjusted P/E ratio is low, the stock market is more likely to produce gains over the following decade. When the P/E ratio is high (it reached an all-time high of about 44 in 1999, for example), you may be looking forward to a decade of very low (or no) returns.

Applying the ratio to your portfolio

Although Shiller's theories have been hotly debated, it stands to reason that, if they are applied carefully, you may just do yourself a favor to slightly overweight all stocks when the P/E ratio is low and to underweight all stocks when the P/E ratio is high. But against the probability that Shiller's formula holds, you need to weigh the very real transaction costs involved in shifting your portfolio. On balance, I wouldn't suggest engaging in tactical asset allocation very often . . . and then only if the numbers seem to be shouting at you to act.

One very quick way to check the P/E ratio for the entire stock market would be to look up an ETF that tracks the entire market, such as the Vanguard Total Stock Market ETF (VTI), on Vanguard's website (www.vanguard.com) or on just about any financial website (such as www.morningstar.com) to see the P/E ratio. Or, to see Shiller's newfangled P/E calculations, go to www.multpl.com. (The P/E ratio is sometimes called the "multiple.")

The historical average for Shiller's adjusted P/E over the past 50 years is 19.5. As I'm writing these words, the P/E for the market is just about at that mark. So, unless that number has changed by the time you're reading this chapter, don't even think about tactical asset allocation. However, if stock prices should race ahead of or fall way behind earnings, and you start to see an adjusted P/E of, say, 30 or more, or 10 or less, you may want to gently — very gently — tweak your portfolio in one direction or another.

Did I remember to say gently?

If, all things being equal, you determine that you should have a portfolio of 60 percent stocks, and if the adjusted P/E falls to the low teens, consider adding 2 to 3 percentage points to your stock allocation, and that's all. If the market P/E falls to 10, then maybe, provided you can stomach the volatility, consider adding yet another percentage point or two, or even three, to your "neutral" allocation. If the adjusted P/E rises to 30 or so, you may want to lighten up on stocks by a few points. Please, keep to these parameters. Tilting more than a few percentage points — particularly on the up side (more stocks than before) — increases your risks beyond the value of any potential gain.

Buying unloved assets

Ever notice how weeds grow so much faster than the plants that you *want* to see grow? For years, Morningstar has advocated, and continues to advocate with varying levels of enthusiasm, something called "Buy the Unloved." It calls not for overweighting asset classes that sport low P/E ratios, but for overweighting asset classes that investors (being the lemmings that they are) have abandoned in droves. In other words, you are encouraged to buy "weeds."

As I'm writing this, for example, Morningstar is listing large cap U.S. stocks as being among the weediest of asset classes. With small cap stocks having outperformed large caps for more than a decade, investors have turned away from large companies, and money has moved out of large cap stock funds.

If you shift from the "loved" to the "unloved" (in other words, you allocate tactically) and hold the "unloved" for three to five years, you'll tend to outperform the market per Morningstar. "From the beginning of 1994 to the end of 2010, the unloved earned 308% cumulatively or 9% annualized. That's far better than the loved, which earned 157% cumulatively or 6.1% annualized," says the company. During this time, the S&P 500 returned 8% annualized.

Investing the SweetSpot way

No matter how well you may tend to the weeds in your garden, they will never win an award at the county fair. The weeds that you buy as an investor, on the other hand, are actually more likely to blossom into big winners than the most highly prized — and high-priced — petunias that tend to wither at the first sign of bad weather.

About a year ago, I encountered a man named Neil Stoloff, a wealth manager outside Detroit, Michigan, who calls his shop SweetSpot Investments LLC. Just as Robert Shiller crunched historical data to come up with a new-and-improved way of measuring P/E, Stoloff crunched historical data and came up with a new-and-improved way of defining "unloved."

Each January, Stoloff examines more than 500 ETFs and mutual funds that track about 100 different U.S. and global industry sectors (from energy to financials to healthcare), as well as entire foreign markets (such as France, South Africa, and Malaysia). He calculates the flow of money into and out of each sector and market over the year that just ended, looking for the greatest outflows. And that's where he invests: into the areas that most investors have decided they wouldn't touch with the proverbial 10-foot pole. These are the weediest weeds Stoloff can find. A year later he repeats the process, and while he's at it he sells whatever was bought three years prior.

Given that he tinkers just once a year, I would classify Stoloff as a professional tactical asset allocator rather than a market timer. You can learn more about what he does and why he does it in a paper published in April 2011: `http://sweetspotinvestments.com/wp-content/uploads/paper.pdf`.

How has SweetSpot performed? Exceptionally well, and far better than Morningstar. For the latest performance figures, go to Stoloff's website, `www.sweetspotinvestments.com`. (Disclosure time: Neil and I have become good friends. At my urging, Neil had his return figures audited by an independent accounting firm, and I believe I'm being objective in saying that this guy may be on to something.)

Stoloff's strategy is not one that do-it-yourselfers can easily employ. Finding and making sense of the data on flows for each of 500 funds isn't nearly as easy as finding market-sector P/E ratios. Stoloff is a money manager whose fee is a percentage of assets under management, but he began his career as a do-it-yourself investor, just like you. When I told him that I planned to feature him in this book, we had a back-and-forth that culminated in an offer: For a relatively modest subscription fee, any do-it-yourselfers who learn about SweetSpot from this book (just tell him so) can subscribe to the information needed to place their own annual SweetSpot trades. For details, contact Neil directly at `neil@sweetspotinvestments.com`. (Disclosure #2: In exchange for this endorsement — ringing or not — I stand to receive zero compensation from Neil or anyone else associated with SweetSpot Investments LLC. Dang it.)

Even if SweetSpot isn't your cup of tea, you can still benefit from the wisdom of investing contrarily. Often you can get a sense of the direction in which the herd is running simply by keeping your ears open at cocktail parties. Just move opposite the crowd — slowly — and you'll likely outperform over time. As with any other kind of tactical asset allocation, I urge you to always consider your total allocation and make certain that you remain well diversified.

Harvesting Tax Losses, and the IRS's Oh-So-Tricky "Wash Rule"

So you had a bad year on a particular investment? You had a bad year on *many* of your investments? Allow Uncle Sam to share your pain. You only need to sell the investment(s) by December 31st, and you can use the loss to offset any capital gains. Or, if you've had no capital gains, you can deduct the loss from your taxable ordinary income for the year, up to $3,000.

But there's a problem. Because of the IRS's "wash rule," you can't sell an investment on December 31st and claim a loss if you buy back that same investment or any "substantially identical" investment within 30 days of the sale. You may simply want to leave the sale proceeds in cash. That way, you save on any transaction costs and avoid the hassle of trading.

On the other hand, January is historically a very good time for stocks. You may not want to be out of the market that month. What to do?

ETFs to the rescue!

What the heck is "substantially identical" anyway?

The IRS rules are a bit hazy when it comes to identifying "substantially identical" investments. Clearly, you can't sell and then buy back the same stock. But if you sell $10,000 of Exxon Mobil Corp. (XOM) stock, you *can* buy $10,000 of an ETF that covers the energy industry, such as the Energy Select Sector SPDR (XLE) or the Vanguard Energy ETF (VDE). They're not the same thing, for sure, but either one can be expected to perform in line with XOM (and its competitors as well) for the 30 days that you must live without your stock. And rest assured, no ETF could reasonably be deemed to be "substantially identical" to any individual stock.

I, of course, would prefer that you keep most of your portfolio in ETFs in the first place. Even then, if you follow my advice, and one year turns out to be especially bad for, say, large cap value stocks, no problem. If you are holding the iShares S&P 500 Value Index Fund (IVE) and you sell it at a loss, you can buy the Vanguard Value ETF (VTV), hold it for a month, and then switch back if you wish.

Two ETFs that track similar indexes are going to be very, very similar but not "substantially identical." At least the IRS *so far* has not deemed them substantially identical. But the IRS changes its rules often, and what constitutes "substantially identical" could change tomorrow or the next day. It's usually a good idea to consult with a tax professional (which I am not) before proceeding with any tax harvesting plans.

As always, consider cost

I'll remind you again that trading an ETF may require you to pay a trading commission to a brokerage house. Harvesting a tax loss generally requires four trades. (Sell the original holding, buy the replacement, sell the replacement, buy back the original holding.) If you're paying $10 per trade, that adds up to $40. Plus, you lose a bit of money on each trade with the *spread* (the difference between the ask and bid prices on a security). If you are in the 25 percent tax bracket, your loss on a particular investment should be *at least* $250 or so before you should bother even to *think* about tax harvesting with ETFs.

Revamping Your Portfolio with Life Changes: Marriage, Divorce, and Babies

Rebalancing to bring your portfolio back to its original allocations, making tactical adjustments, and harvesting losses for tax purposes aren't the only times it may make sense to trade ETFs. Just as you may need a new suit if you lose or gain weight, sometimes you need to tailor your portfolio in response to changes in your life.

As I discuss in Chapter 16, the prime consideration in portfolio construction is whether you can and should take risks in the hope of garnering high returns or whether you must limit your risk with the understanding that your returns will likely be modest. (Diversification can certainly help to reduce investment risk, but it can't eliminate it.) Certain events may occur in your life that warrant a reassessment of where you belong on the risk/return continuum.

If a single person of marrying age walks into my office and asks me to help build a portfolio, I will want to know if wedding bells will be ringing in the near future. A married couple walks into my office, and one of the first things I take note of is how close they sit together. And if the woman has a swollen belly, I really take notice.

No, I'm not being nosy. Marriage, divorce, and the arrival of babies are major life changes and need to be weighed heavily in any investment decisions. So too are the death of a spouse or parent (especially if that parent has left a hefty portfolio to the adult child); a child's decision to attend college; any major career changes; or the imminent purchase of a new house, new car, or Fabergé egg.

Betsy and Mark: A fairly typical couple

Betsy and Mark are engaged to be married. They don't have a lot of money. But both are young (early 30s), in good health, gainfully employed, and without debt. They plan to merge their savings of roughly $37,500 and asked me to help them invest it for the long haul.

The first thing we do is to decide how much money to take out to cover emergencies. Given their monthly expenses of roughly $3,500, we decide to earmark five months' of living expenses — $17,500 — and plunk that into an online savings account. That leaves us with $20,000 to invest.

Normally, I wouldn't consider an ETF portfolio for $20,000, but this is money they tell me they aren't going to touch until retirement. I urge them both to open a Roth IRA. (Any money you put into a Roth IRA grows tax-free for as long as you wish, and withdrawals are likewise tax-free; more on retirement accounts in the next chapter.) I ask them to divide the $20,000 between the two accounts. Since each of them can contribute $5,000 per year, I have them both make double contributions — one for the past year (for example, you can make your 2012 contribution until April 15, 2013), and one for the current year.

To save on transaction costs and keep things simple for now, I limit the number of investments and give each partner a "partial" portfolio. Neither account alone is well-diversified, but together, they are.

Betsy's Roth IRA

Vanguard Mega Cap 300 ETF (MGC)	$4,000
Vanguard FTSE All-World ex-US Small Cap Index ETF (VSS)	$3,000
Vanguard Total Bond Market ETF (BND)	$3,000

Mark's Roth IRA

Vanguard FTSE All-World ex-US ETF (VEU)	$4,000
Vanguard Small Cap ETF (VB)	$3,000
Vanguard Total Bond Market ETF (BND)	$3,000

As Betsy and Mark's portfolio grows, I would plan to add other asset classes (real estate investment trusts, natural resource stocks, inflation-protected securities, and so on) and other accounts.

One year later

Betsy is pregnant with twins! The couple is saving up for their first home, with a goal of making that purchase within 18 months. Although IRAs are normally not to be touched (without stiff penalty) before age 59½, an exception is made for first-time home purchases. Betsy and Mark could take out as much as $10,000 without penalty.

I'd rather that they leave their Roth IRA money untouched, but the couple informs me that they think the money may need to be tapped. At this point, the money in the Roth IRA has grown from $20,000 to $22,000 (for illustration purposes, I'm pretending that each investment grew by an equal amount), and Betsy and Mark can each contribute another $5,000 in fresh money, bringing the total of both accounts to $32,000. Since there is a possibility that $10,000 will need to be yanked in one year, I decide to earmark any fresh money to a fairly nonvolatile short-term bond ETF.

Betsy's Roth IRA

Vanguard Mega Cap 300 ETF (MGC)	$4,400
Vanguard FTSE All-World ex-US Small Cap Index ETF (VSS)	$3,300
Vanguard Total Bond Market ETF (BND)	$3,300
Vanguard Short-Term Bond ETF (BSV)	$5,000

Mark's Roth IRA

Vanguard FTSE All-World ex-US ETF (VEU)	$4,400
Vanguard Small Cap ETF (VB)	$3,300
Vanguard Total Bond Market ETF (BND)	$3,300
Vanguard Short-Term Bond ETF (BSV)	$5,000

Yet one year later

The twins (Aiden and Ella) have arrived! Much to their surprise, Betsy's parents have gifted the couple $10,000 for the purchase of the home. The Roth IRA money needn't be touched. At this point, I would sell the short-term bond fund and add to their other positions. Also, provided the couple had another $5,000 each to contribute, I'd begin adding asset classes to the mix, perhaps starting with the iShares Barclays TIPS Bond Fund (TIP), the SPDR S&P Global Natural Resources ETF (GNR), the Vanguard REIT ETF (VNQ), and the Vanguard Global ex-US Real Estate ETF (VNQI).

Hopefully, Betsy and Mark (and Aiden and Ella) will have many happy years together. And with each major life event, I would urge them to adjust their portfolio appropriately.

Are Options an Option for You?

Beyond the world of exchange-traded funds, an entirely different universe is filled with things called *exchange-traded derivatives*. A *derivative* is a financial instrument that has no real value in and of itself; rather, its value is directly tied to some underlying item of value, be it a commodity, a stock, a currency, or an ETF.

The most popular derivative is called an *option*. Think of an option as sort of a movie ticket. You give the cashier $8.50 to see the movie, not to hold some dumb little piece of cardboard. Certainly the ticket itself has no intrinsic value. But the ticket gives access (the option) to see the movie.

Most options in the investment world give you the right either to buy or sell a security at a certain price (*the strike price*) up to a certain specified date (*the expiration date*). Options are a prime example of a *leveraged* investment. In other words, if you buy an option, you're leveraging the little bit of money that you pay for the option — the *premium* — in hopes of winning big money. If you're an option seller, you stand to make the amount of the small premium, but you risk losing big money. For the system to work, the sellers have to win much more often than the buyers . . . and they do.

Lately, options on ETFs have been hot, hot, hot . . . and growing hotter. Options on certain ETFs, most notably the SPY (which represents the S&P 500) and the QQQ (which represents the 100 largest company stocks traded on the NASDAQ), typically trade just as many shares on an average day as the ETFs themselves. (See the sidebar "SPY, QQQ, and SPX are the options champs.") On most days, options on ETFs like the QQQ and SPY trade more shares than any other kind of options, including options on individual stocks, commodities, and currencies.

SPY, QQQ, and SPX are the options champs

ETFs are a *huge* part of the options market. The most commonly traded options on U.S. exchanges include many individual stocks, but the most active of the active are all ETFs. The five most frequently traded, of late, are these:

ETF	Ticker Symbol
SPDR S&P 500	SPY
PowerShares QQQ Trust Series 1	QQQ
S&P 500 Index (An index option created and managed by the Chicago Board Options Exchange)	SPX
iShares Russell 2000	IWM
ProShares VIX Mid-Term Futures	VIXM

You see, ETFs provide traders with the opportunity to trade the entire stock market, or large pieces of it, rather than merely individual securities. In the past, this was doable but difficult. You cannot trade a mutual fund on the options market as you can an ETF.

Much of this often frenetic trading in ETF options, at least on the buying side, is being done by speculators, not investors. If you have an itch to gamble in the hopes of hitting it big, options may be for you. In that case, I'll refer you to *Futures & Options For Dummies* by Joe Duarte, M.D. (Wiley). Dr. Duarte will warn you, as I am warning you, that successful option trading takes an iron gut, a lot of capital, and a lot of expertise. And even if you have all that, you may still end up getting hurt.

Understanding puts and calls

All kinds of options exist, including options on options (sort of). The derivatives market almost seems infinite — as does the number of ways you can play it. But the two most basic kinds of options, and the two most popular by far, are *put options* and *call options,* otherwise known simply as *puts* and *calls.* I'm going to take just a moment to describe how these babies work.

Calls: Options to buy

With a call option in hand, you may, for example, have bought yourself the right to buy 100 shares of the PowerShares QQQ Trust (currently trading at $50) at $55 (the strike price) a share at any point between now and, say, December 18 (the expiration date). If QQQ rises above $55, you would, of course, take the option and buy the 100 shares at $55. After all, you can then turn around and sell them immediately on the open market for a nifty profit. If, however, the price of QQQ does not rise to $55 or above, you are not going to exercise your option. Why in the world would you? You can buy the stock cheaper on the market. In that case, your option expires worthless.

Puts: Options to sell

With a put option in hand, you may, for example, have bought yourself the right to sell 100 shares of QQQ (currently trading at $40) at $35 (the strike price) a share at any point between now and December 15 (the expiration date). By December 15, if QQQ has fallen to any price under $35, you will likely choose to sell. If QQQ is trading above $35, you'd be a fool to sell. In the latter case, your option will simply expire, unused.

Using options to make gains without risk

Those people who use calls as an investment (as opposed to gambling) strategy are assuming (as do most investors) that the market is going to continue its historical upward trajectory. But instead of banking perhaps 60 or 70 percent of their portfolio on stocks, as many of us do, they take a much smaller percentage of their money and buy calls. If the stock market goes up, they may collect many times what they invested. If the stock market doesn't go up, they lose it all — but only a modest amount. Meanwhile, the bulk of their money can be invested in something much less volatile than the stock market, such as bonds.

Zvi Bodie, Professor of Finance and Economics at Boston University School of Management, wrote a book with Michael J. Clowes entitled *Worry-Free Investing: A Safe Approach to Achieving Your Lifetime Financial Goals* (Prentice Hall) in which he suggests an investment strategy using long-term stock options and Treasury Inflation-Protected Securities (TIPS). If you have $100,000 to invest, says Bodie, you might consider putting roughly 90 percent of it into TIPS. (A very convenient way to do that would be to purchase the iShares Barclays TIPS Bond Fund ETF.) That way, he asserts, your principal is protected.

To shoot for growth, says Bodie, take the other 10 percent or so and invest it in long-term call options (otherwise know as *Long-Term Anticipation Securities* or *LEAPS*), going about three years out. If the market soars, you take home the bacon. If, however, the market sinks, your call options merely expire, and you still have your TIPS, which by this point, three years later, have grown to match your original $100,000.

It's an intriguing strategy that just may make sense, especially for older investors tapping into their savings who can't wait for the stock market to come back after a serious bear market.

Interestingly, a similar kind of "worry-free investing" may be achieved by owning *all* stocks (or close to it) but using put options to protect yourself from the downside. Certain "inverse" ETFs exist that should, in theory, allow you to achieve the same end. As I discuss in Chapter 11, these funds haven't worked so well in the real world.

Insuring yourself against big, bad bears

The put option is an option to sell. This investment strategy allows you to have money in the stock market (all of it, if you so desire), but you carry insurance in the form of puts. If the market tumbles, you're covered.

Suppose you want to invest everything in the NASDAQ index through the QQQ. Normally, an investor would have to be insane to bet everything on such a volatile asset. But with the right put options in place, you can actually enjoy explosive growth but limit your losses to whatever you wish: 5 percent, 10 percent, 15 percent.

With a pocketful of puts, you can laugh a bear market in the face. If the QQQ drops by, say, 50 percent in the next week, you will have checked out long before, smiling as you hold your cash.

Seeming almost too good to be true

So options allow you to capture the gains of the stock market with very limited risk. They allow you to invest in the market and not have to worry about downturns. What's not to love about options?

Whoaaa. Not so fast! You need to know a couple little things about options:

- ✔ **They are expensive.** Every time you buy either a put or a call, you pay. The price can vary enormously depending on the strike price, the expiration date you choose, and the volatility of the ETF the option is based on. But in no case are options cheap. And the *vast majority* of options reach their expiration date and simply expire.

  So, yes, options can save you in a bear market, and they can help you to capture a bull market, but either way, you're going to pay. Free lunches are very hard to come by!

- ✔ **If you happen to make a gain on an option, the income will usually be considered a short-term gain by the IRS.** As such, you may pay twice the tax on it that you would on the long-term appreciation of a stock.

Weighing options strategies against the diversified ETF portfolio

Don't misunderstand me. I'm not saying that the price you pay for options isn't worth it — even after taxes are considered. Options do provide investors with a variety of viable strategies. The real question, though, is whether using puts and calls makes any more sense than investing in a well-diversified portfolio of low-cost ETFs. Most financial professionals I know are skeptical. And that includes several who have traded heavily in options only to learn the hard way that it is a very tricky business.

To be sure, if I knew a bear market were coming, I would definitely buy myself a slew of put options. If I knew a bull market were in the offing, I would certainly buy a fistful of call options. But here's the problem: I don't know which way the market is going, and neither do you. And if I buy both puts and calls on a regular basis, I'm going to be forever bleeding cash.

Not only that, but if the market stagnates, then both my puts and calls will expire worthless. In that case, I'm really going to be one unhappy camper.

So here's the way I look at it: The chances of success with a steady call strategy are one in three: I win if there's a bull market; I lose if there's a bear market; I lose if the market stagnates. Ditto for a put option strategy: I win if there's a bear market; I lose if there's a bull market; I lose if the market stagnates. It's hard to like those odds.

With a well-diversified portfolio of low-cost ETFs — stock, bond, REIT, and commodity ETFs — I reckon my chances of success are more like two in three: I lose if there's a bear market; I win if there's a bull market; in the case of a stagnant stock market, *something* in my portfolio will likely continue to make money for me anyway.

You may recall my saying earlier in the chapter that the derivatives market almost seems infinite, as does the number of ways you can play it. If you wish, ETF options strategies exist that allow you to make money in a stagnant market, too. The most common such strategy is called a *buy-write strategy* or *selling a covered call.* I explain how that strategy works (but don't necessarily advocate it) in the sidebar "How to profit with ETF options in a stagnant market."

Factoring in time and hassle

One final (but fairly major) consideration: Options trading generally requires much more time and effort than does buy-and-hold investing in a diversified portfolio. Let me ask you this: Would you rather spend your spare time at your computer tinkering with your investments, or would you rather do just about anything *but* that?

How to profit with ETF options in a stagnant market

Selling covered calls is a traditional way that many people get started in the world of options, says Jim Bittman, an instructor with the Chicago Board Options Exchange's Options Institute. "You can take a non-dividend paying ETF and turn it into an income-generating asset," he says. Here is how selling a covered call, otherwise known as a *buy-write strategy,* works:

You buy, say, 1,000 shares of the PowerShares QQQ Trust Series 1 ETF(QQQ). Let's assume that the current price is $50 a share. You've just invested $50,000 (plus a small trading commission of perhaps $10 or so, which, for simplicity's sake, we'll ignore for the moment).

Now you sell a covered call. This means that, through a brokerage house, you offer someone else the right to purchase your shares at a certain price in the future. You may, for example, offer the right to purchase your 1,000 shares at $52 (the strike price) within 90 days (the expiration date). You get paid for selling this right. In this scenario, you may be paid something in the ballpark of 75 cents a share for a total of $750 (roughly 2 percent of your original investment).

If, in the next 90 days, the QQQ stays between $50 and $52 (the market is relatively flat), your covered call expires worthless. You walk away with your $750, and life is good. (However, you will have to pay the IRS a short-term capital gains tax on that money. The short-term capital gains tax is usually the same as your marginal income tax rate. In many cases, that will be about twice as high as the tax you would pay after cashing out a long-term investment.)

But now suppose that the market tanks: You are left holding 1,000 shares of the QQQ that may be worth much less than $50,000, the only offset being the $750 (before taxes) that you received.

And suppose the market soars: You just lost out, too. The QQQ may be selling at $60 a share, but the guy who bought your contract can buy your shares from you (and certainly *will* buy them from you, or will sell the option to someone else who will buy them from you) at the agreed-upon price of $52 a share. In the end you will lose the difference between the actual value of your QQQ shares and their value at the strike price, again offset only by the soon-to-be-reduced-by-taxes $750 that you received when you sold the option.

And there's the catch. I've known a good number of investors who *rave* about their experiences with covered calls . . . as long as the markets are relatively stagnant. As soon as there is major movement either up or down — which has been known to happen — they stop raving and start ranting.

In the past few years, we've seen the introduction of several exchange-traded products that allow you to buy a basket of covered calls. These include the PowerShares S&P 500 BuyWrite Portfolio ETF (PBP) and the iPath CBOE S&P 500 BuyWrite Index ETN (BWV). Both have expense ratios of 0.75 percent. Both were introduced in 2007. Both have lost money. A third, similar fund, the PowerShares NASDAQ-100 BuyWrite Portfolio ETF, was delisted (i.e., it folded) in 2010. Will these funds ever make money? Yes . . . if we see several years of a flat market. What are the chances of that?

Chapter 19

Using ETFs to Fund Your Golden Years

• •

• •

I have this imaginary script that often runs in my head when a client asks me to look at his or her 401(k) plan. In this make-believe play, the benefits manager at my client's place of employment is speaking with a representative of an investment company that runs retirement plans.

Benefits manager: Our employees work hard, and we really don't ever want to lose them.

Investment company rep: No problemo! We offer a retirement plan so incredibly bad that your employees will *never* be able to retire! Just take a look at this array of some of the most expensive and poorly performing mutual funds available on the market today. That's what we offer!

Benefits manager: Good. And what about portfolio diversification?

Investment company rep: None. Four of the nine mutual funds under our umbrella are large U.S. growth funds. We offer no small cap. No international anything. Just large U.S. growth, a few ridiculously expensive and volatile bond funds, and an overpriced lifestyle fund with wholly inappropriate allocations for employees of all ages.

Benefits manager: Excellent! Will the fees wipe out any potential gains?

Investment company rep: Absolutely! Each mutual fund in the plan charges at least a 5 percent load, a good chunk of cash each year beyond that in operating fees, and then we slap on yet *another* high "wrap" fee on top of it all! And did I mention that several of the mutual fund companies we use have recently been involved in legal scandals? I can almost guarantee you that your employees' investments won't earn squat, and they'll be working for you forever.

Benefits manager: You're hired!

Okay, maybe this is a paranoid fantasy on my part, but sometimes I wonder. Many of the 401(k) plans I see — and I see many — are so manifestly terrible, so ridiculously designed and priced, and so poorly managed that you can't help but imagine that someone set out to make them that way.

And that makes me sad. The traditional company pension — grandpa's retirement plan that provided him with a steady paycheck from the day he retired till the day he died — is disappearing from the land. Social Security typically provides a modest income, and no more, and even that is at risk. That leaves the omnipresent 401(k) plan (and the lottery ticket) as many working people's last hope for a comfortable retirement.

My advice: Read this chapter. It's about the use of ETFs in retirement plans — potential financial knights in shining armor.

ETFs alone are not going to allow everyone to retire to the golf course. But they could take you a very long way in that direction. In this chapter, I discuss how you should be using your ETFs in tax-advantaged retirement accounts to get the most bang for your investment buck, and I offer advice for those who are stuck with crappy 401(k) plans at work. (**Hint:** Corner that benefits manager by the water cooler and hand him this book.) And I escort you into your retirement years to see how an ETF portfolio may provide you with the income you need to replace your current paycheck.

Aiming for Economic Self-Sufficiency

I've got all the money I'll ever need — if I die by four o'clock this afternoon.

— Henny Youngman

How much you need in your portfolio to call yourself economically self-sufficient ("retired," if you prefer) starts off with a very simple formula: $A \times B = \$\$\$\$$. A is the amount of money you need to live on for one year. B is the number of years you plan to live without a paycheck. $\$\$\$\$$ is the amount you should have before bidding the boss adieu. There you have it.

Of course, that formula is waaay oversimplified. You also need to factor in such things as return on your future portfolio, inflation, Social Security, and (for the very lucky) potential inheritances. For a more detailed reckoning of how much money you should be looking to save, I'll refer you to some fairly decent online retirement calculators; see the sidebar "How much is enough?"

Taking the basic steps

Whatever amount you set as your goal, you need to do three basic things to achieve it:

- ✔ Perhaps obvious, although most people prefer to ignore it: You have to *save.* A retirement portfolio doesn't just pop up from out of nowhere and grow like Jack's beanstalk. You need to feed it. Regularly.

- ✔ You need to invest your money wisely. That's where a well-diversified portfolio of ETFs comes in.

- ✔ It behooves you to take maximum advantage of retirement plans such as your company 401(k) plan — even if it's sub-par — IRAs, and (my favorite) Roth IRAs. If your 401(k) plan offers only pitiful options, you still need to do the best you can with what you've got. I provide some specific advice on that situation later in this chapter.

Choosing the right vessels

If you will, try to think of your retirement plans — your 401(k), your IRA — as separate vessels of money. How much your nest egg grows depends not just on how much you put into it and which investments you choose, but also which vessels you have. Three basic kinds of vessels exist. (I'm big into threes all of a sudden.)

- ✔ First are your basic vanilla retirement plans, such as the company 401(k), the traditional IRA, or, for the self-employed, the SEP-IRA or Individual 401(k). These are all *tax-deferred* vessels: You don't pay taxes on the money in the year you earn it; rather, you pay taxes at whatever point you withdraw money from your account, typically only after you retire.

- ✔ Next are the Roth IRA and the 529 college plans. Those are *tax-free* vessels: As long as you play by certain rules (discuss them with your accountant), anything you plunk into these two vessels (money on which you've generally already paid taxes) can double, triple, or (oh please!) quadruple, and you'll never owe the IRS a cent.

- ✔ Third is your non-retirement brokerage or savings bank account. Except for certain select investments, such as municipal bonds ("munis"), all earnings on your holdings in these vessels are taxable.

Why your choice of vessels matters — a whole lot

How much can your choice of vessels affect the ultimate condition of your nest egg? *Lots.* Even in a portfolio of all ETFs.

How much is enough?

A reasonable accumulation goal for most couples is 20 times the amount you spend in a year. To reach that goal, you may have to set aside a minimum of 15 percent of your salaries for a minimum of two to three decades. For more accurate (but still ballpark) numbers, I can refer you to a number of online retirement calculators. Note that none of these is perfect; I recommend that you use several. Take note that you'll get different — in some cases, vastly different — numbers. Consider each a ballpark figure. Average them for another ballpark-of-ballparks figure.

✔ Good (and quick!): Employee Benefit Research Institute at www.choosetosave.org/ballpark.

✔ Better: AARP at www.aarp.org/work/retirement-planning/retirement_calculator

✔ Best (but still not perfect): FIRECalc at www.firecalc.com

Note: If you use the first calculator, be realistic about your expected rate of return. (The AARP calculator and FIRECalc will help figure out a realistic return for you.)

If you use FIRECalc (*FIRE* stands for "financial independence/retire early"), please contribute a few dollars as I have. But take note: Although I love this guy's free website, I disagree with his assertion that you will need less to live on after retiring than you needed before. That may hold true for Canadians and Brits, but most people in the United States are likely going to be shelling out small fortunes on healthcare in their older years. (According to a recent study from Fidelity Investments, a 65-year-old couple retiring today should have at least $230,000 saved just to cover out-of-pocket medical expenses during their retirement years. For younger people planning to leave the workforce at 65, the number jumps higher.) Even as baseline inflation has remained in the low single digits, premiums for health insurance, as well as the costs of healthcare, have increased by double-digit percentages every year for many years. Recently enacted healthcare legislation may help, possibly, but it will not address the core of this problem: unfettered greed. You should expect the trend to continue, at least for a while.

One more bit of advice for getting the most out of FIRECalc: When the program asks you for the total annual investment expenses (as a percentage of total value), type in *1.4* percent if you currently have most of your money in mutual funds (or even if you don't). If you intend to follow my advice in this book and move to a portfolio of ETFs, you can lower that to, oh, let's say 0.30 percent. Note how much of a difference that one change can make in your retirement projections!

True, ETFs are marvelously tax-efficient instruments. Often, in the case of stock ETFs, they eliminate the need to pay any capital gains tax (as you would with most mutual funds) for as long as you hold the ETF. Still, there may be taxes to pay at the end of the game when you finally cash out. And in the case of certain ETFs (such as any of the bond ETFs) that pay either interest or high dividends, you will certainly pay taxes along the way.

Suppose you're an average middle-class guy or gal with a marginal income tax rate of 30 percent (federal + state + local). Next, suppose that you have $50,000 on which you've already paid taxes, and you're ready to squirrel it away for the future. You invest this money in the iShares GS $ InvesTop Corporate Bond Fund (LQD), which yields (hypothetically) 6 percent over the life of the investment, and you keep it for the next 15 years. Now, if that ETF were held in your regular brokerage account, and you had to pay taxes on the interest every year, at the end of 15 years you'd have a pot worth $92,680. Not too shabby. But if you held that very same $50,000 bond ETF in your Roth IRA and let it compound tax free, after 15 years you'd have $119,828 — an extra *$27,148. And* you would pay no income tax on this cash hoard when you eventually draw from it.

Unfortunately, the amount of money that you can put into retirement accounts is limited, although the law has allowed the sum to grow in recent years. For example, as I write this book, the maximum annual contribution to the most commonly used retirement accounts, the IRA and the Roth IRA, is $5,000 if you're younger than 50 and $6,000 if you're 50 or older. (The amount is subject to change each year.) Other retirement plans, such as the 401(k) or SIMPLE plan, have higher limits, but there is always a cap. (Ask your accountant about these plan limits; the formulas can get terribly complicated.)

What should go where?

Given these limitations, which ETFs (and other investments) should get dibs on becoming retirement assets, and which are best deployed elsewhere? Follow these four primary principles (I've given up on threes), and you can't go too wrong:

- ✔ **Any investment that generates a lot of (otherwise taxable) income belongs in your retirement account.** Any of the bond ETFs, REIT ETFs, or high-dividend ETFs are probably best held in your retirement account. Note: Value stocks generally yield more in dividends than growth stocks.

- ✔ **Keep your emergency funds out of your IRA.** Any money that you think you may need to withdraw in a hurry should be kept out of your retirement accounts. Withdrawing money from a retirement account can often be tricky, possibly involving penalties if done before age 59½, and usually triggering taxation. You don't want to have to worry about such things when you need money by noon tomorrow because your teenage son just totaled the family car.

- ✔ **House investments with the greatest potential for growth in your tax-free Roth IRA.** This may include your small cap value ETF, your technology stock fund, or your emerging markets ETF. Roth IRA money won't ever be taxed (presuming no change in the law), so why not try to get the most bang for your ETF buck?

- ✔ **Foreign-stock ETFs are perhaps best kept in your taxable account.** That's because the U.S. government will reimburse you for any taxes your fund paid out to foreign governments, but only if you have that fund in a taxable account. Over the long run, this "rebate" can add about half a percentage point a year to the returns you get on these funds; it doesn't sound like a lot, but it can add up over time.

Before you decide where to plunk your investments, refer to the following two sections for the basic rules.

Caveat: Tax laws change all the time. For example, the current low rates on capital gains and dividends, unless Congress steps in to intervene, are subject to a boost in 2013. Because of the constant changes in tax laws, I advise you (and your accountant) to review your portfolio every year or two to make sure that you have your assets in the right "vessels." Of course, there are other good reasons to review your portfolio, as well.

Retirement accounts

Here are ETFs and other investments generally best kept in a retirement account:

- **Taxable bond ETFs.** Examples include
    - iShares IBoxx $ Investment Grade Corporate Bond (LQD)
    - iShares Barclays TIPS Bond Fund (TIP)
    - PowerShares Emerging Markets Sovereign Debt Portfolio (PCY)
- **ETFs that invest in real estate investment trusts (REITs).** Examples include
    - Vanguard REIT Index ETF (VNQ)
    - iShares Cohen & Steers Realty Majors Index Fund (ICF)
    - SPDR Dow Jones Global Real Estate (RWO)
- **High-dividend ETFs.** Examples include
    - WisdomTree Total Dividend Fund (DTD)
    - SPDR Dividend (SDY)
    - iShares Dow Jones Select Dividend Index Fund (DVY)
- **Actively managed funds, whether mutual funds or ETFs**

Taxable accounts

Here are ETFs and other investments generally best kept in a taxable account:

- **Cash reserve for emergencies.**
- **Stock ETFs, except for the highest dividend-paying funds.** Examples include
    - Vanguard Russell 3000 ETF (VTHR)
    - iShares Morningstar Large Growth (JKE)
    - Guggenheim S&P 500 Pure Growth (RPG)

✔ **Foreign-stock ETFs.** Examples include

- iShares S&P Europe 350 (IEV)

- Vanguard Pacific ETF (VPL)

- BLDRS Emerging Markets 50 ADR (ADRE)

✔ **Municipal-bond ETFs.** Examples include

- iShares S&P National Municipal Bond Fund (MUB)

- SPDR Nuveen Barclays Capital Municipal Bond (TFI)

- PowerShares Insured National Municipal Bond Portfolio (PZA)

✔ **Exchange-traded notes (ETNs),** other than currency ETNs, which are not nearly as tax-efficient as other ETNs. Examples include

- ELEMENTS S&P Commodity Trends Indicator ETN (LSC)

- iPath Dow Jones-USB Commodity Index Total Return ETN (DJP)

- iPath MSCI India Index ETN (INP)

Curing the 401(k) Blues

Got one of those plans at work that I describe in the intro to this chapter, certain to eat you up alive in fees, about as well-diversified as a lunar landscape? Don't despair. All is not lost. Here's what I suggest:

✔ **Take the boss's money with a smile.** Make a big effort to shovel in at least the minimum required to get your full company match (which will differ from company to company). If you do not contribute enough to receive your employer's full matching contribution, you are, in essence, leaving free money on the table. Even if the investment options are horrible, you'll still end up well ahead of the game if your employer is kicking in an extra 25 or 50 percent.

✔ **Invest to the best of your ability, however poor the menu.** Among the horrible choices, pick the least horrible. Choose those that will give you exposure to different asset classes. Choose index funds if available. Strongly favor whichever funds are least expensive.

If you need help understanding the different offerings in your 401(k) plan, ask someone in the human resources department, or the plan administrator, to help you. If you can't get a clear answer (you very well may not), perhaps hire a financial planner for at least a short consult.

✔ **Argue for better options.** Tell the human resources people (diplomatically, of course) if their plan is a dog. They should look for another plan that includes either ETFs or (sometimes just as good) low-cost index mutual funds. Not sure what to say or where to send them? Specific advice is coming in the next section.

✔ **Check your statements.** It doesn't happen often, thank goodness, but yes, sometimes employers steal from their employees' retirement funds. Or give your employer the benefit of the doubt: Maybe they're just incompetent (and it's just a coincidence that mistakes seem always to reduce your account balance and never go in your favor). Check your statements with some regularity, and make certain that the money you are contributing is actually being credited to your account.

✔ **Plan your rollover.** If you leave your job, you may have the option of keeping your 401(k) plan right where it is. But 90 percent of the time, you will do much better by rolling your 401(k) into a self-directed IRA and then building yourself a well-diversified ETF portfolio.

One important caveat: You can't withdraw IRA money without penalty until you are 59½, whereas some (but not all) 401(k) plans allow you to withdraw your money penalty-free at age 55 if you decide to retire at that point. Don't be too quick to initiate a rollover if you think you may need to tap your funds in the years between 55 and 59½.

If you do initiate a rollover, and you have your own company's stock in your 401(k), you may want to leave just that part behind. You'll get a nice tax break at retirement.

Lobbying the benefits manager

Okay, you have a 401(k) plan. The plan is so bad you want to cry. Your first job is to educate the benefits manager at your office as to why. Don't assume that the people in HR have any more knowledge of personal finance than you do. If you have a lousy 401(k) plan, chances are they don't have a clue. They were likely bamboozled into accepting a high-priced, poorly constructed plan by a fast-talking sales rep from a financial institution (often a large financial institution with a well-known name) that specializes in milking — and/or bilking — the public. An even more sinister explanation is that palms were greased. Rattle some cages, and you never know what may fall out.

I started this chapter with a hypothetical dialogue between the benefits manager of your company and a representative from a financial institution looking to sell its crappy retirement plan. Here I present a hypothetical dialogue between *you* and your benefits manager:

You: Hey, Joe!

Benefits manager: Hey, You! What's that black and yellow thing in your hand, a copy of *Goldbricking For Dummies*? [Har har har.]

You: Actually, Joe, this is a book called *Exchange-Traded Funds For Dummies,* and I've been meaning to share it with you.

Benefits manager: Whoa! Exchange-traded whaa?

You: Exchange-Traded Funds For Dummies. It's all about exchange-traded funds — they're the hottest thing on Wall Street, and Main Street has been catching on lately, too. They're basically like index mutual funds that trade like stocks, and they are very inexpensive and have many other benefits for the investor. In fact, I've done a little bit of calculation, and I believe that we could slash the expenses on our company's 401(k) plan by as much as three-quarters, while giving participants an opportunity to build much better diversified portfolios than they can under the present plan.

Benefits manager: [Mouth open wide, bit of coffee dribbling down the side of his chin.]

You: Here, take this, Joe. [You pass him this book.] I want you to read especially Chapter 19, and particularly the sidebar "ETFs and 401(k) plans," where the author gives specific advice for where really sharp and industrious HR managers like you can turn for more information. Oh, see the sidebar "What a 401(k) plan *can* look like," too.

ETFs and 401(k) plans

Not many 401(k) retirement plans offer ETFs, but the market is "exploding" according to one industry insider. You'd think that would make me — great lover of ETFs that I am — jump for joy.

I'm not jumping.

The problem with ETFs in 401(k) plans isn't what you may think. Even though you may be making weekly contributions, the trading fees that you might normally be hit with can easily be overcome in an employee retirement plan. By consolidating all the employees' trades, the plan sponsor can actually cut trading costs down to almost nothing.

No, the problem is that from what I've seen, many 401(k) plan sponsors are packing their ETFs into nonsensical allocations and slapping on charges (as high as 2 percentage points!) that pretty much negate most of the benefits of ETFs. Why do they do that? Because ETFs are hot, and they make for a good sales presentation, but the plan sponsor may care more about its bottom line than yours.

There are exceptions, however. One company called Invest n Retire, LLC, based in Portland, Oregon puts together ETF-based 401(k) plans with decent allocations and a total cost to the participant of less than 1 percent. Tell your human resources people to contact this company! Here's the URL: www.investnretire.com.

Introducing the Roth 401 (k)

On January 1, 2006, a new kid on the retirement block came into being: the Roth 401(k). While you're chatting with your benefits manager, you may want to bring up this subject, too.

By now, many companies have started to offer Roth 401(k) plans to employees. This type of plan is similar to the existing Roth IRA in that the money you put in is *after-tax* money. In other words, you won't get a tax deduction up front, as you do with your existing 401(k).

So why do it? There are two main reasons:

- ✔ First, you aren't going to have to pay any income tax when you withdraw the money in retirement, as you will with your existing 401(k).

- ✔ Second, you aren't going to have to sweat about taking minimum required distributions starting at age 70½ like you do now with a 401(k). You can keep the money in the Roth for as long as you wish. Indeed, you can opt never to touch it, leaving it instead as an inheritance, tax-free to your heirs.

I'd say the Roth 401(k) will prove to be the better long-term option, maybe in most cases, but especially if you are currently in a low tax bracket. With federal debt and deficits that are huge and growing, sooner or later the government is likely to raise tax rates, and maybe by a lot. At that point, even if you are retired and living on a fixed income, you may well be paying taxes at a (much) higher rate than you are today. If so, tax-free income later will be worth a lot more than it is now.

On the other hand, if you are currently in a high tax bracket and expect to be in a lower tax bracket in the future, the Roth may not make sense. If you are single and make over $75,000 a year, or if you and your spouse together make over $100,000, I suggest that you ask your financial planner or accountant which plan is best for you.

Unfortunately, as with many 401(k) plans, your investment options may not be the best. If you leave the company, I suggest that you roll over your 401(k) Roth into a self-directed Roth IRA.

What A 401(k) plan can look like

Most of the 401(k) plans I see are horrible: high expenses, hidden expenses, impossible to properly diversify. A few companies, however, have begun to offer excellent 401(k) plans built from ETFs.

Invest n Retire LLC, of Portland, Oregon allows investment managers to use ETFs to build low-cost portfolios in 401(k) plans. Following are examples of two such portfolios, one of moderate risk (and moderate return potential) and the other more conservative. These particular allocations were designed by Michael Glackin of InR Advisory Services in Media, Pennsylvania.

The total fees for the actual ETFs are 0.14 percent for the conservative allocation portfolio and 0.16 percent for the moderate portfolio.

The total costs to an employee for an ETF plan (depending on the employer) would typically run 0.94 percent a year. In contrast, the average 401(k) plan cost employees 1.6 percent, with some fees running as high as 3.0 percent.

What's the difference between a retirement plan that charges 0.94 percent in management fees and one that charges 3.0 percent? Start with the average 401(k) account balance of $45,519, and invest $10,000 a year for 20 years in the lower-fee (0.94 percent) ETF plan. If you assume an 8 percent annual return, you'll wind up at retirement age with an account worth $590,781. Invest the same way but in a plan that charges the higher (3.0 percent) fee, and you'll be left with $451,346. That's a difference of $139,346 — well beyond chump change.

Moderate Portfolio (Total Annual Fees for ETFs: 0.16 Percent)

Ticker	Asset Class	Fund	Allocation %
CASH	Cash	CASH	1%
BND	Fixed income	Vanguard Total Bond Market ETF	15%
TIP	Fixed income	iShares Barclays TIPS Bond	12%
VBK	U.S. small cap	Vanguard Small Cap Growth ETF	3%
VBR	U.S. small cap	Vanguard Small Cap Value ETF	2%
VCIT	Fixed income	Vanguard Intermediate-Term Corporate Bond ETF	9%
VCSH	Fixed income	Vanguard Short-Term Corporate Bond ETF	3%
VEU	International	Vanguard FTSE All-World ex-US ETF	18%
VNQ	U.S. small cap	Vanguard REIT ETF	2%
VO	U.S. mid cap	Vanguard Mid-Cap ETF	4%
VTV	U.S. large cap	Vanguard Value ETF	13%
VUG	U.S. large cap	Vanguard Growth ETF	15%
VWO	International	Vanguard MSCI Emerging Markets ETF	3%

(continued)

(continued)

Conservative Portfolio (Total Annual Fees for ETFs: 0.14 Percent)			
Ticker	*Asset Class*	*Fund*	*Allocation %*
CASH	Cash	CASH	1%
BND	Fixed income	Vanguard Total Bond Market ETF	31%
TIP	Fixed income	iShares Barclays TIPS Bond	23%
VCIT	Fixed income	Vanguard Intermediate-Term Corporate Bond ETF	18%
VCSH	Fixed income	Vanguard Short-Term Corporate Bond ETF	6%
VEU	International	Vanguard FTSE All-World ex-US ETF	5%
VTV	U.S. large cap	Vanguard Value ETF	7%
VUG	U.S. large cap	Vanguard Growth ETF	9%

Strategies for the Self-Employed

Although the self-employed have several retirement plan options, the two most popular, by far, are the traditional IRA and the Roth IRA. (Company employees can also contribute to these plans, but few do, and the deductibility of an IRA becomes a complicated matter if you have a retirement plan at work.) Let me compare the two different IRA options.

The traditional IRA versus the Roth IRA

The traditional IRA currently allows you to sock away $5,000 a year if you're younger than 50 and $6,000 if you're 50 or older. The money you contribute to a traditional IRA is generally tax-deductible. Until you turn 59½, you can't touch that money without paying a penalty. At that point, you can start to withdraw it, but you'll pay income tax on both the principal and any growth in the account.

The Roth IRA is available to couples with an adjusted gross income (AGI) of less than $179,000 a year. It allows you to sock away the very same amount as the traditional IRA, but the Roth allows your money to grow *tax-free*. You will never have to pay taxes on any of the money you put into your Roth or on any of the gains. You don't, however, get any tax deductions on the money you contribute to the Roth.

A couple that makes under $55,550 may qualify for a savings tax credit of up to $2,000 regardless of which type of IRA you choose. See your tax advisor, or visit www.irs.gov for details.

Taxes now or taxes later?

So . . . do you want to pay taxes now and not have to worry about them when you retire? (You want a Roth.) Or do you want to hold off on paying the taxes until after you retire? (You want a traditional IRA.)

Which is the better option depends on a few things, but first and foremost is your current level of income versus your income expectations for whenever you plan to withdraw the funds. If you expect that your income will be less — and/or your tax rate will be lower — in retirement, you are likely better off with the traditional IRA; take the deduction now. If you are currently in a low tax bracket, and you think (or pray) that you will be in a higher one in years to come, go with the Roth.

If it seems like a toss-up, choose the Roth because it offers certain non-tax advantages. With a traditional IRA, for example, you need to start withdrawing money at age 70½. But with a Roth, you'll be able to keep your money growing tax-free for as long as you are still breathing, and then your heirs can continue that tradition once you stop — breathing, that is.

Ushering Your Portfolio into Retirement Readiness

A fellow fee-only financial planner and member of NAPFA, William P. Bengen, CFP, wrote a book for financial planners called *Conserving Client Portfolios During Retirement* (FPA Press). Bengen did an enormous amount of number crunching, reviewing historical return figures going back to 1926. He and his computer played out scenario after scenario: If you retired in year X, and you took out $Y for Z years . . . that sort of fun analysis. His conclusion: The conventional wisdom is both right and wrong. Right, stocks drive a portfolio. Wrong, once you retire, you should live off bonds.

15+ years and counting

If you have 15 years or longer until retirement, the money in your retirement account — if history is our guide — should be pretty close to fully invested in stocks. If it is, and we look back over many years, your odds of coming out ahead in any 15-year period seem to be pretty close to a certainty. Forget the bonds. But, but, but . . . the future may *not* be like the past, which is why I never advocate a portfolio that isn't invested at least 20 percent in bonds or cash or some other kind of hedge against a potential stock market tumble.

Less than 15 years to retirement

Every year, starting 15 years from retirement, says Bengen, you may want to tilt your asset mix a bit more conservatively. Once you retire, assuming you're looking at a life expectancy of 30 or so years at that point, you should be thinking not about the conventional mostly bonds retirement portfolio but, rather, something closer to 60 percent stocks and 40 percent bonds. With that mix, your portfolio has the best chance of being around as long as you are.

Throughout his book (as I do throughout this book), Bengen urges investors not to be "wooden" and not to adhere to any strict formulas. The percentages suggested here can, and should, vary with your individual circumstances.

Given the incredible volatility in stocks of late, and some rather serious economic issues facing both the United States and most other nations, I've been leaning my portfolios a bit toward the more conservative side. For a retired or soon-to-be-retired client who may have warranted a 60/40 (stocks/ bonds) portfolio several years ago, I might now suggest a 60/40 portfolio only if that portfolio were very, very well-diversified with different kinds of stocks and bonds, and the client had at least two years of living expenses in cash and near-cash (short-term CDs, high quality and very short-term bonds). But in most cases, I'd prefer to see a 50/50 portfolio.

I also urge you to think of *stocks* and *bonds* in the broadest sense of "growth investments" and "security investments." Growth investments may include commodities or real estate, as well as stocks. Security investments may include a fixed annuity or a market-neutral mutual fund (with a proven track record), as well as government and corporate bonds. Of course, both your stock and bond positions can — and likely should — be held in ETFs.

Withdrawing Funds to Replace Your Paycheck

How much can you withdraw from your retirement funds each year and have a good chance of not running out of money? That, of course, is one of the biggest financial questions retirees have. According to Bengen, the answer, at least for people in their 60s, is somewhere around 4 to 5 percent, depending on your health, your investment choices, market conditions, the rate of inflation, how much you'll pay in taxes, and how much you want to leave behind for those rotten children of yours who never come to visit anymore.

I say, go with Bengen's rough estimate of 4 to 5 percent and use some of the retirement calculators I mention in the sidebar "How much is enough?" to smooth out the estimate a bit, but do plan to sit down with a financial planner at least once to get some better idea of where you stand. You don't want to run out of money!

Know that Bengen's work has been hotly, hotly disputed in financial-planning circles, with some researchers claiming that 4 to 5 percent is way too high (and you risk running out of money by withdrawing so much); while others claim it is too low (and you risk not enjoying your money as much as you could). But as someone who loves irony, I think the fact that both camps feel so strongly about the issue means that 4 to 5 percent is probably about right . . . although I highly recommend regular monitoring and some flexibility in your spending. Did the market boom last year? Take that vacation to Maui. Did it bust? Sorry — no new car for you this year (sigh).

As far as withdrawing funds from your ETF portfolio, in the following sections I offer a few special words of advice that could make life easier.

Don't obsess over maintaining principal or drawing from dividends

I'm not quite sure where this absurd division of the nest egg into *principal* and *interest* got started. It's seemingly some form of mass hysteria that began many years ago and continues to delude the populace.

Listen: If you have an account with, say, $100,000, and you withdraw $5,000, how much do you have left? The answer is **$95,000.** Got it? The answer will *always* be $95,000. It doesn't matter in the slightest whether that $5,000 came from principal or you took it out of recently received dividends or interest. (There may be a tax difference in a nonretirement brokerage account, but in a retirement account, there is absolutely no difference.)

So what does this mean in terms of withdrawing funds to live on in retirement?

 The best way to achieve that end is to rebalance your portfolio with some regularity (perhaps every six months), tapping into whichever funds have performed the best and effectively create your own "artificial dividend." For example, say that you have an IRA with a balance of $100,000. The money is invested (for simplicity's sake) in three ETFs thusly:

✔ Vanguard Total Stock Market ETF (VTI): $25,000 (25 percent)

✔ Vanguard FTSE All World ex-US ETF (VEU): $25,000 (25 percent)

✔ iShares Barclays Aggregate Bond Fund (AGG): $50,000 (50 percent)

You determine that you need to withdraw $7,500. Your portfolio master plan calls for only 45 percent bonds, but after a horrible year for stocks and a good one for bonds, your bond allocation is now 50 percent. The source of your $7,500 withdrawal is clear: Take it out of the bond ETF. Doing so will not only generate the cash you need but will also bring your portfolio into alignment with your target allocations.

(Becuse your new portfolio balance after withdrawing the $7,500 will be $92,500, your bond fund, now with $42,500, will represent 45.9 percent of the portfolio. That's close enough in my book. Literally.)

Fast-forward six months . . .

Stocks have been on a recent tear, and the "principal" you now have invested in stocks has grown considerably relative to your bonds. Your AGG bond fund has also grown (from its starting position of $42,500), due mostly to earned interest, which has been reinvested in the ETF. Your bond fund is now worth $45,000.

Your portfolio, even though you withdrew $7,500 in cash during the year, is now worth $115,000. It now looks like this:

✔ Vanguard Total Stock Market ETF (VTI): $34,500 (30 percent)

✔ Vanguard FTSE All World ex-US ETF (VEU): $34,500 (30 percent)

✔ iShares Barclays Aggregate Bond Fund (AGG): $46,000 (40 percent)

Nothing has really changed in your life (except that you are now a bit older and grayer), so you determine that you don't need to shake up your original target portfolio allocation: 45 percent AGG, 27.5 percent VTI, and 27.5 percent VEU. You now figure that you are going to need yet another $10,000. Do you take it out of the bond fund because its growth was due to interest, and not the stock funds because their growth was in principal? Many people would say yes. Mass hysteria, I say! That makes no sense.

In this case, I would have you take $5,000 each from your two stock ETFs. That leaves you with a portfolio of $105,000, invested as follows:

✔ Vanguard Total Stock Market ETF (VTI): $29,500 (28 percent)

✔ Vanguard FTSE All World ex-US ETF (VEU): $29,500 (28 percent)

✔ iShares Barclays Aggregate Bond Fund (AGG): $46,000 (44 percent)

You have provided yourself with the $10,000 you need, *and* you've brought your portfolio back into near-perfect balance. And near-perfect is good enough, because . . .

As always, watch the fees

In the scenario presented in the previous section, to bring your portfolio into pitch-perfect balance would require shaving a few hundred dollars from each stock fund to move into the bond fund. That would require you to pay commissions on three trades, at a cost (if you trade online, which you certainly should) of perhaps $30. (If you're paying much more than that, you are with the wrong brokerage house.) And on top of that, there will be minor other transaction costs. That money spends. Why give it away for no good reason? Given the volatility of the markets, your portfolio will be out of perfect balance the day after you get it into perfect balance, so let it be!

In general, I'd say that you never want to spend more than one-half of 1 percent on a trade, and — unless you have a teensy-weensy portfolio, this second part shouldn't hinder you in complying with the first part — you never want to let your portfolio get too out of balance. Let's express this in percentages: If your biggest allocation factor — stocks versus bonds — is out of whack by more than 5 percentage points (bonds should be 40 percent, but instead they've dipped to less than 35 percent or risen to more than 45 percent), you need to make a move.

Take your minimum required distributions

After you turn age 59½, you can start taking money out of your 401(k) or traditional IRA. (You can do so before that age, but you usually pay a stiff penalty, or at least you have to convince the IRS why you shouldn't. That's always fun.) When you turn 70½, you *must* start taking money out of your 401(k) or traditional IRA (but not your Roth IRA). If you don't take out at least the minimum required distribution (MRD), you will pay a very nasty penalty. The MRD is based on your portfolio total and your age. There are MRD calculators all over the web; simply Google the words "minimum required distribution calculator," and you'll have many to choose from. Unlike some other calculators, these are all essentially the same.

IRA, 401(k), or regular (taxable) brokerage account: Which to tap first?

For those of you over 70½, your cash needs will come first from Social Security, any pension you may have, and the minimum required distribution on your traditional IRA or 401(k). After that, you can draw additional cash from any available source. For those of you between 59½ and 70½, the choices are all yours. You decide when to begin receiving Social Security benefits; whether and when to take distributions from your retirement account(s); and whether or when to start tapping your taxable account(s). Most money managers suggest pulling money from your taxable accounts first and holding off on drawing down your tax-advantaged accounts. I'm not so sure.

Sure, leaving a tax-deferred account untouched will keep this year's taxes to a minimum. But those taxes will be paid eventually, if not by you then by your heirs. If you care about what you'll be leaving behind, you should know that a large taxable inheritance can create real headaches with the IRS. In the end, for many families it may make the most sense to take needed cash from both types of accounts — taxable and tax-deferred — more or less equally. But there are many factors involved. It would be worth your while to discuss the matter with your financial planner, accountant, and, if you have a sizeable estate, an estate attorney.

Caveat: From my experience, accountants sometimes tend to focus a wee bit too much on your present taxes, while estate attorneys can focus a tad too much on your legacy. Let their counsel, as well as mine, guide you. But ultimately, you need to be the judge.

Part V
The Part of Tens

The 5th Wave   By Rich Tennant

"We believe in all-American investments. Take a look at this Grandma's apple pie chart..."

In this part . . .

Time now to wrap up this book with some practical tips (just in case I haven't provided you with enough in previous chapters). I begin by answering the ten most common questions I get about ETFs. That is followed by a discussion of the ten mistakes that most investors — yes, even smart ETF investors! — often make. And finally, I could hardly call myself a financial professional unless I (like seemingly all other financial professionals) made some predictions! And so, I end Part V by pulling out my crystal ball and making ten forecasts about the future of ETFs. Only time will tell if I am right.

Chapter 20

Ten FAQs about ETFs

*O*h, it's been fun writing a book about exchange-traded funds! Often when someone asks me what I'm working on, and I say, "The second edition of *Exchange-Traded Funds For Dummies,*" I see the eyes glaze over, and then, if the topic isn't immediately steered in a new direction, I'm inevitably asked what the heck an exchange-traded fund is. And so I explain (essentially quoting, from memory, a few lines from this book's Introduction). The *next* question I'm asked is invariably one of the following.

Are ETFs Appropriate for Individual Investors?

You bet they are. Although the name *exchange-traded funds* sounds highly technical and maybe a little bit scary, ETFs are essentially friendly index mutual funds with a few spicy perks. They are *more* than appropriate for individual investors. In fact, given the low expense ratios and high tax efficiency of most ETFs, as well as the ease with which you can use them to construct a diversified portfolio, these babies can be the perfect building blocks for just about any individual investor's portfolio.

Are ETFs Risky?

That all depends.

Some ETFs are way riskier than others. It's a question of what kind of ETF we're talking about. Most ETFs track stock indexes, and some of those stock indexes can be extremely volatile, such as individual sectors of the U.S. economy (technology, energy, defense and aerospace, and so on) or the stock markets of emerging-market nations. Other ETFs track broader segments of the U.S. stock market, such as the S&P 500. Those can be volatile, too, but less so. Commodity ETFs can be more jumpy than stocks.

But other ETFs track bond indexes. Those tend to be considerably less volatile (and less potentially rewarding) than stock ETFs. One ETF (ticker symbol SHY) tracks short-term Treasury bonds, and as such is only a little bit more volatile than a money market fund.

Many of the newer generation ETFs are *leveraged,* using borrowed money or financial derivatives to increase volatility (and potential performance). Those leveraged ETFs can be so wildly volatile that you are taking on risk of Las Vegas proportions.

When putting together a portfolio, a diversity of investments can temper risk. Although it seems freakily paradoxical, you can sometimes add a risky ETF to a portfolio (such as an ETF that tracks the price of a basket of commodities, or the stocks of foreign small companies) and lower your overall risk! How so? If the value of your newly added ETF tends to rise as your other investments fall, that addition will lower the volatility of your entire portfolio. (Financial professionals refer to this strange but sweet phenomenon as *Modern Portfolio Theory.*)

Do I Need a Financial Professional to Set Up and Monitor an ETF Portfolio?

Do you need an auto mechanic to service your car? I don't know. It depends on both your particular skills and your inclination to spend a Sunday afternoon getting greasy under the hood. Setting up a decent ETF portfolio, with the aid of this book, is very doable. You can certainly monitor such a portfolio, as well. A professional, however, has special tools and (I hope) objectivity to help you understand investment risk and construct a portfolio that fits you like a glove, or at least a sock. A financial planner can also help you properly estimate your retirement needs and plan your savings accordingly.

Do be aware that many investment "advisors" out there are nothing more than salespeople in disguise. Don't be at all surprised if you bump into a few who express their disgust of ETFs! ETFs make no money for those salespeople, who make their living hawking expensive (often inferior) investment products. Your best bet for good advice is to find a *fee-only* (takes no commissions) financial planner. If you are more or less a do-it-yourselfer but simply wish for a little guidance, try to find a fee-only planner who will work with you on an hourly basis.

How Much Money Do 1 Need to Invest in ETFs?

You can buy one share of any number of ETFs for as low as the price of a share. But since you usually pay a commission to trade (I'd say the average trading commission is about $10), buying one $20 share (and thus paying a 50 percent commission) would hardly make good sense. Starting at about $3,000 perhaps, it may be worth investing in ETFs, but only if you plan to keep that money invested for at least several years. Smaller amounts are best invested in mutual funds (preferably low-cost index mutual funds), money markets, or other instruments that incur no trading costs.

If you wish to invest in an ETF at a brokerage house that doesn't charge trading commissions for that particular ETF (Vanguard, for example, doesn't charge you to trade Vanguard ETFs; and Charles Schwab doesn't charge you to trade Schwab ETFs), then you can buy one share at a time with impunity.

With Hundreds of ETFs to Choose From, Where Do 1 Start?

The answer depends on your objective. If you are looking to round out an existing portfolio of stocks or mutual funds, your ETF should complement that. Your goal is always to have a well-diversified collection of investments. If you are starting to build a portfolio, you want to make sure to include stocks and bonds and to diversify within those two broad asset classes.

There is not much in the world of stocks, bonds, and commodities that can't be satisfied with ETFs. Try to have both U.S. and international stock ETFs. And within the U.S. stock arena, aim to have large cap growth, small cap growth, large cap value, and small cap value. (I explain these terms in Chapters 5 through 8.) You can also diversify your stock ETFs by industry sector: consumer staples, energy, financials, and so on. (See Chapter 10 for a discussion of sector diversification.) Generally, I wouldn't attempt to use separate ETFs to accomplish both grid diversification and sector diversification; doing so would require an unwieldy number of holdings.

On the bond side of your portfolio, you want both government-issued bonds and corporate bonds, and if you're in a higher tax bracket, you want municipal bonds as well. For more conservative portfolios in which bonds play a major role, foreign bonds may offer added diversification.

Although most ETFs are somewhat reasonably priced, some are more reasonably priced than others. If you are going to pay 0.50 percent a year in operating expenses for a certain ETF, you should have a good reason for doing so. Many ETFs are available for under 0.30 percent, and some for even less than 0.10 percent.

Where Is the Best Place for Me to Buy ETFs?

I suggest setting up an account with a financial supermarket such as Fidelity, Vanguard, T. Rowe Price, Charles Schwab, or TD Ameritrade. Each of these allows you to hold ETFs, along with other investments — such as mutual funds or individual stocks and bonds — in one account. (You probably don't need or want individual securities. I'm just saying . . .)

Different financial supermarkets offer different services and charge different prices depending on how much you have to invest, how often you trade, and whether you do everything online or by phone. You need to do some shopping around to find the brokerage house that works best for you. I provide more suggestions for shopping financial supermarkets in Chapter 3, where you'll also find contact information. Their websites are listed in Appendix A.

Is There an Especially Good or Bad Time to Buy ETFs?

Nope, not really, at least not that can be determined in advance. Studies show rather conclusively that the stock and bond markets (or any segment of the stock or bond markets) is just about as likely to go up after a good day as it is after a bad day (week, month, year, or any other piece of the calendar). Trying to time the market tends to be a fool's game — or, just as often, a game that some like to play with other people's money.

Do ETFs Have Any Disadvantages?

Because most ETFs follow an index, you probably won't see your ETF (or any of your index mutual funds) winding up number one on *Wise Money* magazine's list of Top Funds for the Year. (But you probably won't find any of your ETFs at the bottom of such a list, either.) The bigger disadvantage of ETFs — compared with mutual funds — is the cost of trading them, although that cost should be minimal.

Building a well-diversified portfolio of ETFs — stocks, bonds, large cap, small cap, U.S., international — may also seem to have the disadvantage that in any given year, some of your ETFs are going to do poorly. Just remember that *next* year those particular investments, the ones that look so disgustingly dull (or worse) right now, may be the shiniest things in your portfolio.

Does It Matter Which Exchange My ETF Is Traded On?

No. Most ETFs are traded on the NYSE Arca (Archipelago) exchange, but plenty of others are traded on the NASDAQ. It doesn't matter in the slightest to you, the individual investor. The cost of your trade is determined by the brokerage house you use. The *spread* (the difference between the price a buyer pays and the price the seller receives) is determined in large part by the share volume of the ETF being traded. Regardless of the exchange, if the volume is small (such as would be the case for, say, the Global X Nigeria ETF), you may want to place a *limit order* rather than a *market order.* I explain the different kinds of orders in a sidebar in Chapter 2.

Which ETFs Are Best in My IRA, and Which Are Best in My Taxable Account?

Generally, investments that generate income — whether interest, dividends, or capital gains — are best kept in a tax-advantaged retirement account, such as your IRA or 401(k) plan. That would include any bond, REIT, or high-dividend paying ETF. You'll eventually need to pay income tax on any money you withdraw from those accounts, but it is generally better to pay later than sooner. In the case of a Roth IRA, which is often the best case of all, you will never have to pay taxes on the earnings, the principal, what is in the account, or what you withdraw. Try to put your ETFs that have the greatest potential for growth — REIT ETFs are great candidates — into your Roth IRA.

Because retirement accounts generally penalize you if you take money out before age 59½, anyone younger than that would want to keep all emergency money in a non-retirement account.

Chapter 21

Ten Mistakes Most Investors (Even Smart Ones) Make

. . . .

In This Chapter

▶ Paying and risking too much

▶ Trading too frequently

▶ Saving too little and expecting too much from the market

▶ Ignoring inflation and IRS rules

. . . .

Remember that personal investing course you took in high school? Of course you don't! Your high school never offered such a course. Chances are that you've never taken such a course. Few of us middle-agers have. And that lack of education — combined with a surfeit of cheesy and oft-advertised investment industry products, plus an irresponsible and lazy financial press — leads many investors to make some very costly mistakes.

Paying Too Much for an Investment

Most investors pay way, way too much to middlemen who suck the lifeblood out of portfolios, leaving too many folks with too little to show for their investments. By investing primarily in ETFs, you can spare yourself and your family this tragic fate. The typical ETF costs a fraction of what you would typically pay in yearly management fees to a mutual fund company. You never pay any *loads* (high commissions). And trading fees, as long as you're not dealing in dribs and drabs, and being charged for each drib and drab, should be minimal.

Failing to Properly Diversify

Thou shalt not put all thy eggs in one basket is perhaps the first commandment of investing, but it is astonishing how many sinners there are among us. ETFs allow for easy and effective diversification. By investing in ETFs rather than individual securities, you have already taken a step in the right direction. Don't blow it by pouring all your money into one ETF in a single hot sector! You want to invest in both stock and bond ETFs, and both U.S. and international securities. You want diversification on all sides. Invest, to the extent possible, mostly in *broad* markets: value, growth, small cap, large cap. On the international side of your portfolio, aim to invest more in regions than in individual countries (see Part II). ETFs make such diversification easy.

Taking on Inappropriate Risks

Some people take on way too much risk, investing perhaps everything in highly volatile technology or biotech stocks. But many people don't take enough risk, leaving their money to sit in secure but low-yielding money market funds or, worse, in the vault of their local savings and loan. If you want your money to grow, you may have to stomach some volatility. In general, the longer you can tie your money up, and the less likely you are to need to tap into your portfolio anytime soon, the more volatile your portfolio can be. A portfolio of ETFs can be amazingly fine-tuned to achieve the levels of risk and return that are appropriate for you.

Selling Out When the Going Gets Tough

It can be a scary thing, for sure, when your portfolio's value drops 10 or 20 percent . . . never mind the 40 percent that an all-stock portfolio would have lost in 2008 (demonstrating graphically why you shouldn't have an all-stock portfolio). Keep in mind that if you invest in stock ETFs, that scenario is going to happen. It has happened many times in the past; it will happen many times in the future. That's just the nature of the beast. If you sell when the going gets tough (as many investors do), you lose the game. The stock market is resilient. Hang tough. Bears are followed by bulls (think 2009 and 2010). Your portfolio — as long as you are well diversified — will almost surely bounce back, given enough time.

Paying Too Much Attention to Recent Performance

Many investors make a habit of bailing out of whatever market segment has recently taken a dive. Conversely, they often look for whatever market segment has recently shot through the roof, and that's the one they buy. Then, when *that* market segment tanks, they sell once again. By forever buying high and selling low, their portfolios dwindle over time to nothing.

When you build your portfolio, don't overload it with last year's ETF superstars. You don't know what will happen next year. Stay cool. You may notice that in this book, I do not include performance figures for any of the ETFs discussed (except in one or two circumstances to make a specific point). That omission was intentional. Many of the ETFs I discuss are only a few years old, and a few years' returns tell you *nothing*. On the other hand, the indexes tracked by certain ETFs go back decades. In those cases, I often do provide performance figures.

Not Saving Enough for Retirement

Compared to spending, saving doesn't offer a whole lot of joy. But you can't build a portfolio out of thin air. If your goal is one day to be financially independent, to retire with dignity, you probably need to build a nest egg equal to about 20 times your yearly budget (more on that subject in Chapter 19). Doing so won't be easy. It may mean saving 15 percent of your paycheck for several decades. The earlier you start, the easier it will be.

Savings come from the difference between what you earn and what you spend. Remember that both are adjustable figures. One great way to save is to contribute at least enough to your 401(k) plan at work to get your employer's full match, if any. Do it! Another is to remember that material goodies, above and beyond the basics, do not buy happiness and fulfillment. Honest. Psychologists have studied the matter, and their findings are rather conclusive.

Having Unrealistic Expectations of Market Returns

One reason many people don't save enough is that they have unrealistic expectations; they believe fervently that they are going to win the lottery or (next best thing) earn 25 percent a year on their investments. The truth: The stock market, over the past 80 years, has returned nearly 10 percent a year before inflation and 7 percent a year after inflation. Bonds have returned about 5 percent before inflation and 2 to 3 percent after inflation. A well-balanced portfolio, therefore, may have returned 7 or 8 percent before inflation and maybe 5 percent or so after inflation.

Five percent growth after inflation — with interest compounded every year — isn't too shabby. In 20 years time, an investment of $10,000 growing at 5 percent will turn into $26,530 in constant dollars. Most of us in the investment field expect future returns to be more modest. But with a very well-diversified, ultra-low-cost portfolio, leaning toward higher-yielding asset classes (see Part II), you may be able to do just as well as Mom and Dad did. If you want to earn 25 percent a year, however, you are going to have to take on inordinate risk. And even then, I wouldn't bank on it.

Discounting the Damaging Effect of Inflation

No, a dollar certainly doesn't buy what it used to. Think of what a candy bar cost when you were a kid. Think of what you earned on your first job. Are you old enough to remember when gas was 32 cents a gallon? Now look into the future, and realize that your nest egg, unless it's wisely invested, will shrivel and shrink. Historically, certain investments do a better job of keeping up with inflation than others. Those investments, which include stocks, tend to be somewhat volatile. It's a price you need to pay, however, to keep the inflation monster at bay. The world of ETFs includes many ways to invest in stocks, but if you find the volatility hard to take, you might temper it with a position in Treasury Inflation-Protected Securities (TIPS). The iShares Barclays TIPS Bond Fund (TIP) tracks an index of TIPS. You can read about TIPS in Chapter 12.

Not Following the IRS's Rules

When they leave their jobs, many employees cash out their 401(k) accounts, thereupon paying the IRS a stiff penalty and immediately losing the great benefit of tax deferral. The government allows certain tax breaks for special kinds of accounts, and you really need to play by the rules or you can wind up worse off than if you had never invested in the first place.

People over 70½ must be especially careful to take the Minimum Required Distributions (MRDs) from their IRAs or 401(k) plans. Calculators are available online; simply type "MRD calculator" into your favorite search engine. Unlike a retirement calculator, based on all kinds of assumptions, the MRD is a straightforward equation. Any online calculator can take you there, or ask your accountant or the institution where you have your IRA.

Failing to Incorporate Investments into a Broader Financial Plan

Have you paid off all your high-interest credit card debt? Do you have proper disability insurance? Do you have enough life insurance so that, if necessary, your co-parent and children could survive without you? A finely manicured investment portfolio is only part of a larger picture that includes issues such as debt management, insurance, and estate planning. Don't spend too much time tinkering with your ETF portfolio and ignore these other very important financial issues.

Chapter 22

Ten Forecasts about the Future of ETFs and Personal Investing

I try not to watch any of the investment shows on television. Stock "Expert" Number One gives his prediction of the future. Then "Expert" Number Two gives her (often contradictory) opinion. Viewers may be amused by the heated debate but never know what to do in the end.

I also usually try not to make predictions about the future, but I'll ask you to please indulge me now. I can't resist. It just seems like sooo much fun!

Here are my predictions, for whatever they are worth, about the world of ETFs.

ETF Assets Will Continue to Grow . . . for Better or Worse

Most people should be investing most of their money in index mutual funds or ETFs, but I don't see that happening — not now, not ever. The initial popularity of ETFs was due largely to the interest of educated institutional investors and savvy individual investors, like you, who loved ETFs for their low-cost indexing and diversification power.

In the past few years, educated and savvy investors have continued to invest in ETFs, but there has also been a huge inflow of money from investors who have little if any idea of what they're getting into. Much of this recent inflow is going into the leveraged and inverse leveraged and other pricey and complex and largely pointless if not outright dangerous ETFs. I warn you about these products throughout this book.

The vast majority of investors will *never, never* give up their belief that they can garner huge returns without huge risk. They'll try any which way they can. They will attend expensive workshops that promise to teach them how to double their money overnight. They will subscribe to newsletters and magazines telling them which stocks or mutual funds to buy this week for sure-fire rapid appreciation. They will buy high-priced mutual funds and will actually pay a fat commission for the honor of doing so. They will hire Bernie Madoff types who make promises that they can't hope to fulfill. And they will buy these newfangled ETFs that they don't understand and that will only wind up hurting them.

That's their problem, not yours. For the intelligent investor like you, there will always be sensible, low-cost, well-diversified ETFs from which you can construct a sensible portfolio.

More Players May Enter the Field, but Only a Few

State Street, iShares, and Vanguard got the jump on ETFs, with others, like PowerShares and WisdomTree, riding close behind. Other investment houses have joined in the fun in the past few years. Unlike the world of mutual funds, however, the profit margin on ETFs is fairly modest, so I don't think we'll see hundreds of issuers of ETFs, as we do mutual funds. Recently, large players such as PIMCO and T. Rowe Price have jumped into the fray with actively managed funds. I expect that some of these active funds will do well. But the exponential growth we've seen in the number of ETFs and ETF providers will certainly start to slow.

Investors Will Get Suckered into Buying Packaged Products

Alas, even good ETFs can be turned into bad financial products. It's happening with some of the ETF offerings in 401(k) plans. In that case, perfectly good ETFs are packaged in such a way that the investor (trapped like a fly in a bowl of milk in his company's plan) is paying as much as 3 percent in management fees. Good ETFs are similarly popping up in crappy annuity plans, 529 college plans, and other investments where someone somewhere stands to make a big buck off the small investor. PowerShares several years back tried to slap loads on ETFs. It didn't work. Someone may try again. Remember Dr. Malcolm's line in *Jurassic Park*? "If there is one thing the history of evolution has taught us it's that life will not be contained. Life breaks free, expands to new territory, and crashes through barriers, painfully, maybe even dangerously." The same can be said of greed.

ETF Investors Will Have More, and Better, Options

Despite all the questionable recent offerings in the ETF world, some of the newer ETFs have been quite pleasant surprises, and I discuss those in every chapter of this book. I'm looking forward to seeing more offerings in the tax-free municipal bond area (Vanguard, in particular, is on my radar); and I also anticipate the introduction of a number of *market-neutral* ETFs (which, like hedge funds, have little to no correlation to the broad stock market, even though they may invest in stocks). Thus the advantages (and, alas, the perils) of hedge-fund investing — once limited to institutions and high-net-worth individuals — will be available to the retail investor. We will also see ETFs that represent certain asset classes that don't even exist yet, and some of those may make excellent investments. (Shuttlecraft and warp-drive production ETFs, perhaps?)

The Markets Will (Unfortunately) See Greater Correlation than in the Past

As the world continues to become a smaller place, and the economies of nations become yet more interdependent, so too will stock and bond markets around the world tend to move up and down in unison. This is not a good thing for investors because it lessens the power of diversification to moderate risk.

I want to emphasize, however, that diversification is not dead! Although world markets in 2008 were distressingly correlated (in other words, they took a collective swan dive), some markets recovered much faster than others. And the next market swoon may not see such correlation; we simply don't know. But I think it is fairly safe to say that investors will find a growing need to tap into new ways to diversify a portfolio. An expanded menu of ETFs will make it that much easier for anyone to implement such a strategy.

Asset Class Returns Will Revert toward Their Historic Means

Astronomical rises in the price of certain commodities (silver and gold in particular) may continue for a while, but not forever. We can also expect an end to the seemingly permanent sag of the U.S. housing market. When commodity prices fall, they may fall hard. And when housing prices rise, they may rise swiftly. At some point in the distant future, commodity prices will rise again, and housing will fall. And so on and so forth. All asset class returns tend to revert to their historical norms.

The price of gold, for example, has just about kept up with inflation over the past 100 years. The double-digit returns of the past few years are an anomaly. Anomalies are, by definition, temporary.

In terms of an ETF portfolio, this may be a good time to slightly underweight commodities and overweight those asset classes that have lagged their historical returns over the past several years. (Tilt your portfolio oh-so-slightly because these are only one man's predictions! Moreover, by the time this book appears in print, new information may have caused me to revise these predictions.)

Taxes Will Rise

Let's see . . . The United States has a raging federal deficit; public and private debt that's way out of control; an aging population; a medical "system" (if you can even call it that) that has left millions unable to pay their doctor, dentist, and hospital bills; a sagging Social Security system; and a seriously challenged public school system. After huge tax cuts (mostly for the very wealthy), these problems persist and worsen. Sooner or later, *something* has to give.

As I write this chapter, most politicians in Congress and the White House are trying to figure out how to fix the mess we are in. Others seem bent on sabotaging any fix, having stated for the record that their first priority is to doom their opponents' prospects in the next election. My hope is that they doom themselves.

I'm hearing the same platitudes that I've heard for decades: "We'll cut waste and government will become more efficient." Yeah, right.

I believe that future administrations will have no option but to raise taxes. I would hope that they will start with the super wealthy, who have saved a bundle in tax breaks over the past years. But who knows? Tax rates may be raised across the board. I advocate squirreling away as much of your ETF portfolio as you can into a tax-free Roth IRA (and then pray that Congress doesn't change the rules on Roths).

Inflation Will Remain Tame

Although I'm certainly concerned about inflation and recognize that it can devastate a paycheck or a portfolio, I'm not too worried about a return to the double-digit inflation of the 1980s. There is a good reason that we saw double-digit inflation back then: The United States decided to abandon the gold standard in the 1970s, and the new monetary system was walking on its baby legs.

Today, we have forces at play that argue for greater inflation (such as the national debt), and we also have forces at play working in the other direction (such as high unemployment). But the monetary system isn't walking on baby legs. I anticipate that inflation in the next decade or two will be similar to what it has been in the past decade or two: somewhere in the ballpark of 3 percent.

Whether I'm right about the 3 percent, or whether inflation runs higher, you can protect yourself with a good helping of stock ETFs (stocks have a very good track record of keeping up with inflation) and a position in the iShares Barclays TIPS Bond ETF (TIP), which tracks an index of U.S. Treasury Inflation-Protected Securities (see Chapter 12).

Private Pensions (of Sorts) May Emerge from the Rubble

There's one kind of risk against which all the good saving and wise investing in the world can only go so far to protect you. That is "longevity risk." In order to live a life of comfort post-retirement, you need to save and invest as if you could live to be 105 . . . because you just may. But, in point of fact, you probably won't live nearly that long. Wouldn't it be nice if we could all save just enough to get us through to the average life expectancy (mid 80s), and the money from those who die sooner could help support those who live longer? That's the basic idea behind Social Security, which I'd like to see strengthened, not weakened. Alas, politics being politics, that seems unlikely.

But I have hope that even if the government doesn't come through, private industry may offer us even better "old age insurance" in the form of reasonably priced annuities instead of the horribly overpriced, confusing, restrictive, inflexible, locked-in, complicated, and tricky annuities that have come to dominate the insurance market. Certain companies, such as Vanguard, Fidelity, and Jefferson National, have taken positive strides in the direction. But I'd like to see the day — and we may get there yet — when annuities, just like ETFs, become simple, transparent, inexpensive, and sensible. Perhaps ETFs themselves may evolve into such instruments. I can dream.

Hype Will Prevail!

Of all my predictions, this is the one I'd put money on.

We'll be seeing more magazine articles, websites, blogs, television clips, and advertisements with headings and leads such as "Build Instant Wealth and Retire Early with ETFs!" And there will be books with titles such as *Beat the Market with ETFs!* and *You Can Make a Killing in ETFs!* One of them may become a bestseller, which means that it will make a lot of money for someone — but not for the people who read it.

Bull markets are followed by bear markets, which are followed by bull markets. Trading floors are replaced by electronic trading platforms. Mutual funds are challenged by ETFs. The world of investing keeps changing, morphing into something hardly recognizable from the days when just about all investors were men who wore funny hats, smoked cigars, and spent hours reading tickertapes.

But one thing remains constant: The financial industry will continue to produce hype in the hope that you will buy their new products, and sell, and buy, and sell, and buy, regardless of how ridiculously complex and expensive whatever products they are pushing happen to be.

Having read this book, you now know better. Put your knowledge to good use. Build a diversified portfolio of low-cost, transparent, tax-efficient ETFs. Keep an eye on your nest egg, but don't make changes very often. Just be sure to rebalance at regular intervals. Sit back and relax. Let the hype pass over you like a summer breeze.

Part VI
Appendixes

The 5th Wave   By Rich Tennant

"I'm not familiar with investment terms. What does that mean?"

In this part . . .

In this part, you get some handy reference info: I start with a list of websites to check whenever you're craving even more ETF or general investment info. I follow with a glossary that can help you navigate this book and any other ETF or finance resource.

Appendix A

Great Web Resources to Help You Invest in ETFs

● ●

*Y*ou can find anything online: gobs and gobs of information — and misinformation. And in the world of finance, there is more misinformation than information. If you pressed me, I'd put the ratio at 7:2. Following are some websites you can trust to keep you informed about ETFs and other investment issues.

Independent, ETF-Specific Websites

`http://finance.yahoo.com/etf`: Features a search function with intimate details on individual funds, an ETF glossary, and regularly updated news and commentary.

`http://seekingalpha.com/dashboard/etfs`: Features some the smartest commentary on fund investing you'll find anywhere.

`www.etfdb.com`: Boasts daily ETF news, educational articles, analysis, and an ETF screener. Find out which ETFs represent what asset classes for the lowest fees.

`www.etfguide.com`: A good, quick summary of the entire ETF world. Contains a complete listing of all ETFs available, along with ticker symbols.

`www.etftrends.com`: A gossip column of sorts for ETF enthusiasts. There's chitchat about new ETFs on the market, ETFs pending approval of the SEC, behind-the-scenes industry workings, and rumors.

`www.etfzone.com`: An extremely convenient and quick way to get a scope on what's available in the ETF world.

www.indexuniverse.com: See "News" under the Sections heading for the most up-to-date information on ETFs and index mutual funds. See the "Data" section to help screen for ETFs of your liking.

www.morningstar.com **(Click the ETF icon at top of screen):** Thorough information on individual funds, along with Morningstar's trademarked rating system. (One star is bad, five stars is grand.) See also http://etf.morning star.com, which is the link to Morningstar's ETFInvestor newsletter. It's a paid publication, but there's a fair amount of information that's free.

Websites of ETF Providers

About 85 percent of all ETFs come from BlackRock, State Street, and Vanguard. The remaining 15 or so percent of the market is split among a number of players.

The biggies

www.ishares.com: BlackRock's iShares are the biggest in the business.

www.spdrs.com: The SPDRs are issued by State Street Global Advisors (SSgA).

www.vanguard.com: The King of Indexing produces some of the lowest-cost ETFs.

Some of the lesser players

www.direxionshares.com: Leveraging is their game.

www.elementsetn.com: Exchange-traded notes that tracks commodities and stocks.

www.globalxfunds.com: They seem to be issuing a new ETF every day.

www.guggenheimfunds.com: Featuring narrow segments of markets.

www.ipathetn.com: Barclays' lineup of exchange-traded notes.

www.pimcoetfs.com: Bond people. Purely bond people.

`www.powershares.com`: A host of unusual indexes, for better or worse.

`www.proshares.com`: ETFs for a wild ride.

`www.wisdomtree.com`: You say you like dividends?

`www.vaneck.com`: Specializing in metals and other hard assets.

Retirement Calculators

How large a portfolio are you going to need to retire in style? How much are you going to have to sock away, and what kind of rate of return do you need to get there? None of the online calculators is perfect, so I suggest you use a few and average the answers. Start with this one:

`www.firecalc.com`: *FIRE* stands for *financial independence/retire early*. If you didn't realize it, there is an entire movement out there devoted to financial independence. Use this website as your entry point. You find what is arguably the best free retirement calculator on the Web, along with an Early Retirement Forum where other *FIRE* fans passionately discuss their strategies.

Then use one or more of the following calculators as well:

- ✔ `https://www3.troweprice.com/ric/ricweb/public/ric.do`
- ✔ `www.aarp.org/work/retirement-planning/retirement_calculator`
- ✔ `www.choosetosave.org/ballpark`

Financial Supermarkets

Otherwise known as large brokerage houses, here are some places where you can buy, sell, and house your ETFs — as well as other investments, such as mutual funds and individual stocks and bonds.

`www.fidelity.com`: Or telephone Fidelity at 1-800-343-3548.

`www.schwab.com`: Or telephone Charles Schwab at 1-866-232-9890.

`www.scottrade.com`: Or telephone Scottrade at 1-800-619-7283.

`www.tdameritrade.com`: Or telephone TD Ameritrade at 1-800-454-9272.

`www.troweprice.com`: Or telephone T. Rowe Price at 1-800-638-5660.

`www.vanguard.com`: Or telephone Vanguard at 1-800-662-7447.

Stock Exchanges

`www.nasdaq.com`: Despite the fact that not many ETFs are listed on the NASDAQ, the website has some very cool ETF-related things. Check out especially the "ETF Dynamic Heatmap" (found by clicking Market Activity and ETFs).

`www.nyse.com`: Most ETFs are traded on the NYSE platforms. Surprisingly, there isn't a lot of ETF information on the website, but there is a wealth of general information about the world of finance.

Specialty Websites

`www.bogleheads.org`: This is the forum where index investors go to (respectfully, for the most part) debate other index investors.

`www.cboe.com`: The Chicago Board Options Exchange — if options trading is your kind of thing.

`www.investinginbonds.com`: Get a quickie education on bond investing from The Securities Industry and Financial Markets Association (SIFMA).

`www.investnretire.com`: A company that sets up ETF-based retirement plans for employers. Let it serve as a model to others.

`www.multpl.com`: Robert Shiller's modified P/E index for tactical asset allocators (see Chapter 18).

`www.reit.com`: Everything you could want to know about real estate investment trusts (REITs), including REIT ETFs. Brought to you by The National Association of REITs. Very rah-rah.

`www.ussif.org`. A wealth of information on investing for social good from The Forum for Sustainable and Responsible Investment.

`www.sweetspotinvestments.com`: Provides an interesting twist on contrarian investing.

Where to Find a Financial Planner

www.cambridgeadvisors.com: A national network of *fee-onlies* (financial people who work for a straight fee rather than commissions) who are eager to work with middle-class folk.

www.cfainstitute.org: CFA Institute is where you want to go to find a Chartered Financial Analyst (CFA), which is not as well-known but very similar to a Certified Financial Planner (CFP).

www.cfp.net: The Certified Financial Planner Board of Standards. Lists Certified Financial Planners (CFPs) nationwide. The CFP designation assures that the person has a fair amount of education and experience, and passed a wicked 10-hour exam.

www.fpanet.org: Financial Planning Association, the nation's largest organization of financial planners. It doesn't take much to join.

www.garrettplanningnetwork.com: A network of 250 financial advisors who charge for services on an hourly, as-needed basis.

www.napfa.org: National Association of Personal Financial Advisors. This is the association for *fee-onlies:* financial people who don't take commissions but, rather, work for a straight fee. About four out of ten financial planners are fee-onlies.

Regulatory Agencies

www.finra.org: The Financial Industry Regulatory Authority website. If you click on the Investors tab, it has all sorts of helpful information for do-it-yourselfers. The Fund Analyzer is a great way to see the impact of management fees on a fund's total return over time.

www.sec.gov: The U.S. Securities and Exchange Commission. Under Investor Information, click on Check Out Brokers & Advisers to make sure a financial planner is fully licensed. You'll also find out if your candidate has any disciplinary history for unethical conduct.

The People Who Create the Indexes

Dow Jones, Russell, Standard & Poor's, and others create the indexes that ETFs track. Just in case you're interested:

- www.djindexes.com
- www.ftse.com
- www.indexes.morningstar.com
- www.msci.com
- www.russell.com
- www.standardandpoors.com
- www.wilshire.com

Good Places to Go for General Financial News, Advice, and Education

http://finance.yahoo.com: Extensive information and analysis, all for free.

www.bloomberg.com: Hardcore financial data.

www.cnnfn.com: Get your daily fix of everything money-related.

www.efficientfrontier.com: Some illuminating thoughts from investment guru William Bernstein.

www.moneychimp.com: For the more advanced investor.

www.morningstar.com: Anything and everything about stocks, mutual funds, and ETFs.

www.sensible-investor.com: A gateway to other financial websites, including the most esoteric (gay and lesbian investors, black investors, Christian investors . . .).

Yours Truly

www.globalportfolios.net or www.russellwild.com: Both URLs will take you to the same place: the author's own website. Feel free to visit me anytime.

Appendix B

Glossary

· ·

*I*f you're going to be an ETF investor, you need to know the lingo. If you're not going to be an ETF investor, you can still use the following phrases to impress at cocktail parties and Republican fundraising events. Please note that any word in *italic* (except for the word *italic*) appears as its own entry elsewhere in the glossary.

Active investing. Ah, to beat the market. Isn't it every investor's dream? Through stock picking or market timing, or both strategies, active investing offers hope of market-beating returns. Alas, it sounds a lot easier than it really is. Compare to *passive investing*.

Alpha. Given a certain level of risk, you should expect a certain rate of return. If your stock/fund/portfolio return exceeds that expectation, congratulations! You've just achieved what people in the finance world call "positive alpha." Pass the caviar. If your stock/fund/portfolio return falls shy of that expectation, you are in the dark and depressing land of "negative alpha." Pass the herring.

Ask price. The rock-bottom price that any stock or ETF seller is willing to accept. If any buyer is willing to fork over that amount, a sale is made. If no buyers are willing to match the ask price, gravity will eventually start to drag down the price of the stock. Compare to *bid price* and *spread*.

Asset class. To build a diversified portfolio (meaning not having all your eggs in one flimsy straw basket), you want to have your investments spread out among different asset classes. An asset class is any group of similar investments. Examples may include small value stocks, utility stocks, high-yield bonds, Japanese small company stocks, or Rembrandts (paintings, not the toothpaste).

Beta. A common measurement of the volatility of an investment. If your ETF has a beta of 1.5, it tends to move up 15 percent whenever the market as a whole (usually represented, somewhat clumsily, by the S&P 500 Index) goes up 10 percent. If the market as a whole goes down 10 percent, your ETF will fall 15 percent. Note that beta is a relative measure of risk, while *standard deviation* (a generally more useful tool) is an absolute measure of risk.

Bid price. The highest price that any buyer is willing to spend to purchase shares of a stock or ETF. Compare to *ask price* and *spread*.

Black swan. A term popularized by mathematician Nassim Taleb, it refers to a rare and extreme event (think nasty — think act of God or of madmen) that has the potential to throw financial markets into turmoil. Many alternative investments (including Taleb's own hedge fund) advertise that they protect investors against such events.

Cap size. A less fancy way of saying "market capitalization." It refers to the size of a company as measured by the total number of stock outstanding times the market price of each share. In general, stocks are classified as either large cap (over $5 billion), small cap (under $1 billion), or mid cap (anything in between).

Closed-end fund. Like a mutual fund or an exchange-traded fund, a closed-end fund pools securities, but it differs from its open-ended cousins in that it rarely creates or redeems new shares. Because of the fixed supply of shares, eager investors who want into the fund may wind up paying a significant premium over the market value of the pooled securities. On the other hand, if investor demand lags, the shares of a closed-end fund could sell for a hefty discount.

Closet index fund. A mutual fund may call itself actively managed and may charge you a boatload of money, but it may be, in essence, an index fund. Shhhhhh. The manager doesn't want to come out of the closet, lest he lose his excuse for charging you what he charges you and be forced to surrender the keys to the Mercedes.

Correlation. The degree to which two investments — such as two ETFs — move up and down at the same time. A correlation of 1 means that the two investments move up and down together, like the Rockettes. A correlation of –1 means that when one goes up, the other goes down, like two pistons. A correlation of 0 means that there is no correlation between the two, like the price of bananas and the Philadelphia Eagles.

Diversification. It means dividing your investments into different *asset classes* with limited *correlation*. Diversification is good. Very good. ETFs make it easy. Did I already mention that diversification is good?

EAFE index. EAFE stands for Europe, Australia, and Far East. This index is often used (incorrectly) to represent foreign stocks. What it really tracks are large cap stocks of developed foreign nations.

Emerging markets. This is a common euphemism for "countries where most people live on rice and corn." People who invest in emerging markets hope that these nations (mostly in Africa, South America, and Asia) are, in fact, emerging. No one knows. The fortunes of emerging market stocks are closely tied to the markets for natural resources. Emerging market ETFs tend to be rather volatile but offer excellent return possibilities.

Expense ratio. Sometimes referred to as the "management fee," this is a yearly bill you pay to a mutual fund or ETF. The money is taken directly out of your account. The expense ratio for ETFs is usually much, much less than that of mutual funds. If the expense ratio for your entire portfolio is more than 1 percent, you're paying too much.

Fundamental analysis. If you're going to be picking stocks, it makes sense, I suppose, to do some fundamental analysis: an analysis of the company's profitability both present and future. Just know that fundamental analysis is an awfully fuzzy science. And, ironically, the strongest, fastest-growing companies don't always make for the most profitable stocks. See *value premium*.

Growth fund. A fund that invests in stocks of companies that have been fast-growing and are expected (by fundamental analysts) to continue to be fast-growing. In its day, Enron was a growth stock. You never know . . .

Hedging. If you expect that Asset A may zig, and you purchase Asset B in the hope that it will simultaneously zag, you've just hedged your position. A common hedging strategy is to use *short* positions (selling stock shares you don't own, but borrow) to offset any potential loss you may suffer by holding a *long* (buy and hold) position. Hedging reduces risk, but it also tends to mute returns. The term "inflation-hedge" refers to any asset or type of asset, such as commodities, expected to appreciate in value in a climate of rising prices.

Indexing. This term is synonymous with *passive investing*. Index investing has been around for a good while; ETFs simply make it easier, less expensive, and more *tax efficient*.

iShares. This is the brand name for ETFs issued by BlackRock, the largest purveyor of ETFs in the world. A little more than 40 percent of all money invested in ETFs is invested in iShares.

Leverage. An investment made with borrowed funds is said to be leveraged. A common type of leveraged investment, although usually not thought of as such, is a home purchased with little money down and a big mortgage. Leveraged investments offer great potential for profit or — as many homeowners have found out the hard way in recent years — risk of loss.

Liquidity. A liquid asset can readily be turned into cash. Examples include money market funds and very short-term bond funds. *Il*liquid assets are trickier things to turn into cash. The classic example of an illiquid asset is the family home.

Load. A wad of cash that you need to fork over in order to purchase certain mutual funds. Study after study shows that load funds perform no better than no-load funds, yet people are willing to pay rather huge loads. Go figure. ETFs never charge loads. Gotta love that about them.

Modern Portfolio Theory. It says that a portfolio doesn't have to be excessively risky, even if its separate components are riskier than skydiving without a parachute. The trick is to fill your portfolio with investments that have low *correlation* to one another. When one crashes, another soars — or at least hovers.

Passive investing. You buy an index of stocks (preferably through an ETF), and you hold them. And you hold them. And you hold them. It's as boring as a game of bingo in which none of the letters called are the ones you need. And yet passive investors beat the pants off most active investors, year in and year out.

Price/earnings ratio (P/E). Take a company's total earnings over the past 12 months and divide that by the number of shares of stock outstanding. The resulting number represents earnings, the lower number in the equation. Price — the upper number — refers to the market price of the stock. The P/E is the most common way in which stocks are identified as either value stocks or growth stocks. High P/E = growth. Low P/E = value.

Qubes. A nickname for the QQQ, an index that tracks the top 100 companies listed on the NASDAQ stock exchange. QQQ is the *ticker* for the most popular ETF that tracks the QQQ. For years, the ticker was QQQQ and not QQQ. Why? I don't knowww.

R squared. This measurement shows how tightly an investment hugs a certain index. An R squared of .90 means that 90 percent of a fund's movement is attributable to movement in the index to which it is most similar. For an index fund or ETF, an R squared of 1.00 is usually the goal. For an allegedly actively managed fund, an R squared of 1.00 (or anything higher than .85 or so) means that you have a *closet index fund,* and you are being ripped off.

REIT stock/fund. A stock or fund that invests in a company or companies that make their money in real estate — most often commercial real estate, such as office buildings and shopping malls. REIT funds tend to be interest-rate sensitive and often have limited *correlation* to other funds.

Risk. When we investment types talk of risk, we generally mean but one thing: *volatility,* or the unpredictability of an investment. The higher the risk, the greater the potential return.

Sector investing. If you break up your stock portfolio into different industry sectors — energy, consumer staples, financials — then you are a sector investor. Another option is *style investing.*

Sharpe ratio. A risk-adjusted measure of fund performance. In other words, it measures a fund's average historical return per unit of risk. The higher the number, the happier you should be.

Sophisticated investor. Often mistaken for someone who trades every day and is constantly checking his account balance, or someone who uses charts and graphs and tries to time the markets. In the real world, such "sophisticated" investors rarely do as well as the "dummy" who builds a well-diversified portfolio of low-cost index funds (such as ETFs) and lets it sit undisturbed.

SPDRs. This is the name of the brand line for ETFs issued by State Street Global Advisors (SSgA), the second-largest purveyor of ETFs after BlackRock.

Spread. The difference between the *ask price* and *bid price* for a stock or ETF.

Standard deviation. The most used measure of volatility in the world of investments. The formula is long and complicated with lots of Greek symbols. Suffice to say this: A standard deviation of 5 means that roughly two-thirds of the time, your investment returns will fall within 5 percentage points of the mean. So if your ETF has an historical mean return of 10 percent, two-thirds of the time you can expect to see your returns fall somewhere between 5 percent and 15 percent. If your ETF has an historical mean return of 5 percent, two-thirds of the time you can expect your return to be somewhere between 0 percent and 10 percent.

Style investing. If you divvy up your stock investments into large, small, value, and growth, you are a style investor, as opposed to a sector investor. Which is better? Hard to say.

Style drift. It's 11 p.m. Do you know where your investments are? A manager of an active mutual fund tells you that her fund is, say, a large growth fund. And perhaps it once was. But lately, this gal has been loading up on large value companies. Is she a growth investor or a value investor? Only she knows for sure. Investors, meanwhile, get stuck with her style drift and aren't sure exactly what they are holding. See *transparency*.

Tax efficiency. ETFs are often praised for their tax efficiency. That means the funds generate little in the way of capital gains, so you pay taxes only on dividends until such time as you actually cash out. With many mutual funds, you can wind up paying taxes at the most inopportune moments.

Tax-loss harvesting. Late in the year (most often), you can sell off a losing investment in order to claim a loss on your taxes. You can usually use tax losses to wipe out capital gains of the same amount. If your losses exceed your gains, you can generally take the loss to wipe out ordinary income, up to $3,000. In effect, Uncle Sam is helping to share the burden of your woes.

Technical analysis. The use of charts and graphs to try to predict the stock market. Some people take it very, very seriously — despite a lack of any evidence that it works.

Ticker. The two- to five-letter symbol used for a stock, mutual fund, or ETF. Examples include SPY, QQQ, and EWJ. Some ETF tickers are quite cute. There's one, for example, called DOG (but none yet with the ticker GOD), which allows you to bet that DOW is going down. There's another called MOO, which invests in agribusiness.

Transparency. ETFs are beautifully transparent, which means that you know exactly what stocks or bonds your ETF holds. The same is not always true with mutual funds, hedge funds, or your spouse's safe deposit box.

Turnover. The degree to which a fund changes its investments over the course of a year. A turnover rate of 100 means that the fund starts and ends the year with a completely different set of stocks. Turnover generally creates unpleasant tax liabilities for investors. Turnover, almost always, also involves hidden trading costs.

Value fund. A mutual fund or ETF that invests in companies whose recent growth may be less than eye-popping but whose stock prices are believed to be cheap in comparison to the prices of stocks of other like companies.

Value premium. Over the past century or so, ever since the birth of organized stock markets, value stocks have performed much better than growth stocks, with relatively the same degree of *risk*. Theories abound, but to date, economists can't seem to agree on why this apparent value premium exists or whether it is likely to continue.

Volatility. Whoooeee. What goes up fast often comes down just as fast. A stock or ETF that gained 40 percent last year can lose 40 percent this year. It is volatile. It is risky. It can bring you great joy or great misery. Hope for the former, but be prepared for the latter.

Yield. This term is most often used to mean the income derived from an investment over the past 12 months, as a percentage of the total investment. Income may come from dividends (most often the case with stocks or stock ETFs) or interest (from a bond or bond ETF). If you sink $10,000 into an ETF and it generates $500 in yearly income, your yield is 5 percent. If it generates $600, your yield is 6 percent, and so on.

YTD. Year-to-date return, or the total return (dividends plus any rise in the price of the stock or ETF) from January 1 of the present year until today.

Index